What role does food play in how people imagine themselves and their communities? In this book, Wendy Wall argues that representations of housework in the early modern period helped to forge crucial conceptions of national identity. Rich with a detailed account of household practices in the period, *Staging Domesticity* reads plays on the London stage in the light of the first printed cookbooks in England. Working from original historical sources on wetnursing, laundering, sewing, medical care, and butchery, Wall shows that domesticity was represented as deeply familiar but also enticingly alien. This is a fascinating journey in itself but is especially engrossing when Renaissance daily life is further evaluated as it was portrayed on the English stage at the time. Wall analyzes a wide range of the repertoire, including some now little-known plays such as *Gammer Gurton's Needle*, performed by and for the boys at Cambridge in the late 1560s, as well as key works in the period by Shakespeare and others. Wall concludes that dramatizations of the period represented the common household – rather than only court-based and aristocratic domestic life – as crucial to conceptions of emotion and identity. This study not only sheds new light on early modern literature but, in turn, enhances our understanding of daily life in early modern England.

WENDY WALL is Professor of English Literature at Northwestern University and a scholar of early modern literature and culture. She is author of *The Imprint of Gender: Authorship and Publication in the English Renaissance* (Cornell University Press, 1993) and co-editor of the journal *Renaissance Drama*. Wendy Wall has published widely on print technology, voyeurism, women's writing, poetry, housework, and early modern culture.

*Cambridge Studies in Renaissance Literature and Culture 41*

Staging Domesticity

*Cambridge Studies in Renaissance Literature and Culture*

Since the 1970s there has been a broad and vital reinterpretation of the nature of literary texts, a move away from formalism to a sense of literature as an aspect of social, economic, political and cultural history. While the earliest New Historicist work was criticized for a narrow and anecdotal view of history, it also served as an important stimulus for post-structuralist, feminist, Marxist and psychoanalytical work, which in turn has increasingly informed and redirected it. Recent writing on the nature of representation, the historical construction of gender and of the concept of identity itself, on theatre as a political and economic phenomenon and on the ideologies of art generally, reveals the breadth of the field. Cambridge Studies in Renaissance Literature and Culture is designed to offer historically oriented studies of Renaissance literature and theatre which make use of the insights afforded by theoretical perspectives. The view of history envisioned is above all a view of our own history, a reading of the Renaissance for and from our own time.

*Recent titles include*

# Staging Domesticity

*Household Work and English Identity
in Early Modern Drama*

Wendy Wall

CAMBRIDGE
UNIVERSITY PRESS

PUBLISHED BY THE PRESS SYNDICATE OF THE UNIVERSITY OF CAMBRIDGE
The Pitt Building, Trumpington Street, Cambridge, United Kingdom

CAMBRIDGE UNIVERSITY PRESS
The Edinburgh Building, Cambridge CB2 2RU, UK
40 West 20th Street, New York, NY 10011–4211, USA
477 Williamstown Road, Port Melbourne, VIC 3207, Australia
Ruiz de Alarcón 13, 28014 Madrid, Spain
Dock House, The Waterfront, Cape Town 8001, South Africa

http://www.cambridge.org

First published 2002

Printed in the United Kingdom at the University Press, Cambridge

*Typeface* Times 10/12 pt.     *System* LATEX 2$_\varepsilon$   [TB]

*A catalogue record for this book is available from the British Library*

*Library of Congress Cataloguing in Publication data*

Wall, Wendy, 1961–
Staging domesticity: household work and English identity in Early Modern drama/
Wendy Wall.
  p. cm. – (Cambridge studies in Renaissance literature and culture; 41)
Includes bibliogriphical references and index.
ISBN 0 521 80849 9
1. English drama – Early modern and Elizabethan, 1500–1600 – History and criticism.
2. English drama – 17th century – History and criticism.   3. Domestic drama, English –
History and criticism.   4. Housekeeping in literature.   5. Cookery in literature.
6. Women in literature.   7. Home in literature.   I. Title.   II. Series.

PR658.D65 W35   2002
822′.409355–dc21   2001037400

ISBN 0 521 80849 9 hardback

For Jules

# Contents

# Illustrations

# Acknowledgments

The word "recipe," or "receipt" as they would say in the early modern period, originally meant something received. While writing this book, I have been the beneficiary of many receipts and gifts: from the home-made book of family recipes that my sister Bonnie Lessman sent to me years ago, to the lively conversation, affectionate advice, and stern criticism that colleagues and friends have offered over the years, I am exceedingly aware of the heterogeneous ingredients that went into this project. It is indeed a medley, "hodge-pudding," or gallimaufry, as Renaissance writers might say, of ultimately innumerable voices and contributions.

*Staging Domesticity* began with my response to a talk by Juliet Fleming, whose astute comments made early modern housework actually intriguing. Along the way the book has benefited by having keen readers who have added both spice and good measure to it. My thanks to Rebecca Bushnell, Fran Dolan, Jonathan Goldberg, Gil Harris, Jean Howard, Rosemary Kegl, Mary Ellen Lamb, Jules Law, Mary Beth Rose, Valerie Traub, Linda Woodbridge, and Bill Worthen. With wit and patience, Kathy Maus and Stephen Orgel read the entire manuscript and helped me to distill my arguments. Heartfelt thanks go to Gail Paster, whose generative scholarship and vibrant remarks during Folger lunches shaped my thinking more than she knows. And I am indebted, as always, to my ideal colleague Jeff Masten, who generously puts into practice his commitment to collaboration.

I should also acknowledge material support that I have received. A fellowship from Northwestern's Humanities Center allowed me to map the broad contours of this book. With research grants from Northwestern and the Folger Shakespeare Library (and the benefit of Allyson Booth's lovely guestroom), I was able to savor the Folger's treasury of cookbooks, disgusting colleagues at tea as I recounted their gruesome delights. I completed this book with the aid of a fellowship from the National Endowment for the Humanities, which enabled me to sit at home writing about domestic labor but not doing any.

When presenting parts of this project, I have been gratified if a bit surprised at the wealth of information people have about desserts, butchery, breastmilk, needlework, sodomy, and brewing. I am grateful to audiences at the University of Illinois, Brown University, University of Chicago, University of Michigan, Case Western University, and elsewhere for helpful comments. Like many others, I owe much to the work of Margreta de Grazia, Margaret Ferguson, Stephen Greenblatt, Ann Rosalind Jones, Karen Newman, Louis Montrose, Pat Parker, Maureen Quilligan, Phyllis Rackin, and Peter Stallybrass. And again, a special acknowledgment to the book's final reader, Stephen Orgel, who saw the potential for my ruminations on perverse domesticity at a critical time. The account keeper on this book's cover reminds me that my debt to him is exceedingly large.

I am fortunate to have colleagues who challenge me to read differently. My thanks go especially to Martin Mueller, Reg Gibbons, Barbara Newman, Betsy Erkkila, and Chris Herbert for encouragement on this book when it wasn't yet fully cooked. Friends such as Chris Castiglia, Mary Finn, Jay Grossman, Mark Long, Susan Manning, Jeff Masten, Chris Reed, Margaret Renkl, Julia Stern, and my ex-Penn crew – Allyson Booth, Susan Greenfield, James Krasner, and Laura Tanner – continue to teach and delight me by sneaking feasts of words into fun events.

The ongoing support of my parents, Martha and Harold Wall, proves that they belong on this page – and any other that I should ever write. And at the risk of positing the sentimental household that this book critiques, I end by turning to the home front. For many years, Matthew Law has surprised me with the joys of domesticity (and I'm convinced that his early love of gummy worms first made me attentive to virtual food). Jules Law, whose extraordinary talents in the kitchen are only a small portion of his many gifts, makes daily life into a banquet. I dedicate this book to him.

Chapter 2 first appeared in revised form as "'Household Stuff': The Sexual Politics of Domesticity and the Advent of English Comedy" in *ELH 65* (1998): 1–45. A version of Chapter 3 appeared as "Why Does Puck Sweep?: Fairylore, Merry Wives and Social Struggle" in *Shakespeare Quarterly* 52 (Spring 2001): 67–106. I thank Johns Hopkins University Press and The Folger Shakespeare Library for permission to reprint this material.

# In the nation's kitchen

> Fantasy is not . . . antagonistic to social reality; it is its precondition or psychic glue . . . There is no way of understanding political identities and destinies without letting fantasy into the frame . . .  Jacqueline Rose[1]

A prince trembles with uncontrollable passion at the sight of a milkmaid with her hands buried deep in milk; a householder hysterically sorts through a basket of soiled laundry to find traces of his sexual humiliation; a journeyman dreams of piping hot pancakes and live food marching in the London streets; a servant gleefully narrates the phantasmagoric tale of people butchered and eaten at the dinner table; a fieldworker panics that a lost needle might sodomize him; a housewife rapaciously medicates boy actors in sexually provocative ways. Dramatizing panicked self-dispossession, uncontrollable yearning – even euphoria – these scenes on the early modern stage might be read as interesting precisely because they defamiliarize ordinary domestic life; that is, we might see them as making banal or unremarkable situations appear weighty, fantastic, suddenly odd.

From this perspective, these plays bolster the view of the post-Reformation household as modeling and providing the training ground for political order, since they comically throw into relief the crucial normalcy and regularity of domesticity.[2] Depicting the household in any manner had weighty consequences, for in English political treatises, conduct books, and sermons, the household was routinely touted as the foremost disciplinary site in the period. "Upon this condition of the Familie, being the Seminarie of all other Societies," writes William Perkins in 1609,

it followeth, that the holie and righteous government thereof, is a direct meane for the good ordering, both of Church and Common-wealth; yea that the lawes thereof . . . are available to prepare and dispose men to the keeping of order in other governements. Hence it is, that the Holie Ghost in the booke of the Scriptures, hath in great wisedome commended both Rules for direction, and examples for imitation, to Husbands and Wives, to Parents and Children, to Masters and Servants in everie point of Christian carriage touching God and man. For this first Societie, is as it were the Schoole, wherein are taught and learned the principles of authoritie and subjection.[3]

1

As the "first Societie" and "Seminarie," the early modern family bore the tremendous burden of inculcating citizenship and virtue in a patriarchal and hierarchical world by structuring the proper dependencies that founded church, state, and body politic. Through this key structure, early modern people learned to rein in chaotic impulses and fantasies and to become full citizens. Representations of domestic disorder on the stage might thus simply be said to anatomize the wayward passions to be mastered or pathologies to be cured so as to ensure the proper ordering of home and polity.

But what if domesticity were already "estranged" in the early modern imagination? What if these scenes of domestic passion and panic simply foregrounded what everyone already, at some level, knew: that ordinary experience could be bizarre and disquieting? Might drama then implicitly unsettle ideologies resting on an ordered domesticity merely by revealing the disorienting nature of everyday practice? Even a glance at the first cookbooks and domestic guides published in England suggests as much, for these manuals probe the very categories that the household was enlisted to support. Hugh Plat's popular *Delightes for Ladies* (1602), to take one example, revels in the joys of a wasteful confectionery by instructing housewives to shape marzipan into "rare and strange devices" such as gloves, keys, beasts, and objects. Heralding a society fortressed by sugar ramparts, Plat calls for nature's preservation on the home front:

> I teach both fruits and flowers to preserve,
> And candie them, so Nutmegs, cloves, and mace:
> To make both marchpaine paste, and sugred plate,
> And cast the same in formes of sweetest grace.
> Each bird and foule, so moulded from the life,
> And after cast in sweet compounds of arte,
> As if the flesh and forme which nature gave,
> Did still remaine in every lim and part.[4]

Elaborate marzipan chickens tellingly boast natural complexions that "remaine" in every limb, as if the housewife reincarnates an actual live form when she sweetly molds sugar paste into lifelike shapes (Plat later instructs ladies on how to dredge the fowl in a breadcrumb and sugar mixture so that dessert will seem to be roasted). Insubstantial dessert, stamped as flesh, repeats dinner, bringing back what has already been consumed in a play of wit. And this trick is part of a broader project, Plat goes on to explain; for housewifery, as performance art, can fortify humankind against the ravages of mortality. A recipe in the 1598 cookbook *Epulario* shows that tinkering with the concept of "life" could be so coy as to border on impropriety. Entitled "To make Pies that the Birds may be alive in them, and flie out when it is cut up," the recipe advises, "Because [the guests] shall not be altogether mocked," the wife should make a small edible pie to accompany the conceit.[5] The fun of defamiliarizing eating, that is, should not be a substitute for gustatory pleasure. Such recipes suggest that an enticing mockery – of household members or the fixities of nature – was built into the production of food, or at least its virtual double. The *trompe l'oeil* dimension of cooking and confectionery playfully invited people into a world of fantasy that could confuse critical categories operative in early modern life, namely by putting quotation marks around the "real."

Yet the housewife's imperative to outdo nature, manifest in recipes for durable foodstuffs and preserves, meshed somewhat uneasily with the destructive domestic practices she was invited to organize. "At the ende of the banquet they may eat al, and breake the platters, dishes, cups, and all thynges: for this paste is delicate," writes John Partridge in his *Good Huswives Closet* (1584), as he solicits readers to imitate the refined food fights carried out in aristocratic after-dinner entertainment.[6] Doubly furnishing the table – first with real trenchers and then their cunning edible doubles – the housewife played on the gap between reality and appearance, creating a game of deceit resolved through a collective assault. Given ubiquitous injunctions for the housewife to "keep," the delight in casually destroying the simulacrum of a material world must have been considerable. Dining thus tapped into desires for durability and whimsical sacrifice, for a world to be safeguarded but one whose destruction could be performed at will. In short, it offered what Michel de Certeau termed as an everyday "tactic" that could recast ideologies underpinning economic and social ordering.[7]

The conjoining of preservation and destruction evident in cooking and confectionery carried over into the job of managing flesh in all of its incarnations. Since each food was thought to contain properties that affected the balance of humors in the body, the housewife manipulated diet as part of medical care. In fact, medical and culinary practices were thoroughly fused within a daily regimen geared toward orchestrating the intake and output of the precarious humoral bodily economy.[8] A range of pleasurable or painful procedures, including eating and purging, allowed people to balance the animal, vital, and natural spirits that mediated between soul and matter. While some home remedies were comprised of tasty narcotic syrups, other recipes involved pouring lemon juice into open sores, lancing boils, serving up urine-based concoctions, or sticking oil-infused feathers deep into a patient's nostrils. Lady Catherine Sedley, Lady Elizabeth Grey, and Lady Grace Mildmay wrote that they placed plasters "as hot as may be endured to the Fundament," and subjected children to three-day regimens that alternated fasting, enemas, vomits, and sweating with bouts of drinking acidic concoctions.[9] Clearly the domesticated subject was not simply passively molded within a fixed hierarchy, but submitted as well to uncomfortable modes of disciplining that set up multiple and discrete lines of dependency.

Part and parcel of physic was the transformation of the kitchen into a slaughterhouse strewn liberally with blood and carcasses. As Hannah Woolley recommends in the following cure for agues, health required specific forms of injury and killing:

Take two Running Cocks, pull them alive, then kill them, Cut them Cross on the Back, when they are almost cold take their Guts, and after you have made them clean, break them all to pieces.[10]

Having plucked, killed, and disemboweled the animal, the housewife quickly beats its guts in a mortar before the spirits dissipate (when "almost cold"), and stuffs the remains into a distillation glass to be boiled with milk, currants, and herbs to make something akin to chicken soup. In her diary, Lady Elinor Fettiplace mentioned routinely flaying cats, whipping cocks, and killing sheep.[11] The ailing human, waiting to ingest home remedies, might well have quivered in the face of the housewife, who so evidently had her finger on the pulse of life and death. Even for housewives who did not regularly slaughter animals, Renaissance guides emphasize their troubling power to interchange human and animal parts. One syrup recipe in the 1595 *Widdowes Treasure* promises to aid the delicate almost alchemical process by which animal flesh mutated into human blood; its promise to "turn meat to pure blood" suggests a process intelligible only through the lens of a premodern humoral theory.[12] If banqueting pressured the boundaries between artifice and reality, medical care partitioned life forms into usable parts. Hearkening toward dinner's vitality or the precariousness of human embodiment, housewifery smacked of an aggressive yet licensed violence.

Woolley's paraphrase of the then well-known 1508 *Book of Kerving* offers cues for conceptualizing kitchen practice. "In cutting up small Birds it is proper to say thigh them," writes Woolley, as she renders butchery into a lexicon to be mastered, "as thigh that Woodcock, thigh that Pigeon":

But as to others say, mince that Plover ... Allay that Pheasant, untack that Curlew, unjoynt that Bittern, disfigure that Peacock, display that Crane, dismember that Hern, unbrace that Mallard, trust that Chicken, spoyl that Hen, sawce that Capon, lift that Swan, reer that Goose ... unlace that Coney, break that Deer, leach that Brawn: For Fish, chine that Salmon, string that Lamprey, splat that Pike, sawce that Plaice, and sawce that Tench, splay that Bream; side that Haddock, tusk that Barbel, culpon that Trout, transon that Eel, tranch that Sturgeon, tame that Crab, barb that Lobster. (*Compleat Servant-Maid*, 35)

Making mutilation a rhetorical tutorial, guides construct the decorum of violence. They can be said to partake of what Jonathan Sawday describes as the autoptic vision of early modern culture, the epistemological drive to dissect and master the body.[13] The engaging iteration of imaginatively "disfiguring" reminds us that "carve" also meant "to take at one's pleasure" (*OED*, 9b). Part of the pleasure of housework, then, might involve the fantasy of taming, displaying, barbing, and splatting bodies. Such practices were not, of course, peculiarly premodern; for modern cultures that don't have regular access to re-frigeration, factory food, or markets, butchery remains a domestic chore. Yet, as I elaborate below, the particular terms by which domesticity was represented for the public had historically distinct contours, as did the stakes of domestic order for theories of nation and governance. In presenting the civilized and upwardly mobile housewife as someone who regularly had blood on her hands or mischief in her thoughts, the first cookbooks called attention to how her chores did not accord with the ideals of femininity articulated elsewhere in the culture. When conduct book writers instructed housewives and servants to remain at home quietly learning subjection, for instance, did they have in mind these scenes of wit or dismemberment? Patricia Fumerton remarks that "the everyday practice of another period (as also our own) can be charged with strangeness even to its practitioners."[14] While these manuals refract the everyday so as to make it available for a reader's consumption, they also hint that domestic practice might itself have appeared at times disturbing or slightly fantastic.

Having glanced at cookbooks, might we then reevaluate those seemingly sensationalized moments on the early modern stage? Rather than simply es-tranging things familiar, these hypercharged dramatic moments tease out alien aspects of routine household rituals, activities, and tasks and thus expose the discrepancy between domestic ideals and an often disorderly lived practice. If we venture more widely into the writing in the period, we find that such scenes also animate points of tension arising when domesticity was positioned contra-dictorily in early modern discourses. The household was, after all, prominent in debates about pedagogical theory, childraising, pastoralism, popular lore, medicine, vocation, English speech, nationalism, and especially the ethic of household management, or *oeconomia*, newly popular with the "middling sort" of the population.[15] As such, texts nominating the housewife as the guardian of a national and Christian stewardship inevitably clashed with discourses that devalued the domestic realm as trivial, effeminate, or infantilizing. How could domesticity be key to preserving the diet, rituals, and methods that constituted English culture but also be the abject realm to be disavowed in the name of progress? What was to be made of the fact that housewifery sometimes reversed "proper" lines of dependency? *Staging Domesticity* isolates such contradictions as they surface in early modern plays so as to make visible the contradictory but powerful identifications they offered to audiences.

My argument rests on a simple observation. In the early modern period, domestic labor was represented in two importantly different ways (if I may offer an overly schematic account): as a reassuringly "common" sphere in which people immersed themselves in familiar rhythms, and as a profoundly alienating site that could never be fully inhabited or comprehended. In its first incarnation, the household harbored supposedly indigenous rituals, languages, and practices that bound the *natio*. In its second form, it was associated with femininity, lower-class servitude, vulgar lore, or a degraded oral culture, and, as such, it constituted a site of shame particularly for elite men. The drama of the period fuses these two representations to show how domesticity, in part because of its disorienting character, paradoxically enabled people to imagine new identities and subject positions.

One central subject position that this book takes up is that of national affiliation, the "domestic" in another sense of the word; for the plays that I discuss locate domesticity, in a deep structural way, as at the core of national identity. Common sense might suggest that the panic and pleasure aired about domestic life on the stage might disqualify the household as a nodal point around which national identifications could be generated. After all, how could Englishness rest on such a chaotic foundation? Yet texts that defamiliarize everydayness paradoxically end up consolidating the supposedly collective experience of English daily life. Focusing on the oddities of household relations may erode idealizations of domesticity and traditional claims for the family, but these texts put other models for national identification in their stead. Domesticity, I argue, emerges as *fantasy* in the period, and by this term I don't mean to suggest its unreal character but instead its ability to provide what Jacqueline Rose terms as the "psychic glue" binding people into a community.[16] Some plays suggest that the affective turmoil surrounding household life paved the way for people to reconsider the terms of national affiliation. Other plays indicate that domestic fantasies made the very idea of a nation less abstract and more compelling for its citizens. Rather than showing the domus simply to be the site of a subject's dispossession or enfranchisement within the familial order, then, sixteenth- and seventeenth-century plays thematically harness now seemingly odd passions – the prince's volatile desire for milk, the servant's euphoria in imagining cannibals in the dining hall – to decidedly domestic constructions of Englishness. This book attempts to credit these dramatic scenes as registering something critical about the process of early modern subjecthood, namely the paradoxical ways domesticity signified in the cultural imagination and how it helped to structure social, sexual, gendered, and national identifications.

*Staging Domesticity* begins with the inception of English drama in the universities and grammar schools, themselves domestic spaces, in the 1550s, and concludes with plays presented around the time that professional theaters closed in 1642. My strategy is to read somewhat noncanonical plays in the context of the first published English household guides and cookbooks. If the overarching polemic of this book is that scholars should expand their understanding of early modern domesticity, my more specific argument is that a "middle-class" national identity was generated out of reflections on the material realities of household work.[17] Making this argument allows me to trace a counter-narrative to criticism that defines early modern national identity as a court-based phenomenon. Englishness, in that body of scholarship, becomes reducible to shared subjection to the crown; and domesticity enters into the picture as a central analogical proving ground for monarchy. "The father is head of household as king is head of state" is the ubiquitous message trumpeted in sermons, conduct manuals, and political pamphlets, where the household was to inculcate a model of citizenship given ultimate meaning by the figure of the sovereign. The much-vaunted theory of patriarchalism established the familial, "natural" roots of monarchy, thus providing a rationale for membership in a stratified political community. After the Reformation, domesticity's importance as a structural model for social order was intensified. As scholars have noted, the early seventeenth century witnessed the transformation of what was in effect a "vaguely articulated societal theory into an intentional political ideology," one so powerful that the family secured a place of importance in political debates for the next one hundred years.[18]

Scholars have usefully shown this state-centered paradigm to underpin canonical drama, poetry, and prose of the period, even as they note ways in which patriarchalism failed to dictate or contain actual practice.[19] Yet if we consider the materiality of household life as well as its inscription in cookbooks, guides, and fictional works, we discover a very different picture of domesticity. While Perkins saw the household as teaching the "principles of authoritie and subjection," other representations depict competing lines of allegiance and dependency at work in the home. While the husband was sovereign over the household, for instance, he found himself in the uncomfortable position of submitting to his wife's and servant's medical ministrations. In college residences as well, lines of authority ran counter to idealized versions of both cross-gendered domesticity and pedagogy. Thus while domesticity was indeed a conceptual ideal in the period, it didn't fully square with the complex realities of domestic work. As a busy, chaotic, threatening, playful, transgressive, and gory *workplace*, the household exceeded the symbolic functions outlined in state and church manifestos.

Nor does early modern domesticity completely accord with modern assumptions about the organization, scope, or even fundamental social role of the home. Scholars have helped us to overcome our "presentist" viewpoint by highlighting precisely those features of the Renaissance household that have become alien to later observers: the lack of hallways and private living spaces; the sharing of beds between household residents, servants, and guests; the inclusion of what would later become professional market production; the household's vital implication in community rituals and economic structures; the normative violence; and the sheer amount of labor required to sustain human life.[20] Sometimes headed up by a single woman, often inclusive of a working husband, servants, children, apprentices, infants to be wetnursed, and live-in guests, and lodged at times in same-sex residential institutions, the early modern "family," itself the primary unit of production in the period, offered diverse "kinship" arrangements.[21] In a world where economics was home economics, domesticity exceeded its caricatured form in the prescriptive ideology of its time.[22]

The less canonical representations that I identify – on stage and in print – tend to accentuate the details of household life and to invoke an indigenous community based on cultural affiliations rather than political institutions. Sharing diet, language, climate, history, and even forms of abjection and pleasure, English people were invited to suspend court-based conceptions of Englishness and imagine communities cohering in unpredictable ways. Scholars agree that the link between household and commonwealth was radically reconfigured in the mid-seventeenth century in the wake of the Civil War, so that by 1700 it was no longer key to providing a doctrine of political legitimation.[23] I suggest that English cookbooks, manuals, and plays in the hundred years prior offered indirect ammunition for the critique that social contract theorists would later wage against the traditional analogies of family and state. These texts eroded domestic ideologies and the state-based theories of Englishness they supported, even as those national theories were in the process of being conceptualized. One of my goals in writing this book, then, is to suspend the central metaphor of patriarchalism in order to reveal other conceptions of domesticity and national identifications available in the period.

Telling the story of domesticity draws me into different critical debates. Since these representations turn up surprising erotic investments, they nudge critics to account for the mobile sexualities residing in and around the household. Insofar as domesticity has been seen as the proper subject of feminist criticism and thinking, I join an ongoing project aimed at refining feminist criticism of Renaissance culture so as to take into account gains made by queer theorists, social historians, and materialist critics.[24] In part this simply entails including in our line of vision spaces such as academic residences or the household-based urban shop. But this revision involves a change in perspective as well: shifting a focus away from the marital dyad frees critics to see other economic and erotic relationships forming in the domus, where companions, male and female servants, wetnurses, children, apprentices, journeymen, and field workers labored alongside the housewife and husband.[25] In past years, queer theorists have prodded feminist critics to discriminate more carefully between gender and sexuality and to examine assumptions that obscure the unconventional erotics underpinning even apparently "normative" relationships. Why not subject domesticity to this type of reconsideration? For we discover that relations of status and dependency, in part shaped in domestic arenas, produced erotic desires that cut across and through gender.[26] We stumble, that is, upon the queer nature of the early modern household, not only the homoeroticism that pervades its turf, but also the unstable passions and irregular desires subtending its relationships.[27]

As I have hinted, one of my aims is also to rescue domesticity from being the sordid spot of retrograde values that feminists sometimes take it to be. In fact, this project grew out of my frustration when otherwise attentive critics dubbed characters as "domesticated" when they meant "powerless," or when they assumed housework to be by definition a trivial and trivializing activity. Though it undoubtedly inculcated regulatory norms, domesticity appears more complicated if we take into account its economic and symbolic centrality in the period. How could women be "relegated" to the household at a time in which it had not yet even superficially withdrawn from economic life or from some yet unborn public sphere? And how did the turbulent energies generated in household work square with prescriptions for an intertwined domestic and state order? Even the term "housewife" bears some reflection, since it is often taken to mean marital status and thus a form of legal and economic disempowerment. Yet in texts of the period it could refer to a vocation and practice, and as such, housewifery might be undertaken by unmarried maids and heads of household.[28] Though women could certainly be politically disenfranchised while economically central, their domestic work was sometimes recognized as a stumbling block to state-sponsored political ideologies. Expanding our knowledge of architecture, inventories, lawsuits, and wills, scholars have devised more historically accurate accounts of domesticity as well as better models for charting how "gender" was produced from within lived practices. Building on this work, *Staging Domesticity* works to unbury domesticity from the residue of 1970s family studies, a body of work designed primarily to critique the modern division of labor in a capitalist regime. When the family unit was at the nerve center of economic production, domesticity was more than the domain of "proper womanhood."

In that it takes up the relation of national to other identifications, this book also speaks to scholarship on early modern English identity. While I am not concerned to argue that nationalism emerged in a period earlier than political theorists have previously thought, or even to nominate nationality as the preeminent identification of the day, I am interested in refining our understanding of the *process* by which Englishness was conferred on and experienced by early modern persons.[29] Modern conceptions of nationalism often do not obtain for this era, given that governmental structures bore vestiges of medieval feudal organization; the nation state was dynastic and thus inhered in the sovereign's body; rigid lines of status cut deeper than national boundaries; and the semi-absolutist Tudor state was at odds with its own absolutist official ideology.[30] Nevertheless numerous texts clearly put forth what Homi Bhaba terms the "national address," as they asked audiences to imagine themselves as a collective bound by territory, racial and moral characteristics, common history, climate, temperament, or shared practices. These age-old gestures were given new meaning in the sixteenth century, with national consciousness heightened by England's divorce from universal Christendom, the merging of church and state, the fragmentation of Latin into national vernaculars, the centralization of administrative structures, and the development of infrastructures enabling the flow of goods, information, and books throughout England.

"In the early Tudor period, national more often means race, or kind," Claire McEachern writes, "the kith and kin of a common nativity, or birth, *natio*. Yet it also hovers near the meaning we have given it, and . . . in the course of the sixteenth century it comes to denote that principle of political self-determination belonging to a people linked (if in nothing else) by a common government."[31] Analyzing republicanism and emergent social contract theory, scholars avidly debate what principles of self-determination would have been available to seventeenth-century English citizens. But I am interested in pursuing McEachern's phrase – "linked (if in nothing else)" – so as to unveil the "something else" that was seen as binding the nation. The "Englishness" bandied about in domestic plays and household manuals rarely forms an argument for a particular mode of governance. In that sense, these texts don't reveal a hitherto veiled liberatory political model. Instead Englishness takes shape discursively as a "cultural glue" formed around the interests of the middling sort of the population. Glancing only perfunctorily at shared allegiance to the crown or opposition to foreigners (the most prevalent logics of affinity and difference), these dramatic scenes insist that English citizens are bound by the seemingly primal scene of the home, with its vexed cultural and economic concerns. Perhaps, these texts suggest, *feeling* English involves an oscillation between alienation and belonging. Perhaps this national vertigo strikes more of a chord than the command to inhabit a proper slot within the social hierarchy.

Just as importantly, my project seeks to complicate standard constellations of gender and national identity assumed in current scholarship: the age-old analogy of woman-as-land that permeates early modern chronicle, cartography, and travel narratives; Queen Elizabeth's equation of the autonomy of the English isle with the inviolability of the ideally chaste female body;[32] and " femininity" as an early modern cultural codeword for national hybridization and difference, the *antithesis* of genuine Englishness.[33] I add to these stories a counter-narrative whereby domestic workers (usually represented under the sign of "woman") model the self-sufficiency, moral fiber, and industry necessary for England's identification as a nation not reducible to state structure. In the representations tying domestic *production* to Englishness, "woman" emerges as a constituent part of what Lauren Berlant terms the National Symbolic.[34] My point is not that such representations bettered the actual status of women or offered revisionary political models. Rather, I suggest, gender is itself shown to be internally riven in the discourses that writers used to set the terms for establishing community and nation. Attending to representations of household work and English identity in fact takes us away from the story of women's (seemingly inevitable) exclusion from political, social, and economic formations and hits home the point that "woman" is used to mark contradictory positions in national and domestic ideologies. Though these texts hardly enfranchised domestic subordinates, they · demonstrated that official or critically dominant representations of the nation-as-the-court did not go uncontested. They did so, in part, by offering sites of fantasy for audiences and readers; thus fantasies, as I see them, allowed for the reformulation of subject positions, enabling, among other things, a citizenly conception of Englishness.

Which brings me to my use of the term "fantasy," a clear red flag in an historically oriented project, for the psychological baggage that the term conveys may seem to contradict my commitment to avoid anachronistic and individualistic frameworks. Psychoanalytic categories can pose problems for historicists, since they are predicated on nineteenth-century bourgeois family structures, or since they depend on a conception of persons as having interior truths that can be abstracted from social conditions. Yet I work with the assumption that fantasies can be read as cutting through and across persons rather than being tethered to the epiphanies of a volitional self: that is, I find it possible to identify *cultural* fantasies.[35] The texts I examine imagine a nostalgic return to national origins vexed precisely because of peculiarly early modern problems that are neither individual nor universal (e.g., the politics of wetnursing and milk, changing service relations, agrarian subsistence economies, humanist pedagogy, the humoral body). Terms such as "fantasy" and "identification" are useful for deciphering how representations reconfigured social issues and how they ignited passions in Renaissance audiences and readers.

What then do I mean by fantasy? While accepting Louis Montrose's formulation of plays themselves as ideological "shaping fantasies," I narrow the term at times to refer to scenes that depict curiously heightened emotional expressions.[36] Such passages unfold like dreamwork where subjects appear in and through the very grammar of the representation. When we discover that domesticity excites and frightens characters, we need a language that will allow us to make sense of that hyper-affect. Psychoanalytic language has allowed me to refine the new historicist and feminist methods (in which I have been trained) so as to elasticize the way that texts mark the interests of particular groups. In *Merry Wives of Windsor*, to take one instance, both a town householder and an aristocrat are humiliated by housewives wielding domestic control. But it isn't enough to sort through which gender or class triumphs in the plot, for while content does establish ideological points of reference, we must look as well to language and affect. In this case, Ford's and Falstaff's intense shame surrounding the housewife's authority over subordinates invites a set of mobile identifications – for servants, husbands, and children – in which domestic care figures a *structure* rather than pointing to the actual interests of early

modern housewives. Embarrassment, experienced as the threat of being laun-
dered and cooked, doesn't simply signify male powerlessness but instead creates
a powerful fantasy of dependency, one that the play connects thematically to
the dilemma of being English (for the citizen must lodge national value in an
"effeminizing" arena).

In one sense, determining the "interests" served by literary works becomes
complicated when fantasy is seen not simply as the wish of an individual (the
*object* of desire) but instead as the cultural setting or syntax for desire, the
slushy repertoire of emotions enabling particular vantage points. "Fantasy . . .
is to be understood not as an activity of an already formed subject, but of the
staging and dispersion of the subject into a variety of identificatory positions,"
Judith Butler writes in elaborating the work of Laplanche and Pontalis. Or, as
Slavoj Žižek puts it, the subjects knows itself through the expression of desire
in fantasy, but this recognition takes place through the process of desiring
rather than the imagined fulfillment.[37] Psychoanalytic terminology thus allows
me to make the case that the dispersed *identifications* of fantasy act as raw
ingredients used to cook up provisional identities.[38] Deployed strategically in
an historicist framework, this vocabulary might elasticize our understanding
of identification as a process through which subjects recognize "themselves"
in speech acts and discourses. In small measure, it allows negative emotions
(such as shame) to be considered part of the "desire," or "interests," that make
a subject recognizable.[39] Designating texts as sites of fantasy also illuminates
the subjective component of political belonging – the "feelings" that fueled an
investment in being English and made abstract identification alluring to early
modern audiences.

### *Housework and its peevish fantasies*

Let's think for a moment about what domestic fantasies might have meant in the
period. In his 1581 translation of Steven Guazzo's courtly *Civil Conversation*,
George Pettie advises that a "woman cannot possibly do any thing that may
make her husband more in love with her, then to play the good huswife . . . [For
her husband] conceiveth a firme opinyon of her honesty, seeing her take paines
and exercise her body in workes belonging to the house, whereby she getteth a
lively natural colour and that vertuous vermilion, which falleth off neither with
sweating . . . nor with washing."[40] Pettie emphasizes the exquisite sweat beading
over the virtuous blush of the working housewife, who labors with the self-
consciousness of herself as an erotic spectacle. In this somewhat conventional
eroticization of housework, we see the relaying of desirability to industry that
usually ends up, in conduct manuals of the period, firmly ensconced in civic
virtue. Labor is imagined as the incarnation of discipline, but one put on display
in an approved circuitry of desire. Generating a glistening blush certain to shoot

Cupid's arrows into the heart of her spouse, the housewife performs her daily work (whose mundane nature is marked by reference to sweating and bathing) with the assurance that her moral and economic honesty guarantees a pleasure that will be neatly funneled into marriage at the exact moment that it is produced.

Sixty years earlier, in his introduction to Margaret Roper's 1526 translation of Erasmus' *Devout Treatise Upon the Pater Noster*, Richard Hyrde implies that he might have found this chain of desire reassuring, given his concern for what was concealed beneath the working housewife's sweaty blush. Hyrde argues that educating women was less dangerous than letting them undertake the potentially radical act of housework, since physical labor allows female minds to wander and drum up peevish fantasies:

Redyng and studyeng of bokes so occupieth the mynde that it can have no leyser [leisure] to muse or delyte in other fantasies. [W]han in all handy werkes that men saye be more mete for a woman the body may be busy in one place and the mynde walkyng in another. While they syt sowing & spinnyng with their fyngers [they] maye caste and compasse many pevysshe fantasyes in their myndes.[41]

When women labor at domestic chores, their minds remain perilously at liberty to entertain potentially rebellious thoughts. Reading, on the other hand, colonized the vacant mind, regulated desire, and guarded against untoward behavior. In Hyrde's spatialized view of the mind/body opposition, the unfilled psyche could detach from corporeality, walk away from work, generate, and lasso ("caste and compasse") wanton thoughts, even while the body appeared to all observers to be rigidly obedient. What we have is a fantasy about fantasies devised by women – an imagined moment when housewives, busy spinning cloth and doing exactly what is said to be "mete" for them to do, mask their production of invisible delights. As in Pettie's text, housework is shown to be the site of pleasure, but here it offers dangerously unbridled indulgences for the worker rather than viewer.

Conventionally writers argued the exact opposite theory: labor guaranteed subordination precisely because it so fully absorbed women that they couldn't entertain idle thoughts. Thomas Overbury, for instance, argued that the bodily exercise required by housewifery fashions a correspondingly sober mind: "Domesticke charge doth best that sex befit, /Contiguous businesse; so to fixe the mind, /That leisure space for fancies not admit."[42] In requiring absolute concentration, Overbury suggested, housework fortified the mind against external distractions and suppressed the creation of fantasy. The phrase "contiguous businesse" implies a mind "side by side" with work, aligned and metonymically inscribed by the weightiness of labor. Other writers similarly affirmed the almost hardwired connection between a body bent at labor and the sobriety, virtue, and industry figured by that posture. But commentators such as Miles Coverdale didn't see the workings of the mind and body as inherently related at all since women could simply attach work to both appropriate and inappropriate forms of mirth. Coverdale wished that "women syttynge at theyr rockes or spynnynge at the wheles, had none other songes to passe theyr tyme withall than soch as Moses sister, Elchanas wife, Debora and Mary the mother of Christ ... [T]hey shulde be better occupied, then with hey nony nony, hey troly loly, & soch lyke fantasies."[43]

For my purposes, this debate is not merely about whether housework was politically oppressive for women or not, since putting the question that way straitjackets criticism into echoing the overly simplistic options that these writers put forth (liberatory or restrictive? worthwhile or fantasy?). I'm also hesitant to posit a politics emanating directly from the economic realities of work. While it is true that representations of desirable working women mystified socioeconomic changes taking place as family industry moved increasingly to wage labor, this account hardly tells the whole story. Instead, as these passages suggest, writers were concerned about how domesticity was experienced and interpreted in a number of contexts. Once housework is imagined as a site of fantasy, might it not have unexpected resonances for a culture where domesticity provided the template for political order?

When we supplement these passages with what we know they occlude – the presence of male and female household residents bound in structures of dependency, same-sex domesticity, the intellectual challenge posed by physic and botany, the creativity of confectionery, the disciplinary practices of beating, or the aggressivity required in butchery – the fear of a libidinal domestic space begins to speak to more than female sexuality in isolation. As we uncover debates about the meaning and nature of household work, that is, we enlarge the range of "peevish fantasies" readily attached to it. How else might we classify one ghastly published recipe for curing eye infections where the housewife is to extract "two or three Lice" from a person's hair and affix them to the eyeball, for louse are said to suck out pestilent "webs" or eyesores? "Put them alive into the Eye that is grieved and so close it up, and most assuredly the Lice will suck out the Web in the eye, and will cure it, and come forth without any hurt."[44] The wife here is to subject the ailing person to a nightmare of the flesh, since lice were associated in the cultural imagination with vampirism, predation, filth, and the threat of being devoured alive. The writer's promise, that this will "assuredly" cure the eye "without any hurt," only raises the specter of possible injury. A second recipe in this manual opens with the following instructions for curing aching joints: "Take a live Fox or Badger, of middle age, or a Full body, wel fed and fat, kill him, bowel and skin him" (104). The casual command, "kill him," overlays dissection with domestic *sprezzatura*. Associated with aristocratic leisure sports, and believed to be crafty enough to outsmart even the most skilled hunter, the fox was the ultimately elusive predator. Downplaying the prowess required to reduce a subtle fox to mere flesh, this recipe implies the ease with which the housewife could outfox a rival even in the banal task of creating a pain reliever.[45] While these recipes may or may not have had a practical basis, printed manuals don't shrink from advertising the almost mythic threat buried in the housewife's management of injury, her ability to constitute the bodies under her care by manipulating cunning forces or taming nightmarish predators. Even pragmatic guides, I suggest, air fantasies about domestic work.

While it would be easy to chalk up Hyrde's, Overbury's, and Coverdale's curiosity about housework to voyeurism or to an everpresent concern with regulating the female body, gender management seems only a partial explanation for how domesticity signified. Instead I suggest that we examine the specific contexts in which writers fantasized about domestic license. Each of the chapters of *Staging Domesticity* takes up this task by locating dramatic works within the debates surrounding specific domestic practices: wetnursing and the English vernacular (Chapter 2), housecleaning and fairylore (Chapter 3), homegrown and imported foodstuffs (Chapter 4), medical care and dependency (Chapter 5), butchery and violence (Chapter 6). Diverging interpretations of the possible pleasures of work also reveal that guidebooks' obsessive prescriptions for industry did not get to the heart of the problem even conceptually, since the question of *how* women worked and what their work meant – both to them and to a broader population – remained unresolved. The drama of the period provides one useful site for broadening the myopic vision of domesticity that these passages suggest. In *Gammer Gurton's Needle*, for instance, Hyrde's isolated housewife finds her own work defined in terms of male–male erotic relationships as well as a community's collective efforts at defining its linguistic currency. In *Knight of the Burning Pestle*, the housewife's pleasure in bossing apprentices around suggests how relationships of eroticized dependency, domestic and otherwise, could overlap in the culture. And in *Woman Killed with Kindness*, the domestic worker materializes as a male servant whose labors threaten the organically unified and homoeroticized household body it maintains.

Which leads me to say something about my object of study and its parameters. Why attend to plays? Do I mean to suggest that drama is the most fertile place to look for emergent ideas about domesticity and nationality? In concentrating on readings of literature, I don't mean to call for a return to the "literary artifact" (or the author) as the most productive object of cultural analysis. While drama is simply one site among many in which domesticity and nationality overlap, it does offer at least two advantages: 1) plays not only license strong expressions of affect but are particularly well suited for airing incompatible social discourses since they imagine a wide range of positions put in conversation with each other; and 2) theater reached a wide array of people in and outside London and was collaboratively produced by people of different social backgrounds.[46] Generalizations about "family life" thus might usefully be revised to take into account the oddly *material* households represented in less canonical plays by Heywood, Beaumont, Dekker, and Greene.

And why attend to these plays in particular? Although this book includes drama performed between 1550 and 1640, most of the plays I discuss were written between 1590 and 1610, the time in which the popular stage was most prolific. While scholars have corrected the view that Caroline drama was simply royalist in nature, they have done so by arguing that post-1625 drama critiqued cavalier and absolutist ideologies precisely by showing the follies of the elite world from *within* that world; this suggests that the reputed "citizen drama" performed primarily at the turn of the century gave way to a courtly focus.[47] In the 1620s, playwrights largely transferred their energies away from public amphitheaters to contribute to indoor and more exclusive theaters. One result was that few new plays were written for the amphitheaters in the last two decades before theaters closed. For my purposes this explains why representations of household labor waned in plays written after the 1620s. Yet, even though there was a decrease in *new* plays boasting stewards, housewives, and citizens as champions of Englishness, the earlier "citizen" repertoire of the 1590s continued to be revived and printed in the first part of the seventeenth century. Since only private playhouses would reopen in the 1660s, it isn't surprising that housewifery failed to take center stage in the Restoration drama of social manners and wit. And by the beginning of the eighteenth century, when "bourgeois" comedies by writers such as Lillo and Rowe became fashionable, household work had not only changed, but domesticity had largely vanished as a key term in political debates about government and nationality.

Finally, a word about the type of claim I hope to make. Researching this book has immersed me in the fascinating traces of domestic material culture. I have sifted through accounts of early modern people's casual use of urine, umbilical cords, skulls, and breastmilk as kitchen ingredients, of their penchant for constructing virtual worlds entirely of sugar, and of their ease in disemboweling animals. I have been intrigued by their need to regulate a humoral body always in danger of going awry. In short, my own dis-identification with these practices has become an important means for me to grapple with definitions of early modern or premodern life. Yet, despite the temptation to do so, I don't attempt to write a history of the empirical realities of domesticity. Instead I use primary and secondary sources to characterize household life as part of an argument about the tenor and force of representations. While it does limn a set of practices that may be suggestive for other kinds of studies, *Staging Domesticity* explores the somewhat alien discourse of domesticity in order to say something about the fraught identifications it enabled.

In *Othello*, Iago famously quips that housewifery is really only wayward sexuality. "You are pictures out [a'doors]," he tells Emilia and Desdemona, "Bells in your parlors, wild-cats in your kitchens . . . Players in your huswifery, and huswives in your beds."[48] Here the most notorious domestic disturber evokes the image of a ferocious female kitchen tiger to play on the double meaning of "housewife": a thrifty, economical manager and a loose, disorderly wanton. In doing so, Iago airs a familiar brand of Renaissance misogyny: beneath every housewife resides a huswife, her idealized industry masking the true wildness of her passions (the unstable lexical meanings of housewife/huswife attest to this duality). But numerous texts remind us that the early modern English world could readily implicate household labor in less predictable desires; and in doing so, they revised domesticity's moral, social, and national stakes. Attending to these texts allows us to supplement scholarship that has examined the "hussy" as a momentous figure but has overlooked her counterpart, the "housewife," and the symbolic power she lent for shaping identifications. Analyzing the passions hovering around the banal practices of physic, cookery, confectionery, wetnursing, distilling, and dairying, *Staging Domesticity* investigates ways in which subjects took shape from within domestic fantasies. Rather than restricting domesticity to the "first school" in which political, sexual, and social subjection was inculcated, then, might we see the household as implicated in various modes of subjection and identification? When we characterize early modern domesticity, that is, might we include in our vision the image of Lady Macbeth consulting a Renaissance cookbook as she whipped up a narcotic for Duncan's guards?

# 1 Familiarity and pleasure in the English household guide, 1500–1700

## I. Canning and the uncanny

In his 1919 paper, "The Uncanny," Freud famously undertakes a semantic analysis of the German word "heimlich," tracing its transformation from one set of related meanings – as intimate, familiar, comfortable, and belonging to the home – into superficially opposite definitions. First denoting a private chamber, "heimlich" wandered linguistically so as to signify those mystical things dangerously concealed from sight. Freud's exercise wonderfully demonstrates how the comfort secured by a home's privacy could shade into the threat of something sinister precisely because of its recessivity; that is, the assurance of inhabiting an exclusive terrain could give way to the perspective of the outsider wistfully peering into that domain.[1] Freud's commentary assumes a modern division of public and private that does not obtain in the early modern world, yet his linguistic analysis corresponds to the historical claim that I outlined in the introduction: that domestic life was represented as accessible but also forcefully estranged from its practitioners, and this instability was given meaning, in part, by the early modern struggle to define domesticity's role in shaping national and social identifications.

In this chapter I outline the history of the first English published cookbooks and domestic manuals in order to investigate how household advice defined the publics they addressed. In representing "back" in written form supposedly everyday activities, these manuals necessarily made readers self-conscious about the already potentially peculiar nature of daily tasks as well as the radically different frameworks through which those tasks might be experienced. Less predictably, we discover that books labored precisely (and out of particular political interests) to fashion the conception of "everyday domesticity" that Freud so blithely assumes. In part these books shaped domestic information as part of their appeal to various audiences: newly urbanized wives who wanted to mask country practices; citizens interested in European novelties; daughters of cashpoor aristocratic families in need of positions; yeomen and country gentry interested in efficient agrarian work; men who delighted in viewing tasks designated as female. The cumulative effect was that guidebook writers represented household practices in two different ways: familiarized as native culture and the ur-basis for identity; and defamiliarized as a curiously desirable but inaccessible zone – from the point of view of men who wrote about domesticity, women who sought to emulate the "everydayness" of another social class, and general practitioners who witnessed their behaviors in highly mediated form. While seeking to attract a wide range of readers, writers implicitly or explicitly classified domesticity in ways that positioned it differently in relation to English identity.

Before turning to printed guides themselves I want to outline the contours of the historical reality to which they refer. Recent work by Patricia Fumerton in particular helps to illuminate some of the circumstantial oddities of domestic life, for she describes how members of great households might savor a live goose as it slowly dies at the dinner table, or engage in elaborate and violent banqueting rituals. Though the intricately crafted sugar sculptures and tortured animals that Fumerton mentions were not common fare in most English homes, they have affinities with the practices that did constitute everyday life, for housewifery did include unassuming acts of brutality and creativity.[2] Preindustrial European housewifery ranged beyond the practices of modern housework to include medical service, distillation, water purification, dairying, confectionery, brewing, butchery, slaughter, textile-making, veterinary care, and the production of simple goods. To understand the conception of domesticity underpinning this work, a modern reader has to dispense with now common assumptions and taxonomies. What were the daily activities of a housewife from the middling sort in early seventeenth-century London?

*You rise early in the morning to fix breakfast for the journeymen, apprentice, servants, children, and spouse who constitute your family. Sometime this week you will need to starch linens in preparation for the Lord Mayor's procession, supervise laundering at the river, instruct the children, buy goods from the peddler and grocer, fetch water from the conduit (and get the latest gossip), weed the kitchen garden, and work in the shoemaking shop in your house. For now, however, you've arranged objects on the kitchen dresser as reminders of specific chores that must be done today.*

*The first is a vial filled with breastmilk. You discovered yesterday that one of your children has an infected eye, so you set out to make a milk-based eyewash. While you usually buy cow's, ass's or mare's milk from peddling women, you were fortunate enough to have a neighbor, Mistress Henney, nursing her third child. Happy to spare her excess, she availed herself of the glass tube for drawing milk that you used to help suck out the colostrum, or beestings, after she gave birth. While your mother made eyewashes with milk freshly drawn from the cow in the countryside, here in town you rely on cow's milk to make cheeses and pies (some of which you sell for extra pin money). But you've been able to improve your recipes with access to local wetnurses and nursing neighbors.*

*The second object on the dresser is a glister-pipe, used to administer enemas to servants, guests, and family. You have promised to make a senna emetic to give to your neighbor Ison's servant, so you will use a limbeck for distilling and then loan her a spare glister-pipe. You make a mental note to ask tomorrow for a full report on its effectiveness, since you are thinking of altering the amounts of fennel and linseeds used. Beside the glister-pipe is a bowl filled with squirming snails and slugs that you brought in from the garden yesterday. You need to pound them with a mortar and pestle to make a hemorrhoid salve. And next to the snails is a tiny fragment of a human jawbone. At the funeral of your uncle James last week, the gravedigger exposed a few bones from a previous inhabitant, so you neatly pocketed one of the pieces; Mistress Evans' cure for the falling sickness recommends that you dry a bone fragment in the oven slowly for a few days and then grind it into distilled water.*

*But now you must attend to tonight's dinner and so you turn to the next items: a live capon penned in a wire cage and a freshly slaughtered rabbit bought from the butcher. You wrestle the screeching capon to the table in order to pluck its feathers. The gore and noise from this denuding is intensified when you slit its throat in preparation for making a delicious stew. After dressing the capon, you decapitate and disembowel the rabbit in preparation for roasting. This work brings a stench to the kitchen which you try to combat with a perfumed pomander that you made from home-grown lavender. But you only make matters worse by inadvertently tipping over the capon's blood when reaching for the pomander, so you spend the next half hour strewing rushes on the floor and trying to clean the stains with a home-made urine-based astringent. While scouring the floor, you remember to tell your maid to empty the chamberpot into the street.*

*Glancing at the next item, a paste of sugar, gum, and almonds, you realize that this is the task you have anticipated eagerly for days. You carefully get your banqueting ingredients from a locked closet and prepare the cinnamon, goldleaf, conserved quinces, comfits, and spices so as to fashion and decorate your marzipan, which you mold into the shape of two strips of bacon. You use home-made dyes to create red and white variegations on the collops and you plop an egg-shaped bit of saffron-yellow marzipan on top. While delicious fake bacon and eggs are a certain delight, you'd like to try your hand later at making a confectionery walnut that will contain the poem that you and Mistress Rawlinson composed while making lemon conserves. You'll use one dish for a banquet and save the other for a few months. In the interim, it can serve as a room decoration.*

*You then consult an almanac to find out if it's a good month for blood-letting. While the barber-surgeon usually does phlebotomy, your serving woman Susan needs a minor purge. This morning you had to punish her for oversleeping by uncovering her naked in bed in front of the other workers (and they made up a jingle teasing her about it) but your reprimand didn't rid her of her sluggishness. Your husband thinks that a sound beating is in order, but you insist that cleansing her tardy spirits is a sure-fire remedy.*

*Other kitchen items remind you of future tasks: a glass tube for brewing Dr. Steven's water (the equivalent of aspirin) and hippocras (spiced wine); fresh dog dung and the lungs of a fox used to make plasters; lye to give to the laundry maid for cleaning soiled linens; urine for concocting a pungent ague water (not your husband's favorite drink); pears for canning preserves; tallow to make candles; and a piece of shoe-thread that the maids created for the shop.[3]*

Of course, a housewife would have undertaken tasks, such as sweeping and cooking that fall more readily within the domain of modern housework. Yet some of her chores required the public exchange of now intimate materials (such as urine and breastmilk) and the use of now taboo items such as human bones and umbilical cords. Violating modern expectations of propriety and privacy, premodern housework established only loose boundaries around the body and the household; for it included activities subsequently taken over by professionals. Some aspects of housewifery, now unrecognizable to later readers, involved aggression, inventiveness, strength, specialized knowledges (chemical, mathematical, philosophical, and anatomical) and skill in manipulating people.

Early modern women of even high rank attended to domestic chores. "All the afternone I was busie about some Huswiffrie tell night," Lady Margaret Hoby records in her diary. "Huswiffrie," her diary indicates, included distilling aqua vitae, pulling hemp, preserving quinces, overseeing candle-making, making sweetmeats, gardening, dying fabrics, mending linens, keeping accounts, dressing meat, performing surgery, designing buildings, and administering purgatives.[4] Lady Ann Clifford similarly comments on her housework and her interaction with local working women: she visits "Goodwife Syslies" to eat cheese, has Mistress Frances Pate make preserves of apples and lemons, gathers cherries, oversees laundry maids, whips up pancakes with her servants, and describes her daughter and granddaughter taking turns breastfeeding her great-grandchild. Maria Thynne, mistress of Longleat estate, sent letters to her husband anxiously pleading that he keep on hand home-made dragon water as a plague preventive. And Elinor Fettiplace, part of an old but impoverished Berkshire family, scribbled recipes for concocting beer, flea powder, rat poison, weed killer, soap, and toothpaste.[5] Ladies of high station concerned themselves with fattening chickens and making cheese despite their other more refined interests.[6] Bolstered by the post-Reformation glorification of the household, women of status took interest in the details of domestic labor.

Women of the lower ranks and middling sort, such as the wives of farmers, artisans, husbandman, yeomen, and lower gentry, played more than a supervisory role in these duties. They sold surplus eggs, dairy, and cheeses at local markets, and, despite their limited resources, worked with medical and culinary recipes that differed little from those used by upper-class ladies or doctors.[7] If Hannah Woolley's experience was representative, many girls refined the domestic arts they learned from mothers and housekeepers when placed in households in their early teens (the wealthier as a finishing school or transitional stage toward adulthood, and others as the starting point for lifelong service). Servants apparently learned from both hands-on tutorials and published advice books.[8] Versions of these practices – including herbal knowledge and physic – were undertaken by poor wage laborers who, along with farmer's and yeomen's wives, combined domestic industry with work-for-sale in agricultural and retail trades.[9] And housewifery, despite its coding as "feminine," involved a cadre of workers of both sexes.

In rolling up their sleeves for work, women sought to follow the model of the "good wife," the woman who was not hesitant, as Solomon prescribed, to "put her hand to the wheel" (Figs. 1–2). Though often not literally spinning, the wife could live up to this biblical injunction by being productive. In *A Godly Forme of Houshold Government*, John Dod and Robert Cleaver write:

And though nice Dames think it an unseemely thing for them to soyl their hands about any houshold matters, . . . yet the vertuous woman (As Proverbs 31.17) girdeth her loines with strength and strengthenth her armes . . . She seeketh wooll and flax &c. She putteth her hand to the wheele . . . The meaning is: that she getteth some matter to worke on, that she may exercise her selfe and her family in, and it is not some idle toy, to make the world gay withall, but some matter of good use.[10]

Common appeals to "women" as a group that bridged social ranks were routinely made: "the virtuous woman" labored, if only in a supervisory position, to display a commitment to utility or "good use." The newly popularized post-Reformation ideal of femininity, so clearly indebted to medieval and classical elaborations, attempted to counter aristocrat investment in leisure and instead rest female virtue firmly on diligence and industry.

As Margaret Ezell documents, the ideology of the "good wife" pervaded conduct manuals, character books, plays, sermons, and proverbs, even if that ideology only imperfectly restricted actual female practice.[11] While attempting to instill meek obedience as a by-product of work, these texts necessarily emphasized the fundamental role domestic labor played in England's socioeconomic system. Character books accused ladies who were feeble, dainty, and indulgent (or "nice," in Dod and Cleaver's terms) of draining resources from Christian households, and writers designated labor as indispensable to a healthy moral and national economy.[12] Building on the slogan, "To thrive ye must wive," these texts portrayed marriage as a combined economic and spiritual partnership. Nicholas Breton thus could idealize the Renaissance wife as:

Fig. 1  Kitchen scene of women preparing pastries, vegetables and broths. From Nicholas de Bonnefons, *The French Gardiner*, trans. John Evelyn (London, 1658).

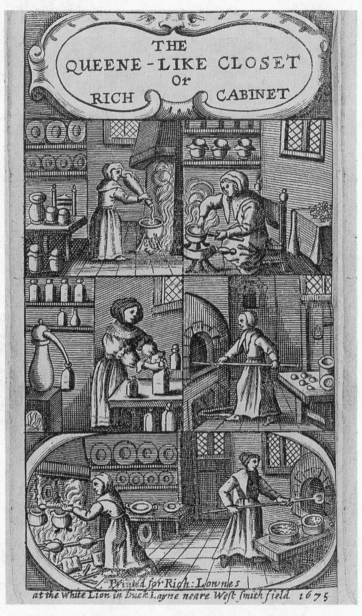

Fig. 2   Hannah Woolley's domestic guide shows the housewife busy in the art of distilling, baking, cooking and preserving. From *The Queene-like Closet or Rich Cabinet* (London, 1675).

the kitchin physician, the chamber comfort, the hall's care, and the parlour's grace. She is the dairie's neatnesse, the brue-house wholsomness, the garner's provision, and the garden's plantation. She is Povertie's praier and Charities praise ... a course of thrift; a booke of huswifery and a mirror of modestie. In summe, she is God's blessing and man's happinesse.[13]

Spirituality and profit emanate even within the lowly chores of milking and brewing, Breton suggests. Deigning even to oversee the dairy's cleaning, the housewife became eligible to bestow grace on her family.

The attempt to rehabilitate domestic work was part of a broader movement in which people of rank took new interest in the cultivation of land and commercial trade. Old gentry found their wealth threatened by an encroaching yeomanry who exhibited an entrepreneurial spirit about land management.[14] Due to changes in labor population, namely the shift from feudal to wage labor and the shrinkage of large households, elite property owners were forced to develop more efficient methods in order to keep their lands. In the wake of increased urbanization, specialized production, and the rise of service centers, the economy enlarged to include, in part, the infamous rise of a middling sort of the population as well as mounting profits among the yeomanry.[15] Guides concerned with household production flooded the book market in sixteenth-century England. Charging that aristocratic consumption was a moral and national flaw, husbandry books sought to instill a work ethic in country gentry and thus champion England's anti-courtly character. The first English *cookbooks* that subsequently appeared tellingly distinguished themselves from their continental counterparts by addressing non-courtly and female readers.[16] Early French printed domestic guides, by contrast, were medieval manuscripts directed toward aristocratic male chefs. In her study of French cuisine, Barbara Ketcham Wheaton ponders the significance of this fact: "Apart from collections of recipes for confectionary, preserving, and distillation ... there apparently were no new French cookbooks in the entire sixteenth century. Why, indeed, should there have been any? Who would have written them, and for whom?"[17] In producing cookbooks for a prosperous household managed by the housewife, English writers made domesticity a public concern. Specifically, they transferred the work of specialists to an imagined heterogeneous male and female population unified in their shared interest in up-to-date household work. Domesticity was placed at the fore of economic and status issues, and "housewifery" (as the labor of male and female servants in households of many ranks) was used to debate and mark "proper" definitions for social groups.

In the two sections that follow, I trace the history of guidebook publication as an oscillation between two conceptual poles epitomized by Hugh Plat's *Delightes for Ladies* and Gervase Markham's *English House-wife*. Plat's manual offers women advice on "the art of preserving" (candying fruits, pastries, jellies); "secrets in distillation" (wines, syrups); "cookery and house-wifery" (brewing, candle-making, baking); and "sweete powders and oint-ments" (lotions, toothpaste, cosmetics). Plat is concerned with the pleasures of inventiveness and with proper "taste" rather than frugal household man-agement. Stunningly popular, this tiny and crafted book object (small enough to fit into the pocket of a gown) went through thirteen editions in fifty years. Housewifery, defined as the making of domestic objects, became one of several skills necessary for social advancement, including the crafting of expensive conserves and banqueting dishes that displayed conspicuous consumption and marked social status. Plat assumes a "lady" not overly preoccupied with thrift (one who likes to shop and throw parties), but who still invested enough in the home economy to make her own cheese and worry over the family health. What Plat does is to offer formerly aristocratic and medical confectionery to a larger populace – particularly to the urban citizenry, country gentry, and yeomanry with leisure time and recourse to markets. In this way he contributes to the wave of self-fashioning books offering social climbers tools for achieving "inherited" class status. Chatty and flirtatious, Plat's narrator embodies the coyness that he imagines clever readers to possess; he dis-closes the admirable mysteries that "ladies" know. To buy the book is to engage in the luxurious delights that he takes pleasure in imagining women performing.

Markham's *English House-wife* couldn't be more different. This encyclo-pedic tome, published first as part of a gentlemen's recreational guide called *Countrey Contentments*, places housewifery within a labor-intensive agrarian production (Fig. 3). Covering a full range of tasks except for the controversial art of cosmetic-making, the book forays beyond cooking, preserving, and dis-tilling to include chapters on physic and surgery, spinning, woolmaking and dyeing, maltmaking, brewing, wine-making, and dairying. Also popular, this text went through six editions in relatively cheap form between 1615 and 1637. Markham's unprecedented orderly format makes the book available as a handy reference guide. In fact, his central goal is to promote efficiency and thrift so that the English home can remain as insulated as possible from professionalization and the market economy. Pointedly at odds with Plat's urban-female consumer, Markham's housewife exemplifies a country frugality that he touts as model-ing national character. Rather than the delights that housewifery affords, this text emphasizes the order, morals, and intelligence required in highly technical procedures. Echoing post-Reformation celebrations of household life, the book presents a non-elite narrator and wife who are sober, active, and busy with pro-tecting home-grown values. While Plat's narrator delights in performing home's pleasures, Markham's narrator thriftily embodies good housewifery by conserv-ing, in textual form, the age-old habits constituting sound English practice.

# THE
# ENGLISH
## Huſ-wife,

*Contayning,*

The inward and outward vertues which
*ought to be in a compleat woman.*

As, her skill in Phyſicke, Cookery, Banqueting-
ſtuffe, Diſtillation, Perfumes, VVooll, Hemp, Flax,
Dayries, Brewing, Baking, *and all other things*
*belonging to an Houſhould.*

*A Worke very profitable and neceſſarie, gathered for*
*the generall good of this kingdome.*

Printed at London by *Iohn Beale*, for *Roger Iackſon*,
and are to bee ſold at his ſhop neere the great
*Cunduit in Fleet-ſtreete.* 1615.

Fig. 3    Gervase Markham, title page to *The English Hus-wife* (London, 1615).
This encyclopedic book describes the virtues of the ideal wife in terms of her
labors.

The history of domestic guides can be simplified to the following story: housewifery was first published as a subset of husbandry and therefore necessarily defined within the goals of estate management. Emerging out of the discourse of husbandry in the late sixteenth century, cookbooks began to promote specialized work, address female readers, and cater to an urban population. Between 1570 and 1650, two importantly different domestic discourses, exemplified nicely by the works of Markham and Plat, evidenced a lively debate about the definition and scope of household labor. When women and elite chefs took over authorship of cookbooks in the late seventeenth century, some of the issues raised by this debate were resolved. Increased specialization segmented husbandry and housewifery into distinct knowledges and separated men's from women's domestic "space" more thoroughly. Portraying domesticity as less tied to a closed home and national, later books participated explicitly in the "civilizing process," as well as the domestic ideologies it supported, by emphasizing the social negotiations and self-regulation that underwrote household work.

The relationship between manners and domesticity is a story taken up by other critics.[18] This chapter attends to a period when the household *economy* was central to its meaning and when domestic order was said to legitimate monarchy. In patriarchalism, as I have described, the state's "natural" roots rest in a fixed domestic hierarchy. Yet sixteenth- and seventeenth-century guides sometimes ignore or confuse the tenets of patriarchalism. Guides offer contrasting ideological frames through which their readers could experience domesticity and community; for these books make the everyday available for a reader's consumption and scrutiny in multiple ways. Clinging to old-fashioned methods, Markham makes the productive household the place in which the middling sort could rescue the national rhythms of days past. Plat, on the other hand, places the household at the forefront of a malleable social order dependent on innovation and the market. And while Markham disciplines his readers to duplicate the most familiar habits of life, Plat advertises exotic novelties for the home. Both offer "delights" for domestic practitioners – fantasies of recovery or of infinite alterability – that unsettle aristocratic claims to an inherent national culture.

When domestic guides encourage people to inhabit a realm that was "properly" their own (but has mysteriously slipped away) or, conversely, when they render the everyday the province of some other group, they shape domesticity as a paradoxically self-alienating but fundamental core knowledge. In the sections that follow I trace this dynamic as it emerges within the two main frameworks structuring domestic guides, and I note how tension between the familiar and unfamiliar provides the material and conditions of a domestic, and sometimes national, fantasy.

## II. Memory and home-born knowledge

> All you who are knowing already, and vers'd in such things, I beseech you to
> take it only as Memorandum.        Woolley, *The Queen-like Closet* (1675)[19]

In the first English estate manual, Fitzherbert's 1523 *Boke of Husbandry*, housewifery formed a subset of household management, which included animal
care, agriculture, grafting, gaming, timber production, accounting, surveying,
distillation, gardening, and physic.[20] With his intended readership as country
gentlemen slowly beginning to farm their own land, Fitzherbert offers a calendar for organizing the rural estate. Not content to speak of Christian stewardship
generally, Fitzherbert explains specific practices by which households could be
run efficiently. In his account, domestic work both allegorizes spiritual processes and earns a divine blessing. Opening with the maxim that man is born
to labor, Fitzherbert inaugurates a spate of vernacular manuals celebrating economic individualism and private property. In his vision, agriculture embodies
a newly important georgic ethic.

Fitzherbert's text is sober and pragmatic, stripped of what we might identify
as rhetorical density or playfulness. Yet even this utilitarian text reveals the
tremendous rhetorical energy required to resolve a key problem in representing
domestic experience. For when Fitzherbert attempts to authorize his advice,
particularly, as we shall see, his recommendations on housewifery, he runs into
a dilemma. While peppering his text with biblical citation, Latin maxims, and
classical *sententiae*, Fitzherbert claims that experience trumps philosophical
advice. To this end, he translates Latin citations into English and assures his
reader that written advice must always be verified by hands-on farming. "It
is better the practice or knowledge of an husband-man well proued, than the
science or connynge of a philosopher not proued," Fitzherbert writes when
questioning some bit of wisdom, "for there is nothynge touchyng husbandry, and
other profytes conteyned in this presente booke, but I haue hadde the experyence
therof, and proued the same" (91).

We might notice as well that "Englishing" a text and documenting "experyence" begin to collapse into each other in Fitzherbert's account. Busily
testing authoritative sayings against his knowledge, Fitzherbert pauses to consider his reader's access to such authorities. Citing Paul's injunction – "Make
thyne expenses . . . after thy faculty" – he offers this gloss:

This texte toucheth euery manne, from the hyest degree to the loweste; wherefore it
is necessary to euerye manne and womanne to remembre and take good hede there-
vnto . . . to . . . kepe, and folowe the same; but bycause this texte of sayncte Paule
is in latyn, and husbandes commonly can but lyttell laten, I fere leaste they can-not
vnderstande it. And thoughe it were declared ones or twyse to theym, theat they wolde

forgette it: Wherefore I shall shewe to theym a texte in englysshe, and that they maye well vnderstande, and that is this, Eate within thy tedure [tether]. (99)

In replacing the Latin biblical text with an English proverb, Fitzherbert instances the conservation required by good husbandry. While claiming to offer a stay against forgetting, he observes that householders may not have ever really known the adage that he enjoins them to remember, and thus he affirms the importance of translating practices into vernacular speech. Fitzherbert's double translation – from experience to print commodity and from Latin to proverbial English – did, as later writers testify, establish an English tradition of husbandry, with "English" referring to both the content and medium.[21]

Yet throughout his book, Fitzherbert engages with Latin texts, verifying them wholesale as they pertain to spiritual matters and conditionally recommending them as practical technique. In doing so, he classifies "old sayings" as either authorized (attributable) or part of oral culture. In three passages, Fitzherbert refutes tenets of "common wisdom," while in three other instances, he accepts the wisdom of an old saying since it accords with his knowledge.[22] But only once does he run into the problem of having to rely on an "olde common seyenge" without being able to verify its information. This problem tellingly occurs when Fitzherbert turns, after 142 chapters, to his 6 chapters on housewifery. Here he is forced to contradict his entire rationale for publishing since he must present something other than personal experience to justify his advice. "There is an old common sayenge," he begins, "Seldom doth the housbande thryue, withoute the leue of his wyfe" (93). In this unprecedented moment, unanchored sayings substitute for hands-on knowledge. The careful taxonomy of citation set up by the text collapses as the book merges into the unverified world of oral culture, the world of women. The male writer finds himself unable to explain the grounds for a knowledge that, by his own definition, he cannot know, except by authorizing a brand of knowledge that the book has disavowed. Fitzherbert's departure from convention was noteworthy enough for the publisher of the 1598 edition to amend the text so that the "old common saying" authorizing housewifery became "an olde proofe-made true saying."[23]

As his object of study opens onto the common world of orality to which *he* nevertheless is not fully privy, it magnifies the tension between axiom and experience latent in the book. He glosses his proverb:

By this sayenge it shoulde seme, that there be other occupations and labours, that be moste conuenient for the wyues to do. And howe be it that I haue not experyence of al theyr occupations and warkes, as I haue of husbandry, yet a lyttell wyl I speke what they ought to do, though I tel them nat howe they shulde doo and exercyse theyr labours. (93)

While speaking "a lyttell" about essential domestic work, the author nervously explains that he won't tell wives "how" to perform their mysterious labors. The experience that Fitzherbert has lauded now becomes the province of female orality and practice. This leads him, in one instance, to reassure the female reader of her "lyberty" in choosing to heed his advice or not (94). At another point, he teasingly "leue[s] the wyues" to their own discretion rather than giving them ammunition in the arts of marital deception, for he refuses to tell how some wives cheat husbands out of pin money (98). He later labels his instruction as a form of cultural hearsay: "For I haue harde olde houswyues saye, that better is Marche hurdes than Apryll flaxe . . . but howe [linens] Shulde be sowen, weded, pulled, repeyled, watred, wasshen, dryed, beaten, braked, tawed, hecheled, spon, wounden, wrapped, and wouen, it nedeth not for me to shew, for [old house-wives] be wise ynough" (96). How is the husband to understand his purchase of unnecessary instruction? We can imagine the embarrassing scenario when the householder reads the book aloud only to find that he must defer to the experi-ence of his domestic pupils. Coming across the adage – "Seldom doth the hous-bande thruye, withoute the leue of his wyfe" – the householder is required to give "leue" to domestic workers to do their jobs so that they may give him "leue" to prosper.

Fitzherbert's section on housewifery functions in the way that Derrida sug-gests the supplement works: while flaunting its secondary nature, the text ex-poses what is lacking in husbandry (what it cannot do) and in the published text (what it cannot know). Just as the husband cannot thrive without the leave (i.e., help, abandonment, permission) of the wife, so the writer can know gen-erally but not particularly his subject matter. In this sense, the book commodity reveals a fissure that perhaps mirrors a practical problem posed by the di-vision of household labor. The writer's recourse is to defer to a seemingly inaccessible but foundational world of proverbial lore and everydayness. The housewife thus marks the site of the vernacular broadly defined – something so familiar that it can't be grasped within the realm of (here, masculinized) print. Fitzherbert's construction of a profoundly alien but utterly familiar domestic-ity is significant, since his book, appearing in twelve editions before 1600, had a strong impact on how agrarian and domestic work was conceived in the period.

When writers of later guides abruptly offer disclaimers or flounder in their attempt to footnote knowledge about women's labor, they underscore this same predicament. In his translated agricultural guide, *The Countrie Farme*, Richard Surflet admits his reliance on country housewives: "You must not doubt but that I my self have learned many remedies from the experiments and observation of those sorts of women." "It shall not be thought strange," he says at another point, "if we touch in a word the dressing and tilling of some few [physic herbs], such as are most usuall and familiar amongst women." John Partridge's 1573 *Treasurie of Commodious Conceites* includes a recipe for an elaborate glazed cake which is amazingly guaranteed to last several years. The icing,

Partridge notes, "will make it shine like Ice, as Ladies report." The sudden distancing effected by the phrase "as Ladies report," unwittingly raises the possibility that the neighboring recipes remain unverified, or that the icing might not be guaranteed, indeed, to shine at all.[24] The odd intensifiers and disclaimers that these writers use (e.g., "you must not doubt," "it must not be thought strange") signal apprehension: if merely acknowledging a source, why mark it so uneasily? In each case, the text veers unsteadily when citing a source, crossing back on itself so as to suggest the problem of knowing, or not knowing, women's work. And in turn, this quandary leads to the problem of truly apprehending domesticity, despite its reputed status as something almost inbred.

In one sense, this rhetorical confusion mimics the practical problem of how a man could rule over a domain defined as outside his domain. Post-Reformation marital guides present this puzzle when they insist on the symbiosis of the husband's and wife's work but then strictly divide tasks in terms of gender. In *Christian Oeconomie* (1609), William Perkins writes that while the "father and chief head of the family" has all rights of governance, he "ought not in modesty to challenge the privilege of preserving and advertising his wife in all matters domestical, but in some to leave her to her own will and judgment." In *A Godly Forme of Houshold Government* (1630), Dod and Cleaver establish areas of household responsibility "in which the husband giveth over his right unto his wife: as to rule and governe her maidens: to see to those things that belong unto the kitchin, and to huswiferie, and to their household stuffe; other mean things." And William Whately writes that the husband might compromise his superior position were he to assume total control of the home. The husband "should permit his wife to rule under him," Whately declares, "and give her leave to know more than himself, who hath weightier matters."[25] As such, these writers confirm Fitzherbert's anxious decision to "leue" the wife to her own, more informed though less momentous, resources. Compelled to explain the simultaneous importance *and* inferiority of housewifery, they fall back on the default existence of "mean" knowledges that the husband can't allow himself to know. If claims about the material importance of housewifery came into conflict with prescriptions about marital hierarchy, a similar tension was registered rhetorically when writers attempted to codify housewifery in print. Many writers end up positing a fraught domestic culture lodged somewhere beyond the purview of the book commodity or husbandly sovereignty.

In part, domestic how-to books run into the problem that "femininity" historically represented the place of non-knowledge itself. It was common for writers, that is, to label non-elite populations or non-authoritative knowledges as "feminine," a gendering enhanced by the fact that Latin, taught primarily to boys, traditionally marked intellectual competency. As the print industry and educational reform facilitated a market of English readers in the sixteenth century, however, they challenged the linguistic faultline separating learned and barbarous people. The increasing affordability of books spawned debates about who should have access to particular kinds of knowledge. This controversy was especially heated in the field of medicine, given that Latin was often the skill that distinguished doctor from amateur. While some writers argued for disseminating information "downward" in the vernacular, others protested that translations encouraged amateur practitioners. William Turner offers this justification for his English herbal:

> Dyd Dioscorides and Galene gyve occasion for every old wyfe to take in hand the practice of Phisick? Dyd they gyve any just occasyon of murther? . . . If they gave no occasyon unto every old wyfe to practyse physike, then gyve I none . . . then am I no hyundrer wryting unto the English my countremen, an Englysh herball.[26]

Esteemed Greek and Latin writers, Turner argues, were not frightened of audiences who spoke their language.[27] In his account "every old wyf" figures the dangerous denizen of popular culture whose misuse of information threatens the stability of the realm. Turner evokes this figure in hopes of creating a third category of reader, the learned man or "anti-wife" who nevertheless cannot speak Latin. In his argument, the English tongue becomes valid currency for exchanging wisdom, and readers are *de facto* inhabitants of a linguistic community. But the "old wife" figuratively haunts the process of disseminating knowledge in the print-vernacular, for she is positioned beyond the national borders of erudition. Husbandry books that address female labor, such as Fitzherbert's, obviously cannot use stereotypical methods for distinguishing oral culture from professional expertise. In fact, their use of the vernacular tongue, a language insistently defined as female, proverbial, and *domestic* (because taught in the home) intensifies this predicament. In debates about the validity of specific knowledges, domesticity emerges as a heuristically handy term, but one always verging on deconstructing the categories it cements. It is no wonder that when domesticity becomes the subject of the printed guide, it produces a set of epistemological, ideological, and rhetorical quandaries for English readers and writers.

### A cow is being milked

When Bartholomew Dowe authored a 1588 book on cheesemaking, he put his own expertise about housewifery on trial and justified his book as based on knowledge gleaned in childhood. *A Dairie Booke for Good Huswives* was written as a dialogue in which a female character begins by explicitly challenging the male writer's competence to dispense advice:

THE WOMAN. I heard of late, you have had much . . . talk . . . concerning the making
    of . . . Cheese. I pray you show me, if ever you used to make Cheese your self?
THE MAN. Never in my life, good wife, I have made any, but I have in my youth in
    the Country where I was borne, seen much made: for in the very house . . . that I
    was borne in, my Mother and her maids made all the Whitemeate of sevenscore
    kine.[28]

As Juliet Fleming has demonstrated, published domestic instructions raised
the specific question of how the male-authored book commodity "framed"
information previously transmitted in oral culture.[29] The writer answers this
challenge by evoking the domestic-making suffused in childhood memory, a
world of yore now lost to him. The image of mother and maids fashioning
cheese floats into the conversation to prove the writer's competency, one predicated on being a native and intimate eyewitness rather than a practitioner.
Downplaying personal experience, Dowe banks on memory as the hallmark of
expertise.

But the issue is not then put to rest, for after offering practical advice Dowe
nervously implores his female readers to speak of him kindly:

I praie you reporte that I have not taken upon me to teach you or others, how ye should
make whitemeate, for it were unseemely that a Man that never made anie, (but hath
seene and behelde others in dooing thereof) should take upon him to teache women
that hath most knowledge and experience in that arte. I have but onlie made unto you
rehearsall of the order and fashion how it is used in the Countreie where I was borne,
to the ende that you and others, understanding bothe, may use your owne mindes and
discretions therein, for sure I am, olde custome and usages of things bee not easie to bee
broken. (B4[r])

Attempting to appear less presumptuous in educating women about their experience, Dowe ends up evoking the staying power of "olde custome" as at odds
with printed advice. Leaving women to their own minds liberated them from
male expertise precisely by tying them to the past custom that the printed object both disavowed and furiously imitated. As Dowe's memory of his mother's
practice is pit against custom we see a subtle redefinition of domesticity. Transforming mother's cheesemaking into print, Dowe reinhabits the past to model
the "efficient manner" that he hopes to inspire in workers, who, he says, might
use the text as a distraction from their "sullen fantasies."

Or perhaps this is merely his own escapist fantasy. For he publishes his book,
as he admits sadly, to "avoid idleness" "[b]ecause . . . I am unapt to doo any good
labour or worke, and nowe none other thing in effect can doe but onely write"
(A2[r]). Having become the housewife that he remembers from childhood, Dowe
translates household industry into observation, memory, then the commodity.
As such, women are invited to "read" rather than remember the everyday, itself

now implicated in a web of longing and desire and packaged in a form that can be distributed widely and preserved.

Dowe's manual was appended to a translation of Torquato Tasso's *The House-holders Philosophie*, a humanist work outlining the universal principles of cosmic ordering underlying metaphysical and material worlds rather than detailing pragmatic tasks. Tasso suggests that good housekeeping is governed by the codes of stewardship and hospitality documented in the most authoritative texts of Western tradition – the Bible, Petrarch, Virgil. More specifically, he imagines stewardship as transmitted through the father's catechism of his son, a process that his book supplements and imitates. Committing instructions to memory, the good son not only learns wisdom but demonstrates the grand memory-system evidenced in the housewife's ordering of goods or the poet's proportioning of art. Appearing as an appendix to Tasso's work, Dowe's text turns to mother rather than classical maxims and thus lodges domesticity squarely in her purview. Concluding with jingles that his mother sang as she worked, Dowe offers a vernacular counterpart to the classical guide to which his work is bound; his reader thus encounters competing fantasies about domesticity, familiarity, and memory. Refusing to credit humanist charges that cross-gendered domesticity damaged the young boy's character (a theory expounded by Erasmus and Elyot),[30] Dowe imagines an instructive domestic experience in which children fruitfully absorb the rhythms and habits of home. Dowe's homey pamphlet appears definitively English when paired with Tasso's text. Women's work emerges as the most basic source of a native knowledge lodged deep in the recesses of memory, and domesticity becomes instrumental in fantasies about national identity.

Comparing Suffolk and "South-Hamshire" cheesemaking, Dowe's text also engages print's potential to forge uniform practices out of regional variety, while piecing together a reading public from local communities. In differentiating practices by region, Dowe fractures Tasso's universalism, yet he establishes local custom as the basis for a widespread, indeed national, dairy practice. Regional variation fades, for dairying is presented as a seemingly naturalized activity that everyone experienced in their youth, *where they were born*. Of course, Dowe implies that one only finds access to the memory of English domesticity by buying a book. As the book forges a vernacular community, it names household work as the feminized signifier for the "us" who speak and practice Englishness. The process of establishing national commonality may begin with the phantom of domestic memory but it is to be completed in the circulation of the book commodity.

We find hints of Dowe's Englished "everydayness" in Thomas Tusser's *Hundreth Goode Points of Husbandrie* (1557), which was expanded into a Tudor and seventeenth-century bestseller called *Fiue Hundreth Points of Good Husbandry*.[31] First organized as a calendar for the husbandman and then enlarged to include housewifery, cross-seasonal tasks, and moral advice, this book became the single most popular book of poetry published in sixteenth-century England and one of the fifteen most popular books on any subject in the Elizabethan era.[32] Tusser describes dairying, baking, distilling, gardening, cheesemaking, childraising, and religious meditation, yet he almost always circles back to thrift as the centerpiece of sound domestic practice. He recommends using table scraps, parings, and stubble to feed chickens; urges the wife to regulate the diet of workers so as to insure their best output; scorns using too many spices in baking; and argues for using human sewage to create compost. Explicitly writing to help tenant farmers and landowners make a profit, Tusser produces a miscellany of household tips whose appeal rests partly in their lack of sophistication and memorable quality. Writing in rhymed anapestic jingles, he creates a book commodity designed to resemble the "sayings" of oral culture.[33] Unlike the sober Fitzherbert, Tusser playfully delves into the banal details and mistakes of housework. Framing his advice with confessions about his school beatings, illnesses, and wife's death, Tusser implies a "can-do" mentality that accords with his unadorned speech. While increasing the individualist tenor of agrarian "thriving," Tusser also enhances the wife's economic role, with the result that housewifery helped to articulate what McRae terms "the newly radical potential of a language of improvement" (*God Speed*, 151).

Yet while building the basis for an agricultural reformation, the book also had cultural effects. When enlarged in 1573, *Fiue Hundreth Points* bordered on old-fashioned, but in subsequent reprintings over the next one hundred years, it appeared increasingly quaint in its outworn assumption that most everything could be produced at home. Charmingly outmoded as well was its representation of agrarian folk as tied to the "natural" rhythms of the seasons. Detailing the rituals of feastdays, Tusser mythologizes the countryside – the wafers and cakes devoured at sheepshearing rituals in Northamptonshire; the harvest home goose eaten in Leicestershire; and seedcake banquets celebrated at wheat sowing in Essex and Suffolk. The result is a reading public fully acquainted with the regional domestic practices cherished because of their historical longevity. Mixing spiritual precepts with a georgic ethic, Tusser produces English lore about everyday life. The book also begins to function as a dictionary preserving a delightfully antique and colloquial country lexicon. He mentions "creekes" (servants); "beene" (wealth); "filbellie" (culinary extravagance); "laggoose" (lazy servant); "gove" (laid up in the barn in a stack); and "aumbrie" (cupboard). Undoubtedly consulted by readers for useful advice, the book begins to speak to antiquarian interest in the preservation of English custom as well as to general nostalgia for a pastoral life always feared to be in jeopardy. As Tusser's book commodity illustrates a universally familiar and imperiled "slice of life," domestic hominess, the work of country husband and housewife, comes to represent the heart of English living.

### Marketing Englishness

'Twill much enrich the Company of Stationers,
'Tis thought 'twill prove a lasting Benefit,
Like the *Wise Masters*, and the *Almanacks*,
The hundred *Novels*, and the Book of *Cookery*.

Lapet, in Francis Beaumont and John Fletcher, The Nice Valour[34]

Finally we come to Markham, whose particular vision of domestic English-ness now has a history. When he writes his *English House-wife*, Markham constructs a national grid for the ideas latent in works by Fitzherbert, Dowe, and Tusser. By choosing to accentuate the wife's nationality (rather than pre-senting the "moral" or "good" housewife), Markham brings to the fore the faint associations found in earlier works – namely by nominating industri-ous domestic labor, especially the more historically continuous work of the housewife, as the backbone of indigenous culture. Seeking to reach the "gen-eral and gentle reader," Markham writes for the wife of a large landed estate, but assumes her to have yeoman's values. He includes both lavish and plain fare in his recipes; and by suppressing class and regional differences, Markham hails a group united in the national imaginary. Though his publisher displays, in one edition, nervousness about a man's intimacy with female chores, Markham's appeal to the nation generally cuts across his focus on gendered labor.[35] In this way, the home becomes a fantasized foundational site of commonality.

Markham was such a prolific author of books of horsemanship, veterinary medicine, and husbandry that agricultural historian G. E. Fussell labels the period between 1600 and 1640 as the "age of Markham."[36] In fact, Markham had the dubious privilege of being one of the few individuals explicitly prohibited by the Stationers Company from publishing books on a specific topic. In 1617 the Company made him foreswear writing books on veterinary medicine since they considered the market oversaturated with his advice on the subject. Author of *The English Arcadia* (1607) and *The English Husbandman*, Markham also was a key player in the rampant Englishing of print commodities. He consistently compared the numerous husbandry books he published to continental guides such as *The Countrie Farme*. Originally a Latin treatise by Charles Estienne that Jean Liébault adapted into French as *The Maison Rustique* in 1564, *The Countrie Farme* appeared in England in Richard Surflet's translation in 1600. Complaining about the inadequacy of Virgil's *Georgics* (which only bespeaks the "Italian Climbe") and *The Countrie Farme* ("a worke of infinit excellency, yet only proper and naturall to the French, and not to us"), Markham sought to rescue the English way of life suppressed in outlandish, foreign manuals and to outline a genuinely profitable and native tradition.[37] As he explains in his 1613 *English Husbandman*:

when . . . I beheld . . . that every man was dumbe to speake any thing of the Husbandry of our owne kingdome, I could not but imagine it a worke most acceptable to men, and most profitable to the kingdome, to set downe the true manner and nature of our right English Husbandry. (A1ᵛ)

Markham claims that foreign advice does not transfer to English soil and weather conditions. Admittedly Barnabe Googe's translated husbandry book did include an entire section on camels that might have amused the East Anglian farmer.

Markham spent the next years refusing to acknowledge material that he garnered from *The Countrie Farme*.[38] After echoing its recommendations in *The English House-wife* and criticizing it in *The English Husbandman*, Markham surprisingly decided to publish his own edition of the French text in 1616. Markham's rationale for this about-face was that only *he* could properly adjust foreign methods to an English lifestyle, for Surflet had left the *Maison Rustique*, he quips, "all French except the language."[39] Forging a collective "we" out of disparate book readers, Markham justifies his change of heart at greater length:

My countreymen of England may object against this Worke, that albeit it may sort well with any soyle that is in any degree . . . allyed to this temper, clyme, & mixture of the French: yet to us that are so much remote in nature and qualitie, and whose Earth giveth unto us, for our most general profit, things and fruits, either little, or very stranger-wise, acquainted with them . . . [Yet] I will, after the faithfull translation of their noble experiences, adde the difference of our customes, and to their labors adde the experience and knowledge of our best Husbandmen, hoping thereby to give a publike content to our Nation, who seeing the true difference of both Kingdomes, may, out of an easie judgement, both compare and collect that which shall be fittest for his use and commodity. (2)

Acting as comparison shopper, the smart reader will find what is truly English within the options for estate governance, and thus will uncover the English farm buried within its French trappings. And when Markham reprints his housewifery guide in 1623, he includes passages from *The Countrie Farme*. There is, then, a cross-fertilization between the distinctly English Housewife and Husband and their embarrassingly evident French guide.[40] Insisting on the natural difference of the nation, Markham evokes but then glosses over variations in regional practices and instead foregrounds the particularity of soil, topography, and climate. Working to increase profits, display English know-how to the continent and sell books, Markham puts forth "true" Englishness as a critical theoretical space that authorizes his work and consolidates his readership.

Markham's housewifery book emerged from within this ongoing nationalist project. Although first published alongside a sporting manual for rural gentlemen, Markham's *English House-wife* was clearly differentiated from her more leisurely textual counterpart; for she was expected to shy away from the aristocratic ideals of stasis, otium, and ornamentation.[41] Both the content and format of this book appropriately emphasize practicality: the culinary recipes consist largely of traditional country puddings and pies, and the guide is organized to an unprecedented degree. The medical recipes are arranged by the part of the body they address, ranging from head to toe; and the cooking recipes are classified according to methods of preparation and the order of serving. "Our housewife," the book obsessively repeats, presides over a newly Englished and systematized field of knowledge. As such, the book is a reference tool for readers who, failing to find all of the advice useful, look to navigate efficiently through the text.

Markham's pragmatic goals occasionally give way, however, to the nostalgia he airs under the name of national culture. Although he claims to pare away everything that doesn't have direct use-value for citizens, Markham oddly includes descriptions of chores that he knows housewives no longer undertook, chores recently taken over by village specialists such as maltsters, vintners, and textile workers. In the late sixteenth century, these industries began to produce goods cheaper and more efficiently than the individual housewife could. Although aware of these changes, Markham fantasizes that the housewife still controls all forms of production. In his section on wines, he transcribes a professional vintner's handbook, admitting in one moment that "one profest skillfull in the trade" devised this "secret."[42] Although he explains that "it is necessary that our *English House-wife* be skilful in the election, preservation and curing of all sorts of Wines" (155), Markham measures his recipes in terms of butts (126 gallons) and tuns (252 gallons), quantities larger than even the most tipple-happy grand estate might viably use.[43] Similarly, in his section on textiles, Markham seems to slip out of the household and into the world of artisanal skill; for he includes instructions on how to dye wool despite his acknowledgment that the wife would have commissioned a dyer to perform this task (167–9). While Markham may certainly have sought to train the housewife to be a knowledgable negotiator in business deals, he fails to offer this explanation. Why would he teach his reader unnecessary knowledges?

*The English House-wife* restages this dilemma when Markham admits that the housewife would have a weaver make cloth from spun thread, yet he nevertheless steams ahead with a complete account of warping, as if his book will be read by apprentices in the trade. When writing of brewing, Markham even begins to mix male and female pronouns, as if acknowledging the male maltster silently working beneath the veneer of the housewife. "This office or place of knowledge belongeth particularly to the Hous-wife," he protests too much, "and though we have many excellent Men-malsters, yet it is properly the worke and care of the woman, for it is a house-worke, and done altogether within dores, where generally lieth her charge" (207). As Alice Clark and Susan Cahn have argued, malt-making and brewing were increasingly centralized in large towns during Markham's life, such that only a rapidly diminishing percentage of the population brewed all the beer necessary for home use by 1650.[44] Rather than explaining when beer should be bought and when brewed, Markham allows his longing for the self-contained household to overcome his investment in efficiency.[45] Like Dowe, he longs to recover a past domesticity as part of the project of validating native efficiency. In these moments, the housewife marks the site of a fading domestic fullness threatened by new modes of production.[46] His printed advice book, like others, evokes a loss for which publishing promises compensation – the childhood world of pots and pans revivified in written accounts. Yet, despite the assuring quality of this fantasy, his text exposes its own projection of familiar and fundamental knowledges onto the past and thus hints at the estranging potential of domestic experience.

Markham's dual interest in patrolling English practices and insulating the home from the market merge in his discussion of the housewife's diet:

Let it proceede more from the provision of her owne yard, then the furniture of the Markets; and let it be rather esteemed for the familiar acquaintance she hath with it, then for the strangenesse and rarity it bringeth from other Countries. (*English House-wife*, 4)

Overlooking the possible native goods that could be purchased at local fairs, Markham equates shopping with foreignness. Although he does separate these commands with the conjunction "and," the two genres of goods – home-grown and English – join rhetorically. Throughout the book, the wife is advised to produce and recycle a world of goods fortified within the confines of her yard and nation. Calling upon the home (rather than the sovereign's body) to mark the boundaries of England, Markham has his housewife guard national- and self-integrity, in short, the "domestic" in its multiple meanings. In this way, his guide is intelligible in the context of widespread xenophobic polemics against importing luxury goods.[47] Markham simply frames typical injunctions for the ideal female body to remain "enclosed" within a broader national imaginary ("Let huswifery appear. Keep close," Pistol commands Mistress Quickly in *Henry V*);[48] Markham asks readers to imagine national resources as kept "close" by female *production*. Thus while Markham's principled objection to marketing consolidates a standard opposition between female urban porousness and country enclosure,[49] it repositions femininity within the story of national prosperity.[50] Since she transforms raw products into utensils, goods, and medicines, the housewife, even more than the husbandman, emblemizes a cherished self-sufficiency. When historians cite Markham to document the housewife's experience, they must maneuver around powerful fantasies – of femininity, nation, production, rural life – that skew his advice.[51]

Kim Hall has underscored the fundamental sleight of hand in works such as Markham's which celebrate national insularity while presenting recipes that require imported goods such as sugar, cinnamon, cloves, goldleaf, and nutmeg. Hall argues that the housewife functioned figuratively to "national-ize" goods by laundering foreign products into home-born forms. By process-ing foodstuffs (especially sugar) into "national staples," the European wife promoted the international trade system and emergent slave trade.[52] Yet this entire conceptual trick depended on the perception that the household was in-deed the preserve of indigenous practices. Markham labors to construct this idea in one instance when he instructs his reader on making broths: "though men may coine strange names, and faine strange Arts, yet be assured she that can doe these may make any other whatsoever" (*English House-wife*, 84); that is, housewives should be heartened to recognize baseline practices that only superficially appear to be "strange." In uncovering the process by which the home was encoded as "non-strange," we elaborate Hall's point so as to see a corresponding contradiction in the marketing of domestic in-formation. Hall's observation that English cookbooks bury the true foreign origins of food has a textual counterpart, for Markham's fetishization of na-tive practices masks his borrowing from foreign books. Cookbooks didn't just "English" cuisine, then, but also showed how the book market helped to nation-alize domesticity and its practitioners. Supplementing "still-room manuscripts" handed down in the family (named for the distillery), published guides neces-sarily ushered in a new mode of authorization for domestic practices. No longer part of a particular family tradition, they became, in many accounts, a signi-fier of authentic national methods. Addressed to a rising gentry and yeomanry, Markham amalgamates readers of different status groups by insisting that they share the desire to thwart a nationally corrosive modernization. Book commodi-ties and female practice join as key factors in this rescue mission.

With Markham as such an influential writer, it is no wonder that later guides such as Thomas Tryon's *The Good Housewife Made a Doctor* (1685) rou-tinely accentuate the nationalist component of diet. "The compounding of these *Forreign Ingredients* with our *Domestick Productions* . . . chiefly destroys the Health of our people," wrote Tryon. "For all the Wayes of God, and his Hand-Maid Nature are plain and familiar."[53] Although Tryon departs from other guidebook writers in promoting vegetarianism, his belief in a distinctly national body was shared by medical and culinary writers. The English body is endangered, Tryon argues, when elite people insist on a rich diet that decays the essential oils of the stomach. Chief in Tryon's list of dietary mistakes is recourse to foreign foods like raisins, which could overheat the blood. "Our Women, who are the chief promoters of such things," he observes,

ought to consider that the Fruits that are grown in hot Climates, are nothing so agreeable to our constitutions, as those of our own Growth . . . There is such a vast difference between the Regions and Climates, both in respect of Coelestial Influences, and the

Nature of Soil and Constitutions of Air whence those Spices come, and ours, that it amounts to almost a perfect Opposition. (83, 90)

In Tryon's schema, women of all ranks patrol the borders of the body politic by regulating diet, and what they are invited to maintain is a non-elite English body. By the late seventeenth century, however, guidebook writers largely defined housework as an occupation acquired by studied training rather than a return to a personal or national past; the idea of "our" customs as tied to the world of women had largely lost its conceptual force. For over one hundred years, however, as men sought to market the first English cookbooks and domestic guides, they trumpeted the importance of native habits as the signifier of an unstable commonality that was being forged, perhaps, by print itself.

### III. Delights for ladies

While estate guides and Tusser's poetic jingles were published throughout the sixteenth century, it was only in the 1570s that cookbooks boasting specific recipes appeared in England. Unlike their French and Italian counterparts, these medical and culinary books were addressed to housewives and read, though not exclusively, by them.[54] Unlike husbandry guides, these texts were largely unconcerned with the authenticity or uniformity of the practices they recommended; that is, they didn't partake of the dream of national unity or the erasure of social divisions that Markham's text evidenced. The whole problem of male domestic expertise was also easily disposed of when claims to experience were eschewed. Severing housewifery from production, these guides made female work a site of pleasure – both for women who undertook creative arts and spectators invited to peek into territory coded as intimately female or elite. While the housewife was still seen as undertaking practical work, her access to markets and lack of livestock responsibilities allowed her to indulge in leisure arts, beautification, shopping, manners, and entertainment. Dedicated largely to the *joy* of cooking rather than its ethical value, these books thus emphasized novelty and sophistication, focusing on methods, even foreign or ostentatious culinary arts, that might catch the imagination of class-conscious practitioners.

John Partridge's 1573 *Treasurie of Commodious Conceites & Hidden Secrets, and may be called, The Huswives Closet of Healthful Provision* made its debut as the first cookbook in England written specifically for women. In this manual, Partridge presents himself not as an experienced farmer or a citizen interested in preserving tried and true English custom, but as a gentleman eager to disclose elite mysteries to all classes. The engraved frontispiece to the text boasts a fashionably dressed man writing in his book-filled closet, his high-heeled foot elegantly displayed (Fig. 4). Professing to publish these recipes at the command of a gentlewoman, the author seeks "to teach all maner of persones & Degrees to

Fig. 4   Frontispiece to John Partridge, *The Treasurie of Commodious Conceites & Hidden Secrets* (London, 1573). Notice that the book is authorized as the knowledge of an erudite and aristocratic man, though this copy is signed by a female reader named Mary.

know perfectly the maner to make divers & sundrie sortes of fine Conceites."[55] The 1584 edition addresses "all that covet the practice of good Huswiferie":

> Good huswives here you have a Jewell for your joy,
> A closet meete your Huswivery to practice and imploy,
> As wel the gentles of degree, as eke the meaner sort,
> May practise here to purchase helth, their houshold to comfort.
>
> (1584, A1$^r$)

Having been the object of an elite woman's desire, the book is available for broader consumption, but in the process housework comes to signify property and wealth – a compendium of "fine conceits," a "jewell," and "closet."

Defined by the trappings of commendatory poems (stripped away in subsequent editions), envoys, and prefaces that boast the courtly language of patronage, this gentrified guide hints that the author delights in cultivating previously inaccessible mysteries for the nation. The author's "seede is sown /To pleasure all," Thomas Curtesye writes in a prefatory poem (1573, A5$^r$), with fruition complementing the book's effort to "frame /A happy common weale" that will "pleasure every one" (1573, A2$^v$). Thomas Blanck explains that the recipes steer clear of expensive foreign goods; for the author "Hath in these dayes: from forrayne soyle, / Brought home to thee, pleasure & gain" (1573, A5$^r$). Urging the importance of recreation, Partridge nationalizes a domesticity organized around the pleasures of acquisitiveness. Admittedly even in his frugal household vision, Tusser eroticized housewifery and husbandry as joining "as lovers should" (*Fiue Hundreth Points*, B2$^r$). While Tusser sexualized forms of labor, Partridge tutors readers to take delight in newfound access to aristocratic and foreign methods. Carefully providing Latin terms with English translations, Partridge urges his reader to assimilate the expertise of clerks, professionals, and physicians by mastering the elements of kitchen physic that were intellectually difficult (e.g., reading urine, astrology) or useful specifically for women (e.g., gynecology). While facilitating social emulation, cookbooks estranged domestic work as having to be "brought home."

Partridge concentrates, however, on the creativity involved in making costly preserves, sweetmeats, marmalades, distillations, and desserts. One recipe for edible kitchen art instructs the wife to print "the forme of an Hert, or the name of JESUS or any other thing whatsoever" on a marzipan tart (1573, B5$^r$). I have already touched on a striking feature of this practice – the ingenious culinary "conceit." In *Delightes for Ladies*, Plat directs women to mold marzipan into "rare and strange device[s]" such as "Rabbets, Pigeons, or any other little birde or beast" (1602, B3$^v$-B4$^r$). The 1608 *Closet for Ladies and Gentlewomen* revels in designing sugar birds and beasts that actually stand on their legs and boast realistic colors;[56] and numerous guides describe desserts shaped as letters, knots and castles. In creating a decorative rabbit, an upright bird or a divinely signed cake, the housewife proved her ingenuity and orchestrated sheer wastefulness. Given pervasive instructions for the housewife to conserve resources, she might readily have appreciated the freedom to expend time on "any . . . thing whatsoever." While conduct books directed women to be practical, these books invited housewives to mock ideologies resting on "proper" work. "Put what you please in the nut," *A Closet for Ladies* commands, "print [the cake] with your molds" (B4$^r$). *The Ladies Cabinet Enlarged* similarly charges the housewife to "make [marzipan] pies, birds, fruits, flowers, or any pretty things printed with Moulds, and so gild them and put them into your stove, and use them at your pleasure."[57] As she "printed" art forms in a surrogate craft shop keyed to her "pleasure," the housewife reimagined the ideal domestic space and its protocols.

Domestic guides thus inaugurate readers into a world with a premium on decadence, malleability, and spectacle. In creating pies containing live birds, the housewife made domestic inhabitants into self-conscious audiences. Promising to trick those at the dinner table, *trompe l'oeil* pastries reveal the control that food providers possessed in devising social rituals.[58] *The Whole Duty of a Woman* instructs housewives to make marzipan rashers of bacon that "will deceive the Curious, who cannot but take them for Bacon, unless you Taste or Smell them."[59] And Plat cleverly describes a paste made from Isinglass, a gelatin derived from sturgeons, mixed with fish guts, spices, and flour and shaped into schools of miniature fish (*Delightes*, 1608, 14). The wit of the recipe is that the dish reconstitutes and resembles its live source. The cultivation of sophisticated taste, in its broader sense, involved navigating through a world of culinary facades that tested the limits of the "real." And the fact that virtual desserts were often made of aphrodisiacs only heightened the impractical pleasures they were imagined to offer. Banquets comprised of wine, distilled waters, and sugar might inflame the very passions that conduct writers saw domestic duties as quenching and ordering. One guide goes so far as to suggest that the housewife create a simulacrum of the entire universe. In an experiment designed to "make the representation of the whole world in a glass," the reader is to mix chemicals so as to produce attractive vapors: "close [the mixture] hermetically, and make a lampe fire under it, and you will see presented in it the Sun, Moone, Stars, Fountaines, Flowers, Trees, Fruits, and Indeed, even all things: which is a glorious sight to behold."[60] With wealth and inventiveness, the housewife could reproduce the world by rummaging through the materials in her kitchen, using them to toy with the taxonomies supposedly underwriting the proper household.

Partridge's text was followed by like-minded texts – Thomas Dawson's 1585 *Good Huswifes Jewell*, the 1594 *Good Huswifes Handmaide for the Kitchin*, the 1608 *Closet for Ladies and Gentlewomen*, and John Murrell's 1617 *Daily Exercise for Ladies and Gentlewomen* – that featured syrups, wet suckets (citrus peels and fruits in syrup), dry suckets (fruit candies), and preserves. Sugar, at first a prohibitively expensive spice, became cheaper throughout the sixteenth century and spread beyond wealthiest classes just at the time that cookbooks flourished.[61] Delicacies that were originally rarities were advertised as affordable fare for the middling sort in seventeenth-century England.

As part of the civilizing process enabling the mapping of social distinctions, culinary artifice became a signifier of taste itself. Promising to teach a way to make a "Marmelade very comfortable for any Lord or Lady whatsoever," *A Closet for Ladies* offers a humble version of the spectacular banquets held at court and in noble households.[62] Here the banquet centerpiece was a marzipan pastry consisting of a large disc of almond paste decorated with three-dimensional figures to resemble cities, castles, and battlefields. The lavish progress entertainment for Queen Elizabeth at the Earl of Hertford's estate in 1591, for instance, included a playlet, fireworks, and a "banket" made up of one *thousand* dishes, including sugarworks shaped as the Queen's arms, drummers, soldiers, lions, unicorns, camels, tigers, snakes, mermaids, and dolphins.[63] In households where such ornate displays were beyond the budget, an occasional banquet dish could modestly mark status. The subtitle to Murrell's 1615 *New Booke of Cookerie* captures the cultural capital vested in these practices – "Wherein is set forth the newest and most commendable Fashion for Dressing or Sowcing . . . Together with making of all sorts of Jellyes . . . to beautifie and adorne eyther Nobleman or Gentlemans Table . . . All set forth according to the now, new, English and French Fashion." Murrell appears as an international traveler well-versed in the protocols of gentle eating. Partridge's celebrity recipes – "To make a Conserve or Jellie of Quinces, after my Lady Gray Clements sort"; "To preserve Quinces all the yeere, as it was used for King Edward" (B4ᵛ) – similarly promise to tutor housewives about chic fashions that might help them to accrue cultural capital.

While domestic guides emphasize the preservation of custom, cookbooks such as Partridge's hint at other forms of "keeping." First heralded as a restorative medicine for the body, sugar, even in its elaborate dessert forms, was said to thwart nature in many ways (Fig. 5). Highly sugared preserves aided digestion and safeguarded the human body from ill health. Many cookbooks conclude recipes for preserves, candies, and conserves with the reassuring mantra that a fresh fruit or vegetable might survive even into winter months – "it will keep throughout the year." Yet cookbooks also indulge in less utilitarian forms of preservation. Partridge's claim for an elaborately iced cake – "If it be through dried, and kept in a dry and warme aire: a Marchpane will laste many yeares" – makes dessert into an *objet d'art* (*Commodious Conceites*, 1573, B5ʳ). As part of their interest in social standing, guides also focus on how the housewife might maintain personal and household appearance by creating cosmetics, perfumes, and sweating baths as well as scouring expensive fabrics. In short, she is to lavish care on her appearance and safeguard refined goods. Plastering her face with boar's grease, almonds, egg whites, bran, and wine, the

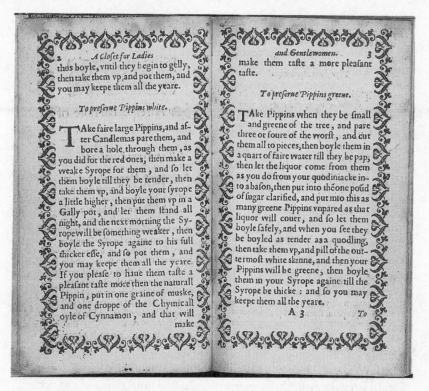

Fig. 5 Anonymous, *A Closet for Ladies and Gentlewomen* (London, 1608), bound with Hugh Plat's *Delightes for Ladies*. Notice that the text sports an artful decorative border.

housewife could whiten skin and erase the traces of dirt, labor, aging, disease, and sunburn. Partridge, for example, offers advice on how "To make a water that taketh off all stayning, dying and spots from the hands of Artificers, that get them by working, and maketh them white and faire" (F4ʳ). Housewifery thus offered the possibility of reconstituting the body and its cultural markers. With urine used to clean stains and lard applied to mask wrinkles, early modern people paradoxically immersed themselves in waste products as part of the patrol of civilized life. Since filth and its antidotes mingle freely in a refined existence, the housewife protects the often tenuous borderline between abject and genteel states of being.

Yet here we return to the fact that cookbooks also indulge destructive or seemingly "improper" domestic whims. Banqueting involved more than merely being the admiring spectator to a virtual world; for aristocratic meals were regularly punctuated with a highly refined food fight carried out in the "void" or banqueting room designed for after-dinner entertainment.[64] With cookbooks in hand, citizens could imitate these collective frenzies by smashing edible dishes: "At the ende of the banquet they may eat al, and breake the platters, dishes, cups, and all thynges: for this paste is delicate," Partridge writes (1584, A8ʳ). Confectionery, it seems, might constitute a sphere of ephemeral production as well as a scene of studied impropriety. At the heart of domesticity, these books suggest, rests violent impulses best incorporated into the material practices of daily ritual. One of the interesting contradictions emerging from the move toward refinement is that the banquet promised a set of legible status codes (to be performed by careful self-control) that unleash a seemingly unlicensed energy. This exuberant if ruled disorder pressures the stability of the "polite" society it helps to mark and define.[65]

Printed twelve times between 1602 and 1683, Plat's *Delightes for Ladies* readily became the most popular cookbook of the period.[66] In this beautifully crafted book, each page of the tiny *Delightes for Ladies* frames recipes for creative household arts within a pretty border design. Plat opens his book with an aphrodisiac (eryngo, the candied root of the sea holly) followed by recipes for preserves, distillations, cosmetics, and "pretie conceits" (B9ᵛ). His prefatory poem celebrates the ephemeral perfumes and sweets that he associates with femininity itself. Fleming has pointed out the theoretical implications of Plat's desire to cater to a feminized world, to be, in her terms, a "ladies' man."[67] Imitating Virgillian language in his claim to abandon serious projects to attend to mere "sweetness," Plat presents himself as succumbing to the frivolity of his age. "I scorne to write with Coppres or with galle," he proclaims and instead turns

> To sweetest creatures that the earth doth beare:
> These are the Saints to whom I sacrifice
> Preserves and conserves both of plum and peare.
> Empalings now adew, tush, marchpaine wals
> Are strong enough, and best befits our age:
> Let piercing bullets turne to sugar bals.

(A2ᵛ)

The inconsequentiality of the times dictates his transformation from "masculine" activities like impaling and shooting to the delicate practices of housewifery. In this inflated prefatory ode to housewifery, "sweetness" (as opposed to "galle") is a characteristic of both the practitioner and her ingredients.

I have commented on the fact that Plat endows domestic practice with the heroic ability to stay time, but he also frames housework within literary tradition. When birds and fowls are cast "in formes of sweetest grace" they transcend death and mutate into an artificial world that is miraculously lifelike:

> Of Marmelade and paste of Genua,
> Of musked Sugars, I intend to wright:

Of Leach, of Sucket, and Quidinea,
Affording to each Lady, her delight.
I teach both fruits and flowers to preserve,
And candie them, so Nutmegs, cloves, and mace:
To make both marchpaine, paste, and sugred plate,
And cast the same in formes of sweetest grace.
Each bird and foule, so moulded from the life,
And after cast in sweet compounds of arte,
As if the flesh and forme which Nature gave,
Did still remaine in every lim and part.

                                                        (A2$^v$-A3$^r$)

Plat uses choice syntactical allusions to Virgil's *Aeneid* to create an epic language designed to clash playfully with the triviality of his subject. Domestic
work imitates the heroic feats of epic largely by blurring foundational line between animation and artifice. Marshaling a tone of deferential awe, Plat offers
sacrifices in the form of insubstantial desserts; and his newfound campaign rests
on manufacturing an invincible female "delight" in household work. Recreation
rather than epic heroism must now arbitrate weighty issues, for in the microcosm
of the home, the parameters of life and death can be obscured.

The comic awe that Plat displays in his poem hints at, while it also neutral-
izes, the force of housewifery. Yet while Plat's initial poem finally suggests
domesticity's sweet insubstantiality, his text then argues against the kitchen's
insignificance; for his book nominates domestic work as a critical *social* art and
suggests pointedly that what one does in the home determines social standing.
Plat hints that the housewife can evidence her familiarity with the right crowd
by how she makes cakes. In one instance, he shows himself to be a terrible
tease, interrupting a recipe to tell readers that he could, if he wished, gossip
mercilessly about his circle of lady friends: "There is a countrie Gentlewoman
whome I could name, which venteth great store of sugar cakes made of this
composition. But the onely faulte which I finde in this paste is, that it tasteth
too much of the sugar, and too little of the almonds" (B5$^r$). Alluding to a bad
confectioner whom he valiantly refuses to name, Plat coyly hints of a social
life glimmering with possible indiscretions. In both this text and his *Jewell
House of Art and Nature* (a book that includes domestic tips), Plat flirtatiously
conscripts his reader as a partner in crime; he brags that he risks "betraying"
his friends' secret cheese recipes in print: "I have beene as bold as *I* dare, in
discoverie hereof," he writes, "because I would be loath to offend a Gentlewoman that presumeth of a great secret herein, and she is the more daintie
of her skil, because shee hath found it out by many labors, and losses of her
owne."[68] The male writer's uneasiness about "knowing the dairy" surfaces in
these passages; and imagined female losses fuel the commodity's exchange
value.[69] In purchasing stolen secrets, readers are invited to fantasize about joining and besting their social superiors. Plat thus enjoins readers to savor the

power vested in owning a domestic wisdom based not on custom but on clandestine knowledge. Housework, as well as its elaboration, becomes a site of intrigue.

And desire as well. When describing how to preserve fruits in his *Jewell House*, Plat slips into a wild reverie:

Nowe me thinkes I see a whole troupe of gallant dames attending with their listning eares, or rather longing with their great bellies, to learne some new found skil, how they may play at chopcherrie, when cherrie time is past. Wel, to give these Ladies some content, I will unfolde a scroule which I had long since as carefully wrapped up as ever any of the Sybels did their fatall prophesies, wherein I will make them as cunning as my selfe (saving onelie that I will reserve one strange venue to foile a scholler withal if need be.) The secret is short, let one element be included within another, so as the one may have no accesse nor participate with the other. But this paradventure is too philosophical for women. Then receive it Ladies with plaine tearms into your open lappes. For want of Glasses with broade skirts . . . cause new Pewter vessels of some large reception to be made. (C2$^r$)

In this extravagant meditation, Plat deems female readers a devouring crowd hungry to satisfy their appetite for carnal knowledge and culinary treats. What the guide offers is a male fantasy about a harem of women who desire the narrator for his domestic know-how and "cunning" (a common term for female genitalia). Assuming the female sibyl's powers of prophecy and divination, the narrator stylizes himself as a flirtatious female tutor to somewhat limited domestic pupils. He thus emphasizes how textual transmission repeats the game of desire and satiation seen in playing at "chopcherrie," for the "open lappes" of female readers meld into the broad skirted glass vessels Plat recommends. In this fantasy, gender blending, learning, and housework appear as provocative and mythic activities. The "troop" of discontent women hanging on the writer's every word then interestingly fades into a lengthy and technical description of how to fasten fruit into receptacles so as to regulate proper moisture and temperature. Plat is, after all, simply explaining how to preserve cherries, but the term's erotic valences (found in lyric poetry's evocation of cherry cheeks and lips ripe for the picking) pervade his account. Housewifery, even in its technical inscription, smacks of appetite and scandalous pleasure.

Plat, in short, offers a sensationalist account of his intimacy with women and their work. So it isn't surprising that he closes his prefatory poem on a provocative note. Promising to write "without affected speech," Plat nevertheless presents an image of combined textual and sexual intimacy:

> Accept [these secrets] well and let my wearied muse
> Repose her selfe in Ladies laps a while.
> So when shee wakes, she happely may record,
> Her sweetest dreames in some more pleasing stile.

(A3$^v$)

Plat sends out his female Muse, along with his book commodity, to be lovingly cradled in the laps of readers. Conjuring up a suggestive scenario, like that of Hamlet resting in Ophelia's lap and bantering about country matters, Plat imagines his muse as dreaming up the "pleasing" domestic recipes he will tantalizingly offer to the public. Is it any wonder that subsequent texts echoed Plat's whimsical tone, as they conflated housewifery and reading cookbooks with the pleasure of a romantic rendezvous.[70] Delights for ladies indeed.

Following cues presented in these guides, early modern plays present characters who freely trope culinary dainties as erotic pleasures. "No sweet meat in the world / Is like the conserve of a Ladies hand," declares a character in William Davenant's *Unfortunate Lovers* (1643), a sentiment that seems to gloss the name of a common dessert, "kissing comfits."[71] And when imagining spoiling a city after battle, the soldiers in William Cartwright's 1651 *Siege* dream of ravaging women who squat among their sweetmeats, gallipots, aphrodisiacs, and jellies. Prusias proudly declares, "I'l to the houses where I think I shall / Meet with the best Conserves, and tenderst Virgins; / Sweetmeats and Maidenheads are all I aime at."[72] This clichéd image of the woman as edible dessert could mutate into a fantasy in which housewives perform indecorous work. In John Crowne's *The Married Beau* (1694), for instance, Mrs. Lovely secrets a man in her closet as a favor to a friend, only to have him read this as proof of her desire: "Wou'd you lock me up in your Closet, if / you did not reckon me among your Sweet-meats? . . . I don't think you e're laid up Conserve o' Roses for your Maid, and Conserve o' Man is more luscious."[73] Women's work with sugar might brand them metonymically as delicious, but it could link them to inappropriate cravings. The connection between cooking and lust is precisely what the narrator fears in Robert Anton's *The Philosophers Satyrs* (1616):

> [W]ives covet *bookes*,
> Not penn'd by *Artists*, but the *fruits of Cookes*
> Prescribing *lustie dishes*, to enflame
> Their lustie fighting *broode* unto their game
> *Confections* with *infections* of their *kinde*,
> Rot both their *body*, and corrupts the *minde*.[74]

Reading, eating, and passion merge to create a morally suspect world beneath the veneer of dedicated domestic work. Given the premium placed on pleasure in cookbooks, it's not surprising that when Samuel Pepys frolicked on a summer day by dining, drinking, and carrying ladies to the king's pleasure boat, he entertained passengers by reading aloud from one of the cookbooks he collected. They went "all the way reading in a book of Receipts of making fine meats and sweetmeats; among others, one 'to Make my own sweet water' – which made us good sport," Pepys writes.[75] Even the fact that Pepys *bought* guides addressed to women (including *The Gentlewomans Delight in Cookery, The*

*Gentlewomans Cabinet Unlocked, The Compleat Servant-Maid, The Compleat Cook,* and *The Queens Royal Closet Newly Opened* ) is telling. Although we don't know whether Pepys's choice of amusement was widespread, we might assume that cookbooks could function then, like today, as recreational reading and the site of fantasy.

*As you mold a marzipan pastry in your London home, do you luxuriate in imagining how indulgent, titillating, and coy these desserts might be? Do you worry if your house is properly English? Or as noble as you aspire to be? While you strive to make your household a microcosm of the realm, do you notice that your chores sometimes mock the rules? That they allow you to become the object of curiosity or envy for others? Though creating spectacles is business as usual, does your kitchen work occasionally feel alien (or uncanny) when you think of how it is sometimes described?*

It was partly in reaction to these representations that Markham published his pious domestic counter fantasy – as an attempt to reclaim housewifery as a productive and altruistic enterprise. When pronouncing on diet, for instance, Markham attempts a categorical distinction between hunger and appetite: "Let it be rather to satisfie nature then our affections, and apter to kil hunger than revive new appetites," he states (*English House-wife*, 4). Rather than infecting the mind and breeding untoward desires, food and the housework it synecdochically figures marks for Markham a moral world of production and consumption. Yet even Markham can't resist including a few recipes for banqueting dishes "not of general use," as if admitting the power of certain domestic "affections." He indulges his desire for ornamentation interestingly by including "Sallats for shew only" (boiled carrots shaped into knots, birds, beasts, and coats of arms (69). As we might expect, guides and cookbooks move between the goals of profit and pleasure, as they attempt to capture the widest possible market of readers. A single cookbook might include expensive dishes among homey country pottages, laud the virtue *and* pleasure of labor, or strive to satisfy contradictory expectations. Dawson's *Good Huswifes Jewell,* for instance, seeks to engage but stretch beyond a rural readership by including both luxury recipes and tips on veterinary care. The 1594 *Good Huswifes Handmaide for the Kitchin* and the 1595 *Widdowes Treasure* both mention a few fashionable sugarworks or banquet items among their plain foods and advice on husbandry. The discourses of national virtue, efficiency, social standing, tradition, novelty, and pleasure intermingle and shape contradictory conceptions of housewifery even within a single text. As such, manuals oscillate between definitions of domesticity as familiar and exotic, and they rest various terms – nationality, class, gender – on these shifting definitions.

Books like Markham's, which insist primarily on a closed home economy, eventually gave way to what Lynnette Hunter describes as the "growing specialisation of knowledge as the arts and sciences separated and fragmented" in the seventeenth century.[76] Confectionery split off from medicinal practice, veterinary care was no longer requisite domestic knowledge, and distillation became the province of professionals. Even when later texts point to housewifery's national importance, they no longer assume the comprehensive system of household production that Markham recommends. "By the end of the seventeenth century," Hunter writes, "not only 'banqueting stuffe' but also the books which conveyed receipts about it had accommodated both to a wider audience and a different class, and to the predominant urban division of women's lives into the commercial and the domestic" (57). Before this separation occurred, writers grapple with how the household's economic centrality inflected the cultural divisions it was conscripted to produce.

### Ladies and chefs: housewifery after 1650

By mid-seventeenth century, manuals interested primarily in aristocratic cuisine join these other two types of domestic guide. Addressed to male chefs and dedicated to prominent lords, Robert May's 1660 *Accomplisht Cook*, for example, promotes the value of country hospitality and international feasting. Trained in French noblemen's houses, May bills his domestic knowledge as rarefied information and entertains his reader by describing the most extravagant sugarwork documented in the period: a huge marzipan ship complete with firing guns, streamers, live frogs and birds, and eggshells filled with wine that ladies were invited to throw at each other.[77] Though recommending fairly plain recipes, May writes for a male professional who sees his labor as an aristocratic art. The 1669 *Closet of the Eminently Learned Sir Kenelme Digby Kt. Opened*, William Rabisha's 1673 *Whole Body of Cookery Dissected*, and W. M.'s 1655 *Queens Closet Opened* (which published Henrietta Maria's recipes), similarly emphasize the novel, cosmopolitan, and elite character of their advice. In these books, domestic and foreign recipes are "approved" by the likes of King Edward IV, Queen Elizabeth, Charles V, Sir Walter Ralegh, and the Earl of Arundel. Unlike Partridge, who claims to release elite mysteries to a larger populace, these guides identify themselves as circulating the choice recipes of lords and ladies among their peers (though in practice they could have been read by anyone). Making no attempt to preserve English custom or enhance social mobility, these books assume a fraternity of cooks catering to a privileged clientele. While they mediated economic changes and demeaned female labor, printed cookbooks, as Stephen Mennel observes, helped to create a literate culinary culture that increased the "technical cohesion and social prestige of a professional elite of cooks in the service of members of the upper class."[78] The uneasiness evident in earlier domestic guides was thus dispensed with in different ways by later writers; while some texts redefine housewifery out of the sphere of production or claim a national affinity that overshadows the gendered division of labor, others simply relegate cooking to professionals.

Books directed to housewives continued to outnumber aristocratic guides. When women began authoring cookbooks at the end of the seventeenth century, however, professionals had assumed many formerly domestic labors and the dream of a closed home economy had faltered in the wake of a more developed service market. When Elizabeth Grey's *A Choice Manual, or Rare and Select Secrets in Physick and Chirurgery: Collected, and practised by the Right Honourable the Countess of Kent, late deceased* appeared in 1655, it significantly made no claims on behalf of the gender of its author. Given nervous disclaimers about knowing women's work uttered by earlier writers, we might expect the first cookbook attributed to a woman to champion female expertise in the kitchen, but professional training and social standing instead served as its principles of legitimation. Thus *A Choice Manual* sports an engraved portrait of a bejeweled countess whose wealth could purchase expert knowledge.

Following the publication of Kent's text, Hannah Woolley emerged as the key female writer on domesticity in the 1660s and 1670s. In *The Cook's Guide, The Ladies Dictionary, The Queen-like Closet, The Gentlewomans Companion,*[79] *The Accomplisht Ladys Delight, The Compleat Servant-Maid* and *The Guide to Ladies,* Woolley defines domestic work as concerned with the acquisition of manners and skills necessary for upward social mobility. She doesn't, however, write from an elite position or legitimate her texts as the fruit of a specifically female or indigenous knowledge. Instead she argues for domestic skill as the product of studied training. While including the basics of cooking and physic, Woolley's texts emphasize skills such as accounting, arithmetic, letter-writing, embroidery, picture-framing, conversation, table arrangement, and home decorating (Figs. 6–8). In *The Queen-like Closet,* she shows women how to stencil figures, landscapes, and stories onto plates and flowerpots (1675, 70–72). Instructing maids on how to catch a husband and offering tips for regulating negligent servants, Woolley immerses her reader in a market economy in which domestic work involves social exchange, financial dealings, and contracted services. Basing her book on thirty years of work, she defines "experience" as that garnered in a paid service job. "I have been *Physitian* and *Chyrurgian* in my own House to many, and also, to many of my Neighbours, eight or ten Miles round," she boasts. Locating her skills in the marketplace, Woolley invites readers to hire her services for a small "Gratuity" and to purchase her home-made remedies or letters of recommendation.[80] It is fitting that the 1675 *Queen-like Closet* ends with an advertisement for a cordial powder and purging pills "sold by Richard Lowndes Book-Seller, at the White-Lion in Duck-Lane near West-Smithfield" (372). Domestic wisdom emerges as the product of shopping or study rather than something women garner from their everyday existence.

Fig. 6   Patterns for shaping and arranging pies and dishes at the table. From Hannah Woolley, *The Accomplisht Ladys Delight* (London, 1675).

Contributing to the civilizing process, Woolley's books emphasize deportment, manners, attitude, and gestures. "Most in this depraved later Age think a Woman learned and wife enough if she can distinguish her Husband's bed from anothers," she quips in *The Gentlewomans Companion* when advocating women's education (1). But she doesn't challenge stereotypes as much as argue for women's intellectual and emotional fitness for good behavior. Tossing off references to the classics, Sidney, Agrippa, and women writers, Woolley argues that girls should learn Latin so as to improve their command of English. As if grasping the importance of the Latin puberty rite, Woolley combines a call for housewifery with the educational training to which it was customarily opposed.[81] "Having qualified them for reading, you shall Practice them

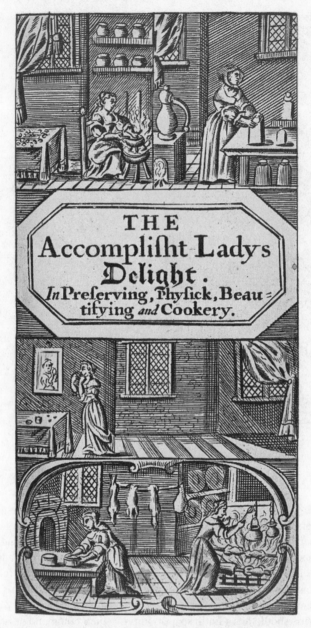

Fig. 7   The title page to Hannah Woolley's *The Accomplisht Ladys Delight* (London, 1675) shows the housewife engaged in the arts of cosmetics along with the standard duties of distilling, preserving and cooking.

Fig. 8 The title page to Hannah Woolley's *The Compleat Servant-Maid* (London, 1683) pictures the maid as taking charge of the nursery and dairy in addition to performing the usual housewifely tasks of distilling, physic, and cooking.

in their pen, as not to be ignorant in a *Point de Venice*, & all the productions of the Needle, with all the curious devices of *Wax-work*, *Rock-work*, *Moss-work* . . . and . . . let them know how to Preserve, Conserve, Distill; with all those laudible Sciences which adorn a compleat Gentlewoman" (*Gentlewomans Companion*, 9). Linking pen and needle as complementary tools, Woolley hints at domesticity's role in social- and self-improvement. Showing the attainability of a model character built around proficiency takes priority over making a case for the pleasure, or patriotism, of domesticity.

Sara Pennel observes that English cookbooks after mid-seventeenth century lose their earlier tone of intimacy. When guide writers preach to the unknowing, they marshal an air of authority that overrides claims to shared experience. One result is that the class divisions masked by writers such as Markham surface as the rationale for transmitting knowledge. In *The Queen-like Closet*,

Woolley, for instance, explains that published domestic advice is necessary because elite families, impoverished by civil war, plagues, and fire, now need to place daughters in positions (1684, 261). "We English" don't, these texts suggest, share a coherent body of domestic knowledge at all, for some portions of the population have never needed to know the basics of home life. Woolley thus defines housewifery as knowledge that has to be self-consciously reproduced within the market rather than simply imbibed in everyday culture. The paradox of learning "familiar" national experiences fades from view. The most noteworthy eighteenth-century cookbook writers – Eliza Smith, Elizabeth Moxon, Mary Kettilby, Elizabeth Raffald, and, especially, Hannah Glasse – join in their disdain for extravagant and/or foreign cuisine, yet they clearly don't mind recommending domestic technique garnered in French-influenced noblemen's homes.[82] The meaning of home-born knowledge, along with the political significance of the home, changed considerably by this time.

Between 1570 and 1650, English readers had the option of buying pocket-size books emphasizing decorative and socially useful arts or extensive husbandry encyclopedias promoting self-sufficient production. A Londoner shopping for books in the stalls of St. Pauls between 1620 and 1630 could choose among Tusser's quaint *Fiue Hundreth Points of Good Husbandry*, Plat's stylish *Delightes for Ladies*, a reprint of Partridge's fashionable *Closet*, or Markham's practical *English House-wife*. The jumbling of these books within the bookseller's wares signals not just different readerships for domestic advice, but mixed desires within the same readership. In these texts, domesticity, in part because of its incarnation as a printed object, was refracted for readers in myriad ways: framed as nostalgia, relegated to a country past, linked to a culture of expertise, tied to foreignness, eroticized as secret delights, championed as the backbone of national culture.

The primary discursive frameworks that I have outlined helped to generate a dynamic that underwrites the dramatic representations explored in the remainder of this book. For plays overlay social debates – about wetnursing, laundering, physic, butchery, and service – onto the paradoxical representation of domesticity emerging in early print forms. As we shall see in the following chapters, theater audiences were entertained with scenes in which household labors were exoticized but celebrated as the cornerstone of community-formation. These representations suggest that different social groups vied to control the meaning of domesticity and the fraught conceptions of English identity it enabled. It wouldn't be until modern formations of domesticity emerged, along with Freud's commentary, that we would interpret this dynamic as the uncanny.

# 2 Needles and birches: pedagogy, domesticity, and the advent of English comedy

> *Lingua* is declined with *haec*, the feminine, because it is household stuff, particularly belonging and most commonly resident under the roof of women's mouths.
>
> John Marston, *What You Will*[1]

## Back to the vernacular

On December 2, 1592, Lord Burghley requested that a group of Cambridge academics provide an English comedy for Queen Elizabeth's Christmas entertainment. The Vice-Chancellor and Heads of Houses responded indignantly by telling Burghley that the request, as stated, was out of the question:

> How fitt wee shalbe for this that is moved, havinge no practize in this Englishe vaine, and beinge (as we thinke) nothing beseeming our students ... wee much doubt; And do finde our principale Actors ... very unwillinge to playe in Englishe ... Englishe Comedies for that wee never used any, wee presentlie have none. To make or translate one in such shortness of time, wee shall not be able; And therefore yf wee must needes undertake the busines ... These two thinges wee would gladly desire, some further limitacion of time for due preparacion, And liberty to play in latyn.[2]

Concerned to distinguish humanist theatrical practice from that of the professional playhouses, these scholars glibly air their condescension toward English, a medium perceived to be below the academy's level, inferior to Latin, and secondary (English drama, it seems, requires translation). If they must perform, he grudgingly concedes, it must at least be in Latin. In claiming that they had "no practize in this Englishe vaine," the Cambridge masters, however, had simply forgotten their stage history. While documenting that Tudor universities occasionally performed Latin and Italian comedies in translation, Frederick Boas notes that the first play written in English, *Gammer Gurton's Needle,* was performed at Christ's College thirty or so years before the dons refused Burghley's request. Although the two universities produced about 150 Elizabethan and Jacobean Latin plays, Cambridge did not present English comedy as a regular part of their offerings until the 1590s when the University became embroiled

59

in the town/gown controversy and sought to insult their town audience in terms the audience could understand.

Disdain for English was not isolated to the universities but infiltrated the entire educational system. Not only was the grammar taught in grammar schools exclusively Latin, but these schools' primary self-identification turned on their almost single-minded curricular devotion to Latin. Mandated to couch all lessons *in* Latin, schools dictated punishments for boys who spoke English in the classroom or in transit to school. As historians have noted, policing speech according to such strict guidelines was virtually impossible. Prompted by the nationalist effects of the Reformation, the vernacular increasingly was employed as a necessary part of sixteenth-century pedagogy, especially for younger boys. Yet Latin remained the espoused cornerstone of the grammar school curriculum.[3]

In this chapter I analyze Mr. S.'s *Gammer Gurton's Needle* (*c*. 1550–60) as a means of asking how a linguistic nationalism tied to domestic life troubled the sex and gender identifications that pedagogical institutions offered.[4] My broadest argument is that housewifery had a deep structural discursive link to a particular kind of national identification by virtue of its connection to the native tongue learned in early childhood. Since it was taught to children by women who also were busy running the household, English speech became fused conceptually with the material practices of the home. But this identification, between domestic spaces and English tongues, contradicted the gender, class, and sexual identifications advocated by humanist teachers; for schools suggested that household life was precisely the element that had to be disavowed in the making of proper civic masculinity.[5] The problems raised by these contradictory identifications inform the work of writers who sought to produce and define English comedy in the late sixteenth century.

Critics nominate *Gammer* as a candidate for the "first English play" because no previous plays followed Latin precedent in terms of act and scene division, secular subject matter, and respect for unities of time and place.[6] It is provocative, then, that when a playwright chose to introduce the very first English play to undergraduates steeped in Latin, he chose the topic of a housewife's mischances. Following classical, epic-sounding, and foreign works tied to Latin and Greek (*Microcosmus, Plutus, and Penulus*), *Gammer Gurton's Needle* marks a departure in a newly forming secular dramatic tradition. Signaling its distinction from the usual dramatic fare by its title, the play announces itself as trivial, home-grown, English, and clearly *new*. What did an English play mean within an academic environment? Why the pointed use of rusticity and femininity to mark the advent of a newly Englished form? If the vernacular was suspect, how was the play's linguistic naughtiness addressed? While we may assume that class snobbery motivated the presentation of yokels bumbling through life with exaggerated dialects, negotiating trivial losses, and displaying coarse behavior, "snobbery" does not adequately account for the complexity of the social relations portrayed in the play and produced through its performance. I suggest that we think about this performance in light of what Walter Ong has termed the "male puberty ritual" of Latin learning and (later in this chapter) what Juliet Fleming has described as a nationalist project built upon the "rumor" of a "female-specific vernacular activity."[7] My interest is in investigating the gendering and sexualizing of community that surfaces when we posit a possible connection between the play's unusual status as English academic drama and its thematic obsession with domesticity.

Ong argues that Latin was taught in conjunction with violent floggings de-signed to instill physical hardiment in young boys and to separate them from the domain of women. Certainly historical accounts of grammar school education support Ong's dual emphases on ritualized beatings and the sustained separa-tion of genders in schooling.[8] Although Renaissance humanists urged sexual segregation on intellectual grounds, they also sought to gender young chil-dren through pedagogy. Marking his separation from both the "mother tongue" and the traditional family, the boy's initiation into a public world depended on Latin's historical divorce from the discourse of "everyday life." The famed sixteenth-century schoolmaster Roger Ascham writes, for instance, that "the Greek and Latin tongue" are "the two only learned tongues which be kept not in *common* talk but in private books."[9] Latin marked the division between what was "common" and "private," "male" and "female," spoken and read. As "the language of those on the 'inside,'" Ong writes, "Latin [learned] at even an infra-university level was the first step toward initiation into [a] closed world" (109). Numerous pedagogical theorists warn about the damage caused by the speech of female childcare providers, faults that the rigor and purity of the Latin curriculum was designed to correct. We have to remember that this was a world in which proper speaking was more than a superficial sign of good breed-ing; brandishing a classical language signaled that a person had fully ingested tenets crucial to the development of a sound moral and critical intelligence. Hyperdefined against a gender-and class-based "commonality," Latin enabled the production of the "closed male environment" of academia, as well as the professional and courtly institutions it fed. No wonder the Cambridge masters, or bachelors, wanted "liberty" to "play in latyn" when asked to entertain a *fe-male* monarch, for it both separated them from effeminizing court discourse and implicitly flattered a queen who had unusual accomplishments in classical tongues.

To extend his hypothesis to the universities, Ong might have pointed to the 1561 proclamation issued by Elizabeth that sought to institutionalize the divide between the cross-gendered world of domesticity and the scholarly world of men. The edict first defines the university as a secluded environment, "houses ... builded and enclosed in severalty to sustain and keep society of learned men professing study and prayer for the edification of the church of God and so consequently to serve the commonwealth." But this seclusion was violated, the text notes, when "prebendaries, students and members thereof being married *do keep particular households with their wives, children and nurses*, whereof no small offense groweth to the intent of the founders and to the quiet and orderly profession of study and learning within the same."[10] Elizabeth's proclamation goes on to banish wives and women that "abide and dwell in the same, or [that] haunt any lodgings within the college." Unlike *Love's Labor's Lost*, which more conventionally counterpoises eros, appetite, and women to the male life of the mind, this edict explicitly defines "wives, children, and nurses" as obstacles to scholarly learning. It is cross-gendered domestic life rather than sexuality *per se* that threatens the order of university students and faculty. Charles I later issued a 1630 edict that sequesters youthful scholars from the marital seductions of lower-class town girls: women caught flirting with elite men could be deported four miles outside the university. Elizabeth's order cordons off universities not from the influence of women generally, but from the domestic practices of "particular households." She exiles, in short, the nurse.

If we look forward in time to a 1626 boys' play performed at the Hadley Freeschool, we find a clear articulation of the adversarial relationship between Latin and housewifery. William Hawkins' *Apollo Shroving* opens with a prologue repeatedly interrupted by Lala, "a woman spectator," who climbs on stage and protests: "What? shall wee have Latine againe? Master Prologue yongster. I pray you goe to the University, and set up your Stage there."[11] It falls to a boy dressed as a housewife to mock pedantry and inaugurate the grammar school's move from Latin to English. When she later heralds the value of English wares, home cooking, economic protectionism, and "our" countrymen, Lala brings nationalist sentiment to bear on her scorn for "outlandish," barbarous tongues. "This is no English. My Mother never spoke it," she declares, "I proclaim to all my sex, they have leave to depart. I'd rather spin at home, then hear these Barbarians spout Latin" (7). If educators were suspicious of the household tongue, Latin appears, from the perspective of the housewife, to be a foreign and barbaric erosion of "our" practices. Presenting a domestic spectator out of control, *Apollo Shroving* burlesques the cultural antagonism between Latin and domesticity.

Given that the definition and prestige of academic life seems so evidently to rest on the rejection of cross-gendered domesticity and its vernacular, we might find it odd that the first English play in a university presented the story of a housewife. Perhaps by realizing so acutely every schoolmaster's worst nightmare, the play could be said to make English drama a joke at the moment of its inception. But rather than simply mocking the vernacular, *Gammer*, I will argue, erodes the differences between male/female and public/private that the Latin puberty rite upheld, and instead defines the "family" as the economic unit *securing* gender relations. While necessarily probing the divide that safeguarded both masculinity and knowledge, this play thematizes English's intrusion into the college milieu; for it demands that Cambridge undergraduates embrace a strongly renounced domesticity at the exact moment that they first conceptualize drama in their native tongue. Complicating associations between femininity and the "mother tongue," *Gammer* pressures a paradigm in which masculinity and power depend upon the repression of a certain kind of domesticity. Who, after all, wants to be identified as barbaric or "un-English"? But what humanistically trained boy could risk association with the non-elite and feminized world of home?

In the 1550s, when the prestige activities of the culture were largely conducted in Latin, English was by definition a trifle, much like an insignificant needle; its familiarity was estranged within the high world of national culture.[12] In legitimating English comedy, *Gammer* revalues the trifle, and, in so doing, the labor of housewifery that is the play's critical metaphor. Constructing a tissue of puns around domestic labor, *Gammer* announces its role in making much ado about nothing – nothing, that is, except the idea of a national domestic drama.

### Oeconomia's "shameful hole"

Our Mother tongue, which truly of it self is both full enough for prose and stately enough for verse, hath long time been counted most bare and barren of both. Which default when as some endeavored to salve and recur, they patched up the holes with pieces of rags of other languages.

*The Shepheardes Calendar*[13]

And 'ch cannot somewhat to stop this gap, cham utterly undone!

Hodge in *Gammer Gurton's Needle*[14]

*Gammer* tells the story of a domestic mishap in a rural village. Diccon, a bedlam, stirs up trouble by concocting lies about a missing needle's supposed theft. Through Diccon's machinations, Gammer's lost needle ripples through the community and causes a series of disasters: Hodge, Gammer's worker, finds himself hampered by a large whole in his pants and soils himself in fear of the devil; the curate, Dr. Rat, is beaten in a case of mistaken identity; and the two town matriarchs become embroiled in a physical and verbal feud. The play ends when Diccon's hoaxes are discovered, and he, in a perverse act of penance, slaps Hodge's rear to reveal miraculously the needle's heretofore hidden location in Hodge's trousers. Structurally, the play demonstrates the way in which the household economy impinges on the community at large; that is, how a missing needle can become the occasion for a complete breakdown of social relations.

The comedy of the play's opening scenes depends on our sense that the household has an exaggerated response to a missing trifle: it robs Gammer of "her joy and life" (1.3.16), causes massive "sighing and sobbing," and threatens to "undo" order. Hodge complains that the women have shown themselves incapable of accomplishing even the minor tasks accorded within the gendered division of labor: "What devil had you else to do? Ye kept, ich wot, no sheep!/ Cham [I am] fain abroad to dig and delve in water, mire and clay . . . /And four of you sit idle at home and cannot keep a nee'le" (1.4.24–5, 28). Hodge's sense of the insignificance of women's work, however, is glaringly at odds with the trauma that the lost needle causes. Unable to work or, more importantly, to go courting because of his torn pants, Hodge becomes acutely aware of his vulnerable and dependent place in the household economy; his sexual and social contentment rests precisely on the women's ability to "keep a nee'le."[15] As Thomas Tusser recommends in his *Fiue Hundreth Points of Good Husbandry*, "Good semsters be sowing of fine pretie knackes, /good huswifes be mending and peecing their sackes" (173). With Gammer no longer able to mend his trousers and hold together the domestic economy, the disgruntled Hodge pledges his labor to whoever has the needle. In fact, the entire economic system upon which the villagers' social and sexual relations are predicated is momentarily suspended. Hodge thus faces the historical reality that sixteenth-century housewives were the "ultimate guarantors" of the family's economic self-sufficiency.[16]

The play's obvious phallic references encourage us to think of Hodge's economic subordination as bodily lack: the "fair long straight nee'le" (1.4.5), described as a "cock," an "eel" (both puns on male genitalia), is romanticized by Gammer as her lost love ("Alas, my nee'le, we shall never meet – adieu" [1.5.8]), and is finally linked in humorous if indiscriminate ways to Hodge's sexual security. "Rake a cat, Hodge? What wouldst thou do?" Gammer demands of Hodge, who is mysteriously groping the animal while searching for the needle. Hodge, missing the point, snaps defensively, "What, thinkst that cham not able?" (3.4.19–20). Linking the missing needle to a gap in clothing and body that has class and gendered valences, Hodge cries: "And 'ch [I] cannot somewhat . . . stop this gap / Cham [I'm] utterly undone" (2.1.60). He later plaintively demands: "Seest not what is here?" [pointing to his torn breeches] (2.3.29). In the course of the play, as Gail Paster argues, the embarrassment of Hodge's labor dissolves into the shame of self-pollution, seen particularly when Hodge soils himself out of fear of the devil. Unable to undertake her housewifery, Gammer is blamed for endowing Hodge with the "shameful" hole (2.1.49) and unstoppable "gap" that the play then naturalizes as expressing his faulty character.

Hodge's masculinity, however, paradoxically rests in Gammer possessing the needle so that she can enact the constant repair necessary to hide Hodge's subservient position. Paster is thus right to see the needle as a "free-floating talisman of gender difference," but it is also tellingly Gammer's phallus, the tool that guarantees the housewife's authority in her husbandless home (118). Having the needle allows her to cover her own lack by producing the sign of his endowment, to "better agree" with her maid Tib, and to command her servant boy "Cock." Gammer's investment in the needle is, of course, part of the play's joke. "My ... nee'le ... was mine only treasure," she laments, "The first day of my sorrow is, and last end of my pleasure" (1.4.5–6). In one of the play's numerous conflations of erotic gratification and socioeconomic authority, we see the "pleasure" that comes to an "end" (Hodge's) is precisely Gammer's role as patriarch within the primary economic unit of production in the early modern world.

As we see in schoolmaster Richard Mulcaster's prescriptions for educating girls, the needle could synecdochically figure domestic work of all stripes: "I meddle not with needles nor yet with housewifery," Mulcaster assures his readers, "though I think it and know it to be a principal commendation in a woman to be able to govern and direct her household; to look to her house and family; to provide and keep necessaries, though the goodman pay; to know the force of her kitchen, for sickness and health in herself and her charge."[17] While advocating a gender differentiated literacy program for boys and girls, Mulcaster feels compelled to list the tenets of household economy important for women to know (though he, of course, would never "meddle" in such affairs). And while distinguishing needlework from housewifery ("needles nor ... housewifery"), he syntactically aligns them, so that the image of the tiny object bears the weighty responsibilities he delineates. In Anthony Munday's 1585 *Fedele and Fortunio*, when a character named Pedante proposes to the enchantress Medusa, he similarly dwells on needles as a primary sign of segregated schooling: "Give me thy hand," he tells her, "I'll set up a great grammar schoole by and by, / We shall thrive well enough, it will tumble in roundly. / I'll teach boyes the Latin tongue, to write and to read, /And thou, little wenches, their needle and thread. / We'll be as merry as crickets."[18]

While Mulcaster defines sewing as a practical chore, Pedante might have been thinking of ornamental needlework, which included embroidering as well as the making of artful samplers, knots, prints, and letter designs for cushions and boxes. The education of aristocratic girls typically involved instruction in these arts.[19] Robert Greene's *Penelope's Web* shows how easily elite textile skills could be appropriated within the middle-class ideology of the good wife, since Penelope's ornamental labor in tapestry-making becomes a sign of her primary commitment to industry. John Taylor's prefatory poem to a pattern book for needlework, "The Praise of the Needle," assumes an audience who can appreciate the needle's multiple functions – from mending torn clothes to embellishing expensive fabrics. Cloaking his titled instrument in extravagant praise, Taylor argues for the needle as an "instrument /Of profit, pleasure, and of ornament" (A1$^v$), useful "so long as garments shall be made, or worne."[20]

Identified so clearly as a specifically female knowledge and practice, it is no wonder that early modern plays and poems often represent needles as the tools of aggressive or resistant women, or as the female enactment of Cupid's priapic "pricking." Robert Greene's *Scottish History of James the Fourth* (1598) stages conventional sexual bantering around the topic of women's needlework; sewing, this text suggests, calls to mind pricked wounds and concealed delights.[21] When male warriors praise military action and mock the folly of love in William Cartwright's play *The Siege*, one character portrays eros as having threatening "pricking" needles: "No such Labyrinth here," Philostratus says of the maze of unrequited desire absent on the battlefield, "No needles hanging at each others Tailes. / No *Cupid* here preserves the Tears of Lovers / To mix'em with the Ashes of burnt Hearts, / To make a Lie to wash his Mothers smock in / Which silly sighs must dry."[22] The image of needles "hanging at each others Tailes" remains cryptic (are these the magnetic hands of a compass representing the attractions of love? or Cupid's jabs at rumps?). But the needles' proximity to preserves, laundry, and mothers' smocks gives domestic resonances to the mysterious dangers of desire. When Taylor represents the needle in his pattern book, he wishfully converts its transgressive potential into a pacifying force. Comparing the needle to a soldier who gets syphilis from lusty heat, a one-eyed Pygmy, and a tailor's efficient lance, Taylor mockingly recommends the needle as the preferred weapon of women:

> And for my countries quiet, I should like,
> That womenkinde should use no other Pike.
> It will increase their peace, enlarge their store,
> To use their tongues lesse, and their Needles more . . .
> A needle (though it be but small and slender)
> Yet it is both a maker and a mender:
> A grave Reformer of old Rents decayed,
> Stops holes and seames, and desperate cuts displayd.

> (A1[r–v])

The nation's peace is tied, in Taylor's account, to female silence and industry. But while suggesting a common investment, by ladies as well as poor seamstresses, in sewing, his fetishization of the needle renders it a source of male fascination and anxiety. Cutting through the poem's satire and condescension, we discover in Taylor's mock heroic a glimmer of recognition that small items carry great weight; for this "pike, a "grave Reformer," stops the hole of poverty.

Though it later became a metaphor for triviality (one of the Martin Marprelate writers mentions the futility of finding "Gammer Gurton's needle"), the needle was used in aristocratic female artistic production (the "maker," in Taylor's phrase) as well as in the repair of shirts and smocks (the "mender"). One of Anthony Munday's pageants for the Lord Mayor's procession introduces yet another meaning for this tool, for the Drapers oddly honor their own profession and the new mayor with a tableau displaying the crest of the drapers company paired with a "housewifely virgin" who sits and cards as an emblem of

England's best domestic industry. In this incarnation, the needle blends artisanal skill with women's non-professional labor. Gammer prizes her needle not
because it allows her artistic license or promotes national commerce, of course,
but because she lives hand-to-mouth in a subsistence economy. Though the
needle's primary association was with housewifery, *Gammer Gurton's Needle*
could well have suggested the needle's multiple cultural inscriptions, both in its
initial Cambridge performance as well as in seventeenth-century revivals and
reprintings.

Gammer's housewifely "treasure" secures for her prerogatives that married
women and maids did not have during this period, since she serves as head
of a household. "Single and widowed women," Amy Erickson explains, "were
nearly three times as likely as single and widowed men to head up their household, or to live alone," although lone women did form the social group most
vulnerable to poverty.[23] This would put Gammer in the ten to twenty percent of
the population that were unmarried at any given time in the sixteenth century.
Owning her home and having access to land, Gammer serves as both husband
and wife in the conjoined business of household and agricultural management.
Though poor, she supervises her maids, male servant and single fieldworker as
part of the subsistence agrarian economy dominating early sixteenth-century
England. As such, Gammer runs a household that clearly doesn't fit models described in marital conduct books; for the ideal household was organized around
a stable marital hierarchy that could model state order. Although Gammer's
household is not founded on a marital bond, her industry does exemplify the
domestic ethic that advice writers alleged to be key to the moral and national
economy. According to Susan Cahn, the housewife's significant role in economic production was threatened in the sixteenth century by the growth of
market production and changes in attitudes toward family property. By the end
of the eighteenth century, women's increased reliance on their husband's labor
largely excluded them from economic production. In the mid-sixteenth century,
however, female domestic labor of all sorts was still a mainstay of England's
economy.[24] Thomas Heywood's *How a Man may Chuse a Good Wife from a
Bad* (1602) suggests as much; for one Griselda-like wife sees her needle as
holding the family together: "My husband in this humor wel I know / Plaies but
the vnthrift: therefore it behoues me, / To be the better huswife here at home,
/ To saue and get, whilst he doth laugh and spend, / Though for himselfe he riots
it at large, /My needle shall defray my housholds charge."[25] *Gammer* endows
the needle with import precisely by detaching it from the ideology of the "good
wife"; for housewifery does not underwrite the proper marital division of labor
as much as the health of a non-kin "family" unit.

Punning on clothing so as to link gender instabilities, the labor of sewing, and
the household economy, *Gammer* invokes the terms "breech" and "dressing"
to explore contradictions in the identities structured on household practices.

The "breech" was clothing for the loins and thighs, which, in contemporary language signified masculine authority. But the "breech" was also the buttocks beneath the clothing, and the terms "broach" (to sew), "breech," and "breach" named acts of rupture, beating, and violation. "Dressing," a term that surfaces thirteen times in the play, indicated both the state of being covered and the violation of body and clothing.[26] To be breeched or dressed (to wear pants, that is) was to become a man with a gap or breach covered by the dressing of breeches. With this paradox at work in the language, the play suggests that the absent needle invisibly constructs a conception of masculinity in ways that threaten to expose its reliance on its opposite. The problem of breached breeches thus exceeds Hodge's personal embarrassment and points to genuine contradictions in interlocking systems of gender, class, and sexuality: it displays the construction of wholeness from holes, of masculinity from the missing phallus, and of social relations from a trivialized labor. "Keeping the nee'le" may be mere women's work according to Hodge, but maintaining the meaning of the needle is a Herculean feat. Instead of ridiculing the rustics' mistaken idea of the phallus, *Gammer* activates a set of puns that hint at the needle's unexpectedly primary if precarious role in stabilizing social, sexual, and gendered relations.

It is fitting that the character who orchestrates disruptions is a homeless bedlam named after London's hospital for the insane. Although he doesn't look like the typical literary beggar, Diccon's bedlam status suggests that he exists outside the regulating structures of household, ward, or village.[27] The catastrophic consequences of the lost needle are made fully apparent when Hodge transfers his loyalty from his mistress to the homeless Diccon – from the domestic economy to the rootless source of domestic disruption. This change is tellingly solemnized by a ritual in which Hodge is made to kiss Diccon's "whole" breeches in default of a book. Deputized as Hodge's new master, Diccon symbolically inserts himself into the system of newly breached social relations. Hodge swears "always me to dispose / To work . . . [Diccon's] pleasure" (2.1.74–5). Within this new work–pleasure economy, Diccon furthers community antagonisms by cementing male–male relationships that oppose the household economy – inducting Diccon into what Ong would term an "extra-familial" structure.

Armed with a minimum of education, Diccon alternately presents his plotting as a play and as domestic work:

> Here is a matter worthy glozing
> Of Gammer Gurton's needle losing
> And a foul piece of work.
> A man, I think, might make a play
> And need no word to this they say,
> But being half a clerk.                                                (2.2.7–12)

"Ye see, masters," he then tells his clerkly audience, "the one end tapped of this my short device; / Now must we broach t'other too" (2.3.1–2). Attempting to "broach" Dame Chat, Diccon uses the language of domestic labor to turn a "foul piece of work" into a "play." Framing the women as two ends of a single "device," Diccon compares plotting to tapping a barrel of liquor. But the term "broach" also recalls Hodge's use of "broaching" to mean sewing. By broaching the dual female ends of the community, Diccon insists that he exposes the insufficiency within the women's hearts.[28] The play thus self-consciously names its production of male–male relations by appropriating the rhetoric of domestic labor that the university nonetheless rejects in its most culturally prominent self-definitions; plotting and playing are inadequate substitutes for the missing female labor/phallus that the semi-clerk tackles.

*Gammer's* denouement appropriately spotlights Hodge's rump. Inverting the earlier oath-taking scene, Diccon rectifies community relations by swearing on Hodge's britches, an act that reestablishes Hodge's allegiance to Gammer and the domestic economy. When Diccon slaps Hodge's rear end and brings to light the lost needle, the female authority on which the domestic economy depends is righted, and the surrogate masters – both Diccon and the academics – playfully surrender their carnivalesque power back to the fantasized household. Hodge's masculinity is secured at the moment in which the "clerk" loses to the house-wife and the phallus is restored to her hands. This return completes a dazzling set of puns: the "whole" truth is discovered in the "hole" of Hodge's pants, in the form of an object that makes and sews up holes to create an "end" to the "tale"/tail or hole/"whole matter" that Diccon has "enlarged." "He feigneth this tale out of his own guts," Dame Chat says of Rat (5.2.11). Displaying a Bakhtinian grotesque physicality that nevertheless orders the plot, Hodge's body, specifically his rectifying rectum, symbolically marks the breaches and reparations in social organization and dramatic structure.[29] In *Eastward Ho*, the tailor's needle, lauded for its ability to mask abnormalities and defects, "recti-fie[s] the imperfection of proportion."[30] "Most aedefying tailor!" Gertrude ex-claims appreciatively, you "make many crooked thing goe vpright" (1.2.56–7). In *Gammer*, the needle rectifies (from the Latin *rectus*, to make right or straight) but not by concealing the body's flaws. Opening with Hodge's complaints about his exposed rectum, the play closes with characters celebrating the telos of dra-matic action – "when the end is known" (5.2.143).

Paster comments that the phallus is reassuringly found where it should be – in Hodge's pants. But the restored needle is precisely someone else's which has painfully and mistakenly been left in Hodge's trousers. Its violent recovery, aligned in the prologue with the disruptive but productive power of sodomy ("pricking"), once again threatens to expose Hodge's gap: "Chwas almost un-done, 'twas so far in my buttock!" he cries (5.2.307).[31] Re-breached, Hodge has his "hole" displayed before it is secured by the needle's transference to

Gammer for her use in "piecing and patching" sexual, economic, and gender relations. The well-run household merely conceals potentially disorderly practices and perceived sexual lack (who is to say that Hodge didn't always "rake" cats while he also courted maids and where are heterosexual relations in this household anyway?). While the stabilization of gender and sexual relations occurs precisely through a sodomitical moment that "almost" undoes Hodge, it is tellingly Gammer's non-reproductive and economic "pricking" that promises to re-suture social relations. "Hast made me forever," Gammer explains in glee (5.2.310). The needle makes visible the erotic complexity of domestic relations, for it serves as a female economic dildo wielded briefly by the academic playwright Diccon before he relinquishes it to a reconstituted domestic order.

In revealing the class- and gender-identified gap at the core of masculinity, the play thus mocks initiation rites dependent upon the disavowal of cross-gendered domesticity. Because *this* housewife was a student in drag, of course, the play's thematic gendering is necessarily prosthetic. Due to the widespread use of boy actors, early modern English theatrical productions necessarily had a problem with extra and/or missing body parts; and they often staged confrontations between the fetishistic signs of gender presence and their marked absence.[32] But *Gammer's* thematic breaching narrows the meaning for transvestite theater by pointedly reminding academic audience members of their "breeching," the moment when boys graduated from wearing skirts to pants. The audience applauds the fantasy of returning to a domestic world signified by the vernacular and femininity, a world both familiar and alienating. In its comic metonymic chain, the play uncovers the instabilities that the Latin puberty rite sought to anchor: Hodge's power rests in an anality concealed by the woman's prosthetic and "plastic" phallus, one secured by productivity and made intelligible by domestic governance.[33]

### The nurse's tongue

Happily undoing the crippling oath he has sworn on the loss of his "tongue" (2.1.53), Hodge experiences his newfound masculinity at the play's end as the recovery of the *maternal*: "Am I not a good son, Gammer, am I not?" (5.2.309). How do we interpret the fact that Hodge understands his return to domestic hierarchy – to his place as obedient servant – as transformation into a good son? Given the widespread use of wetnursing amongst the elite classes (many of whom would have been students in this play and its audience), the "maternal" constituted an ambivalent psychic formation in early modern England, serving as a double link not only between the male child and female authority, but also between the male child and a lower-class, often rural female servant. The "mother tongue" was, in these cases, taught by the nurse; and thus the vernacular was linked to a set of class anxieties that were often mediated through the category of gender.[34]

According to Richard Wilson, old wives' tales, and gossips' fables were linked in the anxious Renaissance paternal imagination to women's privileged place in birth and child-rearing (Fig. 9). Numerous Renaissance texts indicate concern about a "popular" English culture transmitted in aristocratic households through female speech, one defined as such because of the particular class and gender arrangements of child-rearing.[35] Erasmus, for instance, opposed the wisdom of the ancients with the "old wives' . . . rubbish" of "nursery days," the "chatter" and senseless "babble" of servants that deformed the young mind.[36] Thomas Elyot was unusual in advising nurses and serving women to speak Latin to male infants (or at least "cleane" English), but his concern for the possible damaging effects caused by the poor speech of female childcare providers was echoed by numerous other writers. In humanist pedagogy, Latin was enlisted to suppress the faults inculcated in the realm of early childhood. Elyot writes:

It shall be expedient that a noble mannes sonne, in his infancie, haue with hym continually onely suche as may accustome hym by litle and litle to speake pure and elegant latin. Semblably the nourises and other women aboute hym, if it be possible, to do the same: or, at the leste way, that they speke none englisshe but that which is cleane, polite, perfectly and articulately pronounced, omittinge no lettre or sillable, as folisshe women often times do of a wantonnesse, wherby diuers noble men and gentilmennes chyldren, (as I do at this daye knowe), haue attained corrupte and foule pronuntiation.[37]

Elyot then reinforces the divide between "mother tongue" and learned language by banishing men from the nursery and urging that the child, at 7 years of age, "be taken from the company of women: sauynge that he may haue, one yere, or two at the most, an auncient and sad matrone, attendynge on hym in his chambre." In *The Schoolmaster*, Ascham, chief advocate of a gentler regime of discipline, similarly condemns parents who find their children's imitation of lower-class servant's speech amusing (46). He disagrees with Elyot's suggestion that Latin should be encouraged in daily life, however, since common use might degrade the language. But Ascham does fondly daydream of the ideal household-cum-school where perfect Latin is spoken: "In very deed, if children were brought up in such a house, or such a school, where the Latin tongue were properly and perfectly spoken, as Tiberius and Caius Gracchi were brought up in their mother Cornelia's house, surely then the daily use of speaking were the best and readiest way to learn the Latin tongue" (17). Since Roman mothers like Cornelia no longer exist, he complains, female-taught Latin only instills "barbarousness . . . in young wits" (17). English was a source of moral and intellectual corruption.

But English speech also signified national, religious, and cultural affiliation. In *A View of the Present State of Ireland*, Edmund Spenser worries that Irish

Fig. 9   The wetnurse, framed by the images of the scene of childbirth in the bedchamber and the apothecary's shop. From J.S. [paidon nose-mata], or *Childrens Diseases Both Outward and Inward* (London, 1664).

wetnurses strip English children of their language and its companion, English culture:

The child that sucketh the milk of the nurse must of necessity learn his first speech of her, the which being the first that is inured of his tongue, is ever after the most pleasing unto him insomuch as though he afterwards be taught English, yet the smack of the first will always abide with him and *not only of the speech, but also of the manners and conditions.*[38]

Nursing becomes a powerful act, since it constitutes the transmission of both language and culture. I will return to Spenser's words, in Chapter 4, in considering the specific ways in which popular lore and *milk* figured in cultural fantasies about the reproduction of national culture. But for now we see that humanist texts made the nurse a figure for the foundational but deficient acquisition of language that the schoolmaster had to correct.

Perhaps we see why so many sixteenth-century educational writers, such as Ascham, Elyot, Mulcaster, Nicholas Udall, John Cheke, Edward Grant, William Kempe, and John Brisley, felt compelled to address the issues of wetnursing and early childhood care. In his pedagogical tract *Positions*, Mulcaster insists on the importance of a "fine and well-fitted nursery" when explaining the ancients' view of children: "When their youth shall begin to learn, they do fetch the ground of their training, exceeding far off: as what regard is to be hard to the infant, while he is yet under his nurse? Where they moil themselves sore with the manners and conditions of the nurse, with the fines [penalties] or rudenes of her speech."[39] But such a devaluation of female lower-class speech and manners remained at odds with increasing claims, throughout the sixteenth century, on behalf of the "mother tongue."[40] After mid-century, numerous writers, Richard Jones documents, defended the vernacular as capable of holding the greatest truths of Western culture. Writers thus found themselves performing complicated rhetorical gymnastics when edging toward the fact that their mother tongue was endowed by a nurse. For the Reformation, with its emphasis on literacy, marked not only a return to the "true faith" (in its advocates' words) but also a rejection of Latin, increasingly associated with a demonized Papistry. "For while our religion was restrained to the Latin," Mulcaster writes

it was either the only or the oneliest principal in learning: to learn to read Latin was most appropriate to that effect . . . But now that we are returned home to our English A B Cs as most natural to our soil and most proper to our faith, the restraint being repealed, and we restored to liberty, we are to be directed by nature and property to read that first, which we speak first . . . because we need it most. (61)

Having "returned home" to a faith bolstered by the originary vernacular, English subjects can now form a community consolidated around their embrace of what Mulcaster terms "the familiarity of our ordinary language" (61). He vehemently promotes English speech, not only to refine the tongue of elites, but also as a way of acknowledging a different self-identity. "We understand that tongue best whereunto we are first born, as our first impression is always in English before we do deliver it in Latin" (29). Mulcaster's decision to write in English so as to be accessible to a readership composed of "English people" signifies his investment in the "natural" birth-tongue (the "first impression" that can only be "delivered" or surrendered into Latin). Noting that language unites peoples usually separated along lines of class, Mulcaster demystifies Latin and reveals its possible obstructions: "My meaning is principally to help mine own country, whose language will help me, to be understood of them, whom I would persuade . . . I will serve my country that way, which I do surely think will prove most intelligible unto her" (29). While some avid disseminators of English in print argued that they merely "translated" ideas for the unlearned, Mulcaster joins writers who direct readers well-versed in classical languages to refine the vernacular. The goal of language as communication, or as an indices of an *originary* Englishness tied to authentic belief, clearly conflicted with the aims of the puberty ritual of Latin learning and its attendant gendering. The contradiction built into a reformed humanist curriculum comes to light when the vernacular is held up as the carrier of national identification and the signifier of the true faith but also the corrupt force that education must repel.

Remembering that Elizabeth's Proclamation specifically banned the nurse from the walls of academia, we see that a feminized domestic culture was identified, embraced, and eschewed by educators and pedagogical theorists. If the "maternal," as critics concerned to historicize psychoanalytic categories have noted, is often a composite figure split into female servant and elite birth mother,[41] the "mother tongue" could be similarly divided in this period – attached to both a reassuringly original and "natural" femininity and an anxiety-producing lower-class domain. In the first meaning, the mother embodies the ur-tongue tainted by linguistic borrowing: "Some [men] seek so far for out-landish English, that they forget altogether their mother's language," writes Thomas Wilson.[42] We have seen its second incarnation – as the cheap talk of gossips and wetnurses. "A Nurse's tongue is privileged to talk," the Renaissance proverb would have it. Like the household in which early education and language acquisition took place, the native tongue was both a national ideal and a sign of abjection.

In its unusual identification of language as a staple of national identification, Shakespeare's *Richard II* draws upon the image of the nurse as the guardian of a culture marked by shared language. When Mowbray is exiled, he strikingly mourns the loss of his native tongue as a simultaneous castration and infantilization: "The language I have learnt these forty years, / My native English, now I must forego, /And now my tongue's use is to me no more / Than an unstringed viol or a harp. "Mowbray then cites his regression to a pettie (a boy who knows English but not yet Latin): "I am too old to fawn upon a nurse," he states, "Too far in years to be a pupil now."[43] Bolingbroke appropriately ends the scene by sadly invoking his own loss of "England's ground ... My mother, and my nurse, that bears me yet" (1.3.306–307). Gaunt's famous deathbed elegy to the "blessed plot, this earth, this realm, this England, / This nurse, this teeming womb of royal kings" (2.1.50–1) and the Duchess of York's strategy for begging pardon for her son ("And if I were thy nurse, thy tongue to teach, /'Pardon' should be the first word of thy speech" [5.3.113–14]) both call upon the nurse's foundational role as producer and educator. The cumulative effect is to see the nurse as a primary figure for transmitting English identity, but, as Mowbray's lament about his useless phallus/tongue/viol makes clear, a figure that inspired anxiety. While *Richard II* is exceptional in elevating speech to the status of more familiar indices of English identifications (territory, subjecthood), it uncovers the anxious pride of being *nursed* into Englishness. Like *Gammer*, this play assumes the sexualization of identity-formation; the phallic gains generated by the mother/nurse (speech) must be reconceptualized in terms of other powerful cultural formations (literacy). And the play invests passion into linguistic national identification, showing the citizen's binding tie to the nurse's tongue.

In staging Hodge's return to the mother at the exact moment that students "return" to cross-gendered domesticity and to the vernacular, *Gammer* recovers the class and national concerns triggered by the "maternal" as well as the female labors silently attached to English speech. Most importantly, the play absolutely reverses the value coding of this construct: the double anxiety of the return to the maternal tongue/servant – the "site of deformation and vulnerability," according to Janet Adelman – becomes the means for a happy restitution of comic order and sexual assurance.[44] If students are asked to imagine reentry into a newly legitimate domesticity, they are to experience the potential violence and pleasure of that fantasy, a fantasy tellingly unencumbered by conventional fears of the male's unwilling transformation *back* into a woman/child, as Stephen Orgel has discussed.[45] Instead this return enables a comforting collective identification and reminds the audience of the potential costs of their current identity. *Gammer* demands that Cambridge undergraduates conjure up disavowed household stuff – the "smack of the first" – at the moment that they conceptualize English comedy. It is thus fitting that the rustic speech of the play offers an alienated version of the native tongue, for it marks precisely the type of speech that humanists feared: the rude, "corrupte and foule pronuntiation" that they attributed to "folisshe women." Faced with the dilemma of being unmanned, un-English or non-elite, young scholars were given a chance to act out a cultural contradiction. Watching Hodge's catastrophic loss and recovery of the phallus, the audience might have rehearsed their violent initiation into masculinity/ education/ power, but they were forced to acknowledge the partial and ambivalent status of that initiation, to rethink the gendered codings of their native tongue, and to remember that domesticity involved labors fundamental to the community. In other words, they were asked to think of a national and linguistic community, founded on the home, as superseding and qualifying their academic credentials; they were invited to fantasize about an estranging familiarity that forced them to embrace multiple identifications.

Let us return briefly to Hawkins' *Apollo Shroving*, where we left a "female" spectator Lala attempting to commandeer the stage in a grammar school. Denouncing Latin as an "outlandish" tongue clearly at odds with old-fashioned indigenous practices and wares, Lala grandly pronounces: "I'd rather spin at home, then hear these Barbarians spout Latin" (7). Like *Gammer*, this play offers scholars a housewife as the materialization of their academic leisure. "You scholler must not speake in Englishe in the schoole" Lala rebukes the speaker, who replies: "we are not now at our taske, but wee have leave to play" (5). Although seemingly reinforcing the divide between Latin and housework, Lala ends up eroding pedagogy's construction of gender, for she ends up transformed into a male scholar. Reassured in the end that the play will be conducted in English, she swears: "it shall goe hard but I'le get a part amongst them. I'le into the tyreing house, and scramble and rangle for a mans part. Why should not women act men, as well as boyes act women? I will weare the breeches, so I will" (9). And she does. Startlingly evolving from spinning housewife into a breeched scholar, Lala mimics the boy's acquisition of "breeches," a practice reversed by the transvestite stage. Invading the grammar school, she debunks the prestige of the exclusive male-identified Latin as suspiciously foreign. "My mother never spoke it," Lala declares of Latin, and spurns her housewife's garb to become one of the boys whose breeches cannot completely conceal his/her vernacular and domestic foundations.

### Domesticity among the boys

> Nouns and Pronouns, I pronounce you traitors for a boy's buttocks.
>
> Thomas Nashe[46]

> Chwas almost undone, 'twas so far in my buttock!
>
> Hodge in *Gammer Gurton's Needle*[47]

But how can we read the "joke" of Hodge's sodomitical encounter with the lost needle in the context of an academic play? In order to understand why Hodge's happy reconstitution as a good son follows on the heels of a fearful breaching, we might consider the development of pedagogical domesticity in the period. Alan Bray, Bruce Smith, Lawrence Stone, and Jonathan Goldberg remind us that colleges involved alternative domestic practices and living arrangements.[48] In his 1577 description of England, William Harrison tells readers that English educational institutions differ from those on the continent precisely because students' domestic lives were more regulated and insulated. Students are not enforced he writes, "for want of such houses, to dwell in common inns and taverns without all order or discipline."[49] "Every one of these colleges have in like manner their professors or readers of the tongues and several sciences ... which daily trade up the youth *there abiding, privately in their halls*" (71, my emphasis). Similarly, in 1682 Edward Chamberlayne emphasized the enclosed nature of the university: "All that intend to take any degree are to take their diet and lodging and have a tutor constantly in some college or hall; then they are to perform all exercises, to be subject to all statutes and to the head of the house ... They are to suffer themselves to be shut up by night in their several houses."[50] Shut in at night, abiding privately in halls, living sequestered from common inns – undergraduates formed households. Educational institutions may have defined themselves against cross-gendered domesticity, but the language of academic enclosure insured a same-sex domestic environment that included shared eating and shared beds.

Pedagogical domesticity was, however, relatively new. During the sixteenth century, educational systems in England underwent a set of sweeping changes at all levels. These alterations included the growth of grammar schools (as free schools) that absorbed both poor students and elite boys formerly educated by private tutors, and an expansion of the number of students who lived in school buildings, the schoolmaster's home, and local environs. Universities increased the enrollment of elite boys formerly tutored privately while also newly lodging undergraduates in the college rather than in halls in the adjoining town.[51] Increases in the size and inclusiveness of the educational system occurred simultaneously with the expansion of residential pedagogy. Cambridge's Christ's College was, in fact, a forerunner of residential education. Having been established to train masters of grammar in the first half of the fifteenth century, God's House at Cambridge was newly endowed and refounded as Christ's College in 1506. In its new life, according to historian Kenneth Charlton, it "retained its special characteristic as a place in which undergraduates lived and were taught" (132; see also Simon, *Education and Society*, 81). Site of the production of *Gammer*, Christ's College had a reputation as a place where students lived together within college confines.

The sequestering of universities from cross-gendered domestic life continued a process that originated in grammar schools where Ong's puberty rituals ostensibly began. Young boys entered the rigorous physical and intellectual program of grammar school around age 7. From sunrise to sunset, students attended school six days a week, often 40–44 weeks per year, with holidays. Sitting on upright benches in a long and narrow classroom, boys learned according to a highly scheduled format. Brown describes the intense regulation of even toilet breaks, where students could be made to recite lengthy exercises before running outside to the *campo*.[52] Because learning required a rigid disciplining of body as well as mind, beatings were pervasive even in the new humanist system. As Alan Stewart describes, the schoolhouse was popularly portrayed as a site of torment where the intellect was shaped through violent imprint on the body (92–104). The overarching symbol for this regime became the phallic-like ferula (a cane rod made of a giant fennel stalk) or the birch (branches gathered like a broom). In illustrations from the period, the fetishized rod served as an almost ubiquitous emblem of order (see Fig. 10). John Marston's pedagogical scene in his city comedy *What You Will* (to which I will return) trades on the bawdiness and violence accompanying the recitation of grammar. In this scene, a student puns fervently on the trials of his "ass" (arse) by linking them to his failure to recite *as in presenti* correctly. Part of this scene's comedy turns on the student's attempt to stay the frenzied beating orchestrated by the schoolmaster with the aid of the other pupils, who "mount" and "hold up" the guilty student for the master's rod. Learning Latin grammar was clearly tied in the cultural imagination to the sore plight of buttocks as a signifier for a more comprehensive bodily disciplining.[53]

Redescribing the Latin puberty rite, Smith adds the sexual dimension missing in Ong's account: Latin was not only the language of male power (diplomacy, trade, law) but the "language of sexual knowledge" (83). In other words, the classical tongue was understood in Renaissance culture as the language of Greek love, passionate shepherds, salacious Ovidian elegies, and same-sex desire (84). While Smith's notion of "homosexual desire" has been queried by critics emphasizing a less subject-oriented eroticism, Smith's revision of Ong's paradigm is an important one.[54] In remembering his then dead pupil, Ascham, for instance, insinuates learning Latin within male intimacy: "John Whitney, a young gentleman, was my bedfellow, who, willing by good nature and provoked by mine advice, began to learn the Latin tongue."[55] Indeed, as scholars have observed, the choice of text used by Ascham to teach his bedfellow Whitney was particularly appropriate: Cicero's *De amicitia* became the most influential mastertext on male friendship in the period. The domestic practices surrounding learning, particularly the sharing of beds between masters and pupils, was linked, in Ascham's imagination, to the practice of "provoking" students to learn the language of male desire.[56] What engaged boys when their bodies were subject to the schoolmaster's birch was a training that initiated them into (among other things) a discourse of male intimacy. Erasmus' discussion of pedagogy is helpful: "For it is not by learning rules that we acquire the power of speaking a language, but by daily intercourse with those accustomed to express themselves with exactness and refinement."[57] Men reading, translating, talking, sharing a bedchamber, engaging in a "daily intercourse" that fused language-acquisition with intimacy: these acts particularize what we already know – that the institutional apparatuses of education (along with theaters, apprenticeship,

Fig. 10   The Schoolmaster with pupils, holding a birch. From *Pedantius* (London, 1631).

and service) were sites in which homoeroticism could have been expressed (or found "a place" in Goldberg's terms).[58]

If we go back to the puberty ritual with an eye to sexuality as well as to gender, we may look differently at the fact that boys were gender-segregated from an early age in their education, that they endured a rigid program of bodily discipline that sometimes linked erotics with violence (beatings with "lady birchely"[59]), and that they increasingly lived in communities defined against a reproductive domesticity. Adolescent learning involved initiation rites that transferred authority from the nurse/mother to the schoolmaster, who either taught by the rod, or, in keeping with some humanist prescriptions, taught by "provoking" bedfellows to learn with pleasure.

I have chosen two texts in which we can glimpse the disparate registers of male–male relationships fostered by the pedagogical environment: Steven Bateman's didactic *Crystal Glass of Christian Reformation* (1569) and Marston's city comedy, *What You Will* (1607). Bateman's book consists of short sermons centering on highly allegorical illustrations. After portraying the sins of Wrath, Lechery, and Envy, Bateman turns to the emblem of a school-room to illustrate Sloth (Fig. 11).[60] In this picture, the derelict schoolmaster's nap allows students to abandon their studies, as the gloss elaborates: "He which sitteth sleeping signifieth slothfulness amongst teachers, whose desire being satisfied, careth not for the charge: the children idlenes, whose mindes without a carefull tutor, are bent to nothyng but ease and vanities" (F4$^r$). The accompanying sermonette, peppered with Latin and biblical citation, warns of the dangers of idleness and urges the spiritually rewarding labors of the body. But the picture offers a more specific meaning for "idleness." With the ubiquitous birch missing, the young boys dangle toys that mimic the rod; "lady birchely" mutates into a stick used in a game or a spinning device. The "ease and vanities" that are the fruits of sloth do not encourage isolated entertainment but the shared intimacy of schoolboys, who are pictured as two couples, each linked by the casual embrace of an arm draped around the other. In fact, in the middle pair, it is impossible to determine whose arm rests between the two figures; similarly the proximity of their faces suggests the pleasure of shared whispers (in English, perhaps?). Instead of unruly games, the pairs enjoy a quiet moment free from the rigid schedule maintained by the schoolteacher, whose satiated "desire" is the object of the text's critique.

Linked limbs with heads casually leaning against one another: such bodily posture unwittingly echoes the illustrations of Lechery from the preceding pages in Bateman's text (Figs. 12–13). In one picture, five figures gather around a tavern table, with two pairs overseen by the female figure of Lechery, who, unlike the schoolmaster, is awake to see desire satiated (E2$^r$). In another illustration, a monk and nun embrace in a cloister (D4$^r$). Certainly the postures of these couples are more overtly eroticized than those of the schoolboys (hands actually

# Of Sloth.

*The sleepie minde doth tyme forget : and youth to toyes do most desire:
So tyme once paste 's hard to fet : to late in age learning to require:*

## The signification.

HE which sitteth sleeping signifieth slothfulnes amongest teachers, whose desire being satiffied, careth not for the charge : the children idlenes, whose mindes without a carefull tutor, are bent to nothyng but ease and vanities.

*Out*

Fig. 11 "Of Sloth." A picture of momentary ease found in the classroom. From Steven Bateman, *A Cristall Glasse of Christian Reformation* (London, 1569).

touch faces and hugs tightly knit double interlocking arms). Nevertheless these juxtaposed images throw into relief the potential erotic meaning for the positions allowed young boys. We note that Bateman does not denounce this schoolroom behavior as lecherous; instead it is part of the carnivalesque inversion allowed by absented authority, and as such, it is simply stolen "ease," inappropriate because improperly placed. Such a moment constitutes what Smith might call the "homoerotic pastoral" created in the respite from an oft violent pedagogy and its hierarchized authority. Yet, according to Ascham, this intimacy was not simply available in the respite from learning, but one of its constituent tactics. While denunciations of leisure are common in Christian handbooks, this text discloses, with little moral panic, the particularly intimate milieu of pedagogy.

Marston's *What You Will* offers a violent counterpart to Bateman's school-room scene. Amidst common city comedy themes – greed, sexual rivalry, mistaken identity – we discover a schoolmaster drilling students on grammar

Figs. 12–13   Steven Bateman's illustrations "Of Lechery" from *A Cristall Glasse of Christian Reformation* (London, 1569).

Figs. 12–13

lessons and joking that women's loquacity makes language into "household
stuff." When Holofernes Pippo fails at his recitation, he is ordered to be "held
up" by the other boys for a spanking. "You know now what you ha' done not,"
Holofernes cries, "all the syrup of my brain is run into my buttocks, and ye spill
the juice of my wit well" (2.2.80–3). The schoolmaster responds: "sans tricks,
trifles, delays, demurrers, procrastinations, or retardinations, mount him, mount
him" (2.2.85–6). This bawdy tableau of sexualized beating, punctuated with the
ubiquitous reminder of the schoolboy's vulnerable and fully exposed buttocks,
is interrupted by passing visitors who rescue Holofernes by apprenticing him
for service. Upon seeing the young boy "held up," "bewrayed," "untrussed,"
and "mounted" by peers and teacher, the gentleman Simplicius says, "I am en-
amoured on thee, boy; wilt thou serve me?" "A very pretty child," he comments,
as if the spectacle of beating is a routinely alluring display, "has he not a good
face, ha?" (2.2.98–9, 109, 115). Instructing him on how to become a page,
Simplicius enjoins Holofernes to "hold up" his master's rapier, words that

clearly repeat the rhetoric of the beating ("hold him," "up, up!") and highlight the potential erotics of service. Holofernes' later adventures cement the connection between the disciplining of schoolboys and the erotic trafficking of pages who joke about becoming "ingles" or "cracks" to the urban gentlemen they serve.[61] After donning female garb in the final act in order to seduce and gull his master, Holofernes decides to return to a classroom world punningly identified by reference to buttocks; he chooses to opt out of the eroticized exchange of favors between masters and servants and instead recite *as in presenti*. The play narrates the schoolboy's journey from sexualized language lesson, to sodomitical beating, eroticized service, and finally, cross-dressing.[62] Schoolroom violence is eroticized in the comedy, but in ways that subdue its link to the scandal of sodomy. Bray's work in connecting the valued male friend and "monstrous" sodomite helps us to make sense of Marston's and Bateman's representations;[63] for pedagogical violence seems the flip side of the playful "ease" of this play's pages, who, like the affectionate boys in Bateman's schoolroom, devise games that expose the normative erotic attachments between men in social hierarchies.

Hodge's penetration at the end of *Gammer* then might have posed a joke circling around an "improper" version of the fluid sexual possibilities encouraged by the educational system, possibilities made to seem ludicrous (rather than accusatory[64]) when cast in a rural and lower-class world. *Gammer* not only farcically delves into bodily nondiscipline (farting, excrement) but insistently dwells on nonreproductive sexuality. In fact, Hodge's final piercing suggests conflicts that have been troped throughout the play as sodomy: Dame Chat describes a fellow cardplayer as cheating by having "an eye behind her" (2.2.30); Hodge swears to devote himself to a man's "pleasure" by kissing Diccon's buttocks (2.1.65–70); and Dr. Rat is accused of sneaking in the rear "privy way" of Dame Chat's house (5.2.187), entering by the dangerously inappropriate "black hole" in his plan to "[grope] so deep in Goodwife Chat's hens' nest" (5.2.189, 225). "To come in on the back side when you might go about /I know none such, unless they long to have their brains knocked out," Master Bailey declares (5.1.29–30). Repeatedly referring to anality in ways echoed in representations of pedagogy, the play emphasizes Hodge's exposed buttocks as a resonant symbol. Experienced as the absent sign of authority that produces male trust; feared as the breeching of bared buttocks; and linked to eroticized servitude – the birch-like needle encodes the dangers and pleasures of education within the terms of domestic reproduction. Keeping in mind recent scholars' warnings about disentangling issues of sexuality from those of gender, we see that Hodge's "hole" makes him Diccon's "bondman" rather than a woman (and thus "masculinity," while evoked as a critical category, is not subject to a male–female binary).[65] *Gammer* is not just about the "crisis of gender formation," as Paster suggests (119), but also about education's multiple inscriptions of the

body and sexuality. After all, Hodge's ambiguous shriek in the play's denouement – "Ch was almost undone,' twas so far in my buttock!" – marks the most
productive moment in the play, the climactic revelation of a knowledge that
resecures the community's social, sexual, and economic relations.

Discursive links among language acquisition, nursing, and effeminization
help to make sense of why "proper" domesticity and its attendant sexuality had
to be renounced and yet entertained at precisely the moment that the vernacular
was introduced in academic life. In keeping with the politics of Elizabeth's
1561 edict, the play holds up to scrutiny the universities' banishment of "particular households" in reinforcing an exclusionary "society of men" that had
a different relationship to language, sexuality, and (re)productive domesticity.
But seeing the university as a site in which male–male sexual possibilities
were institutionalized – as sodomitical or homoerotic – complicates the terms
by which household scenes are made comic. In other words, the homoerotic
"familiarity" fostered by the academic world colors its playful representation
of the import and trials of cross-gendered "household stuff." In this play's
fantasy, a female-identified housewifery can intervene in homoerotic domesticity, but neither identification is fully renounced; instead the play exposes
the contingencies of identities resting on this division. Serving as the "low"
eroticized constituent of the culture's fantasy, Hodge's "hole" is a marker that
reveals pedagogy's and domesticity's overlapping and partial codings of the
body.

*Gammer* becomes a peculiar language lesson in which a play about a housekeeper interrupts the Latin-saturated Cambridge environs in order to implode
early modern taxonomies.[66] In making sense of this lesson, it might be helpful to keep in mind Žižek's Lacanian gloss on "fantasy" as that which stages
desire rather than fulfilling a wish denied in reality.[67] For this play suggests
an oscillation between domesticity as the sign of a disavowed identification
and as the source of self-knowledge. The trauma of losing one's identity, indeed of being caught in contradictory modes of identification, gets expressed
in *Gammer* – not so as to restore a vernacular domesticity to young scholars –
but simply to limn its features and display the multiple desires it accommodated. It is important to note as well that *Gammer* carried into print the estranging conditions of its first performance: it was the first published play
to announce on the title page that it was performed in a university, played
on a stage, and defined as a "comedy" rather than an interlude. This textual
self-identification insured that the "joke" of domesticity's intrusion into the
academic world, and the fantasy of the multiple identifications that it carried,
would have been readily accessible to performers and readers later in the century when the play continued to be popular. In reminding readers of the novelty
of English comedy, the title page encoded its inaugural moment as attractively
inappropriate.

### Englishing comedy

Let us return to the play's complicated ends. *Gammer's* obsessive references to anality are linked in Hodge's mental universe to castration, impotency, and class-shame: "Cham always sure of the worst end, whoever have the best," he declares (1.4.32). Yet while Hodge finally redeems his "worst end" by embracing the gap that grants him knowledge, Diccon ends up thrusting the university audience into an ambiguously redeemed "end," the play's now notorious marker for the low: "But now, my good masters . . . we must be gone, / And leave you behind us, here . . . at our last ending." These words have particular meaning in a play full of erroneous, beaten, and soiled ends. The audience's privileged position above the fray erodes as they are asked to see themselves, finally, as the butt of a joke. Making the audience the bearer of its posterous closure, the play demonstrates Stallybrass and White's axiom about cultural hierarchies: "the 'top' attempts to reject and eliminate the 'bottom' for reasons of prestige and status, only to discover, not only that it is in some way frequently dependent upon that low-Other . . . but also that the top *includes* that low symbolically, as a primary eroticized constituent of its own fantasy life" (*Politics*, 4). In this instance, the play self-consciously toys with its eroticized investment in "low" elements as part of a fantasy in which the high/low oppositions upholding potent social divisions are eroded. *Gammer* thus suggests an uneasily shared affinity between rustic characters and Cambridge undergraduates, who do not, strictly, know what their laughter means.[68] The play hails its audience as native speakers whose masculinity and sexuality rest on an uneasy identification. English comedy is not simply born out of a sense of the inappropriateness of lodging homey truths in grand forms, for the play's "trifle" turns out to be central to the maintenance of bodies, sexualities, communities, and genders.

Analyzing the odd phenomenon that the first English dictionaries were addressed to women, Juliet Fleming tells a fascinating story about the vexed role "woman" played in the nationalist project of linguistic elaboration and standardization, a story that the Cambridge audience's act of remembering might disrupt. Fleming uncovers ways in which the fantasy of a woman's distinct language worked in the service of producing a masculine and nationally authorized vernacular. In her account, the "rumor" of a "female-specific vernacular activity" is a chimera created after the fact as the principle upon which a newly ordered English could be established. The vernacular, she writes,

and the right to define it, was . . . later to become an object of desire to the denizens of English culture; but it is tempting to imagine that an early masculine disregard for the 'mother tongue' left space for a female-specific vernacular activity – albeit one that left no better record than that which is recorded in the hard word lists that men produced, after the fact, for women. ("Dictionary English," 301)

Designating English as feminized and hence unruled served as a pretext for linguistic standardization, one designed to substitute for the usual regional contests over a prestige dialect. But did this fantasy only serve as the ground for a masculinized language produced "after the fact? Doesn't a text like *Gammer* exploit the fantasy of a female-identified vernacular in radically different terms, such that associations between women and "natural speech" articulate an alternative idea of community and nation? What Fleming finds tempting – the space made possible by the "rumor" of [women's] special relationship with English – materializes albeit fleetingly in this academic performance. In *Gammer*, the mother tongue and the mother, certainly the objects of nostalgic desire, contest a view of English's feminized (il)legitimacy as its founding repudiation. Still perhaps a strange fiction, the rumor of the domestic tongue serves as a different object of "consumption" (in Michel de Certeau's terms) within academic culture.[69] Holding up to scrutiny the gendered and sexual inflections of the educational system, *Gammer* foregrounds instead the politics of domestic speech.[70]

Even though it is farcical and silly – in fact *because* it justified things silly and farcical – this play lodges fantasy and play in the process of national identification.[71] Recent theorists of nationalism have made clear that while shared language is not a sufficient defining condition of nationality, it is a catalyst in shaping a national community. Benedict Anderson's now classic work, which sees the "fall of Latin" as a precondition for the emergence of national consciousness, underscores the stakes of sixteenth-century negotiations over the status of the vernacular. In its initial performance, *Gammer* argues for a collective identification founded on the alienating familiarity of the mother tongue. Though this identity does not turn out to be a salient feature in the subsequent construction of nationalism, the play shows that English community could be produced in relation to contested meanings of domesticity and free from recourse to conventional logics of difference or iconographies of absolutist power.[72] Years before the first English tragedy was written, Hodge's comic return to the *natio* elliptically hinted at his tie to a protonation defined as the "kingdom of our own language," in Spenser's terms.[73] It is thus unsurprising that critics, caught in their own domestic fantasies, have uncritically endorsed the play's conflation of its medium and content. Labeled a "native" comedy with characters "English through and through," the play is praised for its "authenticity to English experience," prosy style, and comforting presentation of "our" milieu.[74] These discursive ties have become so familiar to us that we can scarcely see their oddity in the early modern world.

### From school to playhouse

*Gammer* self-consciously puts its farcical subject into a model closely associated with the work of Terence (the classical unities of time, place and action;

five-act division; interwoven plots; three-part Donatian structure; and the "knot of errors" paradigm). Since Terence was a staple of the grammar school curriculum, college boys would have appreciated this meshing of authoritative knowledge and rustic subject matter. Nicholas Udall's *Floures for Latin Spekying*, comprised of Latin phrases from Terence's comedies, served as the classic grammar school textbook after its publication in 1533. If reading Terence enabled a mental grasp of proper style, acting his plays, along with those of Plautus, was key to the development of what Cambridge dramatist William Gager called an "embolden" youth. Defending private academic dramatic practice, he explains: "We ... [play] to recreate our selves, our House, and the better part of the University, with some learned *Poem* or other ... honestly to embolden our youth; to try their voices, and confirm their memories; to frame their speech; to conform them to convenient action, to try what mettle is in every one."[75] Acting was increasingly important to humanist efforts to train students in conversational Latin, entertain royalty in a way that displayed erudition without being boring, and test the memory and wit of youths. An approved means of enabling students to master syntax, elocution, and oratory and thus of fashioning mature males, performances were mandated as annual events in colleges founded in the sixteenth century.[76] But playing in English, as the Cambridge masters suggested in the 1590s, was a different matter, for who wanted an emboldened English tongue? What possible "mettle" could English test? *Gammer's* citation of Terence alienates a model designed precisely to separate boys from the vernacular.

In the last decade of the sixteenth century, university authorities did perform plays in English, notably *Club Law* and the Parnassus trilogy, which complemented a general dramatic turn to satire and invective on the London stage.[77] As the vernacular gained prestige, the academy used English to signify the "low" world of professional playing that scholars pretended to hold at bay. These plays differ from *Gammer* in their disdain for Englishness and their intended audience. In the 1550s private production of *Gammer Gurton's Needle*, scholars entertained *themselves* with a story of English people whom they could not fully dismiss. *Gammer* was tellingly the only English comedy acted at Cambridge until the last decade, when universities sought to differentiate their own intellectual "playing" from commercial performances in London.

If universities attempted to use playing to cement the divide between academic and nonacademic communities, we might ask how London's playhouses positioned themselves in relation to educational institutions. Given that they had no stake in consolidating elite sites of learning, these plays might reasonably be expected to be unconcerned with the division between the vernacular and Latin. But since humanism pervaded the culture and London plays were written by former schoolboys, we are not surprised to find that the tensions aired in *Gammer* surface in the professional theater where they were sometimes tailored to accommodate civic or national themes. While domesticity had different resonances within a nonacademic site, it still was part of a social struggle surrounding community-formation and Englishness.

Amidst abundant representations of pedants on the London stage, we discover the topos of the housewife's antagonism with the classroom. In *A Chaste Maid in Cheapside* (1613), for instance, Thomas Middleton presents two scenes emphasizing the divide between academia and female domesticity. In one scene, the city wife Maudline Yellowhammer intervenes in her son Tim's "barbarous" discussions with his Latin tutor. Complaining "Here's nothing but disputing all the day long with 'em," Maudline then mockingly turns logical and rhetorical abstractions to pragmatic use.[78] "I'll prove a whore to be an honest woman," claims Tim, to which his mother comments, "Some in this street would give a thousand pounds that you could prove their wives so" (4.1.42). This comic scene is strikingly paired with the inverse moment in which the Cambridge undergraduate inadvertently stumbles onto a christening ritual populated primarily by wetnurses, gossips, and neighboring wives. Tim returns from university only to suffer unexpected entry into the London world of housewifery, wandering into one of the female-identified ceremonies that so haunted the paternal imagination. When Tim cries that he is "betrayed" on first walking into the female gathering, his mother threatens to spank him and explains to the city women, "In the university they're kept still to men /And ne'er train'd up to women's company" (3.2.121–2). While Tim cries, aghast at this spectacle, "Mother . . . 'Tis against the laws of the university/ For any that has answered under Bachelor / To thrust 'mongst married wives," his mother enjoys the torture of making him "embolden" by submitting him to female company (3.2.127–30, 108). Fleeing what is clearly the play's centerpiece scene, Tim consents to return to the spectacle of wetnursing and banqueting only when allowed to bring his Latin Tutor in tow.

Later showing himself incapable of wooing in the English "Protestant tongue," Tim finds himself tricked into marrying a Welsh courtesan whom he thinks to be an heiress (4.1.151). What is his response? He enlists his Tutor to join the marriage triangle where they all attempt to use Latin and logic to translate the Welsh woman from "whore" into wife. Insisting on a gender- and class-based conflict between Latin and English, Middleton's satiric representation ends with Tim's inscription of homosocial pedagogy within a sexually fluid cross-gendered domestic world: "I perceive then a woman may be honest according to the English print, when she is a whore in the Latin" (5.4.117–18). *A Chaste Maid* comically collides the worlds of Latin and wetnursing in order, finally, to mock the ridiculousness of the academy and its claims to pure language as well as to underscore the tribulations of reproduction (termed "keeping house" in this play); that is, the wetnursing scene feeds the play's primary concern with the comedy of illegitimacy rather than domestic labor. If *Gammer* satirizes both misspeaking rustics and haughty university men, *Chaste Maid* similarly points to the foibles of mercenary city women and foolish erudition; for the Cambridge scholar appears ridiculous as he drags his tutor through London streets without a clue as to how to navigate the tricky social waters outside the university. Tim's return "home" is also more problematic than Hodge's because complicated by a ruinous world of heterosexual relationships alien to his academic training; and his confrontation with the mother tongue is rendered more difficult because linked to a larger linguistic matrix that includes foreigners such as the Welsh. At points in the play, Tim's devotion to Latin in fact brands him as a foreigner (4.1.133) and aligns him with Papistry (1.1.82). *Chaste Maid* thus calls upon the humor of pedagogy's disdain for the vernacular while forcefully underscoring the importance of a national identity based on common speech.

Is it a coincidence, then, that it is in Shakespeare's most domestic play that a notorious housewife interrupts a Latin language lesson? In *The Merry Wives of Windsor*, Mistress Quickly comically comments on Parson Hugh Evans' tutoring of Will Page. The humor of the scene turns on her witting or unwitting sexualization of the act of translation. Mistaking the Latin "horum" for "whore" and "pulcher" for "polecats" (prostitutes), Quickly exposes the possible, perhaps inevitable, errancy within the reproduction of meaning, an errancy that thwarts the goals of pedagogy. Both Patricia Parker and Elizabeth Pittenger cogently read this scene's gendering of key conceptual systems: Parker claims that the scene foregrounds the play's subterranean wordplay organized around the transfer and conveyance of property, pages, boys, trade, and women.[79] Pittenger sees this scene as demonstrating the gendered, sexual, social, and nationalist resistances to an ideal of pure transmission.[80] Both critics persuade us that Quickly's femaleness is central to her intervention in male social relations. But what about her status as housekeeper? Someone introduced not once but twice as Dr. Caius's "dry nurse" concerned with brewing, baking, and laundering? Extending Goldberg's suggestion that scholars rethink their attention to cross-dressing as the privileged site of homosexuality and look instead to scenes such as this one, we might ask how Quickly's disruption of the tutorial, clearly linked to her status as outside reproductive sexuality, turns as well on her role as domestic laborer (*Sodometries*, 143).[81]

This scene occurs in Shakespeare's only comedy set in England, a play highly absorbed with the status of right English speaking, foreigners, and household labor. Obsessed with vernacular speech as well as household practice, *Merry Wives* thematizes the Englishing that *Gammer* marked through its medium – but to some of the same ends; for it also argues for a decidedly domestic basis for community-formation and sexual stability. Critics have debated whether or not *Merry Wives* softens its celebration of housewifery by having the final scene nominate an exceptional and monarchal female as the ultimate source of power.[82] Does the play turn to the court as final arbiter of proper Englishness and community standards? I see the play's references to Windsor, in a sense, as a decoy, for *Merry Wives* insists on shared language and values, rather than courtliness, as the community's central means of cohesion.

*Merry Wives* is a play revolving around "household stuff"; it revels in the details of venison pasties, bakehouses, coffers, chimneys, presses, grease, and laundry. Falstaff's attempts to seduce the two wives, as I discuss in the next chapter, are persistently troped as domestic assaults and the wives' triumphs in humiliating him are tied discursively and thematically to their domestic authority. The play's central theme of cuckoldry, for instance, is provocatively introduced first as a *function of housekeeping* rather than of heterosexuality or marriage. In the first act, the French Dr. Caius returns home and becomes enraged to find a man secreted in his closet: "What shall de honest man do in my closet?" he asks (1.4.73). The scene is played out along the old lines – with the comedy turning on the mistress' failed attempt to steer him away from the "dishonest" intruder and on the householder's rage in becoming "horn mad." But the oddity is that Caius is a bachelor and his female roommate, Mistress Quickly, is his brewer, baker, launderer, and housekeeper rather than his paramour. Since he has no wife whose sexuality he can be interested in policing, Caius's anxieties seem to stem from a concern for *oeconomia*. His jealousy later finds a more expected location when he becomes rivals with two other characters for Ann Page's hand in marriage. But the fear that his housekeeper does not "keep his house" properly (meaning that she has a man concealed within it) frames the play's concern with unauthorized sexual circulation. The doctor's dependence on his housekeeper is also at issue: as his English "dry nurse," she is able to discipline him without the "milk" culturally associated with generosity and the inculcation of native language. Caius's foreignness is simultaneously marked as an infantilizing subjection to a female labor, alienation from the maternal, and anxiety about masculinity.[83] The clichéd scene of the jealous husband encountering the man hidden in the house resurfaces more familiarly when the hysterical Ford, seeking to prove himself a cuckold, searches his home in order to discover what the audience has seen earlier: the man in the closet. Although Ford's preoccupation with imaginary losses makes him unable to discover Falstaff's plots, this topos has already been staged for the audience through the lens of the servant–master relationship; that is, erotic jealousy has been made to speak the language of domestic possession.

When jealousy does find its more customary heterosexual location, it remains cast in terms of domestic practice and property. The pathologically jealous Master Ford interprets his wife's supposed infidelity as the sign of a traumatic failure of a housewifery designed to conserve domestic resources. "There's a hole made in your best coat, Master Ford!" he exclaims to himself, "This 'tis to be married! This 'tis to have linen and buckbaskets" (3.4.141–3). Representing adultery as a tear in his clothing, Ford worries that castration, a "shameful hole" (like Hodge's) might undo him. The labors of laundering and sewing mysteriously surface in Ford's account of marital dependence, property, and manhood – entities threatened by the ubiquitous "hole" necessary for the reproduction of property and lineage. As the object that could remedy this imagined hole, the missing needle again marks an anxious set of domestic relations.

In the next chapter, I discuss how thoroughly fantasies of domesticity saturate this play and its lore; for now, I want to concentrate on how the play's references to language work against its domestic backdrop. If we turn to the scene that critics read as establishing the play's ideological force, the final playlet involving the Order of the Garter, we see that the characters redefine domesticity as Englishness rather than as the sexual and economic conservation of the home *per se*. Peppered with Welsh and French dialects, *Merry Wives* throughout identifies abuses to authority as both linguistic and sexual. In one telling moment, Pistol accuses Falstaff of wanting to "translate" Mrs. Ford "out of honesty into English" (1.3.50). By the conclusion, however, the valences of this translation are clearly reversed: the play's emphasis on powerfully chaste women laundering corruption gives way to a public and co-gendered attempt to manage faulty speakers of the native tongue. Translated into kitchen stuff – a "hodge-pudding" and a "bag of flax"– Falstaff attempts to reposition himself within the community by mocking those on its linguistic margins: "Have I liv'd to stand at the taunt of one that makes fritters of English?" he exclaims not of the housewives who have abused him mercilessly but of the Welsh Hugh Evans (5.5.142–3). Redrawing power divisions in terms of national and ethnic lines, Ford also substitutes foreigners for merry wives: "I will never mistrust my wife again, till thou art able to woo her in good English," he says to Evans (5.5.133–4). Both men convert domestic panic into a collective identification based on shared speech, a community that includes women while marginalizing foreigners. Privileging household allegiance over that owed the crown, the play folds one meaning of the domestic into another – with a non-elite national culture as the result. In struggling to redefine the community so as to include themselves, both men, however, must draw from the world of the vernacular that, as rumor has it, is the province of housewives and nurses.[84]

My incomplete account of *Merry Wives* suggests that it provides an allegory for how English-speaking communities are founded on a cross-gendered and material domesticity. This allegory anchors the social world to the ordinary yet authoritative world of women that, in fact, upholds the position of an eager "middling sort" – innkeepers, justices of the peace, householders, local businessmen. As a self-consciously English comedy, *Merry Wives* inflects locale and speech with overt nationalist sentiment, yet it also freely airs the estranging features of domestic subjectivity. Like *Gammer*, it insists on a national community that stretches to accommodate regional lexicons but rests, finally, on the common experience attributed to the household and the prosy English tongue.

In this sense, the play generates a potent but vexed concept of everydayness as the grounds for collective identification, one tied to the national mythology of "merry old England" that Leah Marcus astutely sees as grounding the play. Presenting our only comedic access to a locale much like the bard's own Stratford, this play is thus required to be mimetic and truly English.[85] Yet critics' presumption of the play's verisimilitude, as my argument implies, overlooks its powerful cultural fantasies and its commentary on the process by which communities and identities were imagined.[86]

Glancing briefly at *Merry Wives* throws into relief *Gammer*'s different but related strategies for probing the terms by which speech and status were made culturally intelligible. In the late sixteenth-century London playhouse where the national potential of the mother tongue was not threatening in the same way, domesticity could be mobilized explicitly in the service of an English community. This largely middle-class fantasy posits a nation founded on a domestic labor that doesn't have to be disavowed in the name of gender maturation. We turn from a play interested in the internal contradictions of humanist pedagogy to one interested in showing the limits of pedagogy for a practical middling-class citizenry. And so, in a text so concerned with beaten buttocks, English speaking, and housewifery, we are not surprised to discover the topos of the language lesson, now understood as richly laced with particular sexual and gender codings, and now condensed into one comic scene. Saturated with malapropisms and comic dialects, *Merry Wives* finally anchors linguistic difference by showing the male puberty ritual disrupted comically by the housekeeper or "dry-nurse," the guardian of good English. "You do ill to teach the child such words," Quickly declares, only to have Parson Evans rebut: "'Oman, art thou [lunatics]? Hast thou no understandings for thy cases, and the numbers of the genders?" (4.1.69–71). Here the lesson is ostentatiously conducted by a Welshman, whose own linguistic errancy makes him the butt of a joke waged by citizens and housewives, one of whom has seemingly lost track of the correct number of genders. In Shakespeare's play, the cultural capital of humanist pedagogy is now explicitly spent by the bawdy female wordplay of Shakespeare's most notorious housewife and the vulgar tongue is pit against an academy thoroughly infected by foreign (mis) speakers. Probing conceptions of gender, speech, sexuality, and community, this domestic fantasy works in the service of defining English comedy.

# 3    Why does Puck sweep?
## Shakespearean fairies and the politics of cleaning

Let me begin with the simple question posed in my title: Why *does* Puck sweep? At the end of *A Midsummer Night's Dream*, Oberon and his troupe of fairies enter the Athenian palace to bless the aristocratic newlyweds as they set out to consummate their marriages. After waxing lyrical about screeching predators and demonic spirits, Puck describes his nocturnal mission as an odd hallowing: "I am sent with broom before, / To sweep the dust behind the door" (5.1.389–90). When the fairies saunter casually into the ducal palace, the magic that had been located specifically within the forest is unleashed onto Theseus' domestic, if hyperrational, human sphere. In this moment, class tensions and marital disputes are also overshadowed by the play's culminating interest in aristocratic reproduction. But why in helping to achieve this closure does the mischievous Puck play the role of housewife? Why does the reproduction of the social world, a goal at the very heart of romantic comedy, rest on a task usually too banal for representation – disposing of dirt left in domestic corners? Why introduce a homey image in a play concerned with the grand affairs of state or the chaotic force of the imagination, one situated, albeit loosely, in the remote world of classical Athens?

I suggest that Puck's sacred sweeping links good housewifery with dramatic closure and political authority, and, for the brief moment that it does so, allows a glimpse of an Englishness founded on principles that the play has not generally endorsed: the vernacular broadly defined. As Puck assumes the part of the very English Robin Goodfellow, the exotic mythological realm to which he is attached expands to include local and domestic associations that reverberate oddly with the flexible civic monarchy that founds social order in *Dream*. This revisionary moment also simultaneously imports an agrarian "native" fairy-lore into a foreign city court. Shakespeare's later comedy *The Merry Wives of Windsor* repeats but perhaps helps to clarify this curiosity, for the fairies who emerge in its final scene illuminate a different but equally unexpected moment of disjunction. Why would housewives, who have figured so prominently in this play, seemingly turn away from their domestic province to dream up a fairy spectacle in the forest? How does attention to ethereal spirits square with the play's lauding of prosaic household life? In this chapter I argue that *A*

*Midsummer Night's Dream* and *The Merry Wives of Windsor* position domesticity and "popular" discourse differently in their formulations of community, and, in doing so, they test the range of early modern connections among housewifery, class status, and fairylore. I should make clear that I attempt neither to recover some discrete entity called "the popular" nor to establish how truly widespread, oppositional, or lower-class a particular belief system might be in a given period. Instead I look at how drama represents the "consumption" or "use" of something designated as popular by different social groups.[1] Fairylore becomes a channel through which Shakespearean drama grapples with the class-specific practices that subtend debates about English community in the late sixteenth and early seventeenth centuries; and it is this broader debate – about domestic ideology and community – that I hope to illuminate by scrutinizing two of its local dramatic instances.

It's appropriate that we turn from a discussion of humanism's longing for the vernacular tongue it so heartily renounces to a play about fairies, those creatures that Erasmus roundly denounced as the "old wives' tales" threatening budding scholars. Theseus and Hippolyta, among whom the impish Puck jarringly dwells, might have earned Erasmus' approval, since they embody the classical tradition recommended to elite boys. Yet in *Dream*, the changeling boy is able to fulfill the humanist dream from *within* the fairyworld; according to Louis Montrose, he goes from "the relatively androgynous or feminized state of infancy into the more decisively gendered state of youth, from the world of mothers and nurses into the world of fathers and masters."[2] What, after all, is the fairy Titania but a shadow of the servant surrogate mothers that humanists love to censure, a creature marked by her shameful desire to eroticize and infantilize a male child? What does Montrose describe if not the puberty ritual revisited, with fairylore instead of the vernacular marking a return to domesticity as well as its necessary renunciation? If this is the case, why then does a broom appear in the play's closure, as if offering a trace of the very domain that must be left behind in the name of refined behavior and status?

When *Merry Wives of Windsor* reanimates the fairies from *Dream*, it invites audiences to debate the place of popular myth in conceptions of Englishness. I thus return to *Merry Wives*, discussed in the previous chapter in terms of pedagogy and national culture, in order to investigate how a tradition designated as popular (by those both sympathetic and hostile to it) could be reconciled with the middle-class ideal of housewifery. What the culture sometimes deemed trivial – domesticity, fairy tales, ballads, and the female imagination – could become handy symbols for writers as they queried the terms of national commonality. Showing how ordinary tasks were as potentially traumatic as they were reassuring, these plays demonstrate how social groups "consumed" domesticity, and its inscription in popular culture, differently. Perhaps it was because they were blatantly labeled a "fantasy" by parts of the culture that fairies could so unobtrusively join the national fantasies staged in London theaters.

Folklorists suggest that fairy discourse spanning many centuries designates belief in spirits as both domestic and fading; that is, it constitutes a belief system held reverently until *just recently*, such that "believers" simply represent the unenlightened part of any given culture. As recipients of fairy tales, children (a term signifying differently over the centuries) constituted a privileged group who could still cling, temporarily, to a belief system that many would be encouraged to renounce when they entered adulthood. Children marked the site of the culture's continuity with a legendary past, even when the myth of this "recently" fading system was false; that is, even when many parts of the population still believed fervently in fairies or never had done so at all. Two evolutionary narratives were at work: early modern writers projected an individual chronological evolution for elite children, who had to renounce folktales as part of their initiation into upper-class adulthood, as well as a broader historical evolution for fairylore. The child's temporary immersion in a domain designated as imaginative (the fantasy space inculcated in the domestic world) rehearsed the historical diachronic tale of the whole culture's march toward enlightenment.[3]

Who served as gatekeepers to this illusory past world? Erasmus points specifically to early childcare when arguing that a boy's proper humanist education should center on "high" canons rather than on lower-class forms:

A boy [may] learn a pretty story from the ancient poets, or a memorable tale from history, just as readily as the stupid and vulgar ballad, or the old wives' fairy rubbish such as most children are steeped in nowadays by nurses and serving women. Who can think without shame of the precious time and energy squandered in listening to ridiculous riddles, stories of dreams, of ghosts, witches, fairies, demons; of foolish tales drawn from popular annals; worthless, nay mischievous stuff of the kind which is poured into children in their nursery days?[4]

Ballads and tales are damaging, according to Erasmus, because of their superstitious content as well as their mode of transmission. In fact, these two features fuse, as the shameful tales of lower-class women supposedly derive from the printed ballads that infantilize adults. What the lower classes are imagined to consume becomes identical with what "old wives" whisper to elite children in their "nursery days," with the result that nondiscriminating readers of cheap print appear immature. Erasmus hints that the aristocratic household also risks class hybridity, since serving women open the door to "mischievous stuff." What Erasmus does is to construct "fairy rubbish" as a discourse of the popular in arguing for its eradication; and he codes the popular as the embarrassing secrets of "our" past. His comment bespeaks a widespread practice, Renaissance and contemporary, in which the reality of multiple social groups is reduced to a two-tiered model: popular *v*. elite, vulgar print *v*. ancient poetry, humanistic pedagogy *v*. vernacular domesticity. If female domestic workers are dangerous conduits for "foolish" popular knowledge, then returning to a home tainted by their influence produces a shame that secures these binaries.

Erasmus' concerns could lead us to recount the story of humanism's transformation of education and its attempt to mark and privilege particular forms of knowledge. Despite this effort, "mischievous stuff" seeped into the poetry and history that Erasmus held dear, intermingling, for instance, with classical traditions in the well-attended London theaters. The fact that *A Midsummer Night's Dream* is steeped in fairylore as well as Ovidian tradition indicates that dramatists readily joined popular influences with erudite lineages of knowledge. But isn't it significant that domestic laborers and popular forms were conjoined in the early modern imagination – even if the association was designed as a slur? That people associated fairy stories with serving women and domestic work – in short, with the material relationships hovering around the household and childhood? Attending to ways in which material relationships were represented in drama introduces us to the domestic fantasies that activated and shaped the audience's mobile identifications. Drawing on the burgeoning fairy tradition of ballads, poems, and oral culture – one in which sprites might represent the values of gentry, yeoman, courtiers, or citizens – plays suggest the complicated role that the household played in the project of conceptualizing England's social order.

### Household "bugs"

Erasmus was not alone in attributing belief in fairies to uneducated people and in using female domestic workers to symbolize that backward population. Numerous self-professed "enlightened" skeptics identify fairies as part of a dead or idolatrous belief system. In *The Discoverie of Witchcraft*, Reginald Scot places fairies both within a past agrarian world and the imagination of contemporary nurses and mothers who seek to use the specter of spirits to frighten children into obedience. "In deede your grandams maides were woont to set a boll of milke before him [an incubus] and his cousine Robin good-fellow, for grinding of malt or mustard, and sweeping the house at midnight," writes Scot about the custom of rewarding fairies for nightime work.[5] Not simply the practice of servants, fairylore formed the past that continues to haunt a tenuously identified "us." "But in our childhood," Scot continues,

our mothers maids have so terrified us with an ouglie divell having hornes on his head, fier in his mouth, and a taile in his breech . . . they have so fraied us with bull beggers, spirits, witches, urches, elves, hags, fairies, satyrs, pans, faunes, sylens . . . dwarfes, giants, imps, calcars, conjurers, nymphes, changlings, *Incubus*, Robin good-fellowe, the spoorne, the mare, the man in the oke . . . and such other bugs, that we are afraid of our owne shadowes. (139)

In their drive to classify fairies as obsolete knowledge or as the domain of a female workforce, early modern writers nevertheless demonstrate how potent and persistent these "bugs" were as figures for a particular kind of influence. Erasmus' suggestion that fairies constituted a vital belief system ("nowadays") is credited by evidence from nonliterary sources, which indicate that parts of the population were avid believers in many types of spirit. Interested in discrediting fairylore, Scot links it to lower-class domestic forms of knowledge and, most generally, to behavioral control – the moment when an earlier and vulnerable self was coerced into obedience through mystification. Recognizing "bugs" as illusory seems to be the first step toward throwing off the shackles of intellectual imprisonment ironically forged by marginal parts of the population. After all, who wants to admit to being controlled by servants and women?

Other writers viewed spirits as a source of collective mirth rather than a tool of domestic tyranny. In *Tarltons Newes out of Purgatory* (1588), the narrator dreams that the ghost of the theatrical clown Richard Tarlton returns, offering tales of the afterlife prefaced by an assurance:

although thou see me heere in likenes of a spirite, yet thinke mee to bee one of those *Familiares Lares* that were rather pleasantly disposed then indued with any hurtfull influence, as *Hob Thrust, Robin Goodfellowe* and such like spirites, (as they tearme them of the buttry), famozed in every old wives Chronicle for their mad merrie prankes. Therefore sith my appearance to thee is in resemblance of a spirite, thinke that I am as Pleasant a Goblin as the rest, [and I] will make thee as merry before I part, as ever *Robin Goodfellow* made the country wenches at their Creamboules.[6]

Tarlton's ghost identifies "pleasant" spirits not only by their domestic habitation (as *Familiares Lares* or Roman household tutelary gods) but also by the "old wives" who behold them. In this appreciative linking of women and the supernatural, Robin Goodfellow is rehabilitated through his classification with the folk heroes of a comfortingly familiar world. In identifying Robin with merry household spirits and rural servants' tales, the narrator, like Erasmus, makes fairies "popular knowledge," but he does so in order to validate the imaginative world of country dwellers as the unofficial chronicle that Londoners are presumed to know.

The impulses to privilege an educated citizenry or to champion the delights of common folk were not as distinct as we might imagine. As the antics of fairies increasingly appeared in ballads, poems, pamphlets, and plays, the reputed beliefs of gossips, old wives, and milkmaids became available for multiple readerships. Michael Drayton's 1609 courtly poem *Nimphidia: The Court Faery* opens by commenting on the stupendous popularity of fairies, whose "Elfish secrets" have never been truly told:

> Another sort there bee, that will
> Be talking of the Fayries still,
> Nor never can they have their fill,
>     As they were wedded to them;
> No Tales of them their thirst can slake,
> So much delight therein they take,
> And some strange thing they faine would make,
>     Knew they the way to doe them.[7]

The pleasure that merry country women take in sprites finds a complementary register in the courtier's eroticized appetite for "strange" subject matter. Drayton's courtly text marks the old wives' tale not as the vulgar subject of household talk but as the alien matter that elite readers hungrily claim and metaphorically marry. If fairies are the purview of children and nurses, then this rapacious thirst for outlandish talk shows how easily the domestic could become the uncanny.

When George Puttenham terms a figure of speech a "changeling" in his *Arte of English Poesie*, he not only consolidates the connection between women and fairies but explains the class hybridity attached to this lore:

The Greekes call this figure (*Hippalage*) the Latins *Submutatio*, we in our vulgar may call him the (*underchange*) but I had rather have him called the [*Changeling*] nothing at all swerving from his original, and . . . pleasanter to beare in memory: specially for you Ladies and pretie mistresse in Court, for whose learning I write, because it is a terme often in their mouthes, and alluding to the opinion of Nurses, who are wont to say, that the Fayries use to steale the fairest children out of their cradles and put other ill favoured in their places, which they called changelings.[8]

In a rhetorical conduct manual here addressed to courtly ladies and an upwardly mobile audience, Puttenham notes that noblewomen perpetuate stories derived from their nurses. The figure of the familiar serving woman haunts the corridors of the court in the form of a local knowledge compelling enough to warrant its inclusion in an anatomy of erudite language. In this sense the vulgar nurse continues to speak through the "pretie" mistress, providing the terms in which she can learn new practices. What "Nurses . . . are wont to say" echoes in the polite speech of courtiers, where it is identified as the feminized vernacular counterpart to Greek and Latin terminology, the repertoire of courtiers as well as country wenches. In this way the text collides social groups (courtier and nurse) and exoticizes conceptions of domesticity.

Thomas Churchyard suggests a similarly ambiguous delight in popular lore when he imports country fairies into his 1592 royal pageant, *A Handeful of Gladsome Verses, given to the Queenes Maiesty at Woodstocke*. Glossing supernatural events hovering around ordinary domestic acts, he writes about wives who discover monsters as they roast crabs at night, maids scared of hobgoblins, Robin Goodfellow skimming cream bowls, and spirits who smash plates when "foule sluts" fail to scour the pewter.[9] The world "full merry was / And gossips made good glee," Churchyard notes nostalgically over this simpler, albeit dizzyingly fantastic, lifestyle. Although he apologizes for including vulgar subjects in royal encomia, he does so only after linking fairies to a golden world –England's pastoral days and each person's domestic roots (B4[r]). Churchyard implies that disregard for his "base" subject matter reveals a pronounced want of taste. Fairies could thus be positioned not only as the abject belief system jettisoned in the march of progress but also as the pastoral life endangered by the social ills of the present world. It is the world, good or bad, that people forgo when they mature, and, as such, it remains the object of fascination as well as disgust.

Fairies made their most frequent appearance in English literature between 1570 and 1625, making the Renaissance a critical period in the establishment of fairylore.[10] Although our impressions of fairies are indelibly colored by those ethereal beings from the Victorian era, it was only in the seventeenth century, following the work of Shakespeare and Drayton, that the concept of the fairy as a delicate, miniature, and essentially benevolent spirit became the norm. Medieval fairies were neither friendly nor cute, but were instead regarded as an arm of evil. By the sixteenth century fairies began to be dissociated from the devil in popular tradition and instead portrayed as child-sized country pranksters who wore coarse clothing and busied themselves with fooling travelers and tinkering with household order. Spenser's vision of the fairy kingdom (populated with creatures derived from medieval romance and Celtic tradition) was not the norm in literary discourse. According to Katharine Briggs, the main types of fairylore available to writers in sixteenth-century England included: 1) the "trooping fairies" of Celtic legend which subdivided into the aristocratic heroic spirits of medieval romance and their rustic descendants, the child-sized fairies of popular tradition; 2) the more ominous hobgoblins associated with witchcraft or paganism; 3) mermaids, water sprites, nature fairies, giants, monsters, and hags; and 4) the miniature fairies of continental oral tradition.[11] The most common fairy incarnation was the rustic creature of folk tradition, who became lumped indiscriminately with hobgoblins, elves, mermaids, giants, fairies, and the English hobgoblin called Robin Goodfellow, a descendant of agricultural deities sometimes attached to evil. As larger fairies began to shrink into those precious spirits familiar to modern audiences, they absorbed the characteristics of country fay, namely a fanaticism about fastidiousness, housework, and chastity as well as a love for waylaying travelers and shapeshifting. Although possessing the power to levitate, these spirits oddly concerned themselves with the material rhythms of human work and leisure.

In its literary incarnations the folk fairy tradition underwent a change in late sixteenth- and early seventeenth-century England.[12] Country fairylore was blended into classical mythology, with the result that demonic spirits became less sinister, elves and hobgoblins were assimilated into the fairy kingdom proper, and domestic nosiness spread to all classes of fairy as their chief identifying feature.[13] Cultivated by a growing national consciousness, this transformation foregrounded precisely those figures, such as Robin Goodfellow, who were hailed as "native English" stock, while downplaying spirits with links to German and Scandinavian folklore.[14] Since those coarse spirits with an interest in domestic work were specific to England, this synthesis of traditions had the effect of diffusing national sentiment into popular legend.[15] Representations of fairies thus began to work in tandem with the domestic discourses that I have described in other chapters of this study.

The best-known hobgoblin of this period found his fullest textual elaboration in a 1628 pamphlet called *Robin Good-fellow his mad prankes, and merry iests*. In this collection of tales fairies make nocturnal visits to households where they reward housemaids for jobs well done or pinch "sluts" for creating "ill ordered houses."[16] Like brownies, those supernatural workers from Scottish tales who inspired the American girl scout troop of that name, fairies would not only compensate good housework but actually join in the tasks of cleaning. In this text Oberon impregnates a devoted country maid, who gives birth to the rough and hairy Robin Goodfellow. Thus assimilated into the fairy kingdom, Robin sheds his sinister and pagan characteristics. While using his formidable shapeshifting powers to aid honest folks and play mischievous pranks, Robin's central preoccupation is with eroticism and domesticity. He disrupts lascivious male courtships, engages in adulterous affairs, and insistently patrols women's work in the home. The frame tale of *Robin Good-fellow* creates him as the product of entertaining female talk in the countryside.[17]

Robin Goodfellow gradually becomes identified as the arbiter of good housekeeping. In Samuel Rowlands' *More Knaues Yet*, this pleasant "deuill" is an inveterate inhabitant of the dairy and mill, someone with privileged knowledge of domains coded as female and lower-class:

> Amongst the rest was a good fellow deuill,
> So cal'd in kindnes, cause he did no euill,
> Knowne by the name of Robin (as we heare)
> And that his eyes as broad as sawcers were,
> Who came a nights and would make Kitchins cleane,
> And in the bed bepinch a lazie queane.
> Was much in Mils about the grinding Meale,
> (And sure (I take it) taught the Miller steale)
> Amongst the Creame bowles & Milke pans would be,
> And with the Country wenches, who but he

> To wash their dishes for some Fresh-cheese hire:
> Or set their Pots and Kettles 'bout the fire.[18]

Located within the landscape of the household, Robin becomes intimately associated with pots, cheese, and, it seems, women's beds. Pinching maids, grinding meal, and scrubbing the kitchen, he makes eroticism and work appear to be natural allies. Both enabling and disrupting daily rhythms, Robin serves as a heuristic device not only for galvanizing women to work but also for rendering a fully anatomized housewifery into exotic myth. The idea that serving women transmitted fairy stories was thus not the only domestic component to fairy fantasy, for their stories' most prominent characteristic was a deep interest in the details of household life. The *content* of fairy tales had a class and gender coding separate from their location in the mouths of nurses and buttery maids. As industrious workers, fairies did not simply constitute the ignorant belief system against which humanists liked to tilt, for they began to be associated with (even as they eroticized) the values of stewardship, diligence, and *oeconomia* so dear to the "middling sort."[19]

When literary and performance texts of the period use fairies to explore collisions between ostensibly "high" and "low" social groups, they engage with the cultural debates about domesticity that I have traced in previous chapters. Drayton's *Nimphidia* presents the almost schizophrenic class divide within fairy representations made to embody chivalric and popular traditions simultaneously, for he burlesques heroic romance by rendering valiant warriors in miniature form, and he shows courtly fairies to belie an interest in the drudgery of housekeeping.[20] In Jonson's "Entertainment at Althrope" (first performed in 1603), Queen Anne and Prince Henry are greeted by a satyr who delights in importing fairies from the dairy into the presence of royalty:

> This is Mab the mistris-Faerie,
> That doth nightly rob the dayrie,
> And can hurt, or helpe the cherning,
> (As shee please) without discerning.[21]

If the fairies' ability to transport a butter churn into a royal encomium is seen here as quaint, Jonson's later masque "Love's Restored" shows that these two worlds are not so easily reconciled. While courtiers are invited to revel in the antics of the rustic Mab at Althorp, they are directed by this later spectacle to scrutinize their own sophistication. As an "honest plaine countery spirit, and harmelesse," Robin Goodfellow is repeatedly excluded from the court, for Whitehall has no place for a spirit that "sweepes the harth, and the house cleane, riddles for the countrey maides, and does all their other drudgerie."[22] Robin succeeds in gaining access to the masque only by having his "costume" of broom and candles mistaken by the audience as a theatrical "deuice" (381). Robin thus ruptures the exclusivity of the court, but the joke is on the court; for

Jonson uses this moment to criticize courtly foibles and satirize the nastiness of elite society.

In *Grim the Collier of Croydon*, Robin's decision to escape the corrupt courtly society and return to his country roots provides a sharp satire of high living. "These silken Girles are all too fine for me," he declares:

> My Master shall report of those in Hell,
> Whilst I go range amongst the Country maids,
> To see if home-spun Lasses milder be
> Than my curst Dame.[23]

In this play, banqueting on exotic foodstuffs is the sign of the bad *oeconomia* that inevitably produces a "loose" house (one simultaneously unproductive, unlocked, and adulterous). Although he takes pleasure in foiling housewives, Robin concludes that modest maids are more true than ladies of means, and thus he chooses country life by choosing its women. Fleeing demonic sophistication, the "home-spun" Robin champions a rural world removed from the depravity of hyperrefined society.

I suggest that two aspects of fairylore blended in the cultural imagination: domesticity and a "low" country workforce defined in patent opposition to the court or the site of humanist "high" learning. Since the countryside was often touted as preserving an agrarian self-sufficiency threatened by market forces, fairies could be enlisted to support a yeomanry faithful to the tenets of good housekeeping; that is, servants' labor might be recruited to ratify the ideology of the middling sort.[24] Yet something remains to be said about the fairies' interest in sexual, as well as class, issues. While fairies sometimes punish licentiousness (as in John Fletcher's *The Faithful Shepherdess*), their activities inevitably engaged them in the erotic life of maids. In John Lyly's 1591 *Endymion* fairies don't merely supervise household work but instead pinch saucy mortals who try to view the Queen of Stars. But in the anonymous play *The Maydes Metamorphosis*, fairies are not the guardians of forbidden and eroticized spaces but their most successful intruders. In their nocturnal appearances spirits leap into maids' gowns, peep beneath their frocks, and nip at their sleeping bodies.[25] And in Thomas Campion's 1601 *Booke of Ayres*, Proserpina is so eager to encourage ladies' amorous delights that she sends out fairy minions to punish those not properly sympathetic to their paramours.[26] In this odd representation, fairies reverse their typical mission of safeguarding female virtue. Whether protecting honor or provoking desire, fairies surface as gatekeepers to an explicitly sexualized and industry-driven world.

As the title image to *Robin Good-fellow* makes strikingly clear, England's popular hobgoblin is defined by both domestic and sexual escapades. In this woodcut, Robin appears as a gigantic bearded satyr with hairy breeches and hoofed feet, holding a priapic scepter in one hand and a broom in the other. Circled by miniature vaguely demonic spirits, he has an erect penis protruding from his pants (Fig. 14). Perhaps this blending of household sweeping with a slightly sinister eroticism is not surprising, since Oberon and his crew are described as regularly swooping down on the mortal world to dally with women's "sluttery," both their domestic shortcuts and their wayward desires.[27] In *Robin Good-fellow*, Robin's bawdy songs are intermixed with provocative advice about housework:

> Maydes in your smockes,
> Looke well to your lockes,
> And your Tinder-boxe,
> Your wheeles and your rockes,
> Your Hens and your Cockes,
> Your Cowes and your Oxe,
> And beware of the Foxe,
> When the Bell-man knockes,
> Put out your fire and candle light,
> So they shall not you affright:
> May you dreame of your delight,
> And in your sleepes see pleasant sights.
>
> (E3$^{r-v}$)

This song veers from practical advice about guarding household property into a fantasy of what young girls in their "smocks" behold in their "pleasant sights." The blessing of dutiful maids mutates into speculation about the pleasure women take in dreaming. In these moments the household is imagined as a place of female enclosure, locked tight and protected by a watchful maid – but not protected from the gaze of the ethereal male advisor. The fantasies and habits of serving women mark the site of a sexualized domestic nostalgia, as Robin's secretive trespass joins stories in which fairylore itself constitutes a foray into a national and personal past. As Drayton's amused description of the court's avid desire for fairy stories implies, the erotics of the fairy world could bleed into their form of representation; that is, stories about fairies' entry into the fantasy life of women might bespeak the wistfulness or disgust that writers feel about old wives' tales.

Fairies were inconsistently represented: they sometimes punished bad housewifery, sometimes worked laboriously, and sometimes simply danced among the trenchers in the kitchen as magical footnotes to the materiality of the house.[28] In the English cultural imagination their attachment to domestic work made them multifaceted emblems of vernacular culture. For elite audiences they signified the exotic or vulgar hominess of serving women; for the middle part of the population they enabled a critique of elite neglect for life's basics; and for general audiences they simply marked a "familiarity" inscribed in the rural roots of Londoners, native traditions, or the mythological space of childhood itself. Rather than merely demonstrating the widening gap between popular and elite cultures, fairylore casts light on how this two-tiered model was constructed

# ROBIN
## GOOD-FELLOVV,
### HIS MAD PRANKES AND MERRY IESTS.

Full of honeſt Mirth, and is a ſit Medicine for Melancholy.

Printed at *London* by *Thomas Cotes*, and are to be ſold by *Francis Grove*, at his ſhop on Snow-hill, neere the Sarazens-head. 1639

Fig. 14  Title page to *Robin Good-fellow His Mad Prankes and Merry Iests* (London, 1628).

discursively in the period, as well as showing the presence of a middling sort that complicated the model.[29] Fairylore consistently occupied different sites within the culture – as "popular" knowledge claimed by lower- and middling-class people who defined themselves against aristocratic finery, but also as the concern of courtiers who assimilated the belief systems they rejected as part of their status-identifications. Because fairy discourse cut across class lines its reputed and intertwined class *assignments* (rather than its "true" class position) should be the object of our inquiry. Fairy belief was not the province of one specific social group but served as a discursive field that could be activated in diverse ways to produce alliances and stratifications. As such, it offered a storehouse of *fantasies of recovery* – popular "home" traditions that could never be fully absorbed nor renounced. As an institution catering to multiple social groups, the London stage presents a particularly interesting site for looking at how fairy discourse was taken up by different constituencies in early modern England.

### Enter Puck

> This is shee, that empties cradles,
> Takes out children, puts in ladles.
>
>                     On Mab, in Jonson's "Entertainment at Althrope" (7:123)

It is the conventional Robin Goodfellow who first appears in *A Midsummer Night's Dream.* "Either I mistake your shape and making quite," an unnamed fairy exclaims,

> Or else you are that shrewd and knavish sprite
> Call'd Robin Goodfellow. Are not you he
> That frights the maidens of the villagery,
> Skim milk, and sometimes labor in the quern,
> And bootless make the breathless huswife churn,
> And sometime make the drink to bear no barm,
> Mislead night-wanderers, laughing at their harm?
> Those that Hobgoblin call you, and sweet Puck.
> You do their work.                    (2.1.32–41)

Typically identified by his rustic interests and pranks, Robin unexpectedly assimilates the names ("Hobgoblin," "Puck") and characteristics ("shrewd," "knavish") of discrete spirits from the medieval period.[30] In addition to his job of amusing Oberon, Puck concurs, he leads an alternative life circling around the country maid or "wisest aunt, telling the saddest tale" (2.1.51):

> And sometime lurk I in a gossip's bowl,
> In very likeness of a roasted crab,

And when she drinks, against her lips I bob,
And on her withered dewlop pour the ale.                    (2.1.47–50)

In the village, Robin playfully teases gossips, spilling ale on their faces or causing them to tumble from stools, especially when they are in the middle of narrating one of those old wives' tales of which he is a product. In this part of his life, Robin is both a character and the figment of the housewife's imagination as she encounters domestic accidents. Through his characterization as "sweet Puck," *Dream* redefines the demonic *puca* (known as the pouk) as the somewhat more benign Robin. The stage directions and speech prefixes in the 1600 quarto and 1623 folio formally endow Robin with an alias that had staying power, for the names Robin and Puck were used interchangeably in subsequent texts. While *Dream* rehabilitates the medieval pouk by only faintly echoing his demonic ties, it also assigns him to two radically different social environments. Equally at home with mermaids or dairy maids, Robin mingles rural everydayness and pastoral romance. As both the literalization of failed work and the exotic spirit happy to circumnavigate the globe, he straddles the provinces of village housewives and mythological royalty.

Although first distinguished from the play's other spirits by his village antics, Puck quickly joins a society of fairies concerned primarily with aristocratic homage. As an attendant to the royal Oberon, he centrally serves as the court jester, appropriately called "*gentle* Puck." For most of the play, *Dream* invites amnesia about this spirit's signature characteristics and instead tailors the fairy world to the image of the court. How are we to read this transformation of popular lore? One interpretation might emphasize the fairies' tie to old wives' tales as a repressed subtext for the play. In this reading the serving woman or nurse that Erasmus links to superstition surfaces in distorted form as the old dowager that Hermia and Lysander seek in their plans for elopement (1.1.157), or the elderly female moon that thwarts Theseus' romance (1.1.5) – two female figures who haunt the play and the elite family. As absent presences, their shadows become legible largely because the play attempts to credit the fairies of "old wives' tales" while stripping them of their class associations.[31] In this account, representations of Oberon and Titania's struggle over the Indian boy (the only description we have of a changeling from the fairies' point of view), smack of both the nurse's domination over children and the class hybridity caused by wetnursing. The gender and class associations of what Erasmus terms "fairy rubbish" help to explain why a play about fairies might belie anxieties about artisans and women, or why the play might want to conscript Robin to serve the interests of royalty. As male servant to a male king at odds with his queen, Robin functions within a masculine and elite sphere.

C. L. Barber's classic *Shakespeare's Festive Comedy* argues that popular festivity – including morris dances, wassailings, mock ceremonies, sports, and seasonal customs – structured early modern experience. In his reading, drama encoded symbolically those patterns of festivity experienced elsewhere in the culture. But Barber also located drama and ritual as epiphenomena of a deep structural need for release from and clarification of the social and natural order.[32] Fairies become part of a folk tradition recruited in the play's exploration of mimesis and the bounds of holiday. Barber's seminal work has been importantly critiqued by Annabel Patterson and Louis Montrose, among others, as naturalizing social categories and restricting the political possibilities of drama, since it, like other forms of festivity, seems to invert norms only in order to "right" them in the end.[33] In such a reading, *Dream*'s fairies symbolically mark the nonreal imaginative order activated by the play before being relegated to the safe sphere of holiday by Theseus.

Revisiting Barber's territory, Montrose defines the "popular" in terms of its competing social interests and draws domestic ideology into the analysis. Seeking to fill the void left by the Tudor state's suppression of religious and amateur theatricality, commercial theater, in his account, gradually absorbed popular forms into a centralized venue. As *Dream* assimilates classical mythology, amateur ritual, native folklore, and popular festivity into its bounds, it affirms a court-centered world organized around conventional marital and class hierarchies. Yet the play also mounts two important critiques: it exposes the tenuous construction of dominant social arrangements, and it shows patriarchalism to be pointedly unavailable to a female queen. The result is an affirmation of a *male* monarch whose power rests precisely on his domestic control over female sexuality and generation. Domesticity and fairylore are two central intersecting variables in Montrose's argument about the gendered representations of state. It is the royal fairy Oberon's power over his *wife* Titania, a mastery achieved by eliciting an "unnatural" desire from her, that settles the domestic dispute over the Indian boy and the social-cosmic crisis it produces. But Montrose notes that the fairies' existence *as fairies* enables the play to challenge the idea of a naturalized social order. Instead of being divinely ordained imperatives of nature, the fairies are overtly artificial, the "humanly constructed imperatives of culture" that undo the "natural" logic of generation binding the political world (*Purpose of Playing*, 145). The fairies thus probe the "normative discourse" of gender that they help to produce. A similar tension marks the play's assimilation of popular tradition, for the fairies merge with artisans at the play's end to serve jointly as figures for actors. Appealing to the audience for applause as a "shadow" (a term for actor), Puck advertises his role in commercial theater, with the result that he foregrounds the stage's reliance on revenue. If *Dream* has shown amateur theater to work in the service of the court, it qualifies that seamless unity by reminding the audience that the theater was indebted to paying customers. The fairies' finale may be one more instance in which figures of popular culture are welcomed into a national courtly sphere, but Puck's address to a paying audience muddles the equation and makes fairies into a figure for the shaping power of commercial theater.

What might complicate this account is the fairies' preexisting association with domestic work and ideologies centering on household production. As a "figure of folklore and village life," in Montrose's words, Puck plays more roles than those of court jester, courtier, actor, or emblem of popular ritual (*Purpose*, 200). With broom in hand, Puck activates that part of fairy discourse that linked spirits to housekeeping, femininity, and a "middling-class" devotion to the materiality of work. In this final incarnation he represents himself as a servant-worker whose domestic labor silently enables the reproduction of the royal family. In Jonson's *Alchemist*, Subtle reminds Face of his rise from low status precisely by identifying the broom as a sign of abjection:

> Thou vermine, haue I tane thee, out of dung,
> So poore, so wretched, when no liuing thing
> Would keepe thee companie, but a spider, or worse?
> Rais'd thee from broomes, and dust, and watring pots?
> *Sublim'd* thee, and *exalted* thee, and *fix'd* thee,
> I' the *third region*, call'd our *state of grace*?[34]

The broom-man or broom-woman (peddlers of cheap household tools) were low on the social ladder. As an impoverished version of the working housewife, the laborer momentarily finds a place within the royal palace in *Dream*, in the figure of a fairy who has given up playing pranks on housewives but who can't completely kick his desire for housewifery. Puck signals the play's overarching interest in those aspects of domesticity – a bourgeois housewifery or menial service class – not completely reducible to aristocratic marital order.

The fairies roughly divide into two social categories: Titania and Oberon derive from the aristocratic world of fairy romance, while Robin Goodfellow evolves from agrarian spirits found in ballad tradition.[35] Yet the two classes of spirits intermix; not only is Puck a dutiful servant to a king, but Titania's fairy attendants incarnate domestic objects. While they protect their queen from evil, they also embody the simples (single ingredients) found in cookbooks and medical guides. Bottom's demystifying narrative about each fairy makes this clear. "If I cut my finger, I shall make bold with you," he tells Cobweb, shrinking the power of the magical sphere to homespun remedies (3.1.183–4). "I promise you your kindred hath made my eyes water ere now" (3.1.194–5), he then tells Master Mustardseed, a substance used, according to *The Englishmans Doctor*, to produce fake tears, "purge the braine," and "[add] unto the stomacke force and heat" although it also threatened good eyesight.[36] If a woman buries an unloved husband, this medical guide offers helpfully, she might find mustardseed just the thing for keeping up civil appearances: "if in shew good manners shee will keepe, / Onyons and Mustardseed will make her weepe" (B6$^r$). From this perspective, the supernatural creatures of the exotic fairy queen devolve into mere mustardseed, peasblossom, cobweb, and moth – the stuff of kitchen gardens, condiments, and homey physic. When Titania orders her minions to gather "apricocks and dewberries, / With purple grapes, green figs, and mulberries" (3.1.166–7), she inventories items commonly purchased at local markets to cure constipation. Gail Paster's reading of Titania's erotic purging of Bottom is instructive, for it makes visible the domestic tenor of their relationship.[37] Though seemingly a mythological foreign space, Titania's bower is shot through with the staples of the contemporary English household and would have smacked of basic home care.[38] The division between dainty fairies and the earthy Bottom is thus complicated by the fact that the ethereal fairies literalize the mundane work of housewives and serving women. The fantasy that fairyland offers is the alternately pleasurable and anxious return to the familiarity of childhood, where a boy may simultaneously submit to a medicating housewife and lord over an exotic, royal realm.

Although Puck sheds his place amid cream bowls to become a player in the crises of courtly fairies and lovers, his tie to domestic work reemerges in the last scene, where he enacts a dignified symbolic sweeping:

> Not a mouse
> Shall disturb this hallowed house.
> I am sent with broom before,
> To sweep the dust behind the door.                    (5.1.387–90)

The mundane task of cleaning resonates allegorically, as fairies create a domestic order that safeguards reproduction. Their specific task in consecrating the bridal chamber is to cleanse newly conceived babies of the "blots of Nature's hand" (5.1.409). Fairies thus function multiply – as a condensation of housewives, servants, and godlike forces – all of whom invisibly cater to the needs of the upper classes. Endowing female labor with holy force, the fairies close the play by integrating housewifery into a comedic social reproduction. Servants (or the "popular" beliefs with which they are aligned) no longer signify domestic disorder but its very opposite.

Although the belief that fairies abducted children was a sixteenth-century invention, fairies in earlier periods were said to "change" infants, meaning that they rendered them deformed or half-witted. Sixteenth-century texts routinely mention charms used to ward off fairies who might steal a mortal child, kidnap a nursing woman, or deform a baby. *Dream* hints at this concern by dramatizing the fairies' quarrel over the mortal Indian changeling. But the play ends by countering the idea that fairies are antagonistic to generation, since they labor to protect the progeny of the newlyweds. *Dream*'s fairies may have sparked its audience to recall the fraught issues of class, gender, and region hovering around fairy discourse – the championing of work, the fear of serving women or housewives, the naughtiness of low knowledges – but the play ends with a cross-gendered housewife named Robin Goodfellow working efficiently in the service of a dynastic civic court. Rescuing fairies from their typically sinister aspects, the play enables spirits to serve as holy caretakers for a social order built on traditional gender and class hierarchies. A pressing concern for the institution of marriage and reproduction is, in all probability, why Theseus changes his mind and allows Hermia to triumph over her father. *Dream* in part recruits fairylore to relax the tie binding the father's domestic control to the monarch's authority. The result is a social world predicated on a newly expanded domesticity that integrates rural tradition with courtly rule and middling-class concerns for work with aristocratic concerns for lineage. But this integration is not seamlessly accomplished. By revealing the palace's faulty housework and the dust it secrets, Robin uncovers the fact that the tidy domestic closure rests on a reproduction as magical and contingent as fairylore. Locating holy practices beneath the notice of aristocrats, Shakespeare makes daily labor the unacknowledged metaphorical basis for social order.

Though critics have found it tempting to categorize the fairies as gossamer beings in contrast to stubbornly earthy artisans,[39] fairylore from the period shows us that they were hardly ethereal. Puck stains an insubstantial world with the traces of domestic effluvia – butter churns, bobbing apples, joint stools, brooms. And the fairies flicker from exotic manifestations into things familiar, local, and native. In one sense, Robin enters *Dream* trailing the anti-elitist residue from his place in the ballad tradition. As a plain country spirit who has no use for social pretensions, *Dream*'s Robin would have been seen as straining against his role as court fool. Domestic fairylore may merely be one folk tradition impressed in the service of monarchical authority by the London theater, but Puck's housewifely gesture at the play's end reminds the audience of his predilection for servants; that is, he registers, at discrete moments, a set of values potentially at one remove from the court. The play's parting suggestion – that fairy housewifery figures social and dramatic harmony – is thus telling, for it acknowledges a discourse in which English social ideals were invested in oral agrarian traditions. Like Puttenham's pretty court mistress who cannot help but repeat her nurse's words, *Dream*'s court festivities are haunted by their perceived tie to a domestic and popular culture – in short, to an anxiously foundational set of old wives' tales. Before they are foreclosed, Puck triggers the audience's worries about the transmission of culture and their shameful delight in viewing a domesticity tied both to *oeconomia* and to Bottom's "childish" enslavement by a surrogate caretaker.

Puck's broom also reminds the audience of his status as a homespun English spirit. Following the imaginative "failure" of the English artisans in their attempt at courtly drama, the fairies import another, more loosely associative English world into the mythological Athenian court. In refiguring popular knowledge, *Dream* shows household work, country living, and true

Englishness to thrive amid a world of foreign traditions. Puck sweeps, it seems, so that the Athenian court can entertain an Englished folk tradition within its bounds, though the court's inability to see its fairy servants suggests a crucial distance between the court's and the play's perspectives. The grandest mythological ruler becomes a version of Bottom, since the artisan's interlude with a dominating exotic herbalist uncovers Theseus' potentially embarrassing reliance on housewives and workers – even in the form of a fairy.

Does Puck's broom also have the priapic meaning so evident in *Robin Goodfellow*? His interest in uniting the Athenian lovers is signaled by his displeasure that they sleep so far apart on the forest floor: "She durst not lie / Near this lack-love, this kill-courtesy," he observes, misinterpreting chaste behavior for sexual rejection (2.2.76–7). If this suggests a sexual interest rather than just a social duty (he is, after all, simply following Oberon's orders), then Puck does faintly register the fairies' traditional immersion in fertility and erotics. Although he himself is somewhat immune from the furious circulation of desire in this play, he orchestrates a set of sinister yet compelling sexual games. In fact, we might see the holy consecration of conjugal relations at the play's end as a necessary compensation for the gross indecencies that the fairies have so thoroughly revealed to the audience: the husband's production of his wife's bestial infidelity, the eroticized maternal desires unleashed in Titania's bower, Puck's salacious interest in his mistress' "hateful fantasies," Bottom's pleasurable sexual bondage. Guided by Puck, Bottom undergoes an eroticized return to childhood, becoming a distorted figure for the audience, who forays into the potentially damaging world of "fairy rubbish" and who is asked to delight in the monstrous and preposterous fantasies that fairies uncover in domestic relations.[40] Engulfed by the nurse and her tales, the audience can experience the fear and pleasure of recovering a familiar reality cast within exoticized trappings. In their tie to perversely unstable desire, infantilization, and dotage, *Dream*'s fairies finally channel the audience's flickering identifications into the order of a palace world propped up by English rustic servants and a middle-class investment in sheer industry.

### The return of the repressed wife

*The Merry Wives of Windsor* works through the contradiction implicit in the incongruous image of a fairy-servant sweeping the court, for it presents faux fairies whose service to the court is simply a ruse orchestrated by pragmatic housewives and citizens. Here the ideology of *oeconomia* that flickers dimly in *Dream* becomes the centerpiece for a play thoroughly immersed in the world of pots and pans. Unlike Puck and his spritely crew, the fairies in *Merry Wives* play a relatively small and belated part in the drama. Yet these fairies significantly emerge as the culmination of the townspeople's domestic and community projects. As illusory projections of the middling sort, these co-gendered fairies extend the merry wives' domestic authority beyond the household into the reach of the court, forest, and myth. Here children posing as spirits rehearse the final court blessing from *Dream* as a hoax designed to establish their fabricated credentials as fairies. Their demystified status, as the real unreal, punctuates the play's interest in the governing power of everydayness, a point to which I will return. While critics have reached opposite conclusions when they look to this scene for evidence of the play's view of monarchy, they tend to agree that the court isn't the determining factor in Windsor's community.[41] Yet the play's climatic fairy performance does offer a salient clue as to how we should read the Windsor citizens' relationship to popular lore, aristocratic status, and English subjecthood.

In the last chapter I argued that *Merry Wives* engages discursive connections among Latin, academia, and domesticity to present a vision of national community founded on the "everyday" language of the home. Since *Merry Wives* lands debates about Latin and education within an explicitly nationalistic terrain structured on proper speaking, Englishness becomes embraided into the play's domestic themes. I revisit *Merry Wives* here with an eye to how its representation of domesticity speaks not only to vernacular nationalism but to the class politics of popular folklore. *Merry Wives*, we might say, introduces fairies who fuse popular myth with the desires of a wealthy village citizenry. While the Windsor fairies extend Puck's casual sweeping into a full-scale cleansing of the royal palace, fairy praise for the court and its esteemed Order of the Garter ritual serves as a mere detour in the drive to purge Falstaff of what is misrecognized as his sexual licentiousness. At the heart of the fairies' disciplining is a story about protecting money and social class as well as correcting the flaw of presumption. Rather than guarding the fertility and status of the aristocracy, as do Oberon and Titania, these fairies dabble with those further down the food chain: they seek to safeguard the property and authority of citizens from encroachment by the upper classes. Thus in *Merry Wives*, Shakespeare returns fairies to a more predictable milieu, showing how a citizenly ethic could assimilate popular myth precisely by foregrounding its domestic components. Commerce, industry, and work pervade the fabric of *Merry Wives*, such that the fairies' regard for housework serves as the culmination, rather than the repressed subtext, of this play. Since citizens enact a project devised by housewives, *Merry Wives* makes the gendered aspect of fairylore congenial to middle-class self-identifications.

In a well-cited study of the play's politics, Peter Erickson suggests that the subversive energies of the wives' control over marital and community relations are contained by conventional class arrangements. Contradictions in gender and in class, he argues, stem from the contradictory authority of Queen Elizabeth, who legitimates female authority only by affirming social hierarchy. Erickson sees this problem as encoded in the folio's final allusion to the Order of the

Garter, the elite chivalric society established by Edward III and used effectively by Queen Elizabeth.[42] In his analysis, the play finally erodes the wives' authority by reinscribing it within the terms of the court. Wives can be merry and powerful only when they invest their chaste power in the iconography of the Queen. While Erickson argues that this middle-class investment in aristocratic ideology belies male anxiety about a female-centered court, it nevertheless makes monarchy the ground of all meaning. Reading the local and national politics of the play, Richard Helgerson supports Erickson's argument by detailing ways in which a highly local early modern domesticity is relentlessly produced in the play as the object of national and aristocratic appropriation.[43]

In my view, however, the play's representation of domesticity and fairylore undermines the endorsement that Erickson and Helgerson describe.[44] Instead of an unhampered celebration of the court, the folio's final fairy scene – which is campy, stylized, and clearly over the top – parodies courtly values. Rather than limiting the power of citizen housewives, this scene shows that housewives and castigating fairies provide the generative grammar enabling the Windsor community's consolidation. In foregrounding faultlines between aristocracy and citizen and between Englishman and foreigner, *Merry Wives* mystifies gradations of status (e.g., collapsing the differing interests of yeoman, townsperson, local and national justices, wage servants). Yet it clearly unsettles any assimilation of popular folklore within a court-centered national mythology.[45] For while the village rejuvenates itself as a merry old England by using everyday practice to patrol linguistic, social, and sexual improprieties, the England it produces is not one defined within the province of the court.[46] Even in the more urban-oriented quarto version of the play, which Leah Marcus has argued persuasively to be a credible and separate variant, a fairylore attached to housewifery ends up underpinning the ideology of citizens in Windsor – or elsewhere.[47]

### Cleaning house in Windsor

In the final scene of the folio *Merry Wives*, Pistol, disguised as a hobgoblin, introduces the puckish spirits who will torture Falstaff for his attempted seduction of Mrs. Page and Mrs. Ford:

> Elves, list your names; silence, you aery toys!
> Cricket, to Windsor chimneys shalt thou leap;
> Where fires thou find'st unrak'd and hearths unswept,
> There pinch the maids as blue as bilberry;
> Our radiant Queen hates sluts and sluttery.          (5.5.42–46)

In this version the debauched knight and slovenly housekeepers are mutually defined in opposition to the stainless chastity of the radiant Elizabeth. By convening fairies to reprimand bad housekeeping and to maintain the hearth, Pistol equates domestic supervision with the sexual management exemplified by the head of state: both reprove "sluttery." And, as Hugh Evans' subsequent instructions make clear, the fairies are sent to oversee moral conduct as well as labor:

> Go you, and where you find a maid
> That ere she sleep has thrice her prayers said,
> Raise up the organs of her fantasy,
> Sleep she as sound as careless infancy;
> But those as sleep and think not on their sins,
> Pinch them, arms, legs, backs, shoulders, sides and shins.          (5.5.49–54)

Although negligent maids are unsurprisingly bruised, pious workers are oddly rewarded with pleasing fantasies that return them to infancy. While a serving maid's excellence in housewifery marks moral innocence, her reward for self-discipline seems to smack of sexual pleasure, the erection of her "organs" of "fantasy." The fairies' nocturnal delights, seen so clearly in *Robin-Goodfellow*, seem strangely out of place in this play, since the performance of popular ritual is designed precisely to banish Falstaff's overweening fantasy. Windsor's expulsion of "lust and luxury," a scapegoating ritual that Jeanne Addison Roberts sees as reenacting ancient seasonal folk rituals and Marcus sees as mimicking the charivari shaming rituals of early modern Europe, becomes a task *performed* as fairy-housewifery (5.5.94). Since Falstaff is made to play the part of the wayward court maid subject to the castigation of housewife and Queen, *Merry Wives* uses popular tradition to analogize community, household, and court.[48]

But the fairies are, of course, putting on an elaborate act for Falstaff, conjuring up a counterfeit supernatural world in order to strike fear into his heart. Falstaff's belief – "They *are* fairies," he exclaims – is the stuff of farce, amplified by his ridiculous headdress of horns and his pathetic daydreams about bestial orgies (5.5.47, emphasis added). Dreaming of aphrodisiacs falling from the heavens, Falstaff cuts a ridiculous figure fully in tune with the fairies' chant about the maid's fantasizing organs. Connecting the fairies' ethical housekeeping with the Queen's chastity is quite evidently a fiction designed to gull someone foolish enough to misread thrifty wives for unchaste ones. Falstaff's actual punishment lies at the hands of a community empowered by women who don't mind engineering a masquerade Fairy Queen.

In the 1602 quarto, Pistol is not present to steer the elves to Windsor. Instead, Parson Evans directs the fairies to commercial as well as rural locations:

> go to the countrie houses,
> And when you finde a slut that lies a sleepe,
> And all her disches foule, and rooms unswept,

With your long nailes pinche her till she crie

. . .

       go you & see where Brokers sleep,
And Foxe-eyed Seriants with their mase,
Goe laie the Proctors in the street,
And pinch the lowsie Seriants face.[49]

Instead of serving a luminous queen who guards the chaste industry of maids, these elves move between countryside and town. "The folio version of *Merry Wives* is a comedy of small-town and rural life, steeped in rustic customs and topography, but also imbued with the 'high' presence of the royal court," Marcus writes; "the quarto version is 'lower,' more urban, close to the pattern of city or 'citizen' comedy" (*Unediting*, 88). Yet even in a commercial environment, fairies are still galvanized to action by the thought of "lowsie" household servants. Fairy interest in domestic management pervades both topographies.

In the folio, Mistress Quickly's role as faux fairy queen extends her role as Shakespeare's most notorious housekeeper and highlights the domestic aspect of popular lore. "[T]here dwells one Mistress Quickly," says Evans of Dr. Caius's house, "which is in the manner of his nurse – or his dry nurse – or his cook – or his laundry – his washer and wringer" (1.2.3–5). Quickly's self-description two scenes later refuses her translation into "laundry" and shows herself cognizant of domestic hierarchy: "I may call him my master, look you," she declares of Caius, "for I keep his house; and I wash, wring, brew, bake, scour, dress meat and drink, make the beds and do all myself" (1.4.94–7). Having been introduced so emphatically as a servant, housekeeper, and nurse, Quickly makes the stylized purgation of sin evident in the Garter motto, "Honi soit qui mal y pense" ("evil to him who evil thinks"), into a purification ritual emanating out of her work. "The several chairs of order look you scour / With juice of balm and every precious flow'r," the folio Quickly commands her fairy helpers (5.5.61–2).

It isn't just through laundering that domesticity makes an appearance in supernatural ritual, for fairies "scour" stalls by labeling them with flower juice. Macbeth's plea for advice from the doctor provides a gloss for this word, for it tellingly links national cleansing with bodily purgation: "What rhubarb, cyme, or what purgative drug, / Would scour these English hence?" (5.3.55–6). Using "flow'rs for their charactery," the fairies marshal the herbal knowledge that every good housewife was enjoined to master (a component part of tending kitchen gardens, physic, and distilling). Collapsing cleaning and healing, Quickly's spirits continue the activities of the two merry wives, who have spent much of the play attempting to repel Falstaff's sexual advances by transmutating him into the objects of housewifery. Described as a barely congealed liquid mass of desires subject to dissolution, Falstaff attempts to frame his "old body" as the gross means to a much needed end (2.2.139), yet the play deflates his bodily pretensions by making him into manageable domestic goods: gross fat puddings (2.1.32), whale oil used for candle wax (2.1.65), and cooking grease (2.1.68). The wives' attempts to purge him of lust consolidates their role as cooks, home doctors, and housecleaners.[50] Or, rather, the depiction of moral ordering never strays too far from that of domestic labor. "I think the best way [for revenge] were to entertain him with hope, till the wicked fire of lust have melted him in his own grease," Mrs. Ford declares (2.1.66–8). Undertaking Falstaff's reformation, the wives move between figurative and literal acts of purgation, with the result that the household swells to define the ethics and boundaries of the community. Is it any wonder that the chastising fairies later appear specifically as house-cleaners?

### The buck(ing) never stops here

If *The Merry Wives of Windsor* can be said to "dilate," in Patricia Parker's terms, on a set of puns that discursively frame its meaning, the fairies provide the terminal point for a central discursive tissue emanating from the word "buck."[51] When caught with Falstaff in her home, Mrs. Ford sneaks him past the search party organized by her husband by hiding him in a buck basket, a tub for soiled laundry on its way to be bucked or bleached. Her husband's blind curiosity about this large, greasy object inspires an odd, somewhat hysterical meditation: "Buck! I would I could wash myself of the buck! Buck, buck, buck! ay, buck! I warrant you, buck, and of the season too, it shall appear" (3.3.157–9). Obsessing on the word "buck" and airing the family's (or rather his own) dirty laundry to his acquaintances, Ford converts soiled wash into the male horned deer that figures both his sexual vulnerability *and* his overly lusty rival. His rage manifests itself as a jealous pun marking his inability to see the obvious: the intruder is *in* the buckbasket. Instead his fixation on the plight of bucks leads him to free-associate on washing the household's sexual threat, identifying Falstaff as a rutting beast and imagining the shape of his own cuckold's horns. It's standard for sexual pathologies in the period to turn on images of deer – "I'll be horn-mad" Ford cries (3.5.152) and he fantasizes Page as a "secure and willful Actaeon" (3.2.43) — but it is highly unusual for domestic labor, in the form of "bucking," to dominate this semiotic network. As Ford later says in disgust later when he imagines his wife's infidelity: "This 'tis to be married! This 'tis to have linen and buckbaskets" (3.5.142–3). Is this pun perhaps what Gervase Markham had in mind when he interjected the unusually animated phrase "drive that buck!" into instructions for washing hemp?[52]

What Ford has to renounce is precisely a single-minded obsession with domestic space and objects as sites of sexual pollution. Dreaming of monsters sequestered in his house, he takes to such an extent the role of "good husband" – someone who was to oversee the ordering of material resources – that he threatens the credit and resources of the family. Going so far as to relinquish possession of his household keys (objects as treasured as a modern police officer's weapon[53]), Ford seems even to his friends to display "fantastical humors and jealousies" (3.3.170–71).[54] When Falstaff, trapped in the Ford house, suggests an escape by creeping up the "kill-hole," Mrs. Ford explains that her husband knows all household recesses by heart: "He will seek there, on my word. Neither press, coffer, chest, trunk, well, vault, but he hath an abstract for the remembrance of such places, and goes to them by his note. There is no hiding you in the house" (4.2.60–4). Long before Falstaff appeared on the scene as a would-be seducer, Mr. Ford apparently acted on this "abstract" by habitually searching his own house. Inventorying the space "by his note," Ford takes stock of his luxurious furniture – chimney, press, coffer, and vault – only by imagining them as defiled. His attempt to patrol the home's purity in fact leads him to produce its tainting. Testing his wife's honesty by asking Falstaff to seduce her, he complains, "She dwells so securely on the excellency of her honor,"

that the folly of my soul dares not present itself; she is too bright to be look'd against. Now, could I come to her with any detection in my hand, my desires had instance and argument to commend themselves. I could drive her then from the ward of her purity, her reputation, her marriage-vow, and a thousand other her defenses, which now are too too strongly embattled against me.                    (2.2.242–51)

In other words, he needs to dig up dirt on Mrs. Ford to give him leverage in overturning her marriage vows. Ford's pretense belies a truth: although he devises this plan when impersonating Master Brooke, he does hope to tarnish his wife's reputation and confirm his humiliating status as a cuckold. Touching on the discourse of dirt and redemptive cleansing evident throughout the play, Ford becomes an anti-housecleaner who hopes to "drive [his wife] from the ward of her purity" and make her shine less "bright." Mrs. Page later acknowledges Ford's twisted ambitions when she encourages Mrs. Ford to "scrape the figures out of your husband's brains" (4.2.216). Scraping dirt out of an impure imagination involves showing Ford that he has overattended to the household in a way that has ruptured his husbandly responsibilities.

In Ford's paranoia driven by self-loathing, desire oddly takes definition in its routing through the interiors of cupboards, furniture, and chests. It is appropriate that the folio text creates a punning joke by having Ford assume the alias "Master Broome" rather than the quarto "Brooke." If editors did not choose the "bad" quarto's "Brooke" over the more editorially respected folio, readers would hear Falstaff declare his allegiance to a household utensil.[55] Puck's broom, linked to the squalid broomsman or menial service, surfaces as Ford's domestic alias. His self-transformation into a household object shows less a general anxiety about emasculation at the hands of women, I would argue, and more a desperate concern over the power of household materiality. Hoping to sully his wife's purity, the broomlike Ford is ironically draped in an ensuing scene with soiled laundry and found crying: "Behold what honest clothes you send forth to bleaching" (4.2.120–1). Deliriously looking to torn clothing and laundry tubs for evidence of his domestic losses, Ford displays a perverse fantasy of wastefulness that sets up the play's prominent dream of domestic recovery.

Ford is not the only character to experience domesticity as a threat. Having been buttered with "greasy napkins" and carried "like a barrow of butcher's offal" (3.5.5) Falstaff describes his dunking in the buckbasket in oddly domestic terms:

I suffer'd the pangs of three several deaths: first, an intolerable fright, to be detected with a jealous rotten bell-wether; next, to be compass'd like a good bilbo in the circumference of a peck, hilt to point, heel to head; and then to be stopp'd in like a strong distillation with stinking clothes that fretted in their own grease. Think of that – a man of my kidney. Think of that – that am as subject to heat as butter; a man of continual dissolution and thaw. It was a miracle to scape suffocation. And in the height of this bath (when I was more than half stew'd in grease like a Dutch dish) to be thrown into the Thames, and cool'd, glowing-hot, in that surge, like a horseshoe; think of that – hissing hot – think of that Master [Brook]!                                                                                                    (3.5.107–22)

In Falstaff's imaginative universe the buckbasket mutates into a limbeck, a dairy cask, a bathtub, and cookpot, all offering brands of kitchen torture. His mind first converts laundering to distilling, another purifying household activity. A 1631 play called *Rhodon and Iris* defined an artful housewife simply by saying: "With limbecks, viols, pots, her Closet's fill'd / Full of strange liquors by rare art distilled."[56] Wielding this equipment, the housewife refined waters, extracted oils from herbs and flowers, and concocted medicines, alcoholic beverages, sweeteners, pain relievers, and perfumes. "[D]istil your water in a Stillitorie, then put it in a faire glasse, and take the buddes of Roses . . . and put the leaues into the stilled water," advises John Partridge in *The Treasurie of Hidden Secrets*; and Thomas Dawson tells the housewife how to stuff a whole young chicken "well fleshed and not fat" into an earthen distilling jar after hacking at its bones.[57] In a pre-Cartesian Galenic world, where the psychological and the material had not yet divided, it isn't surprising that Falstaff's sexual humiliation and fear of castration (becoming a "bell-wether") could register as corporeal liquefaction or that these emotions could find a material correlate in the processes by which the body was routinely tended. The degree to which he attaches destruction to domesticity does, however, signal his affinity with Ford, as he unwittingly notes: "I have had ford enough. I was thrown into the ford" (3.5.35–6). He experiences his purgative baptismal bath as threatening his very constitution or "kidney."

Falstaff's worry about being heated, stewed, and cooled stems from the period's belief that the humoral body churned unpredictably in a state of disequilibrium and required an almost daily regimen of diets, purges, vomits, sweatings, and enemas. An Elizabethan audience would have understood Falstaff's profound fright at being thrown "hissing hot" into the cool Thames, just as they would have seen the interconnection between this purgative treatment (much like a sweating tub) and his venal appetites.[58] As Paster's work demonstrates, affective relations in the early modern period were shaped by the child's bodily dependence on female healers and caregivers. "The repeated bodily phenomenon of the purge," Paster writes, "perhaps calling up unpleasant early memories of... physical subjection, perhaps calling up pleasurable memories of genital/anal stimulation ... helped to constitute normative forms of bodily self-experience."[59] This may explain the sentiment fueling John Cotta's 1612 attack on female medical practitioners, whose deceptively simple staples of milk, broth, and butter were said to mask hidden dangers. In a stunning theological interpretation, Cotta compares the housewife to Eve, whose offering of the apple was the first pharmacological seduction.[60] And maybe this helps to account as well for John Johnson's 1641 *Academy of Love* which depicts men's willing submission to the erotic manipulations of wildly beautiful female purgers, who perform vomits, glisters, and bloodletting as part of courtship ritual. "Prepare my Bath," commands a character in Shirley's 1640 *Humourous Courtier*, "Ile distill and grow amorous."[61] Although meant to purify lust, Falstaff's "bath" is read by him as part and parcel of the discursive tissue binding eros to control and to bodily care. The fantasy of Bottom's erotic encounter in Titania's purgative fairy bower is replayed in this plot through the register of alarm. Yet the controlling forces are not courtly fairies and patriarchal dukes eager to reinstate domestic hierarchy but housewives whose authority in the domus is only credited by the spectacle of male panic.

Describing his symbolic castration (his "crest-fall'n" and dried Fall-staff) as a transformation into the stuff of bootmaking, laundry, and preserving (drying pears), Falstaff imagines the court laughing at him in terms that obsessively repeat acts of housewifery. "If it should come to the ear of the court, how I have been transform'd, and how my transformation hath been *wash'd* and cudgell'd," Falstaff worries, "they would melt me out of my fat drop by drop, and liquor fishermen's boots with me. I warrant they would whip me with their fine wits till I were as crest-fall'n as a dried pear" (4.5.94–100, emphasis added). He feels compelled, that is, to reproduce endlessly an earlier loss of status, money, and land, now interiorized as court gossip and shaped to reflect his liquefying romp in the buckbasket. That Ford's desire to "wash himself of the buck" and Falstaff's claustrophobic buckwashing both betray erotic investments suggests more than the axiom that disgust bears the imprint of desire; it indicates ways in which early modern domesticity profoundly stamped registers of emotion and ways of articulating status. Purgation and purification, as spiritual processes, freely commingled discursively in literature of the period with their more mundane physical incarnations – as bleaching, humoral balancing, distilling.

*Merry Wives* ends up suggesting that male characters have simply perverted an *authentic* middle-class belief in the interrelationship of work and social life; for the play rescues housewifery as key to community formation.[62] Unlike *Dream* where Theseus and Oberon must regain domestic control in order to stabilize the community, Ford and Falstaff learn, through the grammar of domesticity, to cede authority. As its title may lead us to predict, the play offers a female fantasy in which household labor insures pleasure, profit, and social order. "I know not which pleases me better," declares Mistress Ford, "that my husband is deceiv'd, or Sir John" (3.3.178–9). The wife's artful pleasure, emanating from her domestic responsibilities, founds the play's final presentation of social order. For while Falstaff sees his body as put in harm's way by mischance, the wives offer a diagnosis that the play as a whole endorses: Falstaff's excessive heat and moisture make necessary the wives' kitchen physic. "We'll use this unwholesome humidity," says Mrs. Ford, "this gross wat'ry pumpion" (3.3.40–41). Mrs. Page appropriately identifies a curative: "[W]e will yet have more tricks with Falstaff. His dissolute disease will scarce obey this medicine" (3.3.190–92). Alternately presented as negligent maid, gadding "aunt" (the emblem, in Renaissance misogynist stereotypes, of mutability and poor self-control), and unruly object (e.g., a "gallimaufry" or "hodge-pudding"), Falstaff is thoroughly implicated in signifiers of domestic and bodily disorder. Posing as a lusty buck, Falstaff becomes the mere stuff of buckbaskets, putty in the hands of housewives.

In its discursive and thematic interest in bucking, the play implicitly offers a defense of laundering. Such a move was necessary because the early modern laundress was a target of social condescension, often labeled as a prostitute and associated metonymically with the dirt she was charged to expel. Both laundresses and wanton women "took up linen" or stripped gentlemen of clothes.[63] Thus a character book entitled *The Whimzies* bawdily puns when describing the laundress' morning access to gentlemen's bedchambers: "Her *young masters*, whom shee serves with all diligence, neede no Cocke but her: shee'll come to their Chambers, and wake them early; and if they have the *Spirit* to *rise*, may at their pleasure use her help to make them ready."[64] Privy to the family secrets marked on clothing and sheets, and mocked for her compromised physical posture in wading into streams and bending over to beat clothes, the laundress was the object of derision and awe: "Shee must not tell what she sees," warns *The Whimzies* (85). Ford's frightened gaze at laundry may be directed toward his wife's behavior, but, in suggesting that only the paranoid and foolish are overly concerned with laundry, the play undoes a widespread stereotype. Is it any wonder, then, that the buckbasket appears conspicuously, in a play that intensifies *Merry Wives*' themes, as a "cage" in which a Dutch suitor named Vandall is muffled, imprisoned, and symbolically castrated by three women?[65]

John Taylor's 1630 "In praise of clean linen. With the commendable use of the Laundress" similarly reverses the laundress' figurative association with dirt by praising her spotless chastity and capacity for effecting redemption. "I am strucke into admiration," he says in a preface,

at the undaunted valour, that champion-like doth accompany and constantly defend your chastitie; For you dare in a morning to enter a Gentlemans chamber, to strippe him out of his foule shirt in his bed, to have him at your bare and naked mercy, and then like a vertuous victor, in pittie and commiseration, you put a cleane shirt on his backe, leauing him in a clearere and farre sweeter case then you found him; no doubt but such objects are prouacatory temptations to fraile flesh and bloud: but as I said before, your courage and constancie alwaies brings you fairely off and on, though thousands weaker vessels of mortalitie would bee crak'd.[66]

In his text, the laundress' proximity to the "prouacatory temptations" of men's bedchambers only proves her moral fiber. Exposing naked vulnerability, she righteously strips the flesh of its stain and keeps at bay the soiled linen she handles. Dedicating his work to "the most Mondifying, Clarifying, Purifying, and Repurifying, cleanser, Clearer, and Reformer of deformed and polluted Linnen, *Martha Legge* ... Snow-Lilly white Laundresse to the Right worshipfull and generous the Innes of Court," Taylor conflates moral and literal cleansing, with only a hint of the scandal that trails this figure.[67]

The affluent merry wives in Windsor are hardly laundresses. Nevertheless, domestic guides emphasize that the average housewife was expected to oversee the washing of clothes, handwash expensive satins, points, taffeta, lawns and silk stockings, make soaps, and starch special linens. One book offers an antidote to grease spots that reveals the somewhat gory labor necessary in creating detergents: "Take the bones of sheep's feet," the text instructs, "burn them almost to ashes, then bruise them to powder and put it upon your spots, and lay all before the sun when it shines the hottest."[68] In *The English House-wife* Markham gives detailed instructions for "bucking" yarn with strong lye, and his recipes for "washing balls" call for storax (a tree resin), calamus aromaticus (a root), ladanum (a gum), and herbs such as cloves, nutmeg, mace, and saffron (150). "Washing balls" helped not only to perfume fabrics and remove dirt, but also to clear the air of bad vapors that could cause disease. Cleaning and medical care merge in these tasks, showing that customary duties took the housewife into the laundress' territory. As Quickly and the wives safeguard the community, *Merry Wives* elevates washing to a social enterprise akin to the skimmington ritual, in which the community would "dunk" an adulterer, female scold, or husband-beater in a local pond. Falstaff's immersion in Datchet Mead shows that the world can be made safe by a sound bucking controlled by industrious citizens' wives, though fears of the dominating housewife or servant haunt the scene of moral redemption. Falstaff's and Ford's compulsive dread about linens has to do with the domestic worker's command within a newly valued domus, an authority mainly legible in this play as control over sexuality.[69] In the readily identifiable sexual politics of Merry Wives, then, are found traces of household materiality in the grammar structuring social identifications.

Is it surprising that the folio ends this prolonged domestic meditation with a fairy blessing of the Windsor court? That fairies mark the collapse of the vulgar laundress and magisterial monarch? In part, fairies import and tailor the populist aspects of fairy behavior to the enterprise of mocking the aristocrat, for Falstaff's naive belief in fairies overturns the common gesture in which "low" culture is defined by unenlightened superstition. Locating myth in the hands of the citizenry, the play presents fairylore as the endpoint of its extended exploration of domesticity as a foundational discourse for individual experience and social relations. Falstaff thus appropriately emerges dressed as the buck that Ford glimpsed in the laundry, one who can't keep his mind off bodily fat and household candles. Adorned in horns as Herne the Hunter, Falstaff goes into his romantic rendezvous calling for a purgation: "I am here a Windsor stag, and the fattest, I think, i' th' forest. Send me a cool rut-time, Jove, or who can blame me to piss my tallow?" (5.5.12–15).[70] He then lustily imagines a cross-species orgy: "Divide me like a brib'd buck, each a haunch" (5.5.24).[71] Having fairy citizens mortify Falstaff's abundant "waste," the play puns once again on "buck" – in its meaning as a large belly – here dieted in a fitness program of thrift. With Falstaff substituting for a legendary slutty maid, his wastefulness is reproved by Mrs. Page's plan to bring on the fairies. Falstaff's redemption is thus renarrated within popular myth, as the housewife materializes the "old tale" (4.4.28) of Herne the Hunter, urchins, ouphs, and fairies. The wives argue that staging a vernacular tale allows them to punish Falstaff, eke out a public confession, and "dis-horn the spirit" (4.4.63). Gathering "properties" (4.4.78), purchasing vizards, and rehearsing parts, the entire community busies itself with the work of producing the spectacle of fairies.

When the housekeeper-fairy queen grandly hails her minions as the "orphan heirs of fixed destiny" (5.5.39) the ceremonial language of moral-domestic redemption begins. Falstaff falls prostrate on the ground, submits to the torture of pinching and burning, and then is ridiculed by citizens. But the talk still is of buckwashing and bucks: Mrs. Ford lovingly calls Falstaff her "deer," Ford teases Falstaff about laundry, and Falstaff likens all gulled people to deer. Opening with charges of deer-stealing, a crisis deferred by eating "hot venison pasty," Merry Wives circles back to the discourse of bucking in its final moments as way of registering a potentially emasculating domesticity that can be circumscribed within the fantasy of a socially empowering housewifery.[72] Fairies thus complete a fully domestic scouring, as they labor to "pinch the unclean knight."

The baton of domesticity has been handed from paid housekeeper to indignant housewives to co-gendered punitive fairies whose domestic interests now define their character and function.

While the fairies of popular lore serve the purposes of folio citizens, those townspeople are somewhat thwarted in their attempt to ward off the aristocracy; for Anne Page and the aristocrat Fenton use the cover of the night's havoc to gull the Pages. The scope of domestic disorder widens in this scene, as the conflict between genders and classes disappears momentarily in the wake of a generational struggle, and as courtship uncovers the specter of two same-sex marriages brought about by fairy disguises. Both Dr. Caius and Slender steal away a figure whom they believe to be Anne Page only to find themselves with a boy-fairy in tow. The scene thus produces "changelings" of another kind, as the fairy daughter mutates into multiple wayward boys. The daughter's disobedience qualifies the housewives' power in dictating the shape of the community. Folio citizens are bested by a courtier, while the quarto Fenton remains a hometown boy. Either way, the play ends by qualifying the power of housewifery to govern the meaning and use of popular ritual. Positioning Falstaff properly in the social landscape, the fairy pageant pressures parental authority in the Page household and ignites a set of problems not contained by tropes of purification. Dr. Caius has married a boy, and the reproduction of citizens lies with the whims of Anne Page, the only woman in the play not linked to *oeconomia*. While fairies reassuringly bless babies in *Dream*, *Merry Wives'* spirits suggest that reproduction and the property transfer it insures can only be tenuously controlled; that is, the popular ritual it so clearly ties to the fantasies of the middling sort can be made to serve many ends.

In dramatizing an old wives' tale, *Merry Wives* points to the widespread conjunction of female labor, vernacular speech, and popular lore evident in fairy legend, for the play reintegrates Falstaff and Ford into a community founded on right English speaking. The national contours of the community, clearly established by reference to the English tongue and the pointed exclusion of foreigners, are consolidated by having native fairies and English lore affirm citizens' values.[73] As a self-consciously English comedy, *Merry Wives* inflects locale, ritual, and speech with nationalist sentiment. In seeing the drama as a mimetic reproduction of experience, some critics take their cue from the play's construction of Englishness: "There is no play of Shakespeare's which draws so unmistakably on his own experience of English life as this," Felix Schelling argues, "and the dramatist's real source here is indubitably the life of the Elizabethan."[74] Presenting our only comedic access to a locale much like the bard's own Stratford, this play is unsurprisingly required to be mimetic and truly English.[75] The homey atmosphere of English life is conveyed by a return to the housewife's reassuring if alienating domain and by the recoding of popular lore as socially useful for a middle class eager to claim the nation.

No more true than Italianate comedies, of course, *Merry Wives* suggests the audience's (and, apparently, critics' and editors') domestic experience.[76]

Turning away from their predecessors' appreciation of the play's neoclassical unities of time and place, nineteenth-century scholars celebrated *Merry Wives'* folklore as part of the myth of merry old England. A product of the late eighteenth and early nineteenth centuries, folklore was fueled by the project of recovering and preserving indigenous traditions often at a remove from institutional learning. Assuming that they could recover an unchanging oral culture of the "folk," scholars reacted in part against the enlightenment in concord with the nationalist European movements of the nineteenth century.[77] In England, *Merry Wives'* fairies validated the portrayal of a quaint old England characterized by a whimsical queen, pastoral bliss, and mirthful citizens. What was, in fact, part of the play's inscription of popular fairylore within middle-class domesticity became readable later as the bard's immersion in a national lore surely connected to the meads of Stratford. Yet folio references to the court can't obscure the play's mockery of one aspect of the myth of Merry old England that Marcus describes: "a timeless vision of court and countryside in harmonious alliance, of simple rural folk and their superiors, nay even the queen herself, as working reciprocally for mutual prosperity and betterment."[78] Indeed in *Merry Wives* Shakespeare parodies the assimilation of popular forms and courtly lineage seen in *Dream*. As a garrulous laundress directs native fairies to sing chants about the Virgin Queen, the play may be said to produce an "Englishness of everyday life" – one that nominates the values of the emergent middle class as the foundational world for which everyone supposedly yearns. Elite citizens, whether in the quarto town or the folio Windsor, use the popular discourse of country value to position Englishness as the preserve of townspeople.

The play's "mimetic effect" in part explains why fairies must be unmasked as mere mortals. *Dream*'s pastoral magic both allowed for the gentrification of popular ritual and broadcasted the elite humanist male fantasy of returning to domesticity. By having fairies appear as the culmination of the citizens' attempts to protect hearth and well-furnished homes, *Merry Wives* casts a skeptical eye on the imaginative license of pastoral fantasy and instead locates fairylore in a more workaday domestic domain. Without chalking up their "unreality" to the inherent mimeticism of citizen drama, I would argue that the Windsor fairies' explicitly theatrical status reveals the play's interest in the process of producing popular culture. The ideological configuration of court, polis, and fairy world is thus effected in these plays differently: for the homage paid to the court as a fairy blessing turns so evidently into a class-motivated fantasy. If Titania and Oberon immerse the audience in the pleasurable return to the childhood household, *Merry Wives* presents a domestic-national ideology in which housewifery never has to be renounced at all. Indeed domesticity – including sweeping and laundering – remains the cornerstone of community;

and Ford's and Falstaff's misguided anxieties about its influence are mocked as flaws of character. Rather than marking a deliciously transgressive place within the elite imagination, the Windsor town fairies materialize out of the fabric of household life and, as such, they conspicuously challenge aristocratic claims to popular lore. What we have seen is that this materialization turns squarely on the ideological work of fantasy. Airing the affect surrounding domestic work, *Merry Wives* suggests that those who acknowledge domestic paranoia and pleasure are most fit to receive the compensatory bonds of national culture built on shared speech, *oeconomia*, and the everyday. National sentiment, that is, emerges out of a self-knowledge marked as familiar and estranging.

Taken together, these two Shakespeare plays reveal divergent ways in which the class-specific elements of fairylore could be taken to represent household and national relations. In the process, both plays expose the potential uncanniness of domesticity, the fantastical quality of everydayness that made submission to household tasks a precarious but formative activity. During a period when the household was seen as modeling and providing the training ground for political order, such an experiment had potentially important implications. Why would fairies be the logical finale for a plot about housewives and laundry? Why does Puck sweep? Thematically tied to a powerful popular lore, his broom, like the Fords' buckbasket, stubbornly recalls the material grounding for household relations as well as their vexed but critical place in the cultural imagination.

# 4 The erotics of milk and live food, or, ingesting early modern Englishness

"But ah, desire still cries: 'Give me some food.'" After devoting thirteen lines to the joys of Platonic love, Astrophel closes this sonnet by admitting the hunger of passion.[1] His plea may be said to replace one convention with another; for food and desire often merge in Western aesthetics. From Greco-Roman banquet literature to modern feast-based films, texts have lovingly unfolded the rich symbolic universe surrounding culinary pleasure. But how are we to understand a scene in which a prince's appetitive nature is awakened at the sight of a woman making, rather than eating, cheese? Or one in which a worker rhapsodizes about his exhilarating freedom by imagining live food marching in the streets? In such moments, the details of food production seem to puncture the familiar sensual expansiveness found in common fantasies about eating.

In many early modern English guides and plays, images of domestic labor are readily recognizable to modern readers – as chores performed in the interior of a home and managed by the household mistress. In taking up the question of how a specifically early modern view of domesticity becomes significant to class and regional conceptions of Englishness, this chapter analyzes two plays whose representations of domesticity fail to fit this model. Robert Greene's 1589 *Friar Bacon and Friar Bungay* explores a prince's inappropriate desire for a milkmaid, a desire that I track within the elite childraising practices complicating the boundaries of family. Thomas Dekker's 1599 *The Shoemaker's Holiday* invites its audience to see the combined urban household and shop as constituting a domestic space co-extensive with the national economy, one in which fantasies about unfettered eating mark a particular kind of civic desire. Neither play allows us to reduce domesticity to "family" issues (in our modern use of the term). Instead these plays suggest the figurative and symbolic possibilities for the "family production unit" on the London stage. Light-hearted and festive in their tenor, these comedies have sometimes been dismissed as mere flights of fancy, but it is precisely their immersion in fantasies of work that I find compelling.

It is no coincidence that both plays end with a grand banquet. Not simply a dramatic device used to symbolize a regenerative comic world, these concluding feasts help to resolve the class stresses that have been expressed, in part, by reference to edible foodstuffs and the relations established by food exchange. Situated in pastoral and academic environments seemingly phobic about consumerism, *Friar Bacon* demonstrates how household work resonated in the upper-class male imagination and how fantasies of housewifery might expose contradictions in theories of elite manhood. *Shoemaker's Holiday*, on the other hand, uses the household-based urban shop to present a middling-class utopian civic fantasy in which the needs of the nation can be satisfied by domestic production broadly defined, one in which plenty is produced by a housework not controlled by women or the crown. Both plays point, in different ways, to domesticity's role in forging collective identifications, and both locate food in the terrain of a spectacular national mythology.

Culinary taste was often imagined to derive from nationality. In his *Description of England*, William Harrison conventionally explains diet by geography:

The situation of our region, lying near unto the north, doth cause the heat of our stomachs to be of somewhat greater force; therefore our bodies do crave a little more ample nourishment than the inhabitants of the hotter regions are accustomed withal, whose digestive force is not altogether so vehement, because their internal heat is not so strong as ours, which is kept in by the coldness of air.[2]

Assuming a humoral body whose porosity made it susceptible to vicissitudes in air, climate, and temperature, Harrison suggests that location determines a national (or regional) pattern of digestion and appetite. Diet is understood in thermal terms, as cold air insulates the digestive "force" within the English body and shapes its appetites.[3] Harrison's account is predicated on the "climate theory," which had been debated by Aristotle, Hippocrates, and Galen, and revived in Europe with the 1579 publication of Jean Bodin's *Methodus*. In this theory, the continent divides into three zones, each determining its inhabitants' physical appearance, character, and temperament. Medical writers explained digestion and taste by classifying foods in terms of their ability to generate heat. In *The Good Housewife Made a Doctor*, Thomas Tryon articulates a holistic healthcare predicated on the dangers of foreign diet. "There is scarce any one thing so much destroys and hurts our Health, both of Body and Mind, as the eating and drinking *Foreign Ingredients* with and amongst our common Food," he warns.[4] Declaiming against imported fruits, sugar, and spices, Tryon attempts to "return" the humoral body to "fit" its native English soil. Food, diet, and national constitution are, in these discourses, thoroughly intertwined; and the salvation of the English body rests with the food provider.

We have already glimpsed Markham's attempt to create a corpus of authentically English guides that express the "true manner and nature of our right English Husbandry."[5] As he saturates the market with guidebooks linking food production, taste, and temperament, Markham chiefly locates English indigenous practices in the countryside. Yet even cookbooks catering to cosmopolitan readers sometimes authorize rustic practices. *The Good Huswifes Handmaide for the Kitchin*, for instance, recommends expensive foodstuffs necessary for banqueting, but it also assumes that readers would want to know how "To make clowted Cream after Mistres Horsmans way."[6] Being able to impress people with the novelty and cost of her desserts apparently doesn't erase the housewife's need to know tried and true rural practice, to be able, that is, to impersonate "Mistres Horsman" and her frugal ways while marking her financial difference from her. In guides directed to upwardly mobile readers, Plat also doesn't mind confessing his admiration for old-fashioned country cheeses.[7] And *The Closet of Sir Kenelme Digby Opened* assumes that elite ladies will take interest in the details of milking cows. National fantasies invested in particular female domestic skills pervade advice literature of the period.

Yet when London plays weave culinary themes into plots about courtship and social ambition, they often highlight *internal* English differences of opinion about cuisine that are then only indirectly linked to claims to national identity. Less interested in the national determination of taste, these plays examine ways in which populations assess food production and consumption differently. Representing social struggles among aristocrats, manorial lords, civic leaders, artisans, workers, and the king, *Shoemaker's Holiday* and *Friar Bacon* saturate scenes of defamiliarized domesticity with a patriotic fervor that brings English identity, custom, and character to the fore. The banquet rituals that close each play subsume individual fantasies of food into collective attempts to affirm particular conceptions of Englishness.

## I. Milk and the national imaginary

Let's return to Bartholomew Dowe's *Dairie Booke for Good Huswives* (discussed in Chapter 1) so as to consider why this particular task might have captured Dowe's imagination so fully. When challenged by a fictional female interlocutor about his expertise in cheesemaking, Dowe calls forth a fulsome memory of early Suffolk childhood revolving around the image of his mother and her maids milking cows. Since dairying, like laundering, was one of the few activities practiced exclusively by women, instructions on making butter and cheese were usually passed orally from mother to daughter or mistress to servant. Inserting his book into this line of knowledge and fabricating a woman's skeptical inquiry about this intrusion, Dowe calls attention to his unusual access to the dairy. Yet his heated assurance that he has witnessed this task "in the very house that [he] was born" insists on the primary place that milk has in his early childhood (A3[r]); dairying is accessible to men, Dowe implies, at least as remembrance. In *Delightes for Ladies* Plat offers an inflammatory account of how he has stolen his wife's prized cheese recipe in order to gratify female readers (F10[v]–F11[r]). Tied to remote memory or a violated domain, the dairy materializes as a peculiarly female and unavailable province, and, as such, an object of fascination.

Staged as a conversation in "South-hamshire" with a matron of that county, Suffolk-born Dowe compares regional methods by answering a set of questions: do people in Suffolk rise earlier than those in "South-hamshire"? Are Suffolk cheese fats stronger that those from other areas? Why are milking practices in Suffolk so efficient? Here we witness the localism that critics have seen as critical to early modern identity. Yet while the population had a developed sense of belonging to a small social unit – be it parish, village, region, or county – this investment was newly qualified by the sixteenth-century development of internal markets, centralized administrative structures, and a freer trafficking of cultural forms, objects, and people. "The diversity of English provincial society was contained," writes Keith Wrightson, "within a strong framework of national integration."[8] As Dowe seeks to convert his fictional and real audience into Suffolk cheesemakers, regional variation and female dairying emerge as two enclaves of knowledge that threaten to dissolve when aired to a print readership.[9] Or it might be more accurate to say that they simply symbolically mark the subsumption of one set of practices into another. We have already seen that Dowe's publication helps to forge the collective readership that his "memory" enjoins. It was only incidental to my earlier argument that his text concerned cheesemaking. But the dairy had specific cultural meanings in the early modern period that made his interest in milking resonant.

While occasionally yoked to the biblical promised land of honey, early modern milk was a foodstuff more often used to signify simple fare or pastoral plainness. Conjuring the image of lusty swains bouncing in the countryside delighting in ordinary food, Tryon argues that milk, a product "brave" and "friendly in nature," breeds good blood if not adulterated with troublesome ingredients like sugar (28). Harrison bemoans the fact that "white meats, as milk, butter, and cheese, which were never so dear as in my time and wont to be accounted of as one of the chief stays throughout the island, are now reputed as food appertinent only to the inferior sort" (126). He then counterpoises a diet of butter and cheese to the obscenely ridiculous dainties served at wealthy tables:

> geliffes [jellies] of all colors, mixed with a variety in the representations of sundry flowers, herbs, trees, forms of beasts, fish, fowls, and fruits, and thereunto marchpane wrought with no small curiosity, tarts of divers hues and sundry denominations, conserves of old fruits, foreign and homebred, suckets, cordials, marmalades, marchpane, sugarbread, gingerbread, florentines, wild fowl, venison, of all sorts, and sundry outlandish [foreign] confections, altogether seasoned with sugar. (129)

Horrified by the erosion of eating's practical function, Harrison condemns the variety, artificiality, and extravagance of these foods as well as their intermixing of "foreign and homebred" ingredients; he denounces, in short, the "outlandish" food promoted in cookbooks, those desserts "of no small curiosity" that made daily practice into exotic spectacle. What has happened to plain old whitemeats? Harrison asks, eager to rest a sentimental vision of national salvation squarely on the shoulders of husbandmen and artisans. Or rather their wives, who must heroically salvage a native lifestyle by promoting a diet of barnyard animals and cheese (131). The countryside becomes the last hope for maintaining the frugality that underpins sound social custom, national identity, and moral virtue. When the artificer and the husbandman meet, Harrison narrates, "they are so merry, without malice, and plain without inward Italian or French craft and subtlety, that it would do a man good to be in company among them" (131). Hinting that proper diet can prevent Englishmen from transforming into deceptive foreigners, Harrison uses the variables of nation and food to critique particular behaviors. In *A Treatise Wherein is declared the sufficiencie of English Medicines* (1580) Timothy Bright takes up these same issues with regard to curatives. Arguing doggedly for using home-grown medicines rather than "straunge" foodstuffs, Bright offers milk as his chief example of a natural English "home medicine," one which can remedy ulcers, menstrual problems, nervous disorders, inflammations, epilepsy, leprosy, constipation, teething, snakebites, infections, and sores. "Thou seest reader what treasure is hid in Milk."[10] In these texts, milk becomes an unpretentious national foodstuff fully attuned to some "original" body; as such, it is made to bear the weight of a critique of foreign and aristocratic habits.

Besides its affiliation with common folk and national prosperity, milk was also intricately tied to animal and human bodies. When modern recipes call for milk, we assume them to mean the liquid derived from a cow. But in early modern England, human milk was a commodified product detachable from what it would later become in the "intimate" scene of nursing, and therefore human and animal milk grace the pages of recipe books readily and interchangeably. "To provoke sleep," writes Markham in *The English House-wife*, "take of *Saffron* a dramme dried . . . and as much *Letticeseed* also dried . . . and mixe these with womans milke till it be a thick salve, and then bind to the temples of the head." "For ease in childbearing," he recommends, "take foure spooneful of another womans milk, and give it to the woman to drinke in her Labour."[11] Handily providing ointments, eyewashes, and sleeping potions, breastmilk had multiple beneficial effects. One French proverb which begins "No wife, no cow, hence no milk, no cheese" simply means to point to dairying as a female responsibility, but, given these recipes, it also highlights women's privileged bodily connection to milk.[12] No wife, no milk.

Classified as a basic skill of housewifery along with physic, cookery, and baking, dairying was fundamental to household production at all ranks.[13] Even homes that could not afford brewing equipment generally kept, shared, or leased a cow, mainly because dairying was one of the chief ways for the housewife to make extra cash at local markets.[14] Tusser proclaims the importance of dairying for trade practices just shy of bartering: "Sell butter and cheese, / good Faires few leese./At Faires go bie,/home wants to supplie."[15] A rustic character in *A Looking Glass for London and England* thinks instead about how the dairy's bounty renders the market unnecessary: "Why, sir, alasse, my Cow is a Common-wealth to me, for first, sir, she allowes me, my wife, and sonne for to banket our selves withal: Butter Cheese, Whay, Curds, Creame, sod milk, raw milke, sower-milke, sweet-milk and butter-milke."[16] Perhaps recognizing the benefits of this poor man's "banket," Tusser confirms its economic value. "Good dairie doth pleasure," he writes, "Ill dairie spendes treasure" (168). Figuring prominently in domestic work and its textual elaborations, milk was the everyday product most clearly linked to both living bodies and specifically gendered forms of work, and thus it can be said to rest at the intersection of human and cultural reproduction. It is no wonder that this image surfaces in a key moment of sustained fantasy on the London stage.

### Enter the milkmaid

*Friar Bacon and Friar Bungay* consists of two central plots: a conventional love rivalry between a prodigal prince and his friend, and a story about the moral limits of magic. These intertwined narratives conclude with Friar Bacon's conversion from magic and a double wedding, the centerpiece of which is Prince Edward's arranged marriage to a Castillian princess. In one sense, the play is structured through an exchange of women that consolidates domestic and international communities: the prince (Ned) and his friend Lacy reconcile when they sort out who can marry the milkmaid; England and Castille unite through Ned's marriage to Eleanor. Bacon's misguided goal of circling England with a fortress of brass gives way to a national prophecy about the birth of Queen Elizabeth; and Ned's desire, misguidedly spent as lust for a commoner, gives way to a diplomatic marriage. But this account of the play too neatly overlooks how milkmaid Margaret and the "simple fare" with which she is almost without exception associated, troubles the plot's resolution. As an emblem of pastoral home-labor, Margaret remains embarrassingly at odds with the play's closing celebration of the international English court. Greene's play may be said to stage the way that a vision of yeoman England is imagined through scenes of domesticity, but it also reveals the tension created when that ideology comes into conflict with other national discourses.

The play opens with courtiers hunting venison while visiting pastoral Fressingfield in Suffolk (Dowe's epicenter for cheesemaking). Here the prince's unseemly attraction to a gamekeeper's daughter prompts skeptical inquiries from his friends. When asked, "Why, how watch'd you her, my lord?" Ned justifies his desire by recounting an odd spectacle. After "tossing of ale and milk in country cans," he discovers passion, it seems, in the dairy:[17]

> When as she swept like Venus through the house,
> And in her shape fast folded up my thoughts,
> Into the milkhouse went I with the maid,
> And there amongst the cream bowls she did shine
> As Pallas 'mongst her princely huswifery.
> She turn'd her smock over her lily arms
> And dived them into milk to run her cheese;
> But, whiter than the milk, her crystal skin,
> Checked with lines of azure, made her blush.[18]

In this climactic revelation, the prince confesses that his passion was ignited by a stolen glance at cheesemaking. Having mentioned Margaret's "Princely huswifery" and then noting that "beauty play'd the huswife," Ned offers an explanation that appears to restate the problem: in accounting for his desire for a mere laborer, he protests that he discovers Venus in the act of working, and at one of the most menial tasks to boot (1.83).

We might chalk up Ned's odd response to an overinvestment in the pleasures of rural life. Pastoralism was, after all, a well-established literary and cultural convention that saturated the early modern imagination. It left traces in the idealized representations of shepherdesses and shepherds that populate Renaissance drama, masques, entertainments, prose, and poetry. Following Virgilian tradition, poets such as Spenser use pastoral to signal England's Protestant and imperial designs; other writers simply point to country bliss as an antidote to a corrupt society.[19] Queen Elizabeth is reported to have twice called upon the milkmaid to symbolize that class of blessed persons exempt from the burdens of royal life. And in 1602, when the Queen was entertained by the Countess of Derby in Harefield, she was greeted by a dairymaid named Joan who invited her to the dairyhouse for a competition over who was the "best Housewife." Although Joan's invitation was merely a pretext for presenting the Queen with the bejeweled prize in advance (how could Elizabeth not be England's best housewife?), it played into a deep cultural nostalgia for rural life. In this pageant, as in other courtly pastoral representations, only true royalty can effect the recovery of England's past pleasures.[20]

Louis Montrose has argued persuasively that courtiers used pastoralism as part of their own attempts to negotiate the terms of royal rule. Instead of reading the pastoral impulse as mere mystification of class antagonisms, he shows that pastoral served as an "authorized mode of discontent" that could mediate status relationships.[21] Montrose's cogent reading of these symbolic functions is largely based on the period's representations of shepherds and sheep. But what about cows? Although mentioning the dairy briefly,

Montrose does not take up the difference between leisurely gentlemen shepherds and female dairy workers or housewives, differences that might skew the cultural meaning of bucolic imagery. While representations of pastoral *otium* was certainly a topos through which gentlemen expressed social frustration, pastoralism was not just an elite phenomenon attached to royal encomium, for dairying emphasized an arduous manual labor at odds with courtly taste. There was no ennobling classical heritage of milkmaid poetry.

If Ned indulges himself in a pastoral reverie that offers a healthy contrast to the niceties of court life, he chooses an unusual and unusually banal chore as the basis for his fantasy. For it is Margaret's business that arrests Ned's gaze in this scene. Rather than merely standing prettily with milkpail in hand, she flashes before him in a whirl of activity: sweeping, diving her hands, turning her smock. By plunging her bare "lily" arms into milk, the typical analogy for the fetishized whiteness of skin, Margaret also stages a conventional Petrarchan beauty code. Sidney's Astrophel conventionally longs for Stella's "milk hands, rose cheeks" while the *Arcadia*'s Pyrocles praises Philoclea's blush: "Like wine and milk that mingled stood."[22] As if cognizant of this topos, Ned notes the irresistibility of Margaret's "bashful white" face in his first, more courtly praise for her. The milkmaid not only highlights the physicality of a common trope (bathing her arms in liquid) but displays herself as whiter than the substance used as the typical superlative. In literalizing tropes of beauty, Ned takes pleasure in teasing out the "low" practice embedded in "high" language, the material in the figurative, the rural in the courtly, mere milk in divine milkiness. Moving from metonymy to metaphor, Ned isn't simply slumming, taking perverse pleasure in desiring a peasant in the only florid terms he knows. Instead, I argue, he experiences desire *as* a contradiction, one that reveals the way that homey practices and non-elite ideals of work could materialize within the courtly tropes that potentially activated them; and in this sense, both idealizations and workaday realities posed problems for aristocratic claims to national culture.

### Wetnursing and national culture

Since conversation (after the milk) is the first and chiefest thing, both animal as well as rational creatures do most desire and delight in, I shall first advise, as to choice of company.                    *The Gentlewomans Companion*[23]

Let me offer three contexts for interpreting Ned's desire in the dairy. Despite its positive symbolic associations with purity, cow's milk was largely undrinkable in early modern England due to the absence of pasteurization and refrigeration. Numerous medical and domestic guidewriters make precisely this point: people should avoid water and milk except in special circumstances. Given that few people drank cow's milk, it would have triggered two primary associations for an early modern person: an infant feeding from a breast or the raw material for foodstuffs and medicine – in both cases it was tied to the world of housewifery.[24] Suffice it to say that milk fell under the province of women not primarily because of an idealization of "mother" but foremost because of its attachment to particular forms of labor and their products. As I discussed above, aristocratic parents as well as aspiring merchants, lawyers, physicians, and clergymen routinely sent their children away at birth to a wetnurse, a practice that was on the rise in the seventeenth century. The middle portion of the population carefully weighed the economic and social merits of wetnursing when deciding on infant feeding.[25] When writers of household and medical guides offer advice on how to assess the breastmilk of potential nurses, they highlight the commodified nature of this substance. Most popular was the "fingernail test," in which the consistency of nurse's milk was evaluated for its thickness, but parents were also to scrutinize her hair color, disposition, verbosity, and skin clarity, while observing the color and *taste* of her breastmilk. "There by four wayes in women and beasts to know the most nourishing and substantial milk: namely by the colour, smell, consistence, and taste," writes Thomas Muffett.[26] As does Muffett, guidewriters occasionally compare and rate the milk drawn from women, goats, cows, mares, camels, and asses, implying that one can be substituted, in a pinch, for another. While milk thus vividly retained its link to living bodies, it was an exchangeable secretion. Infirm and elderly adults were breastfed in order to aid digestion, and women were called to "dry up the breasts" of post-partum mothers by using intricate glass devices, sucking out the presumably tainted colostrum (or "beestings") themselves, or placing a puppy at the breast.[27] The discourse of maternal obligation that continues today remained in tension with more production-minded discourses about milk; it was part of work, transaction, and business.

Despite the fact that their audience did not seem to be listening, Renaissance commentators, ministers, and doctors urged upper-class mothers to breastfeed (although many of these writers then offered detailed advice, I imagine with a sigh of resignation, about how to choose the best nurse). "The fountains of the earth are made to give water, and the breasts of women are made to give suck," writes Henry Smith in 1598.[28] If lambs are nourished with the milk of goats, they will have coarse wool, notes Thomas Phaire in his *Boke of Chyldren*, "Wherfore ... it is ... necessary & comly for the owne mother to nource [her] owne child" (18). While glancing at the health benefits for the infant, breastfeeding advocates often underscored the importance of vocation: the mother's realization of her "natural" work in lieu of the frivolous vanities of aristocrats or the misplaced priorities of citizens. One effect of these injunctions was to elevate "motherhood" over other household roles and eventually to isolate women from more public forms of economic production. But this is a story that would unfold slowly over the next 150 years. The maternalization of women dovetails with the shift from a family economy to wage labor – the so-called domestication of women which more accurately refers to the perceived extraction of domesticity from the general economy. But in the late sixteenth century, this shift was by no means a given trajectory, nor can calls for mothers to nurse simply be understood within this framework. Tusser, for instance, points not to vocation but to thriftiness as the impetus for maternal nursing: "Good huswives take paine, and doo count it good luck / to make their owne brest their owne childe to give suck, / But one thing I warne thee, let huswife be nurse, / least husband doo find thee too franke with his purse" (180). While such exhortations may have led to restrictions on women, they need to be read, I argue, as part of broader debates about domesticity and culture.

My second observation is that nursing was seen as critical to the formation of a subject whose "nationness" was defined by shared speech and manners. In part breastfeeding supporters were concerned about the overwhelming influence that the nurse had over the child, and not simply because they had a healthy respect for the power of imitation. Numerous medical and religious authors writing between 1500 and 1700 maintain that the nurse's qualities were transmitted to the child primarily through bodily fluid.[29] While Rousseau famously claimed that wetnursing imperils the state because it severed natural bonds of affection, sixteenth-century writers were more likely to worry that the nurse injects questionable lifeblood into the infant's body. Marking a crisis in nature and nurture, the nurse is the external force who paradoxically physically molds the child as a social and personal subject. I have discussed the importance of the nurse as a figure for the vernacular, one who manifested a potential class taint in the mother tongue. What I emphasize now is that the transmission of both culture and language was bound up with the physical act of transferring milk and with housewifery; as such, the white liquid itself triggered a set of responses. We recall Spenser's assumption that nursing endowed the infant with manners, speech, and character. In his *A View of the Present State of Ireland*, Spenser worries that Irish wetnurses corrupt English language and culture: "The child that sucketh the milk of the nurse must of necessity learn his first speech of her, the which being the first that is inured of his tongue, is ever after the most pleasing unto him insomuch as though he afterwards be taught English, yet the smack of the first will always abide with him and not only of the speech, but also of the manners and conditions."[30] Although Spenser seems to differentiate between feeding and language learning, his very term "the smack of the first" makes one a metonymy for the other. In a letter prefacing *The Shepheardes Calendar*, E. K. performs a similar rhetorical operation when complaining about the deterioration of English. Through linguistic borrowing, he says, people reject "their own country and natural speech, which together with their Nurse's milk they sucked."[31] National identification becomes naturalized as the process of acquiring a speech that seemingly flows together with, or through, milk; and the verb "sucked" makes the national identification a corporeal transaction. A poem celebrating King James's return to Scotland thus prophecies his joy on being reacquainted with the native practices that he "sucked" from his nurse.[32]

Numerous writers document the period's fascinating belief in the intensely corporeal means by which English identity and culture were reproduced. Sermons, gynecological tracts, and advice books attempt to patrol class boundaries when they advise against wetnursing; Tasso explicitly warns mothers that wetnursing denies children their proper class status.[33] While Muffet writes that the child's "mind is answerable to the Nurse" (123), Laurent Joubert and James Guillimeau argue that the nurse and parents equally mold the child. "Before a marriage," Joubert then argues,

people look very deeply into the man's and the woman's . . . ancestry, their blood, and . . . conduct . . . But is not the blood that was then in the womb the same as that which is now in the breasts, only whitened with a large amount of spirits through natural heat? . . . This blood acts as the body's liquid craftsman; after forming the child in the lower regions, it turns upward at the time of delivery and flows into the higher parts [namely, the milk glands].[34]

Stating the common belief that milk was humorally transformed and whitened blood, Joubert anticipates barbaric characteristics seeping into the so-called national bloodline via milk. One place to turn in guarding against what Joubert calls "foreign milk" is the regulation of the nurse's diet, particularly her intake of foreign spices. The breast, it seems, was nominated as the guardian of a somewhat illogically interlaced national and aristocratic identity.[35] Joubert also highlights the importance of "resemblance" when thinking about infant feeding: why do so many aristocratic children fail to resemble their parents in breeding, looks, or morals? Because of wetnursing, he concludes, since infants are re-bred with artisans' blood. This leakage signals, in the logic of these writers, the erosion of culture itself as well as the denial of birthright; that is, the language of "foreignness" creeps into complaints about how the upper classes "degenerate," suffer "dimunition," or otherwise lose status because of the nurse's appropriation of the role of parent.[36] As such, commoners and foreigners become interchangeable non-English types. Robert Burton's proposition – that parents use wetnurses as genetic engineering by picking qualities that they want to instill into the child when shopping for a nurse – was exceptional. Instead wetnursing was seen as installing national and class hybridity into the very origin of the subject. It seems that the wetnurse was more than kin, but less than kind.

These texts posit an invisible and vulnerable English community frighteningly perpetuated through the lower-class breast. If nursing was not simply a powerful trope, as it was at times, then early modern people believed that one sucked one's identity. That identity was a cultural, biological, and personal one; that is, nursing shaped the individual according to social norms but also instilled affections and passions. "Together with the milke passeth some smacke of the affection and disposition of the mother . . . Yea we may observe many who have sucked others milk to love those nurses all the daies of their life," writes Gouge.[37] Henry Newcome offers etymological support: "Some Grammarians derive the Latin word *lac* (Milk) from *lacio* (to allure) as concluding no way so likely to allure the child to love its Mother, as Nursing it with her Milk."[38] Desire and affection are produced in the transfer in which children inhabit intelligible subject positions in the culture, but not in simple or predictable ways.

For the third clue to the dairy's allure for Ned, let us turn to Thomas Overbury's 1615 *Characters*, where the milkmaid is the epitome of ideal womanhood, praiseworthy because she endorses labor over consumerism. He presents "a country wench, that is so far from making herself beautiful by art, that one look of hers is able to put all face-physic out of countenance . . . although she be not arrayed in the spoil of the silk-worm, she is decked in innocence." In Overbury's description, the milkmaid's innocence is intricately tied to labor, both signified and constituted by it. "She doth not," he continues,

with lying along abed spoil both her complexion and conditions . . . In milking a cow, and straining the teats through her fingers, it seems that so sweet a milk-press makes the milk the whiter or sweeter; for never came almond glove or aromatic ointment in her palm to taint it. She makes her hand hard with labour and her heart soft with pity . . . The garden and the bee hive are all her physic and surgery, and she lives the longer for't.[39]

The milkmaid's fetishized "white" hand is yoked indistinguishably with the milk that rivals it in whiteness. This idealization of labor is in fact a testimony to self-sufficiency, for the milkmaid's fair hand is milky and able to purify cow's milk because it has not been tainted with ointments. In harmony with nature, the milkmaid eschews the commercial world of silks, lotions, and cosmetics; in short, she does not shop. Overbury's milkmaid, like *Friar Bacon*'s Margaret, serves as an eroticized image of the insular English economy that appealed to Markham and others.[40] The idealization of *this kind of* labor avoids the controversies of wetnursing and instead makes milk serve the interests of middle-class domestic ideology.

We can reread scenes of upper-class desire in the dairy, such as Ned's, through the lens of the formative power associated with, and feared in, milk. Keeping in mind Peter Stallybrass and Allon White's axiom – that "disgust bears the impress of desire" (*Politics*) – we see that disgust for the nurse modulated into desire at times, but that desire was often cordoned off into safe idealizations of the rural milkmaid, the guardian of "pure" milk. Together these representations reveal a contradiction in codes of masculinity, since they forced the elite male to choose between being English and having social status, between seeing a milkmaid as the emblem of an age-old pastoralism or seeing her as the middle-class ideal of industrious housewife. Perhaps this cultural quandary explains some of the now odd fantasies that pervade early modern texts. In John Dunton's 1691 *Voyage Round the World*, for instance, an urban gallant is uncontrollably aroused at the sight of a milkmaid. I saw, he states,

kneeling by a Cow, and singing to her (whilst she Milk'd her) a Person who in the habit of a *Milkmaid*, seem'd to disguise, and yet make good the Character of one of those *Nymphs* the Poets are wont to describe: I need not tell you this fair Crea-ture had *the Blushes of the Morning in her Cheeks* . . . the whiteness of the Milk (she had before her) in her Skin . . . without any assistance of Ornament . . . In a word she looked at once so Innocent and Pretty that she seem'd like to do Mischief, without at all intending it.[41]

This scene is rehearsed more salaciously in Richard Head's 1665 *English Rogue* where the narrator experiences an insatiable desire and seduces a working coun-try girl:

Riding along the Road I met with a young Girl with a milk-pail on her head, but I was amazed to see such perfection in one mortal face. I rid up to her very near, purposely to entertain some discourse with her . . . She opening a gate to milk her cows, I followed . . . begged her an excuse for being so rude, and beseeched her charitable opinion of my present actions, assuring her I would not offer the least injury nor prejudice to her chastity . . . She admitted me to sit down and discourse with her whilst she performed the office of a milkmaid. I could hardly contain my self within bounds, when I viewed her pretty little hand stroking the dugs, which indeed so heightened my amorous passion that I soon forgot my oaths and promises.[42]

Dunton's and Head's narrators testify to an erotics of dairying: one sees "Mischief" in "the whiteness of the Milk" while the other can hardly "contain" himself when witnessing the "pretty little hand stroking the dugs." In the anony-mous play *Two Merry Milke-Maids* (1620), a courtier rebuffed by two gentle-women disguised as milkmaids, complains of them in terms that disclose the mental merger between dairying and nursing: "beleive it my Lord, they are a brace of the / rudest Babies that euer drew or suckt the Milke of Innocence."[43] The speaker moves easily from milkmaids to nursing babes, as if a deep struc-tural logic connected what modern readers divide taxonomically. The dairy was a variant of the nursery.

Keeping in mind these scenes, we might consider Sidney's choice of phrase when he praises his mistress' "milken breasts, the nurse of child-like love."[44] In this sonnet, breasts are "milken" because of their pure white color but they are also oddly identified as the source, or "nurse," of a love implicitly figured as milk. To desire is to be in the perpetual childlike condition of being nursed or nourished with the sight of the white breast. Common figures of speech in courtly poetry thus reveal a set of desires implicated in the material substance of milk. For in the ubiquitous blazons that appeared in Renaissance love poetry, female breasts are routinely eroticized in ways that *recall* their potential function for nursing. Robert Herrick describes his beloved's breasts in terms of the erotic value of orality, maternity, and whiteness, as:

> twoe globes where love and pleasure sitt
> Which headed with twoe rich, round rubies showe
> like wanton rose buds growing out of snowe
> And in the milky vally that's betweene
> sits Cupid kissing of his mother Queene
> Fingring the paps that feele like sleeded (sleaved) silke
> And prest a little they will weepe new milke.

Elsewhere Herrick's speaker commands: "Display thy breasts, my *Julia*, there let me / Behold that circummortall purity: / Betweene whose glories, there my lips Ile lay, / Ravisht, in that faire *Via Lactea*."[45] And Thomas Lodge's sonnet speaker confesses the origin of his mistress' desirability as the moment when Cupid sucks from the beloved's breasts: "Let *Venus* seeke another sonne, / For heare my onely matchlesse Mother is. / From whose fayre orient Orbes the drinke doth ronne, / That deifies my state with greater blis: / Thys said, he suckt, my Mistress blushing smyled, / Since Love was both her prisoner and child."[46] Such fraught idealizations – maternal or no – raise the specter of milk that they might well have sought to repress. In short, these passages called to mind the substance that made the breast contaminate socially and biologically, as Paster has demonstrated. The breast was a conduit through which the "lower" social stratum could infect, imprison, mold, and allure upper-class subjects.[47] Courtly love poetry oddly foregrounds the breast's link to orality and milk, *oddly* I say, given the controversial status of wetnursing.

As if recognizing this contradiction, Shakespeare's *Two Gentlemen of Verona* bases the humor of one scene on a collision between "high" and "low" registers of milk, on its double incarnation in poetic praise and country work. When servant Launce offers a comic blazon of his mistress' parts and merits, he includes a simple but telling boast: "She can milk." It is no coincidence that this parody of courtly praise follows twenty five lines after Proteus promises to deliver Valentine's Petrarchan love letters to the "milk white bosom of thy love" Silvia. In literalizing Proteus' adjective, the play points to the vexed class valences of milk and thus exposes possible contradictions harbored in elite grammars of praise. What do courtiers know of milk? the play seems to ask, and this incongruity is what makes the echoing word humorous. Domestic labor is thus figured contradictorily as the safeguard or origin of national culture and its potential contaminant; milk is attached to lower-class work, pastoral innocence, female desirability, national character, and non-elite self-sufficiency. It constitutes a highly eroticized but abject zone of identification and disavowal.

Ned's desire for Margaret is not just a sexualized replaying of infant pleasure or horror, but an eroticization of the gender and class codes that upper-class males experienced *contradictorily* because of wetnursing's supposed role in subject-formation. Ned's description of his rapture in the milkhouse tellingly ends with a metaphor that reminds us of its threat; for he stylizes himself as Tarquin who will rape Lucrece, ruin idealized femininity, and, in doing so, lose claim to royal position.

> Ermsby, if thou hadst seen as I did note it well,
> How beauty play'd the huswife, how this girl,
> Like Lucrece, laid her fingers to the work,
> Thou wouldest with Tarquin hazard Rome and all
> To win the lovely maid of Fressingfield.                    (1.82–6)

Twenty years later, Thomas Heywood amplifies Greene's eroticization of house-wifery when he dramatizes the myth of Lucretia. Unlike Shakespeare, who uses the story to outline the risks of rhetoric, Heywood presents the heroine's dedication to housework as the act that makes her desirable to Tarquin. Lu-crece's unsurpassed beauty and chastity seemingly follow from her virtuous de-cision to renounce festivity and to undertake good old-fashioned housework. In Heywood's account, the warriors' wager revolves around industry. "Lets mount our steeds," Collatine suggests, "And to our houses all come unprepar'd, / And unexpected by our hie praisd wives, / She of them all that we find best im-ploid, / Devoted and most huswife exercisd, / Let her be held most vertuous."[48] Collatine wins the bet because Lucrece epitomizes the ideal of housewifery. In a world of rampant injustice and moral chaos, it is only the disruption of do-mestic work – an event apparently more egregious than patricide – that incites the warrior-courtiers to reclaim Rome from tyranny. In making the detection of housewifery the catalyst for political revolution, Heywood intensifies the force of what is in Greene's work the mere threat of self-alienation. This danger sur-faces when Ned, caught in a state of milky desire, likens himself to Tarquin; and the threat materializes when Ned splinters into a series of counterfeit doubles. It is no surprise that he is identified throughout the play not as the prince but as the "courtier . . . That help'd [Margaret] handsomely to run her cheese" (1.143–4). His princely status is temporary unmired, dispersed by the domestic labor that seemingly founds desire itself.

It may seem as if I am veering toward the familiar argument that English elite men were constituted through a process that required inordinate attachment to and disavowal of the maternal. But I hope it's clear that I understand this paired fixation and renunciation as intelligible through the frame of the *labor* practice of infant feeding, specifically its supposed link to national subjecthood. Critics have rightly pointed to the ambivalent cultural fantasies about birth, maternity, and maternal lactation that saturate writing in the period (and here you may mentally conjure up an image of Lady Macbeth exchanging milk for gall or Cleopatra with the asp at her breast). But early modern concerns about milk were not reducible to problems with "the maternal." What Ned flirts with is an eroticized return to the moment in which he was supplied with manners, personhood, and desires – the fused national, social, personal, and sexual inculcation of nursing. And mother wasn't present.

### *"Our" kind of food*

The dairy scene in *Friar Bacon* may seem familiar to modern readers who recall subsequent eroticized representations of working women (such as Freud's case study of the Rat Man). But Ned's stare in *Friar Bacon* is framed in specifically early modern terms, for the play gradually detaches this desire from the prince's individual erotic life and associates it with a general cultural longing for a pastoral simplicity that critiques courtly and upper-class consumerism; that is, it turns desire back on the prince to reveal its potentially self-consuming dimension.

Before Ned confesses the allure of something as base as cheesemaking, he offers a conventional Petrarchan description of Margaret that is more readily familiar to his courtly friends. Her "sparkling eyes / Do lighten forth love's alluring fire" (1.50–1), he exclaims:

> Her bashful white mix'd with the morning's red
> Luna doth boast upon her lovely cheeks;
> Her front is beauty's table, where she paints
> The glories of her gorgeous excellence;
> Her teeth are shelves of precious margarites
> Richly enclosed with ruddy coral cleeves.
> Tush, Lacy, she is beauty's over-match,
> If thou survey'st her curious imagery.                    (1.54–61)

Resembling a sonnet mistress, Margaret takes shape as fragments of nature, artifice, and myth. Ned's speech departs from Petrarchan language slightly but tellingly – in his emphasis on the mouth as a site of double enclosure. Poetic blazons typically portray the mouth as guarding the mistress' essence or advertising her cherished silence. In Ned's description, however, the dental "shelves" (cliffs) are protected by another barrier – cliff-like gums. Moving from shelves to cleaves, the reader finds Margaret unusually fortressed. In modifying Petrarchan rhetoric so as to emphasize enclosure, Ned forges one of the play's crucial rhetorical associations. The significance of his words only become apparent in the fourth scene when his father, King Henry III, welcomes the foreign entourage "To England's shore, whose promontory cleeves / Shows Albion is another little world" (4.6–7). The "cleaves" of the coastline act as England's distinguishing feature, the hallmark of the island's claim to be otherworldly and autonomous. Henry's speech places Margaret within the conceptual framework of idealized national and erotic enclosure that underwrote so many of the period's poetic representations of Queen Elizabeth and feminized nation-states: Margaret becomes linked to England and takes meaning from that identification.

Even if Henry had not pointed out the national valences of enclosure, *Friar Bacon's* audience would surely have made this association; for, as critics have noted, England's "islandness" was a staple of its national imaginary. Anthony Munday's 1609 Lord Mayor's pageant opens with a description of "a goodly Island styled *Insula Beata*, or the land of Happynes": "This island is round engirt with rich Rockes of Gold Oare and Chrisolytes, the maine Ocean also running naturally about it . . . There, in a golden Feild or Garden, imagined of the nature of the *Hesperides*, where all the Trees and Fruites are of pure golde, do we erect *Majesties* watch Tower."[49] Gaunt's famous elegy to England in *Richard II* celebrates a fortified *hortus conclusus*, "this other Eden, demi-paradise, / This fortress built by Nature for herself"(2.1.42–3); and in *Cymbeline*, England is seen as "Neptune's park, ribb'd and pal'd in / With oaks [or rocks] unscalable and roaring waters" (3.1.19–20). Looking to geography as a sign of national autonomy was not just a literary technique but a strategy used in homilies, state proclamations, and advice books. Even *The Englishmans Doctor* opens with an envoy which describes "the Countrey which the Sea-god saves, / And loves so deare, he bindes it round with waves."[50] Bound by loving waves, ribbed in by rocks, and fortified by impenetrable walls, England appears a citadel. And if England's nationalist ideology was consistently mapped in geographical terms, this tactic was exploited adeptly by a virgin Queen who mystically tied the realm to her own impermeability.[51] In highlighting Margaret's and England's shared impenetrable "cleaves," *Friar Bacon* produces a folk version of idealized state chastity. In fact, when the magician-scholar Friar Bacon takes as his chief goal a bizarre scheme to "[ring] the English strond / From Dover to the market place of Rye," he attempts to duplicate the enclosure supposedly inhering in the land and its monarch (2.65–6).

When Ned's momentary longing for the worker fades from view, the play continues to idealize plain fare and work, or what the text calls Margaret's "princely huswifery." But the fantasy that *Friar Bacon* limns involves another kind of Englishness in which domestic labor *represents* rather than produces subjects, a subjecthood erotically figured through pastoral imagery. This is to say that Ned's prolonged stare at Margaret's cheesemaking suggests resonances for milk that Greene transfers onto a more expected celebration of folksy

Englishness and rural toil. As "rich England's star, / Whose beauty tempered with her huswifery / Makes England talk of merry Fressingfield," Margaret is both a regional celebrity and an embodiment of the nation (10.35–7). In this sense, Greene's milkmaid takes meaning from the pastoralism that I discussed earlier as inadequate for explaining the dairy scene, the idea of a countryside populated with English people tied to "natural" diurnal and seasonal rhythms. Emerging from a venerated tradition stemming back to Virgil's eclogues and georgics, and joining with contemporary idealizations of rural custom, sport, and activities (such as the sheepshearing festival in *A Winter's Tale*), English pastoral represented labor as a signifier of unspoiled national character. Combining beauty and work so as to embody "rich England's star," Margaret becomes a less controversial object of desire. Metonymically connected to milk, butter, and cheese, Margaret expresses a theme bolstered by the play's representations of England's culinary plenty.[52]

But in celebrating the simple life, the play redefines milk and food in a way that makes it easier to stage a rejection of those very values; the issues raised by an eroticized national housewifery, that is, fade into a fairly standard debate about the ideological meanings of food. This trajectory begins in the second scene, when Friar Bacon seeks to punish a scholar skeptical of his powers; for he magically produces a female kitchen worker reeking of carnal circulation and promiscuous flesh. Echoing Ned's revelation of the secret of Margaret's attractiveness, Bacon promises to expose the "secret" learning of an Oxford scholar named Burden (2.110). But he in fact produces Burden's clandestine love interest; she appears as a "woman with a shoulder of mutton on a spit, and a devil," Margaret's ugly double (2.115). The confused Mistress Henley, miraculously drawn from the "kitchen 'mongst the maids, / Spitting the meat against supper," is transformed momentarily into a "she-devil" (2.126–7, 118). Bacon's production of an alien domesticity proves his talents and punishes Burden, for the Hostess mires the scholar to a world of kitchens and muttons far inferior to the intellectual domain of magic. It reveals the renunciation of cross-gendered domesticity and the flesh required by academic institutions, but also colors food preparation as scandalous and embarrassing.

While Bacon's joke rests on the transformation of cerebral study into appetite, it also turns on a pun. "Mutton," a common Renaissance word for prostitute, is glossed as such later in the play when Ermsby misidentifies the nun-to-be Margaret as her father's mistress: "The old lecher hath gotten holy mutton to him" (14.44). Literalizing a bawdy term, Bacon's spectacle displays a horrifying domesticity; the household, having been exoticized as mythic temptation, is now rendered demonic and shameful. Although female sexuality was commonly associated with appetite, it is here part and parcel of the *production* of food and the class status that such work bespeaks. In its two opening scenes, then, *Friar Bacon* stages unauthorized desire by conjuring up striking displays of domestic labor, with the second version standing as a carnivorous and carnal parody of the milky white Margaret. We have only to contemplate Burden's intense humiliation at being associated with the kitchen to see this shift in affect.

The play continues to mock its own pastoral idealizations when the King rejects the lowly "home-fare" that Bacon pretends to serve to the courtly entourage. Suggesting that it isn't only scholars who must renounce "kitchen stuff," the visiting royal party roundly refuses Bacon's "frugal cates" as an insult to social decorum: "What, dost thou taunt us with thy peasants' fare, / And give us cates for country swains?" the Emperor asks (9.227, 229–30). Henry's apology for the Friar's "feeble fare" gives the lie to the pastoral embrace of country milk and cheese (9.236); for country diet signifies the peasant rather than the good citizen. Preparing the way for Ned to exchange homespun Margaret for foreign Eleanor, the elite travelers demand an imported meal. But how can we interpret the dazzlingly lavish meal that Bacon then reveals as the "real" feast designed for the "English Henry" and the other potentates? Served by mythological leaders and conjured from around the world – herbs fetched in Portuguese sailing ships from Egypt, wines richer than Cleopatra's, sugars from Ceylon, dates from Africa – this cornucopia is patently excessive. With seeming amnesia about its former skepticism of luxury foods, the play celebrates an exoticized dining spectacle; or rather, it fails to criticize the demonic kitchen that elevates social hierarchy over folk heroism. "Bacon, thou has honoured England with thy skill," Henry announces (9.165). The play momentarily tries to have it both ways: to preserve England as the purview of simple folk and to locate national honor in its lavish acquisitiveness.

The final scene returns the audience to this voluptuous banquet, as the newly educated prince and newly converted magician join an England ratified by an international marriage and a second lavish feast. Here the court celebrates Ned's marriage to the Castillian Eleanor and his renunciation of the milkmaid, who herself abandons the countryside to marry an earl. Bacon finds his place in English history by renouncing his magic as unholy and instead offering a national prophecy. Bacon predicts that Elizabeth's reign will spring from "the royal garden" of the marriage alliance (16.45). Henry's claim – that foreign dignitaries create "fair England" as "that wealthy isle / Circled with Gihon and swift Euphrates" (16.65–6) – calls to mind the natural enclosure central to representations of milkmaid Margaret. But the King attributes Eden's power to the food it can buy: "The tables all are spread, / And viands such as England's wealth affords / Are ready set to furnish out the boards" (16.69–71). Since Bacon has renounced the magic that formerly produced the demonic banquet, we might expect the final scene to shy away from the embarrassment of feasting. But the play that opens by embedding desire and national value in the milkmaid concludes by displaying purchased foods as the signifier of national destiny. There is, needless to say, no milk in this scene.

*Friar Bacon*'s concluding vision embraces commerce, fluidity, and exchange within a dynastic model of the nation. Bacon's attempt to "[ring] the English strond / From Dover to the market place of Rye" fails because the court-controlled marketplace must remain permeable and free. England must celebrate the "invasion" of Eleanor instead of the local housewifery of Margaret. "England" is constituted not by its insularity but by its stratified assimilation of foreigners, milkmaids, magicians, merchants, aristocrats, and country gentlemen – all of whom celebrate national unity by imagining Europe's envious gaze upon their shared merchandising power.[53] The spectacle of bucolic domesticity transforms an international marketplace controlled by the royal family.

The memory of homespun domesticity lingers in the closing banquet, however, in Henry's final invitation to eat, for he reminds the audience of the controversial meanings attached to food, and, perhaps, the aristocratic decadence that underwrites his new national vision: "the time / Craves that we taste of naught but jouissance. / Thus glories England over all the west" (16.74–6). The final words of the play return us to Spenser's claim for the staying power of the infant's "smack of the first" milk, for Henry's imagined "taste" conjures up a domestic scene only to give it a cosmopolitan flavor. If milk was the site of anxieties about class and national boundaries as well as a key figure in debates about class conceptions of Englishness, *Friar Bacon* alludes to these debates but sweeps them away by integrating pastoral labor into an elite world in which foreignness is controlled by proper authorities. This play, performed in the new commercial playhouses of London for an audience with roots in the countryside, ends by reluctantly turning from the folk image of national authenticity that it has represented so fully and passionately in the dairy. The play's overarching fantasy is telling, however, because it fails to present a personified state that fully endows coherence on a population, establishes terms of social unity, and epitomizes cultural attributes (and here we might think of Shakespeare's *Henry V* as a counterpoint). Instead *Friar Bacon* compels the audience to experience the titillation and shame of unauthorized domestic desire only, finally, to represent the problems that emerge when England, personified as a king, is embarrassingly beholden to its domestic determinants, that is, to the burden of national culture supposedly imparted under the nurse's watch.

## II. The way of all flesh: food in the streets

> I saw him euen now going the way of all flesh (thats to say) towardes the
> Kitchin.                                   Mistress Birdlime, *Westward Ho*[54]

Noteworthy as a precursor to Jacobean city comedy without its biting satire, Thomas Dekker's 1599 *Shoemaker's Holiday* closes with a culminating banquet conspicuously held not at court but spilling from London's most famous marketplace, Leadenhall, into the city streets. The play traces Simon Eyre's meteoric rise from shoemaker-tradesman to Lord Mayor of London while airing the class tensions and social problems invading life in the capital: vagrancy; wounded veterans; wives of soldiers left without pay; competition in the workplace between workers and mistress; shady business practices; class hatred between citizenry and aristocrats. In the final socially harmonious moment, the King appears on stage to endorse Eyre's Shrove Tuesday banquet for workers and thus to consolidate the capitalist social climbing and convivial work relations that Eyre models. This scene conflates a set of holidays into one (Shrovetide Tuesday, St. Hugh's Day, Ascension Day) and designates the true origin for this holiday as an early modern Labor Day, one that foregrounds market production rather than monarchy.

Dekker's downplaying of holiday's royal commemoration is not surprising, given what critics have called the "bourgeois" tenor of this play. In its broadest themes, *Shoemaker's Holiday* presents a counter-narrative to history plays that make state and national welfare commensurate with monarchical interest or that focus on the dynastic struggles of a royal family waging international or civil battles. While positively representing kingship, this play offers glimpses of England's medieval war in France from an unconventional perspective: that of the wounded veteran whose domestic life is ruptured by battle. In this sense, *Shoemaker* shows the economic home front, so to speak, as the nation's most noteworthy resource. The monarch appears at the conclusion to endorse the socially mobile Mayor Eyre, but clearly the monarch's concerns are peripheral to the play's account of social relations, however fanciful and incoherent that account may be. Part of the play's critically noted "double consciousness" rests on the tension between its exuberant festivity and the cynical social realities it so fully airs.[55]

### Live food

*The Shoemaker's Holiday* places food at the fore by offering an extensive catalogue of edible staples. In insults and dialogue, characters readily talk of powder-beef, brewis, entrails, brown-bread, mutton, ale, puddings, chitterling, Islington whitepot (a cream dish), cheese curds, and carbonados (grilled or roasted meat).[56] Near the play's end, Eyre's foreman Firk responds to a bell calling workers to a holiday feast by conjuring up a vision of anthropomorphized kitchen fare unleashed into the streets:

O my brethren! There's cheer for the heavens – venison pasties walk up and down piping hot like sergeants, beef and brewis comes marching in dry-fats, fritters and pancakes come trolling in in wheelbarrows, hens, and oranges hopping in porters' baskets, collops and eggs in scuttles, and tarts and custards come quavering in in malt shovels.[57]

In Firk's imagination, culinary plenty signals a national and civic prosperity made possible by Eyre's hospitality to workers. As domestic production subsumes civic institutions and space, animated food possesses the bodies of soldiers and laborers. In a text where we see war's ability to ravage the soldier's body, the transformation of food into a bustling militia is unnerving; for the play opens by showing the household-based urban shop to be mildly at odds with the royal project of war. Eyre's household together petitions the Earl of Lincoln to release Ralph from conscription: "Keep him at home," says Eyre (1.133). With these words the play sets up the divide between "home" and foreignness, while lodging work in the realm of the household. The final scene's presentation of a food-based army ruptures the dichotomy offered in the first scene, since home production imitates the military expedition to which it had been opposed. The army in France is temporarily visible *at home*, as Eyre marshals a substitute garrison composed of beef and broth, bacon and eggs, poultry and pancakes. It is as if dishes leap from the pages of early modern cookbooks to occupy the city, forming a parade with such splendor that, in Firk's eyes, the community it offers overwhelms hierarchy. "My brethren!" he cries. In one sense, the scene simply toys with meanings associated with Firk's name: "firk" is derived from the Old English "fercian," which meant to feed or to supply with food for a journey; a "firken" was a small keg; and "to firk" meant to whip, often with sexualized overtones. Firk's excited speech activates the eroticism, violence, and sustenance condensed into his name.

The concluding celebratory banquet to which these dishes supposedly march is the site where several plots come together: the King addresses class tensions between the gentleman Lincoln and the citizen Oatley by sanctioning a marriage between their children, and Eyre shores up his political authority as mayor. But the primary rationale for the feast is to honor workers, and thus the apprentices appropriately view the banquet as a celebration of their success in disrupting Hammon's marriage with Jane, Ralph's lost wife. Crying "clubs for apprentices," the workers transform a rallying cry for riot into a battle to protect the marital rights of workers from wealthy encroachers. Leading shoemakers to celebrate this skirmish, Firk and Hodge first march workers/kitchen soldiers toward Eyre's house. "I'll promise you wine enough," says Hodge, "for Madge keeps the cellar." "And I'll promise you meat enough," adds Firk, "for simpering Susan keeps the larder. I'll lead you to victuals my brave soldiers; follow your captain." The apprentices' responding cry, "O rare! Madge is a good wench!" acknowledges female servants as gatekeepers to the resources that transform work into holiday (18.174–9). The workers' fantasy of controlling conscription and war is a decidedly domestic one.

When the pancake bell rings to signal Eyre's holiday feast, Firk claims the right to mark the holiday as the purview of shoemakers, for it becomes Saint

Hugh's Day, named for their patron saint. He then shouts, "Open the doors, my hearts, and shut up the windows [lock the shop]. Keep in the house, let out the pancakes. O rare, my hearts! Let's march together for the honor of Saint Hugh to the great new hall in Gracious Street corner, which our master the new Lord hath built" (18.182–7). Dining at the Lord Mayor's cost, these workers imagine unlocking their boss's larder to the public. To "shut up the windows" is to close the store but rather than "keep[ing goods] in the house," as was the usual meaning of this term, Firk locks out work so as to unleash household plenty. Figuring food as an army, Firk makes the absent forces fighting for the King in France materialize as kitchen soldiers and frenzied beef beholden to the buttery worker and household master alike. What the play presents are home front soldiers who depend on the combined workshop / domestic sphere as their source of power; for even in the depiction of holiday resides traces of the work necessary for a proper celebration – brewers, porters, maltsters. Calling on his officers to wait on the apprentices and his shoemakers to serve the King, Eyre consolidates Firk's metaphors by making men into consumers of live flesh. "Where be these cannibals, these varlets?" he asks (20.2). The hopping, marching, quivering food (sometimes figured as workers themselves) becomes a domestic work force that clearly does what we never see the King's army accomplish: define national prosperity and character. When live foodstuffs joyfully martyr themselves to civic needs, they provide a counterimage to Ralph's and Lacy's reluctance to join the English army. Since Ralph's future – as a wounded veteran separated from his bride – does little to glorify the national project of the French wars, the play's productive homefront takes over the ventures organized by the crown – the making of holidays and the formation of armies. At least the slightly hysterical nature of the culminating feast suggests the excitement of a fantasy of familiar goods exoticized as warriors.

It is telling that the play opens with a non-kinship, co-resident "family" – Simon Eyre, his wife Margery, and their workers Hodge, Firk, Jane, and Ralph – taking to the streets to negotiate Ralph's release from combat duty. This moment establishes the play's interest in the household-based urban workshop as a unit; and it structurally sets up a division of interest between that unit and the crown. Our first glimpse of the Eyre household is their self-presentation as bonded by common interests in opposition to the King's wishes. Eyre's plea to keep Ralph "at home" is given meaning over the course of the play, verified in the closing scene where the apprentices have "gone home" stuffed from the banquet just before the King announces: "Come, lords, a while let's revel it at home, / When all our sports and banquetings are done, / Wars must right wrongs which Frenchmen have begun" (21.185, 192–4). The play's investment in "home" is clear – it is the nation whose interests merge with the productive household. Domesticity is enmeshed in the production, management, and consumption of goods as

well as in the affective bonds of love, loyalty, and affiliation structuring relationships. Eyre's description of his marriage is a case in point: he reminds
Margery that she is obliged to him for lifting her from her lowly position as
street-seller: "Have I not ta'en you from selling tripes in Eastcheap, and set you
in my shop, and made you hail-fellow with Simon Eyre the shoemaker?" he
asks (7.64–7). Setting Margery in his shop defines the marriage and home in
terms of a workspace, the formation of a family/household revolving around its
conjoined productive function and companionate spirit. In the final scene's portrayal of marching food, the play's entire network of production comes alive
as something tied as much to domestic work as to the ethos of aristocratic
hospitality.[58]

If *Friar Bacon* makes imported foods incompatible with the plain fare of
pastoral domesticity, *Shoemaker* presents a commercial ethos that stresses food
*consumption* as overriding the line between home production and trade. Here
merchant-producers combine international trade with local craftsmanship, and,
in Firk's account, imported oranges happily march with English beef toward the
banquet table. Dekker alters his source, Deloney's *Gentle Craft*, so that Eyre
gains his wealth by buying a cargo that includes, among other goods, luxury
*foods* such as "sugar, civet, and almonds." While Deloney's Eyre purchases
only textiles, Dekker's Eyre buys precisely the ingredients that housewives
needed to make those expensive banqueting dishes that some condemned as
harmful to the national economy. Yet the play emphasizes Eyre's shrewd business deal as complementing his skill in running the efficient home-shop. And
while the final banquet is held at the newly established Leadenhall – the emblem of a specialized market economy – it is supplied metaphorically with the
seemingly bottomless fruits of Eyre's household. After Firk commands that the
maids unleash Eyre's private larder, Eyre commands: "Want they [the work-
ers] meat? . . . run, my tall men, beleaguer the shambles, beggar all Eastcheap,
serve me whole oxen in chargers, and let sheep whine upon the tables like
pigs for want of good fellows to eat them. Want meat!" (20.23, 25–8). Leaving aside the oddity of eating live sheep as they whimper and impersonate
pigs at the dinner table, we see that Eyre's words transform all of London
into his larder. This domestic urban fantasy counters the agrarian vision of
husbandry writer Barnabe Googe, who describes a housewife's recourse to
markets as sign of her moral and economic failure: "where they [the old hus-
bands] found the garden out of order, the wife of the house (for unto her belonged the charge thereof) was no good huswife, for they should be forced to
have their vituals from the Shambles or the Market."[59] Eyre's willingness to
"beleaguer the shambles," however, signals the success of domestic production rather than its failure, the triumph of the fraternity of workers dedicated
to principles that allow for isolated moments of extravagance. And though the
King's reference to "taste" in the final speech is reminiscent of the closure in

*Friar Bacon*, it here signifies the glories of urban production and trade rather than the "smack" of the first milk or a rural ethos fading in the wake of internationalism.

As a worker in the household-based shop, Firk had reason to fantasize about food being released from human control and from established lines of dependency. For earlier in the play, Eyre envisions the "family"'s cohesion in terms of food. One scene opens with childless householder Eyre calling his well-populated household to awake:

Where be these boys, these girls, these drabs, these scoundrels? They wallow in the fat brewis of my bounty, and lick up the crumbs of my table, yet will not rise to see my walks cleansed. Come out, you powder-beef queans! What, Nan! What, Madge Mumblecrust! Come out, you fat midriff-swag-belly whores, and sweep me these kennels that the noisome stench offends not the nose of my neighbours. What, Firk, I say! What, Hodge! Open my shop windows! (4.1–9)

Bandying insults and swaggering about the shop, Eyre comically insists on a contractual obligation between his provision of food and the family's duty to work, a family comprised of shoemakers and domestic servants who share a living space and undertake interlaced if gender-segregated duties. Cleaning sidewalks and (as he later adds) preparing food are necessary for the journeyman, foreman, female servants, apprentices, and shoemakers who inhabit the household. The women (branded as "drabs," "whores," "queans," and "beef") are expected to sweep the sidewalk, prepare breakfast, and make shoethread; both male and female servants serve the workers' beer. The tasks performed by domestic workers and apprentices are not differentiated clearly since everyone unites in their common accountability to the house master. Tusser's *Fiue Hundreth Points of Good Husbandry* has the wife regulate the household diet as a way of monitoring labor output: "Poore seggons halfe starved worke faintly and dull," he writes, "and lubbers doo loiter, their bellies too full" (177). Often traveling far from their homes and families into service, workers found the fruits of their labor to be both a skill and a home; they were largely recompensed with clothing, shelter, and food.[60] In this play, the provision and consumption of food is presented as critical to the business of living and working in the shop: Hodge tries to persuade Eyre to hire Hans by telling him that Dutchmen don't eat much beef (4.55–6); Firk threatens to work slowly unless he is given beer (4.25–8); Eyre resolves a dispute between his workers and his wife by calling for "a dozen cans" (7.74); and he uses breakfast as a way to galvanize the men to work (4.125). But it isn't just food that links shop and domestic duty, for it is the job of one of Margery's maids (Cecily Bumtrincket) to make shoethread for the shop. Tasks that modern audiences think of as "domestic" pervade the business sphere and domestic workers make contributions to the leather/shoe trade. This conjoining is imagined by Eyre as undifferentiated workers wallowing in the "fat brewis" of the householder's bounty.

Firk responds to Simon's subsequent order to wash his face and get to work by returning to the issue of food: "Let them wash my face that will eat it – good master, send for a souse-wife, if you'll have my face cleaner" (4.16–17). Instead of wallowing in the bounty that his master provides, Firk imagines himself as food to be consumed – as perhaps the popular calf's head recipe detailed in cookbooks or the offal cleaned and pickled by souse-wives.[61] He refutes his master's claim to his labor by imagining himself, that is, as the object of housewifery. Eyre's suggestion that eating creates ties of dependency mutates into cannibalism, in Firk's language, with the result that it underscores labor struggles taking place around food consumption and distribution. Is it any wonder that Firk later enjoys thinking of Eyre's "brewis" detached from the sphere of obligation and marching to the workers on its own accord? His fantasy of liberated food defamiliarizes domestic routine by disentangling provisions from contractual arrangements. "Let's feed and be fat with my lord's bounty," he exclaims, this time about his own fatness and Eyre's free liberality (18.192–3).

The play demonstrates what Martha Howell (in an analysis of economy of the late Middle Ages) calls the "family production unit" as opposed to the family subsistence unit. In the family production unit, members do not produce principally for household use or work for wages outside the household but instead produce goods and services for sale.[62] In family economies, as Louise A. Tilly and Joan Scott define them, "the labor needs of the household defined the work roles of men, women, and children. Their work, in turn, fed the family. The interdependence of work and residence, of household labor needs, subsistence requirements, and family relationships, constituted the 'family economy.'"[63] Howell refines this definition by looking at the unit's central objective as subsistence or goods for sale. However, the realms of subsistence production (as domestic labor is usually seen) and market production were not, Howell reminds us, as distinct as we might imagine. Eyre's household-based workshop suggests this point: the wife is part of business management and domestic labor provides the infrastructure for the business. If urban housewives had more access to purchasable goods than their rural counterparts, they nevertheless still engaged in housewifery when they regulated expenditures for food, clothing, and provisions, oversaw the maintenance of house and shop, and tended to the health and diet of household members. The family economy did not require common participation of members in a single shared productive effort, but instead was defined by the way that members shared economic, social, and political resources – the "fat brewis" that Eyre holds forth (Tilly and Scott, 29).

Given the play's interest in the material relations of the household, it is fitting that its crises are not restricted simply to the conventional entanglements of erotic jealousy and courtship. While the Rose–Lacy plot offers the audience the ever popular tale of obstructed young love, the Eyre plot shows another dimension to household life. Jealous rivalry, for instance, takes the form of workers and household mistress jockeying for power as they attempt to influence the shop master's business decisions.[64] Twice the play stages Eyre's intervention in disputes between Margery and Firk, in which Eyre acquiesces to his workers' demands over his wife's. In one instance, Eyre responds to his men's preemptive appeal for him to curtail Margery's authority. "By the life of Pharoah, by the Lord of Ludgate, by this beard, every hair whereof I value at a king's ransom, she shall not meddle with you," (7.36–8) he promises, before commanding her: "Peace you bombast-cotton-candle quean – away, Queen of Clubs, quarrel not with me and my men, with me and my fine Firk. I'll firk you if you do" (7.38–41). Promising to "firk" her for interfering with his "fine Firk," Eyre brings out the lewdness and aggressivity harbored in the journeyman's name, and thus the eroticized and violent terms by which the householder and men unite against the mistress. After lambasting his wife as "kitchen-stuff" far beneath his "brave men," however, Eyre ends the scene by reassuring his wife (in an aside) that his liberality to his men does indeed have bounds. Having Margery share the secret that he has halted the free flow of liquor, Simon acknowledges his wife as the co-manager to whom he is accountable despite his exaggerated claims of loyalty to his workers.[65] Natalie Zemon Davis offers an historical example of this rivalry when describing a Genevan proofreader named Guillaume Gueroult who complained in 1549 that his master's wife had too much control over the resources of the print trade. Geuroult specifically objected that the mistress spent money too frivolously and refused to unlock the wine cupboard for him in the middle of the night.[66] In towns such as Bristol, the wife was an equal party in the indenturing contracts for apprentices, but even where this was not so, she often had an unspecified authority over the workers.[67] *Shoemaker* comically focuses on internal disputes between workers and mistress that fade as Eyre rises socially with the result, the audience assumes, that there are more resources to go around. At least Firk's final culinary vision of Eyre's generosity as *enabled* by housewifery suggests as much.

Valuing the domestic dimension of the shop hardly means that *Shoemaker* accords the housewife a privileged place in that environment. Margery appears as one cog in a complex wheel of production and she is subsumed, along with the other workers, into Simon's occupational identity. Yet Dekker makes Margery a constant and active presence (albeit one humiliated and scorned) within the commercial space, as she deliberates in the management and distribution of resources. As Eyre rises to Sheriff and then Lord Mayor, Margery turns into the comic stock figure of consumer wife concerned with feathers, farthingales, French hoods, wigs, and high cork heels, fashions so impractical that they restrict her ability to do work. Reframing her new interest in consumption within the Protestant conception of vocation, she declares, "How costly this world's calling is!" (10.49). Yet since Margery has been designated as the overseer of household food, the final scene might bespeak a more significant part of her "calling," for it shows housewifery expanding out of the domus into civic institutions. The fraternity of men consolidate through Eyre's harsh final invective toward Margery, and she is excluded from a civic harmony figured by food: "Away, you Islington whitepot! Hence, you hopperarse, you barley pudding full of maggots, you broiled carbonado! Avaunt, avaunt, avoid!" Eyre swears, in a speech that turns his wife into spoiled, fleshly, and sexualized edibles (20.49–51). Despite the fact that Eyre uses whitepots, puddings, and carbonados as insults, domestic food and management remain at a premium in the closing feast; they signify the liberal spirit that can harmonize social tensions. Controlling the "fat brewis" of bounty in this world, including its metaphorical meanings, marks power. In the play's final speech, the King somewhat rescues Margery from the fate of being either a consumer or mere food for he puts her back in charge of the rituals surrounding victuals: "Thanks, my kind Lady Mayoress, for our cheer" (21.191). All economics in this play are home economics, it seems, but the home is not simply the purview of women.

### *"Happy Work!"*

Food production makes up only part of the play's general interest in work, an issue taken up in its artisanal incarnation in the scene where city gentleman Hammon, having been rejected by the mayor's daughter, tries to woo a lowly sempstress. As in *Friar Bacon*'s depiction of Ned in the dairy, the scene focuses on Hammon's prolonged stare at a working woman and his paean to a beauty is tied to industry:

> Yonder's the shop, and there my fair love sits.·
> She's fair and lovely, but she is not mine.
> O would she were!
> . . .
> How prettily she works! O pretty hand!
> O happy work! It doth me good to stand
> Unseen to see her. Thus I oft have stood
> In frosty evenings, a light burning by her,
> Enduring biting cold only to eye her.          (12.1–3, 13–17)

Hammon's repeated use of apostrophe and synecdoche elevates the humble scene of shop labor, rendering into poignant comedy his fixation on a menial occupation ("O happy work!"). Pleasurably imagining being transformed into the cloth she holds, Hammon rhetorically fuses Jane's "hand" with her "work." Unable to see him as he watches her, Jane embodies what Hammon conceives of as "not mine": the world of labor, the allure of female beauty.

In its repetition of the word "hand," this scene implicitly glosses the play's exploration of courtship, labor, and London life: Hammon offers to buy Jane's hand; he swears by her white hand to persevere in his suit; his asks for her hand in marriage; he holds her hand prisoner as he woos her. To puzzle the meaning of the working hand, we might look to the scene when Simon consigns Jane to work because her husband has been pressed into military service: "This fine hand, this white hand, these pretty fingers," he tells her, "must spin, must card, must work. Work, you bombast-cotton-candle quean, work for your living" (1.210–13). As in *Friar Bacon*, it is the whiteness of the hand that inspires commentary since it does not accord with the labor that the woman performs. Simon's sense that the "pretty hand" must engage in labor is tantamount to saying that it must harden and be stained with work, but Hammon is excited precisely by the contradiction between what he interprets as the labor of the unassuming worker and the visible beauty of her skin. Later Lincoln threatens to dissolve his nephew's marriage: "Howe'er their hands have made them man and wife, / I will disjoin the match, or lose my life" (18.165–6); the conjugal bond established by reference to the "hand" underscores the fresh context Hammon gives to the working hand as the object of desire. Her "hand" is precisely what the play will not allow Hammon to have, since Jane "belongs" to shoemaker Ralph. But Dekker creates a scene that conveys the intense longing inspired by the sight of labor, making visible an eroticized version of Dowe's memory of childhood dairying. Spinning was, after all, a task carried out routinely in the home, so Hammon's gaze at what is not his, the scene suggests, marks his alienation from an inaccessible but perhaps familiar housewifery.

Hammon's fantasy almost provides a parody of the play's own effervescent idealization of labor. After all, when urging Rose not to marry the aristocrat Lacy, Eyre airs his preference for "real" workers over mere unsewn courtly veneers: "A courtier? – wash, go by! Stand not upon pishery-pashery. Those silken fellows are but painted images – outsides, outsides, Rose; their inner linings are torn. No my fine mouse, marry me with a Gentleman Grocer" (11.39–43). Eyre's endorsement of Lacy is based on the aristocrat's ability to make shoes and his willingness to participate in the humdrum affairs of business. But Hammon's desire for the hand of the worker does not bespeak the play's perspective, since his view of workers is later tainted by his offer to buy Jane from her husband. After this display of superiority, Hammon, like Ned, renounces the desire he conjured at the spectacle of work, not because the play cannot sanction a cross-classed marriage but because Hammon remains detached from the sphere of workaday production that the play endorses. Had he not been standing outside the shop, he might have been in the position to understand the "happiness" of Jane's work.

What the play endorses in Hammon's desire is his momentary appreciation of ordinary objects and tasks. Firk's passionate description of food, for example, similarly singles out for notice mundane containers – "dry-fats," wheelbarrows, "scuttles," and porters' baskets. Here the life of objects takes center stage as they move from harvest to the consumers without the seeming aid of humans. Eyre's merry insults routinely join domestic goods – bombast, cambric, hodge-pudding, powder beef, kitchenstuff, mustard tokens, whitepot – to "learned" terms (Termagent scoundrels, Greeks, Trojans). Firk similarly swears of Lacy and Rose: "they shall be married together, by this rush, or else turn Firk to a firkin of butter to tan leather withall" (16.104–106). Looking around the household, he spies the least valuable objects – the rush strewn casually on the floor, the oily butter bearing his name – and transforms them into an oath. Similarly Ralph invests shoes, objects tied to the lowest body part, with a value that exceeds their function and cost.[68] Telling Jane to remember him "every morning, when thou pull'st them on," Ralph creates a covenant of remembrance (1.236). The play bears out Ralph's faith in the convertibility of banal things, since his ability to recognize this single pair of shoes provides the clue that reunites him with his wife, when, like Cinderella, the shoe materializes the lost person. Juxtaposed to Ralph's crippled legs, the shoe is made precious, a signifier of the personhood threatened by war and urban anomie, as well as the commitment to love and a collective production that promises restoration. *Shoemaker* indulges in an unfettered sentimentality, as it makes the object produced in Eyre's shop into a symbol of enduring value; but the shoes are also the road back to domestic bliss and the marker of an artisanal skill implicated in functional domesticity. The cumulative effect of such scenes is a play in which vibrant household and shop inventories anchor and express emotional conflicts.

*Shoemaker* ends by casting doubt on what "work" will mean in the future, for the shoemakers use the occasion of the final feast to secure the King's support for a petition to trade leather at Leadenhall on two days each week. At this moment, the aristocratic milieu of hospitality disappears, leaving in its wake a business deal. More importantly, the play gestures toward a future shift from work and sale in the craftsman's shop to the public market. What this portends is a more differentiated set of labor practices within the shop, since the housewife and female servants will almost certainly remain at home. Does this change hint of the emergent division of labor that has been charted by Alice Clark? The moment when the nature of the family economy changes as it folds into capitalist market production?[69] While *Shoemaker* exists in a world where neither the family productive unit nor the subsistence unit are about to disappear any time soon, it does end by pointing toward a specialized labor that will alter the domestic flavor of Eyre's shop. All may not be undifferentiated workers wallowing in the master's "fat brewis" for long; and the homey staples that structure fantasies about work and everydayness may accrue new meaning.

If the King is happy to grant this commercial privilege to the shoemakers, he also takes the occasion to reflect upon his current project: the war in France.

Casting an eye over the reveling workers, the King notes ominously:

> With the old troop which there we keep in pay
> We will incorporate a new supply.
> Before one summer more pass o'er my head,
> France shall repent England was injured
> What are all those?                                    (21.138–42)

When Lacy answers, "All shoemakers, my liege," the play loses its festive tone momentarily to imagine the disappearance of Firk, Hodge, and other workers as they become "incorporated" into the royal army; that is, Firk's vision of animated food becoming soldiers is given a bleaker visionary counterpart in which workers become fodder for French cannons. The image of socially mobile apprentices happily supportive of their Lord Mayor is darkened by the threat of a war whose danger has already been made manifest by Ralph's maimed body. Workers will soon "leave home" for battle, taking the place of marching food in an injurious national project that seems at odds with Eyre's collective spirit. When England is personified as the King, workers can be incorporated, in the sweep of an eye, into supplies for royal ingestion.

Dekker's concern is to keep the "home" front in view for the London audience. When Jacobean city comedies later take up plots about sexuality and urban life, they almost always lodge prostitution, rhetorically or thematically, at the heart of the marketplace. All sex is potential business and all business is a form of sex. But in the less satirical age of the 1590s, social cynicism is tempered by an almost hysterical festivity, and the civic market relations of romantic comedy emerge as more convivial than predatory. The play is so blatantly utopian that, as David Kastan argues, it reveals its own designs as wish-fulfillment and flaunts theater's transformation of work into work-as-play.[70] In doing so, this fantasy reveals how the urban household "family" could be recruited to serve as the core of true Englishness.

### Staging Domesticity

*Friar Bacon* and *Shoemaker* present different national fantasies built around household labor, as they activate for audiences multiple points of identification – with region, city, profession, or court. Existing records show that both plays were popular as printed texts or performances, available not only to London audiences but also, through provincial playing and peddlers, to a wider audience outside the metropole.[71] Greene's play reveals an upper-class trauma caused by the social hybridity endemic to transferring nation and culture to the next generation; and it resolves that trauma with a debate about courtly values and correct feasting. Like Dowe's dairy book, *Friar Bacon* evokes a yeomanly Englishness only to fold localism into a national project in which the court is the epicenter of English culture. Yet, this play invites a heterogeneous audience to enjoy the vexed nature of upper-class fantasies (identifying *as* the elite man desiring the milkmaid while watching the contradictions unfold that make this desire as alluring as it is futile). As in *Gammer Gurton's Needle*, the play demonstrates the collision between a status marker (humanist pedagogy's embrace of Latin, aristocratic wetnursing) and emergent nationalist consciousness. But the play's audience is invited to partake in other identifications as well – desiring the milkmaid as an endorsement of middle-class ideology or inhabiting the milkmaid's fantasy of upward social mobility. These contradictory desires seemingly unify in country ideals compatible with the new international market. Pointedly representing the prince's trade of cheese for a lavish banquet and the intellectual's exchange of magic for royal prophecy, *Friar Bacon* ratifies pastoral nationalism and European erudition as constituent parts of a vision in which the court, agrarian economy, and developing urban markets harmonize. Positioning cultural sites in relation to the court – rural Fressingfield, academic Oxford, and the London market – the audience is asked to accept the court as arbiter for competing claims to national definition even as it airs the domestic desires and disgusts that trouble national identifications.

*Shoemaker's Holiday*, on the other hand, repositions the court as peripheral to the urban world of merchandising. Monarchical projects seem mere subsidiaries and, at moments threats, to a genial English commercial and social life best marked by the amazing potency of everyday objects. Dekker thus underscores the *social* value of industry and capital investment in the domestic workspace, one that citizens never have to renounce in the name of elite humanist culture. Rather than exposing contradictions in elite ideologies and practices, *Shoemaker* zeroes in on tensions emanating from London's self-representation as the core of the nation, a "nation of shopkeepers," as Adam Smith would later note. Its fantasy of unbridled production and consumption spiraling out of upward social mobility is tempered only by the reminder that Englishness involved allegiance to a crown whose interests could diverge from the nation's producers. But again Firk's euphoric vision of "live food" subsuming soldiers, workers, civic leaders, and householders, paired with Hammon's inappropriate longing for the working woman, indulges a fantasy of endless surplus and frustrated desire that exceeds (even while it structures) the play's bourgeois vision.

Both plays tutor modern scholars to refine our understanding of early modern domesticity, for they suggest that a definition of the household as cemented by blood lines or marriage is hopelessly inadequate for making sense of sixteenth-century social relations. Feminist critical analyses of the 1970s importantly held up the family unit for scrutiny as part of a broader analysis of the social and economic relations structured by gender. But animus toward the inequalities of the modern family can skew a full understanding of either the economic place of early modern domestic work or its figurative role in shaping identifications.

When literary critics see early modern women as relegated to the domestic sphere, degraded by their inconsequential work, or severed from the public, they assume the household to be a place of leisure in which subordinates are oppressed. And while servants, apprentices, workers, children, and wives were clearly subject to a household master, they occupied complex positions within this unit. A "presentist" view of the household as a place of privacy, unremuner-ated labor, and a recognizable gender oppression doesn't provide an accurate picture of what constituted domesticity in sixteenth-century England.

Jean-Louis Flandrin argues that the European concept of family was divided between notions of co-residence and broad kinship networks from 1500–1800. "One has to wait until the 19th century," he writes, "for the concepts of co-residence and close kinship to be united in concise formulas, in definitions whose very succinctness bears witness to the fact that they no longer consti-tute any problem."[72] Sixteenth-century texts make clear that neither household nor family were reducible to the father–mother–children triad, that scholarly discussions of women's work cannot dismiss domestic labor as trivial, and that men and boys working in the household were oppressed or validated by their institutional status. As Samuel Pepys said of his "family": "I live in Axe Yard, having my wife, and servant Jane, and no more in family than us three."[73] The hybrid family stretches beyond the confines of the house or the ties of blood to encompass wetnurses and shopworkers who populate imaginative, often utopian, spaces and who function to trigger anxiety and aggression about the identifications made possible by the home. In amplifying fantasies circu-lating around domesticity, drama makes visible a non-normative family unit (indeed a queer one, as I discuss later) that modern readers sometimes fail to recognize. What may be more readily evident is the patriotic fervor of these final staged banquets, spectacles in which characters "revel at home" and glorify "England all over the west."

Let me end by speculating about the props used to create such theatrical spec-tacles. Philip Henslowe, who had a hand in producing both *Shoemaker's Holiday* and *Friar Bacon*, undertook an inventory of props owned by the Lord Admiral's Men in 1598. Predominantly comprised of expensive clothing – taffeta suits, satin doublets, velvet gowns, and farthingales – the company also apparently kept on hand swords, drums, trumpets, a hell's mouth, a Jew's cauldron (pre-sumably for *The Jew of Malta*), outfits for particular characters (Phaeton, Neptune, Mohammed), a miniature version of the city of Rome (for *Dr. Faustus*), snakes, crowns, and even spare heads. Amidst these items, Henslowe records "ii marchpanes."[74] Since cookbooks mention that sugarworks could be preserved for years, it makes sense that edible sculptures could serve as stage props. And while we don't know what form these marzipans took, it stands to reason that they were used in banquet scenes such as the ones in *Friar Bacon* and *Shoemaker's Holiday*, either to represent expensive desserts in the form of castles or faux food. Not only do we see that Henslowe's domestic theater business had need for "housewifery" in its very mode of production, but we encounter a *mise-en-abyme* – the illusory tricks of domestic confectionery imported into a theatrical space as a representation of a representation of the real. When Friar Bacon marvels at the exotic foods he serves to royal guests or Firk hallucinates about live food marching to a holiday feast, might the theater audience have been entertained as well by a second trick of the culinary imagination – the fantasy world of the kitchen now so evidently put on stage?

Tending to bodies and boys: queer physic in
       *Knight of the Burning Pestle*

---

> By your leave, gentlemen all, I'm something troublesome; I'm a stranger here;
> I was ne'er at one of these plays, as they say, before . . . I'm bold to sit amongst
> you.                  The Wife, taking the stage in *The Knight of the Burning Pestle*

### The stranger's desires

In a play performed by the Children of the Queen's Revels at the Second
Blackfriars Theater (*c.* 1607), a citizen grocer George and his wife Nell supposedly interrupt the dramatic action, climb on stage, and insist that the company
offer a more citizen-friendly play than the one advertised: "Present something
notably in honour of the commons of the city," the Grocer demands.[1] After com-
mandeering the stage, Nell donates their servant Rafe to the company, directing
him to prove the dignity of citizenry by undertaking chivalric adventures. The
result is three plays grafted uncomfortably together to form *The Knight of the
Burning Pestle*: the stock city comedy planned by the troupe, "The London
Merchant"; the quixotic romance, starring Rafe, manufactured *ad hoc* by the
citizens; and a frame tale in which the citizens attempt to control the entrances
and exits of all performers. Part of the wit of the play turns on a productive
clash between "ordinary" and "spectacular" events. This theme is transparently
evident in the citizens' play, as apprentice Rafe transforms everyday circum-
stance into mythic adventure, but it saturates the entire play experience as well
since the workaday citizens constantly expose the real conditions underwriting
dramatic spectacle. The citizens incessantly remind the audience that the characters are merely English youths playing out theatrical conventions that can
easily be misread, refused, or altered.

*Knight of the Burning Pestle* opens with an induction, a device in which actors masking as audience members comment on the business of theater. Highly
popular in the first decade of the seventeenth century, this self-conscious convention was often used to satirize the conduct of viewers.[2] The inductions in
John Marston's *The Malcontent* (1604), John Day's *Isle of Guls* (1606), and
Ben Jonson's *Cynthia's Revels* (1600) mock the obnoxious behavior of gallants
who drag their stools onto the stage, fill the room with tobacco fumes, gab about

fashion, groom themselves, ridicule the actors, mock the author, and heckle the Prologue. In *The Isle of Guls*, performed by the Children of the Queen's Revels just the year before *Burning Pestle*, one gentlemen demands a seething scene of sex, while another airs his taste for social satire: "Is't any thing Criticall?" he queries the players, "Are Lawyers fees, and Cittizens wives laid open in it: I love to heare vice anatomizd."[3] Scripting the audience-chorus as citizens, *Burning Pestle* redirects the focus of satire downward socially. While analyzing the taste of the "middling sort," the play also alters the convention by introducing the citizen's wife along with the citizen, as if to anticipate a later characterization of bourgeois domesticity as the hallmark of a stifled aesthetic appreciation. Yet a popular target of satire (the citizen's wife usually "laid open") is allowed to turn the tables on her "betters" and question their inclination to see citizen drama.[4] Nell's particular identity – as a housewife – becomes central to the playwright's critique of taste, for she demands the old-fashioned literary fare of romance to which untutored viewers were supposedly mired.[5] But in this chapter I suggest that the housewife's gender, the labors with which she was associated, and the meaning attributed to those practices by the culture, complicate a straightforward send-up of middle-brow taste. Instead the play posits the figure of the housewife as a means of exploring cultural fantasies of dependency, familiarity, and nationality.

We might first observe that the play mocks, as editor Michael Hattaway notes, the citizens' "theatrical naivete" as well as their "terms of endearment, their bawdy, their ignorance of the classics, and the Wife's trust in homely medicines."[6] Hattaway's last remark points to the phenomenon whereby the Wife repeatedly offers remedies to the characters who are wounded or ailing in the play's fiction: "Come hither, Master Humphrey," she consoles one character, "has he hurt you? . . . Here, sweetheart, here's some green ginger for thee" (2.254–6). While Nell's fierce attempt to minister to the players' aches exposes her inability to understand the fictional nature of the play, it also displays her seemingly bottomless desire to import one of the central tasks of housewifery, the maintenance of the body, indecorously into a public arena; that is, staged female practice and the attempt to cure imaginary wounds are doubly marked as "inappropriate." But the act of maintaining the body was perhaps already a fraught domestic experience, and as such the Wife's desire to medicate actors readily blends into seemingly unrelated yet provocative impulses: the urge to sit on stage amongst boys and gentlemen; to "see her man" Rafe parade before her; to flirt outrageously with the actors; and to dote on them as if her wards. "Didst thou ever see a prettier child?" she coos (1.94). When George asks Nell, "How lik'st thou this, wench?" she confesses her single-minded interest, "I cannot tell; I would have Rafe, George; I'll see no more else, indeed" (2.89–90). Rafe's participation in the London stageworld seems to authorize the Wife's intrusion. "I'm something troublesome; I'm a stranger here," she confesses (1.49) and later declares, "I'm bold to sit amongst you" (108). Conduct potentially aggressive but not "strange" within the domus (e.g., passionate concern for bodies and boys) is held up for scrutiny when aired in this environment; for Nell proceeds to pump the actors full of aphrodisiacs and purgatives, deflate the authority of adult characters by calling them cute boys, and sadistically demand that everyone be beaten on cue. As a memorably rapacious character, Nell brings to light the violence, eroticism, nurturance, and dependency all associated with household practice.

Part of the play's conservatism turns on the irregularity of a housewife on stage, whose hunger for chivalric romance clashes with her insistence on the old-fashioned comforts of home. Alternately infantilizing teenage actors and demanding that they battle violently in foreign lands, she wants to be indulged with a brand of exoticism that she can domesticate at will. The result is a humorous collision of things fantastical and familiar as well as the presentation of people whose identities waver, under the housewife's direction, between characters, actors, and family dependants. In *Burning Pestle*, Nell exposes twin desires: to exoticize the world and to anchor everything to the reality principle that she embodies for her culture. While she longs to see *her* servant leave the humdrum reality of the grocery shop and become stage myth, she takes every opportunity to "out" characters as mere boys. Nell thus constantly translates between realms that eventually become nationally inflected. Importing household work to the stage, the Wife invites her audience to become disoriented by the confusion between deeply familiar practices and their fantastical incarnation in theater. Conspicuously displayed as a spectacle for a paying audience at the private theater, the housewife figures the "low" tastes of the unsophisticated theater-goer.

But, as I argue, the "stranger" housewife offers more than a critique of a combined bourgeois and feminine naivete; for she also articulates domestic desires and fears that the play doesn't completely disavow. *Knight of the Burning Pestle* asks its audience to think about the potential fantasies that infiltrate domesticity – the postures of loss, mastery, dependency, and submission played out in strong form in the home regimen of kitchen physic. The play then extends its theme so as to inquire about the fantasies that a children's theater regularly offered its viewers. Not only does it insist on a mythical domestic commonality that it only half seriously attaches to verisimilitude, but *Burning Pestle* also uncovers the titillation and consolation of a queer "everyday" world.[7]

### Tending to bodies

In *The Instruction of a Christen Woman*, Juan Luis Vives describes home medical practice, a domain of knowledge inseparable from food cultivation and production, as the cornerstone of household management. "Because the business and charge within the house lyeth upon the woman's hand," Vives writes,

I wolde she shuld knowe medycines and salves for suche diseases as bee common, and reigne almost daily: and have those medicines ever prepared redy in some closette wherewith she maie helpe hir housebande, hir littell children, and hir householde meny [servants], whan any nedeth, that shee nede not ofte to sende for the phisicion, or bye thynges of the potycaries.[8]

In "The good huswifelie PHYSICKE" in his advice book, Thomas Tusser similarly enjoins thrifty women to have aqua composita, vinegar, rosewater, treacle, endive, conserves of quinces and barberries, and syrups on hand for tending the sick.[9] Early modern cookery books and domestic guides routinely offer cures for bad breath, the ague, worms, consumption, fevers, jaundice, toothache, headache, gout, hemorrhoids, "tight" bellies (constipation), flux (diarrhea), ulcers, and sore breasts. Based on Galenic medicine, this system of healing was largely distinct from the magical-based medicines involving charms and spells that cunning women or "wise women" reputedly used.

The housewife was required to provide basic healthcare for persons in her home and neighborhood. Some texts emphasized the health benefits of simples (single herbs) or foodstuffs that we now categorize as desserts, while others recommended complex syrups concocted from roses, violets, quinces, damasks, sage, and ginger. This knowledge cut across class lines, since wealthy aristocrats were to oversee the practices of female servants: farmers' and citizens' wives to perform their own labor with the help of maids; and poor women to tend to tasks alone with goods they could obtain cheaply. Ladies such as Margaret Hoby, Anne Clifford, Anne Howard, Brilliana Harley, and Elizabeth Grey dressed wounds, prepared drugs, distilled cordials, and attended to internal diseases.[10] Lady Grace Mildmay recorded in her diary: "Every day I spent some time in the herbal and books of physic, and in ministering to one or other by the directions of the best physicians of my acquaintance."[11] Upon her death, Mildmay left manuscripts to her grandchildren, including 2,000 loose papers with writings devoted to the structure of the body, the preparation of medicines, and the nature of diseases. Recommending syrups, balms, oil, tinctures, lotions, cordials, and pastes, Mildmay engaged in medical practices that accord with those of university-trained physicians, despite the emergent medical community's denunciations of amateurs as "quacks" and "mountebanks." Alternating between culinary and medical recipes (or those that embodied both), guidebooks targeted to diverse audiences portrayed the kitchen as a pharmacy and distillery where plants and herbs were processed, a slaughterhouse where animals were skinned and dressed, and a hospital where wounds were attended. The common denominator for these activities was the maintenance of the body in the forms of foods and cures.

Creating and dispensing drugs, housewives were the medical practitioners most likely to come into actual contact with a patient's body, for physicians preferred to make diagnoses without seeing the patient, on the basis of urine samples or descriptions of symptoms. Within the camp of emerging professionals, physicians (licensed by the relatively new College of Physicians) were to attend to major internal diseases; surgeons were to perform the "manual labor" of amputating limbs and treating venereal disease; apothecaries were to prepare and sell drugs; and midwives were to monitor normal childbirths.[12] Yet since "official" medical personnel were in short supply and official training was not seen as a guarantor of sound practice, English people typically relied primarily on amateur healers such as clergy, wise women, and most commonly the housewife. Whether most people agreed with Ann Windsor's declaration that "Kitchen physic . . . is more proper . . . than the Dr's filthy physic" isn't as important as the fact that household physic was the *only* form of medicine available to most people in early modern England.[13] Professionals were new intruders into a longstanding system of medicine based primarily on folk knowledge; and the practices of trained medical personnel did not differ in kind from those performed by lay practitioners – except, that is, for their distance from the patient's body.

While some women confined their medical treatment to simple remedies, others extended their work both in terms of its scope and its reach. Hannah Woolley boasted that she acted as surgeon to her entire parish. Hoby, whose reputation was widespread, felt comfortable attempting an unsuccessful surgery on a child born without an anus.[14] And the Countess of Kent treated strangers who traveled to take advantage of her expertise. It was perhaps the scope of this medical practice that occasioned the panicky warnings that crop up in husbandry books and guides, for here we find injunctions that women should not intrude upon the tasks of physicians or assume to be their equal. Northampton doctor John Cotta devotes an entire chapter of his physic book to declaiming against "she-physicians" who dissuade patients from using physicke "as commeth unknowne unto them, out of Apothecaries shops, or from Physitions hands, and directions: thereby preferring their owne private ointments, plaisters, ceaseclothes, drinkes, potions, glysters and diets because by time and custome they are become familiar and knowne unto them."[15] Even Gervase Markham feels obliged to mention that his competent housewife shouldn't overreach her skills by acting as "professor" of the art. Markham continues:

Neither doe I intend here to lead her minde with al the Symptomes, accidents, and effects which go before or after every sicknesse, as though I would have her to assume the name of a Practitioner, but only relate unto her some approoved medicines, and old doctrines which have beene gathered together . . . and delivered by common and ordinary experience for the curing of those ordinary sicknesses which daily perturbe the health of men and Women.[16]

The collaborative *Countrey Farm* similarly advises women to leave "more exquisite Remedies to . . . professed Physitions"; and John Partridge's *Treasurie of Hidden Secrets* assures readers that it contains medical knowledge "not impertinent for every good Huswife to use in her house, amongst her own familie."[17] If Cotta sees female doctors as dangerous because of their limited knowledge, other writers represent them as perhaps too eager to venture beyond "ordinary" treatments carried out in the home or to attend to the paying customers of professionals. Venturing "outside" set parameters, as Nell in *Burning Pestle* so clearly does, seems an everpresent concern in the period.

Despite the fact that it could be imagined as "impertinent" knowledge, housewives at every rank were enjoined to oversee healthcare. After offering a caveat about the limitations of a housewife's "proper" medical work, Markham puts his lengthy section on medicine at the beginning of *The English House-wife*. "To begin then with one of the most principal vertues which doth belong to our English House-wife," Markham writes:

You shall understand, that sith the preservation and care of the family touching their health and soundnesse of body consisteth most in the diligence: it is meet that shee have a physicall kind of knowledge, how to administer many wholesome receits or medicines for the good of their health as wel to prevent the first occasion of sicknesse, as to take away the effects and evill of the same when it hath made seazure on the body. (4–5)

His complicated recipes hardly seem about "common experience," or rather, we might conclude that the housewife's ordinary medical work was intricate. Markham's relative lack of panic over the housewife's medical know-how seems connected to his investment in the self-sufficiency of the English estate; for in his schema, the housewife is the ultimate guarantor against failures caused by problems in the body (disease) or in the economy (overconsumption). Yet as Doreen Nagy has shown, women's role in seventeenth-century medicine was hardly limited to the occasional philanthropic gentlewoman or exceptional wise woman; instead, housewives at different social levels read medical books, wrote manuscript recipes to be handed down to servants and children, and tended to sick bodies in many capacities; they participated, that is, in medical practice and the circulation of texts surrounding it. Advocated as a moral and economic duty – but also denounced as a potentially hubristic act and a threat to propriety – women's medical work was named as both controversial and routine.

The fact that the housewife was nervously agreed to be the ultimate authority on common ailments could register in early modern discourse in unexpected ways. The 1616 *Maison Rustique* is a case in point. A standard book of household management written for the male householder, *Maison Rustique* offers instructions for how to design a kitchen garden, vinery, park, dairy, henhouse, and barnyard. What is odd, however, is the almost obsessive focus on healing to which the book keeps returning, almost despite its broader designs. Although the housewife's duties are covered in a short section, she stubbornly resurfaces in chapters ostensibly directed to other workers. In a chapter on hunting, for instance, Markham begins to wax on the medical properties of deer meat and to stray into the subject of food preparation. At another point, the author interjects instructions on distillation in the section on gardening. Since all plants, trees, herbs, and animals could be processed into goods that contribute to the maintenance of the body, all husbandry leads back inside the house – into the kitchen.

Markham apologizes for his seemingly compulsive return to the wife's duties, noting at one moment that he keeps wandering "from our scope and platform" to circle back to "the Mistress or good wife of our Countrey Farme" (469). He explains:

Notwithstanding that distillation be the worke rather of a Philosopher or Alchymist . . . than of a farmer or maister of a Countrie Farme: notwithstanding the profit thereof is so great, and the use so laudible and necessarie, as that we take not the chiefe Lord of our countrie house to be furnished with all such singular commodities as we desire, if he lacke the knowledge and practise of distillation; not that I would have him to make it a matter to trouble himselfe much withall, and to be at much cost and charges therewith . . . but onely that we would take his time thereto at his best leasure, and without any great expence; or else to *leave the same to his wife or his farmer's wife*; for indeed such occupation is farre better beseeming either of them than him; for as much as the maistresse or dairie-woman hath the pettie affaires and businesses belonging to our countrie Farme, and lying within the doores, resigned and put over to her. *Therefore let it not seem strange in this point*, if after our briefe intreatie of Oyles, we discourse somewhat briefely . . . of the manner of distilling of waters, and extracting of oylie quintessences, out of such matter as our Countrie Farme shall afford; which we would should serve for the use of the Farmers wife, as well to relieve her folke withall, as to succour her needie neighbours in the time of sickenesse; as we see it to be the ordinarie custome of great Ladies, Gentlewomen, and Farmers wives well and charitably disposed, who distill waters and prepare oyntments, and such other remedies, to succour and relieve the poore. (438, emphasis mine)

The writer's anxiety in allowing the farmer's wife to overstep her authority presses through this passage. The husband cannot be expected to master a difficult, costly, and complex art that appropriately is the concern of professionals, philosophers, alchemists – or housewives, the text says puzzlingly. "Let it not seem strange," he beseeches his reader, to speak at length of the "pettie affaires and businesses" of female workers, trivial duties that are also "laudible and necessarie." The entire work of agriculture finds its telos in raw products, the "matter" that the farm affords, so a proper estate manual must not mention farm materials without explaining their use value. Since the wife is in charge of the body, what then truly lies beyond her purview? *Maison Rustique* suggests that housewifery could loom large in the cultural imagination as well as in actual practice, taking center stage as a foundational economic activity.

Is it surprising, then, that when a character introduced as "the Wife" takes the stage in *Knight of the Burning Pestle*, she hastens to demonstrate her mastery of the tasks chiefly recommended to her? Throughout the play, Nell attempts to minister to the ailments of both actors who need help in performing, and characters who suffer fictional beatings; she fills the stage with the medical wisdom standard in how-to books. Before servant-turned-actor Rafe makes his entrance, Nell insists on sending a piece of liquorice into the tiring house: "Tell him his mistress sent it him," she instructs a boy actor, "and bid him bite a piece; 'twill open his pipes the better, say" (1.71–3). Eating liquorice, according to Partridge's *Treasurie of Commodious Conceites* and W. M.'s *Queens Closet Opened*, could indeed cleanse the windpipe, lungs, and chest. Nell's later decision to use mare's milk to cure worms comes straight out of the *Closet for Ladies* (though she adds the popular *Carduus benedictus*, or blessed thistle, to this remedy); and she reflects standard practice when she uses sugar candy lozenges to heal wounds (3.303–306; 2.329). John Murrell's *Daily Exercise* validates her decision to staunch the blood with green ginger suckets, for ginger was a powerful "warming spice" used to heat the body and decrease inflammations (2.255–6).[18]

Nell's most unexpected intrusion into the play's action comes when she advises Mistress Merrythought to cure her son's (fictional) chilblains by rubbing them with a mouse skin. Having attended to this symptom, she then throws in additional tips for how to help his (non-existent) constipation. Although Michael hasn't displayed any signs of "tightness," Nell is eager to loosen his body. Peppering her speech with references to the growth-stunting power of "knot-grass" (an herb used in making cordial waters), Nell imports kitchen wisdom into the theatrical arena. Since the title pestle was in fact an instrument used not only by grocers but by housewives, Rafe's quixotic tasks are defined within the domain of both guild and household.[19] The audience would have readily identified the popular but somewhat controversial discourse of home medicine that preoccupies Nell and her questing knight.

According to marital guides and sermons, the wife's authority in the home was qualified by her husband's superior rule. Although she was to be subject to him in all areas, the housewife could command matters in which the husband had little or no knowledge. In *A Godly Forme of Houshold Government*, Dod and Cleaver establish areas of household responsibility "in which the husband giveth over his right unto his wife: as to rule and governe her maidens: to see to those things that belong unto the kitchin, and to huswiferie."[20] Medical care was one of the tasks that "belonged" to the kitchen. Yet the prestige of medicine, bolstered by its appropriation by professionals, put it at odds with the other work undertaken by housewives, with the result that the home physic had an ambivalent cultural status. In *Burning Pestle*, when the Wife takes every opportunity to spew medical knowledge, she locates her authority to comment on theater within a domestic expertise deemed both prestigious and contentious.

It wasn't just the housewife's increasing rivalry with professionals but also the nature of physic that made her medical interventions noteworthy. Highly soluble, the early modern body was in constant need of evacuations: enemas, laxatives, and emetics for the lower body stratum; herbs, changes in thermal conditions, and air for upper body "purges" (vomiting, coughing, burping); bloodletting, exercise, and orgasm for all around purification. In the Galenic model, disease resulted when the humors were imbalanced and thus bodies required constant maintenance. In the new medical theories derived from Theophrastus Paracelsus, disease was caused by agents located in particular body parts; yet in practice Paracelsian methods closely resembled humoral treatments. Housewifery guides regularly assign multiple benefits to purgatives (Nell's preferred method of treatment): they cured a "dim" head, bellyache, fevers, difficulty in breathing, pains in the joints, problems in digestion. Even poor vision was treated with an expulsitive since it was said to be caused by gaseous spirits that had risen to the head. Texts such as *The Compleat Servant-Maid, The Queens Closet Opened, The Ladies Cabinet Opened* and *A Choice Manual* repeatedly point out that the housewife must "keep the body open."[21] George Hartman includes 35 fairly complex recipes for purgatives and enemas in his 1696 *The Family Physitian*, noting that a clister once a month kept the body in good order.[22] In *The Castel of Health*, Thomas Elyot notes that enemas are safer than swallowed purgatives, since they don't have the opportunity to boil within the stomach and produce harmful superfluities.[23] Indeed *The Charitable Physitian* opens with eighteen different recipes for enemas, suppositories, and laxatives, all of which would have been concocted and administered by the housewife.

The housewife's ministrations granted her intimate knowledge of, and control over, these desperately needy early modern bodies. Cotta implies that it was a routine event for women to offer household members (including guests and servants) doses of "purge comfits" (sweet laxatives) and then monitor the progress of the drugs in detailed terms.[24] Markham instructs his reader on the secret of having "two stooles a day and no more" (32). Guibert's *The Charitable Physitian*, addressed to lay practitioners who wanted to avail themselves of the latest doctor's methods in their homes, includes among its list of necessary household instruments "two syringes or bladders fitted with pipes to give Clysters, the one for great folks, the other for children" as well as "another bladder and boxe pipe to lend charitably to the poore" (41). Guibert hastens to mention that enema pipes loaned to people should be warmed and washed upon their return (44). Margaret Hoby indicates that these were not fanciful instructions, for she records preparing a purgative for "my cousin Isons woman" as well as her own glisters.[25] Given these exchanges, it seems that the housewife regularly scrutinized the (now privatized) bodily secretions of household members and neighbors.

Submitting to such ministrations meant acknowledging a lack of control over one's chaotic body, but this moment of physical subjection might bring the pleasures of bodily attention, stimulation, and release; that is, common dietary and medical regimens were said to produce feelings of laxation. Since the body was thought to be under constant pressures, the patient might associate treatments with a much needed relief from tightness, looseness, or windiness (treatments that might include massaging and bathing a patient's back, head, and buttocks).[26] Narcotics such as alcohol-based syrups served as pain relievers; and sugar, still an important medicinal spice, made cordials hardly unpleasant to the palate. In early modern usage, the word "purge" in fact generally suggests a redemptive moment, the blessed cleansing of defilement.

Here we might recall Paster's analysis of how affective relations were shaped by people's peculiarly humoral bodily experience and the social practices surrounding it. The child's early relationship with the female caregiver (nurse, mother, wise woman, or servant) shaped feelings of dependence, pleasure, and self-mastery that persisted throughout the subject's life. Practices of bodily maintenance such as purges constituted one of the domestic interactions through which the child's struggle for autonomy was waged. "The repeated bodily phenomenon of the purge," Paster writes, "helped to constitute normative forms of bodily self-experience."[27] The fact that the ingredients for enemas did double duty as aphrodisiacs and banqueting materials (e.g., sugar candy, milk, rosewater) emphasizes the complex pleasure tied to the housewife's jurisdiction. In John Ford's *Love's Sacrifice* (1633), a servant responds sarcastically to his preening master, Mauruchio, who asks, "Am I all sweet behinde? . . . with what grace doe my words proceed out of my mouth?" "I doe feele a savour as pleasant as a Glister-pipe," servant Giacopia responds, "Calamus or Ciuet" (perfumes).[28] Cosmo Manuche's *The Loyal Lovers* (1652) expands the meaning of the glister-pipe's "sweetness" when a character named Sodome dimly recalls a night of debauchery: "They have given me purging comfits too, for I'me / Damnable moist behinde; What company was I in? / I remember nothing but a whore."[29] Apparently the delights of a carnivalesque release from propriety could call to mind the "savour" of a glister-pipe or the taste of purgatives. In this period, a wild night might include desserts, sex, and laxatives, and a servant might attend to the sweetness of his master's "behinde" by thinking of the "savour" of an enema. As I have mentioned, John Johnson's *Academy of Love* (1641) presents an elaborate dream in which a lover tours a Dante-like University of *amor*, where lovers are shown satirical versions of academic "disciplines." This tour includes having "Batcherlorists, Licentiates and Doctoresses" administer glisters and purgatives. Johnson's poem serves as the fantasy par excellence of male submission to the erotic manipulations of wildly beautiful female purgers who perform vomits, glisters, and bloodletting as seduction.[30] The postures of dependency, vulnerability, and mastery so prevalent in early modern erotic representations found one register in the practices of home physic.

Yet some recipes tested the very threshold of the patient's pain by requiring that plasters – as hot as the patient could stand – be repeatedly laid to sensitive areas (e.g., the anus, vagina, tongue, penis). *The Closet for Ladies'* remedy for vaginal infections requires endurance on the part of the patient: "Fry Hemlock in fresh swines grease. Lay it as hotte as shee may suffer it to the secret place," the text instructs (71). *The Queens Closet Opened* advises the healer to cure the plague by forcing a feverish patient to drink treacle and malmsey, which causes sporadic vomiting for days. "You must apply the same very often day and night till he brook it," the writer advises (25–6). It also recommends loosening a patient's belly by repeatedly applying hot boiled eggs to the anus: "put the smaller end of it hot to the Fundament or Arse-hole then when that is cold, take another such hot, fresh, hard and peeled Egg and apply it as aforesaid" (130). Grey's *Choice Manual* tells housewives how to cure an ague in the breast: "Take the patients own water, or any others that is very young, and set it on the fire, put therein a good handful of Rosemary, and let it boil." After soaking a cloth in steaming urine, the housewife lays it on the patient's breast "as hot as it may be endured" (64). In addition to recommending that women cut the patient's navel to absorb drugs, guidebooks prescribed a host of intrusive and painful therapies.[31] Some subjected patients to a cycle of sweats, enemas, fasting, and bloodletting from veins in the head. Mildmay offers a cure "for the red face" that tells how to crush pimples with a needle, squeeze out blood and pus, and then fill up the skin sack with ink. "If it smart it is the better," she observes, suggesting that pain would be an index of the body's recovery of health (Pollock, 26). The repeated call for "gentle physic" by characters on stage suggests the commonplace early modern association of healing with a harsh counter-experience.

Remedies that were not necessarily painful may simply have been perceived as uncomfortable. People were urged to drink concoctions made of rancid milk left to steep for weeks, place fresh warm dog excrement against sore throats, bind dead pigeons to the soles of their feet, and sip broths composed of animal flesh that had been buried for days, exhumed, and ground into cullises or jellies. Despite the resilience of an early modern nose accustomed to strong odors, practitioners and patients may well have noticed the smell of rotting eggs, putrefying animal flesh, urine, and excrement hovering around the kitchen.[32] Urine (human and animal) was also an important ingredient for cleansing the body and adjusting its temperature. Trinculo's complaint to Caliban in *The Tempest* – "Monster, I do smell all horse-piss, at which my nose is in great indignation" – suggests that these ingredients might have been noticed by patients (4.1.199–200). In *The Queens Closet Opened* (1658), housewifery brings the stench of death along with the annoyance of spoiled flesh. One of its plague remedies requires the housewife to plaster a bare-rumped chicken over the patient's ulcerous sore until the animal labors and dies: it "will gape and labour for life, and in the end dye; then take another, and the third and so long as any do dye: for when the poyson is quite drawn out, the Chick will live, the sore presently will asswage, and the party recover" (31–2). Swallowing bitter herbs, being scalded by hot plasters, drinking lye, and imagining tortured chickens dying as they cleave to pestilent sores – early modern people submitted to a corporeal trial under the housewife's command. The housewife's privileged relationship to the body embedded her in early modern negotiations over autonomy and dependence.

In previous chapters, I have examined plays that place the audience in the position of a male subject who finds himself forced to reckon with a seemingly lost, intimate, or frightening domesticity. *Merry Wives of Windsor*, for instance, portrays housewifery as empowered enough to remold social relations, but it does so by focusing on the householder's and male aristocrat's feelings of titillating masochism as they are made to submit to domestic authority. But what about the fantasies and feelings of the woman administering kitchen physic? Or to put it differently: how might we think about representations that show traces of early modern interest in the psychic and social investments of *both* parties in these corporeal exchanges? *Burning Pestle* vividly depicts the housewife's domestic desires and passions. Titania's pleasure in "purging" Bottom in *Midsummer Night's Dream* may finally be a humiliating joke, but in *Knight of the Burning Pestle*, Nell's strange passion for the players – her gleeful desire to make everyone into an ailing dependant that she can medicate – is lightly satirized but never demonized as a threat to male subjectivity. Instead the play explores and delights in the strange cathexis that the housewife has for dependants. Rather than tracing the male subject's separation from the infant–female caregiver dyad (as did *Gammer* and *Friar Bacon*), *Burning Pestle* displays the domestic woman's *ongoing* psychic investment in managing bodies. Thus while Paster focuses her discussion on infantile dependency and its translation into symbolic forms, we may also consider the housewife's perceived dominant role in healthcare, not necessarily as a "regressive bodily memory" but as an ongoing event in the lives of adults (125).

Let me give two examples of how kitchen physic emerges as the site of fantasy in *Burning Pestle*. The unabashed social ambition that Nell displays in boldly stepping onto the stage with gentlemen is first expressed as her desire to make Rafe's voice "swell." Offering liquorice to "open his pipes" and ventilate his upper body enough for clear oratory and projection, her first advice to her servant is a purge.[33] The Wife's pride and nervousness about Rafe's (and by extension her own) performance emerges, in this moment, as a rehearsal of a conventional household task, now shown to underpin good acting and public speech. The spectacle of Nell's apparent breach of decorum, that of appearing on stage, is displaced onto her servant's healthy bodily "expansion." Having given ambition this domestic register, the play then goes on to present the metaphorics of purging in "The London Merchant"; for the Merchant Venturewell compares his apprentice Jasper to a "bladder" [enema bag] who "blew himself with love" and now requires a "cure": "I have let out," he confides to his would-be son-in-law Humphrey, meaning that he has fired Jasper and saved his daughter from the downward class mobility that such a marriage would bring (1.77–80). Here purgation figures the master's regulation of the inappropriate sexual desires of household subordinates (their unsuitable self-expansion) as well as his right to purify disorderly elements. Nell's positive image of purgation as enabling full expression contrasts with the Merchant's vision of deflation as social discipline.

Later Nell reminds the audience of the Merchant's figurative appropriation of the purge by insistently literalizing it. Carried away in dispensing medical wisdom, she recommends a purge for Michael to help constipation even though the character only has sore feet. Her call for a purgative is not a way of registering a character flaw, as did the Merchant in the first scene; instead her advice is merely a digression that she comes to associatively, since smelling feet is supposed to aid in evacuating the body. Since the Merchant's authority in the first scene relies on the grammar of housewifery, Nell's subsequent obsession with purging implies a claim that home care is the prior activity on which such figurations are built; that is, the play figures her "literal" purging by associating it with the fantasized ambitions of subordinates. Presenting a housewife almost out of control (expanding and loosening the bounds of the play, its actors, and their bodies), the audience is reminded of the processes of subjection that shaped early modern subjects.

A similar oscillation between fictional plot and frame tale occurs around another moment of purgative housewifery. In "The London Merchant" Luce sarcastically pretends to minister to the wounds of Humphrey, her despised fiancé who has been beaten by her true love. "Get thee some wholesome broth with sage and comfrey; / A little oil of roses and a feather," she advises, "to 'noint thy back withal" (2.237–9). Advising Humphrey on how to salve his wounds, Luce quotes a familiar poultice used to staunch bleeding.[34] What is interesting is that the Wife then echoes Luce, replacing the character's mockery with a genuinely offered cure for the stomach and head. Reaching into her pocket to find candied ginger, she pleads: "Come hither, Master Humphrey; has he hurt you? Now beshrew his fingers fo'rt. Here, sweetheart, here's some green ginger for thee. Now beshrew my heart, but 'a has peppernel in's head as big as a pullet's egg" (2. 254–7). Luce ridicules Humphrey by mimicking the role that she refuses to undertake – that of good wife – but audience member Nell steps in to redefine housewifery not as a marital role but as task-based knowledge. Offering him one of the two most common spices (the other was pepper), Nell downgrades Luce's recipe to a bare simple, one that tellingly involves a "warm" and ingested purge. As a character in Greene and Lodge's 1598 *Looking Glasse for London and England* notes, "the philosophers have written of the nature of ginger, 'tis expulsitive in two degrees . . . it will make a man belch, cough, & fart, and is a great comfort to the heart." Woolley verifies this information: "The biting heat of Ginger is more lasting and durable [than pepper] . . . [it] opens obstructions, and is very expedient for the expulsion of Wind. Green Ginger in the Indies preserved, is excellent good for a watry and windy stomack."[35] Not only does Nell replace a romantic version of nurturance with a vocational one, but she changes the nature of the cure from easeful rose oil to a "biting" expulsitive; her response to physical injury is not to treat the symptom but to alleviate pain by dramatically purging the entire body. Like other "warming spices," ginger aided not only in digestion and the balance of fluids, but was thought to have aphrodisiac qualities. Again in this instance, the housewife recasts the stage action so as to query the play's multiple frames, but that "joke" rests on a highly material and eroticized maternal nurturance. Through her medical interruptions, the housewife seems able to reach deep into the recesses of all bodies, and, by doing so, translate everyone into malleable household dependants.

The housewife's investment in tending to bodies could be represented in a tragic register as well. As she is dying, Webster's Duchess of Malfi begs her female servant Cariola to oversee her children's religious instruction and healthcare: "I pray thee look thou giv'st my little boy / Some syrup for his cold, and let the girl / Say her prayers, ere she sleep."[36] Many of the feminist critics who have grappled with these lines locate them within the conceptual schema of separate private and public spheres: the Duchess is said to conjure up an intimate family life in the face of a corrupt political world, to install a liberal female subject who chooses to submit to heterosexual domesticity, to reveal contradictions between a woman's political station and the power accorded her gender, or to carve out a powerful space from within the position of maternity.[37] But was tending the body a privatized "maternal" act? Guidebooks suggest that it could also constitute *work* within the household, as mistresses and maids collectively made syrups. Tusser instructs the housewife to create a "Conserve of the Barberie, Quinces and such, / With Sirops that easeth the sickly so much" (179); and Plat, Partridge, and Woolley direct all women including aristocrats to make syrups from flowers, roots, and fruits. The Duchess may be acting the part of "good wife" in her final moments, but what a "good wife" entailed was not merely subordination within the marital hierarchy; it also meant a "good worker" in a vocation.

In addition to conjuring up maternal concern, the Duchess' allusion to medical remedies, then, might have invited the audience to recall the labors of shopping, distilling, and gardening that inevitably went into their making. When critics see this gesture as evidence of an emergent maternal role defined primarily by affective bonds, they have to skew the way that affective bonds were attached to labor relations within an expansive notion of "family." What the

Duchess wants Cariola to replay is the bodily care that she herself experienced as a child and then rehearsed in her life by healing household dependants. This memory, cast in the form of an injunction, functions as solace for the Duchess, promising a continuity of everyday acts that overshadow the madness that Bosola has created in the orgy of violence in this scene. He has, after all, made her witness a tableau of her dead family, kiss a dead man's hand, and embrace her tombmaker. Instead of succumbing to despair, as Bosola hopes, the Duchess tries out subject positions – noblewoman, Christian, and housewife. This tragedy poignantly shows the intense *affect* surrounding the seemingly trivial everyday tasks of medical practice and childraising. It can be read, I think, as complementing rather than reducing her other declarations about the futility of death in the face of unwavering belief in heavenly redemption.

When played out in comedy, the housewife's domestic investments are unsurprisingly ribald. Reminding her husband of his wild youth, extracting hugs from him to alleviate her fears, and offering kisses if he will make demands on the actors, Nell blends amorous negotiations with dramatic critique. Labeling Merrythought a "fornicating fellow" that "will not out of [her] mind," Nell later becomes almost "molten with fretting" (Interlude 3.3).[38] Her involvement with the play, and with Rafe as a figure for the playworld, produces violent emotional and physical reactions. "I would have Rafe, George; I'll see no more else indeed" (2.89–90). "I shall be sick if he go away, that I shall. Call Rafe again, George," she pleads (2.131–2). Rafe becomes the citizens' theatrical fetish, naming their eroticized desire to manage spectacle and producing in Nell a longing that manifests itself as somatic symptom. If, in eroticizing domestic tasks, *Burning Pestle* exposes the housewife's investment in tending to bodies, it also makes what Paster refers to as the affect surrounding bodily control a *reciprocal* set of emotions.

Plays that represent physic as an indulgence of consumer-minded women offer a related but slightly different account of the housewife's pleasure. In *Eastward Ho!* gentleman-apprentice Quicksilver warns another character about the demands of aspiring ladies. Discussing a woman's professed need for local cunning women, Quicksilver paints a portrait of female–female relationships based on a scene of intertwined gossip, erotics, and medicine: "what Nurses, what Midwiues, what Fooles, what Phisitions, what cunning women must be sought for (fearing sometimes she is bewitcht, sometimes in a consumption) to tell her tales, to talke bawdy to her, to make her laughe, to give her glisters, to let her bloud vnder the tongue, and betwixt the toes."[39] Quicksilver offers a vision of the housewife being housewived: the dream of being tended materializes in the form of a purgation (anally and arterially) enmeshed in the discursive pleasures of titillating talk, gossip, and stories. This scenario is meant to evidence a lady's social pretensions, since it shows her willingness to relinquish domestic authority in order to become a pampered dependant, an exchange marked by a housewifely erotics (bawdy talk, giggling, purgation). The imagined pleasure of bodily evacuation is here embedded in a female–female relationship, one intimate enough to involve searching the interior of the mouth or handling one's naked foot.

Jonson's portrayal of female physic must be distinguished from the common city comedy representation of professional medication as a luxury good consumed primarily by indulgent and licentious women. In Lording Barry's *Ram-Alley* (1611), taking physic is lumped together with reading romances and other extravagances in a way that makes Nell's bawdy and body talk seem less extraordinary. In this play, when Mistress Taffeta is wooed by Sir Oliver Small-shankes, she bargains with him about what pleasures married life must offer, including, interestingly, medical treatment: "Shall I keepe / My chamber by the moneth, if I bee pleas'd / To take Physicke, to send for Visitants, / To haue my maide read *Amadis de Gaule, /Or Donzel del Phoebo* to me? shall I have /A Carotch [luxury carriage] of the last edition, / The Coatch-mans seate a good way from the Coatch, / That if some other Ladies and my selfe / Chance to talke bawdy, he may not ouer-heare us."[40] Dirty talk, exclusive female company, and humoral purging merge within a fantasy of a truly leisured female life of urban consumerism (and Barry adds romance reading to the equation). This sentiment is legible as well in *Westward Ho* when the bawd Mistress Birdlime attempts to goad a citizen's wife into an adulterous liaison with an earl: "beauty covets rich apparell, choyce dyet, excellent Physicke . . . and what means hath your Husband to allow sweet Doctor *Glister-pipe* his pention."[41] In such scenarios, the doctor's access to the house becomes a source of jealousy for the citizen who craves markers of status but who worries about opening the home to such traffic. Taking physic or not marks a power struggle over controlling access to home and body, which, in city comedies, revolves centrally around the faultline between citizenry and aristocracy as they trade money and wives in early modern London. But Birdlime's glisterpipe fantasy is centered around a desire to escape the traditional housewifery that Nell embodies. Quicksilver instead makes physicians interchangeable with female vernacular practice, and therefore he touches on desires other than status consumerism; it is this fantasy of the multiple pleasures of home-care that *Burning Pestle* so readily engages.

### Tending to boys

Nell's stage housewifery simply exaggerates the complicated dynamics that could develop around household service. Young people comprised the pivotal mobile group yoked into service in the early modern period, as upper-class youths flowed into the households of relatives and patrons and those from non-elite backgrounds entered schools, apprenticeships, domestic service, and wage-labor situations. Apprentices made up about one-fifth of the population at the turn of the century, with approximately 2,800 teens beginning apprenticeships in London each year.[42] Citizenship was not usually conferred until age 24, after an apprenticeship of seven years of service, but official service was itself sometimes a second stage of work. Young people remained single (not a householder or household mistress) for a more prolonged period of time in England than in other pre-industrial societies. Their full participation in adult life was retarded since legal, social, and economic rights could not be conferred until they established a household through marriage. Before that time, they entered domestic situations as subordinates to an institutional, often paternal, authority.

The 10- to 15-year-old boys who appeared in theater productions were conscripted from grammar schools, choirs, and apprenticeships to "serve the Crown," in keeping with the official conception of private theater.[43] Nell even mentions the odd power that theater companies had in impressing children when she says of Rafe, "and he be not inveigled by some of these paltry players I ha' much marvel" (2.202–203). The conscription of boys into companies was a commonplace event, although the kidnapping lawsuit it spurred in one instance makes clear its potential conflict with household authority and elite family expectations.[44] Boys working in supposedly noncommercial companies occupied a different position from those serving in adult theatrical companies; for private theaters ran on the fiction that they were simply rehearsals for the court and thus were outside commercial regulations. Boy actors in public companies, however, were indentured as apprentices to actors who were also guild members (hence Ben Jonson's motivation for continuing to pay membership to the bricklayer's guild). Since boys in the children's companies were not members of guilds, they were dependants within a highly unusual and vague structure of mastering – subject to the authority of the manager but also the royal household and the audience.

Extending the master's and mistress' sway over apprentices (who acted *in loco parentis*) to the stage, *Burning Pestle*'s Nell repeatedly calls attention to the players' juniority, addressing them as "pretty youth," "the boy," "the little boy," and "pretty child." Although the Merchant is an aged senex parent, Nell deflates his authority by infantilizing him. After he struts around displaying his seniority, the Wife remarks, "Well, my youth, you may proceed" (1.100–1). "That's a good boy. See, the little boy can hit it; by my troth, it's a fine child," she later says of apprentice George (1.296–7). The pronoun "it" was routinely applied in the early modern period to infants and children under the age of 7, when the sexes were not yet differentiated by dress. Nell's repeated use of "it" not only infantilizes the actors, but it also levels age distinctions within the fiction. "Didst thou ever see a prettier child? How it behaves itself; I warrant ye, and speaks, and looks, and perts up the head?" Nell exclaims, as if the teenage actors provided an anthropological curiosity, a source of wonder (1.94–6). Her constant fussing over the children's troupe serves to "out" their boyness from their roles as adult and teenage characters. That the Wife is herself played by a boy actor only ironically underscores the humor of this "disidentification."

What Nell puts under the microscope are the practices of "children's theater companies," as they were called. "I pray you, brother, with your favour, were you never none of Master Monkester's scholars?" she questions one of the players (1.96–7). Headmaster of London's two best grammar schools, The Merchant Taylors and St. Paul's, Richard Mulcaster was an esteemed pedagogue known for, among other things, his introduction of acting into the humanist curriculum and his direction of pupils in court plays. Given the conceptual opposition between housewife and humanist, Nell's reference to humanist scholar and teacher Mulcaster is resonant.[45] Her intended compliment might have simply served as the Chapel Children's joke at their own expense, since Mulcaster was associated with a defunct rival theater company, but its overall effect was to call attention to teenage actors as caught up in a business where they straddle different identities – pupil, servant, commercial player, courtier. When she coaxes Rafe, "It's a good boy, hold up thy head and be not afraid" (2.98), Nell defies the humanist view of cross-gendered domesticity as the anti-type of proper learning and instead asserts her authority as a household manager *in charge of children.* Jonson's *Staple of News* stages this opposition more baldly when one of the "female Gossips" of the chorus denounces pedagogy: "I would haue ne'er a cunning Schoolemaster in England . . . They make all their schollers Play-boyes! Is't not a fine sight, to see all our children made Enterluders?"[46] But Nell, a clear advocate of theater, dissolves the opposition between domesticity and academia/theater. Claiming that the home-tutored Rafe can outwit the players even if "they were older than they are," she pictures actors, servants, and students as interchangeable dependants (1.66–7).

In one sense, Nell calls attention to the phenomenon that the audience always, at some level, recognized when they enjoyed "children" (a capacious term in the period) aping adults, plotting intrigue and violence, and spewing invective and bawdy innuendo. As Michael Shapiro argues, it was precisely the incongruity raised by a character who was both child and adult that made the private companies so enjoyable to Renaissance audiences.[47] Part of the energy generated by children's troops, he notes, stemmed from the inappropriateness of youths licensed to act saucily, a lack of decorum noted in the Cambridge play *Lingua* when a character called Common Sense complains: "O times! O manners, when Boies dare to traduce men in authority."[48] Thomas Heywood famously agrees when he writes of the "liberty which some [playwrights] arrogate to themselves, committing their bitternesse and liberall invectives against all estates, to the mouthes of children, supposing their juniority to be a privilege for any rayling."[49] Clearly satiric barbs were intensified when mouthed by audacious teens. Heightened as well was the impropriety of bawdiness, which underwrote much of the humor of early modern drama. *The Isle of Guls* satirizes elite audience's taste for "good baudry . . . jests of an ell deepe, and a fathome broad, good cuckolding . . . a sceane of venery that will make a mans spirits stand on theyr typtoes and die his blood in deepe scarlet" (66–7, 69–70). *Cynthia's Revels* comments on this phenomenon by presenting youths who get into a full brawl when two attempt to stop a third actor from revenging the author by giving away the whole plot. When the assaulted speaker declares, "What, will you rauish me? . . . I'd crie a rape, but that you are children," he highlights the carnivalesque shock afforded by children breaking the rules of everyday life in the theater.[50] Young actors lent an air of absurdity that could momentarily distance the audience from the plot enough to make them aware of the delightful improprieties of theatrical practice.

Since Nell's pleasure in how "it" behaves makes the familiar sight of child actors performing adulthood look eccentric, she teases out a source of humor latent in theatrical practice, subduing the actors' cheekiness with her domestic overtures but also exacerbating a tension that animated the performance. Given that some plays featured adults performing alongside 13-year-olds, the early modern theater clearly found it easy to flaunt fissures in identity in ways that a modern mimetically based theatrical practice might find disruptive. The Wife's commentary in *Burning Pestle*, then, exposes the imaginative dynamic inhering in the audience's relationship with children's troupes, forcing an inquiry into what it was that so piqued audience interest. Her obsessive desire to "see" Rafe may have only exaggerated a posture available to all audiences, a posture reinforced by the fact that theater was one institution among many where boys entered service in a domestic environment. The choirmaster of St. Pauls, Sebastian Westcote, for instance, had seven current and former choristers (ages ranging from 16 to 30) living with him when he died and he remembered them affectionately in his will. *Burning Pestle*'s audience was invited to delight in watching youths whom they knew to "belong" institutionally elsewhere. "The child's a fatherless child," Nell says of Rafe, clearly marking a chain of surrogate dependencies (2.92–3).

Recent work on eroticism in early modern culture has called attention to how issues of status and dependency were explicitly joined to desire in dominant discourses of the period, if for no other reason than the fact that the entire world was refracted through a prism colored by social hierarchy.[51] Since everyone was a mastered person or a master, and networks of patronage defined one's identity, desire was predictably understood and experienced in socially vertical terms that cut across lines of gender. This phenomenon is evidenced, as Lisa Jardine suggests, in Shakespeare's *Twelfth Night*, where the language of courtship and that of household service are shown to be identical. To wait on someone, offer a suit, serve – these residual feudal terms of courtly love implicate eros within the logic of social place. It is no wonder that the two noble characters, Olivia and Orsino, marry people whom they think to be servant-dependants (though, in the case of Sebastian, this turns out to be a mistaken assumption); and that the creation of a fabricated character, servant Cesario, clarifies the drive for mastery and dependency that shapes Olivia's and Orsino's desires.[52] *Twelfth Night* is unusual only in foregrounding the absolute reducibility of the vocabulary of loyal servitude to that of desire – so much so that when Viola reveals her female identity buried beneath her livery garb in the finale, Orsino says that she *has already sworn love to her master* in terms that only need repeating, not alteration. As potential wife, that is, she doesn't need to alter in the least the oath that she swore as servant. While this certainly makes wives and servants homologous and interchangeable positions within the domestic economy (i.e., both equivalently mastered), it reveals more than gender inequity. For it also suggests that desirability – homoerotic or heteroerotic – was experienced and expressed in the grammar of social position and that this grammar could be indifferent to gender. Why else would Malvolio's declaration that Cesario's "mother's milk is scarce out of him" persuade household mistress Olivia to forgo her previous declarations, open her gate, and fall in love with a feminine, vulnerable, and dependent youth? How else does Orsino discover that the best wife for him is indeed a young male servant?

While critics of private theater often target its propensity for satire and topical scandal, the erotic component of boy-players as spectacle does not go unremarked. An anonymous 1569 pamphlet entitled *Children of the Chapel Stript and Whipt* objects to boy troupes' performances in the royal chapel (a practice that ended in the 1570s). Preoccupied with the allure of boys, this pamphlet writer portrays acting as a potentially unholy juvenile orgy: "Plaies will never be supprest while her maijesties unfledg'd minions flaunt it in silkes and sattens . . . Even in her Maiesties chappel do these pretty upstart youthes profane the Lord's day by the lascivious writhing of their tender limbs, and gorgeous decking of their apparell, in feigning bawdie fables gathered from the idolatrous heathen poets."[53] In this account, performance itself ("feigning") merges with dramatic content ("bawdie fables"), and both blend indiscriminately into the seductive danger of male youthfulness; for the degenerate and ungodly nature of these performances seems oddly enhanced by the fact that the boys are "pretty." (Would homely boys performing irreverent matter on the Sabbath be less troublesome?) Not only do the boys' gorgeous costumes make them alluring, but their position as "minions" of the Queen gives them an unattainable and desirable status. Combined with the title of the pamphlet, which suggests the righteous pleasure of unclothing and violently chastising young boys, the focus on the "lascivious writhing of their tender limbs" creates a pornographic and homoerotic tableau predicated on their combined vulnerability and sensuality; they are "unfledg'd" and "tender," yet "lascivious" and "bawdie." The 1606 renewal of the Chapel's writ for impressing choristers similarly includes the perhaps hypocritical pronouncement that boys chosen to sing the praises of God should not also be employed in "lascivious and profane exercises."[54]

While critics interested in eroticism have fruitfully analyzed structures of dependency generated by various institutions, they have largely overlooked the one area of tutelage that was routinely cross-gendered as well as female–female gendered: the potentially queer relationship between household mistress and domestic worker.[55] Instead of acting as the figure of sober prudence familiar to readers of conduct books, Nell unabashedly expresses her desire for the gratifications that theater offers.[56] When she, in one instance, insists on kissing the unfledged boy actor and then immediately thinks to diagnose his breath, she injects eroticism into her prescribed household charge: "Faith, the child hath a sweet breath, George, but I think it be troubled with the worms. *Carduus benedictus* and mare's milke were the only thing in the world for't," she declares, moving easily from kiss to curative (3.303–306). Even without the pun on "mare" ("mère's" or mother's milk), the play flaunts her unabashedly amorous flirtation with the boy she insists on treating. The sensual remarks that Nell makes as part of her running commentary intermingle with her domestic nurturance, practices, as we have seen, that were sometimes already eroticized.[57] While plays such as *Twelfth Night* readily display boys as objects of erotic desire and others eroticize purging, *Burning Pestle* is unusual in locating the wife's "maternal" and domestic authority within this queer field, revealing a free-floating and potentially polymorphous erotics of service that could underwrite household work, theater relations or dramatic spectacle.[58]

Through the self-conscious device of the citizen-as-mock spectator, the audience is invited to recognize their thrill at licensing children to "act up," but also their desire to produce, manage, and subdue the possibly titillating performances of youths. In this manner, *Knight of the Burning Pestle* solicits the audience to shift their identifications between the position of housewife (the audience's usual dominant position vis-à-vis the dependent teen) and the dependency that adults might feel in relation to a female household healer. We might profitably read this play, then, as well as others that explore domestic panic, through the lens of new theorizations of desire and dependency and not just as symptom of the transhistorical "fear of mother" evidenced through the ages. The domestication of the stage foregrounds overlapping and passionate investments in actors and dependants.

While the play obviously crosses into psychosocial territory that roams far beyond any specific form of theater, *Burning Pestle* zeroes in at moments on the particular fantasies afforded by a children's company. The boy actors prompt Nell to recall her favorite freak show anomalies – tellingly the "little child that was of fair grown about the members" and "the hermaphrodite" (3.275, 276). What does this image of monstrously sexualized children refer to if not the theater company? Boys who were amusing because they precociously acted the part of adults, slung insults, and made overtures supposedly beyond their comprehension? The Wife's recollection of a child with abnormally large genitals and a hermaphrodite not only suggests the potential fantasies inspired by young actors, but also specifically anatomizes acting practices – youths as "fornicating" adults wielding phalluses beyond their control and cross-dressed actors. The entire troupe transmutates momentarily, in Nell's imagination, into a traveling freak show that exposes the marvelous erotics of its own brand of spectacle. Yet her gloss was not unique: in *Cynthia's Revels*, the "child actors" in the induction are referred to as "cracks" and "ingles," synonyms for catamites and ganymedes. Willingly donating "her man" Rafe to this world of sexual anomalies and then insisting on the stage's affinity to domesticity, Nell dramatically forces a reimagining of both the domestic and stage world.

By stripping adult status from the characters, Nell not only activates the "dual consciousness" which all theater-goers held, but she also creates a compensatory authority in the theatrical world that is self-professedly alien to her; that is, if she wants, at one level, to call attention to analogous subordinate positions in the household and on stage, she wants at another level to remake the theater into an expansive household over which she has a privileged claim. Perhaps their importation of domesticity into the theater makes citizens into a kind of "reality principle," for they remind the audience that boy actors are never fully absorbed into comedic or quixotic plots. But in other ways, Nell's commentary has the opposite effect: it exposes the strangeness of the child actors' gestures and attitudes, imitated mannerisms that construct fictions of authority in the drama. The structures of dependency on the stage, it seems, are denaturalized in the moment that they are refracted within Nell's domestic fantasy.

I should note that the Wife's desire to repair bodies is matched in intensity with both citizens' bloodthirsty hunger for violence. Prompted to scold and beat disorderly servants and children by some conduct books, the citizens gleefully take up the task of orchestrating injury. Nell's first act is to arm the hero with a pestle and demand that he do battle; and she continues to show a penchant for bloody skirmishes. "Kill, kill, kill, kill, kill, Rafe," the Wife cries (3.348). Indeed erotic desire, violence, and nurturance merge in Nell's fantasies. "I will not have him go away so soon," she says of Rafe, "I shall be sick if he go away, that I shall. Call Rafe again, George, call Rafe again; I prithee, sweetheart, let him come fight before me, and let's ha' some drums and some trumpets, and let him kill all that comes near him, and thou lov'st me, George" (2.131–5). In her plea, affection shades into a yearning for carnage. "Shall Rafe beat nobody again?" Nell later asks plaintively (2.390). The citizens welcome a world where bodies are constantly and dramatically wounded so that they can be repaired, disciplined, judged, and forgiven. "Sick" if Rafe disappears, eager for him to massacre everyone and bossy in ordering his appearance, the Wife embodies the full range of taskmasters' postures. The affection and severity that characterizes good householders becomes convoluted into a fantasy of sadism in which stage players submit to the chastising violence of their loving social betters. But there is another explanation for the housewife's (as opposed to the male householder's) desire for aggression. The entire scene of housewifery smacked of aggressiveness, both on the part of the patient who might well have resented the wife's mandate to poke, probe, and purge the body, and on the part of the housewife who might be imagined to take pleasure in controlling bodies and asserting her medical authority.

Existing in the outermost frame of the play, the housewife-on-stage rhetorically subsumes theatrical and guild apprenticeship into household dependency; while she worries that Rafe is governed by both the audience and the theater company, his ultimate allegiance is to household mistress and master. "I am afraid o' *my* boy," Nell confesses (2.91–2, emphasis mine). Claiming their servant and apprentice as a surrogate child, Nell overtly "maternalizes" her role as stage director. "That's good boy," says Mrs. Merrythought about her son Michael; "'I'faith, it's a fine spoken child," echoes the Wife, collapsing the attributes of character and actor (1.324–5). When Nell defends the young Jasper, she is scolded by her husband for displaying maternal indulgence: "if there were a thousand boys, thou wouldst spoil them all with taking their parts. Let his mother alone with him" (1.383–5). Nell's desire to "spoil" the actors, or, in theatrical terms, to "take their parts," must be read through a larger critical lens – one that not only suggests affinities between mastered servant and nurtured child but projects those fraught relationships onto the business of acting. Collapsing actors, servants, apprentices, and children, the play hints that the child/caregiver relationship is the earliest blueprint on which other social hierarchies are fashioned.

### Running away from home

Along with traditional rituals of courtship, *Knight of the Burning Pestle* unfolds non-normative fantasies underwriting everyday routine; for its vision of the almost out-of-control housewife conjures up a disorderly set of domestic relations. The Oedipal tensions evident everywhere in Renaissance drama surface in *Burning Pestle* when rifts between merchants and apprentices meld into tensions between fathers and sons. But in focusing on Nell's managerial spectatorship, the play specifically shows characters straining, at points, to escape the housewife's authority. When Rafe gives a May Day speech honoring English springtime rituals, he wanders into domestic territory:

> London, to thee I do *present the merry month of May*;
> . . .
> For now the fragrant flowers do spring and pout in seemly sort,
> The little birds do sit and sing, the lambs do make fine sport.
> And now the birchen tree doth bud, that makes the schoolboy cry;

> The morris rings while hobby-horse doth foot feateously
> ...
> Now butter with a leaf of sage is good to purge the blood;
> Fly Venus and phlebotomy, for they are neither good.
>
> (Interlude, 4.26, 36–9, 42–3)

Why does Rafe mix household physic into his declaration of English manhood? Echoing the Wife's proverbial wisdom, Rafe advises his audience to eschew sex and bloodletting in the spring in lieu of herbal purgatives. In calling for a refreshing of bodily spirits, Rafe conflates a patriotic holiday ritual (the morris dance) with the indigenous "natural" knowledge of housewifery. The wife's intimate sponsorship of boys reverberates in Rafe's vision of national manliness. Male anxiety about infantile bodily control, which Paster details so acutely, begins to resonate at the play's end as Rafe takes over Nell's control of the humoral body.

In Rafe's deathbed speech, then, we are not surprised that he meditates on love by recalling a moment of constipation: "When I was mortal, this my costive corpse / Did lap up figs and raisins in the Strand, / Where sitting, I espied a lovely dame ... / Straight did her love prick forth me, tender sprig, / To follow feats of arms in warlike wise" (5.278–80, 283–4). The dying Rafe attempts to render the episodic feats of the play performed at the citizens' whimsy into a coherent plot, with causation yoking individual episodes into a narrative. But he strangely attributes his transformation into a love-stricken knight to a moment of bodily purging: sitting in the Strand in London, eating delicious foods that functioned as laxatives and aphrodisiacs, Rafe falls in love and becomes a knight errant guided by his beloved's influence. In his revision of the origins of the play, Rafe is tellingly not subject to the housewife for bodily remedies. Freed from the directorial cues of the citizens and especially the purging housewife, Rafe remakes himself as a character whose actions have a self-imposed integrity.

As he loosens his attachment to the household at the play's end, Rafe defines himself first as an apprentice and then a *youth*. After losing a climactic bout with death in the Grocer's shop, he flees the confines of the shop into the London streets, addresses "all you good boys in merry London," and revels in the annual ritual of kicking free of household, civic, and commercial authority on festive Shrove Tuesday:

> Farewell, all you good boys in merry London;
> Ne'er shall we more upon Shrove Tuesday meet
> And pluck down houses of iniquity.
> My pain increaseth. – I shall never more
> Hold open, whilst another pumps both legs,
> Nor daub a satin gown with rotten eggs;
> Set up a stake, oh, never more I shall.
> I die; fly, fly, my soul, to Grocers' Hall.          (5.321–8)

Fantasizing about escaping his mistress' and master's authority, Rafe mourns the fact that he can no longer take part in the riotous and defiant activities of teen youths (e.g., throwing rotten eggs, setting up cockfights, razing bawdy houses). While early modern texts frequently characterize apprentices as unruly hoodlums interested in urban bloodshed, *Burning Pestle* links Rafe's rebellion to patriotic impulses and a devotion to trade.[59] His odd and indiscriminately sexual image of holding something open while riotous youths "[pump] both legs" offers yet another metaphoric version of the purge. In this version, however, the pump is evacuated in the homoerotic camaraderie associated with holiday freedom. Even in Rafe's attempt to elude the authority of the citizen dramaturg, his final words falls back on the queer pleasures of a purge, so clearly associated with female domestic authority in this play.

Merrythought's constant invitations to mirth also qualify and redefine the housewife's control over the body. Singing that people ensure good health through sustained hilarity rather than diet, Merrythought celebrates the paradoxical self-mastery evidenced in release:

> 'Tis mirth that fills the veins with blood,
> More than wine, or sleep, or food;
> Let each man keep his heart at ease,
> No man dies of that disease.
> He that would his body keep
> From diseases, must not weep;
> But whoever laughs and sings,
> Never he his body brings
> Into fevers, gouts or rheums.                                    (2.449–57)

Later Merrythought reiterates the health benefits of what seems to be theater itself when he leads the actors in a final song: "Let each other that hath been / Troubled with the gall or spleen, / Learn of us to keep his brow / Smooth and plain as ours are now. / Sing ..." (5.338–42). Laughing, playing, and caroling, according to this stock character, purge the body and animate the spirits travelling in the blood. His refrain is seconded by the prologue's promise that the play will "move inward delight." Thought to cleanse the body and relax the muscles that held in fluids, laughter could be, in effect, a purgative (Paster, 122–5). The play thus attempts, albeit faintly, to aestheticize or commercialize kitchen physic into an effect of stage business.

But *Knight of the Burning Pestle* ends with the Wife reasserting her claim to domestic authority, for in her final speech Nell invites audience and actors to her home after the performance. Having occupied many subject positions – consumer, housewife, Protestant companionate wife, English woman, citizen – the Wife ends as a spokesperson for gentle manners. If she has demanded, along with George, that her tastes prevail to shape the performance, she now makes a gesture of catering to the tastes of a higher class. During the play, the citizens balance Nell's offers of homey medicines with a reminder that theater is a relentlessly commercial enterprise – they buy plots and music, and bribe players. Yet supposedly outside the fictional frame, Nell turns to the "real" arbiters of performance where offers of money may be inadequate. Her attempt to counterbalance exotic plots with the staples of domesticity culminates in a final invitation to the gentleman of the audience to return – literally – to a domesticity in which housewifery gracefully gives way to hospitality. Let's imagine returning to the household, since we have never left it in crucial ways, she seems to tell the gentleman. Or as fatherless Rafe affirms, "To a resolved mind, his home is everywhere" (3.145).

### *Ordinary Englishness*

While revealing that housewifery and playgoing could both be eroticized around the issue of dependency, *Burning Pestle* also offers a second discourse that champions domesticity as the staple of true Englishness. As part of its critique of taste, *Knight of the Burning Pestle* renders comic the Wife's divided interest in unleashing magical otherworlds and then harnessing them to an arena that is simultaneously familiar, domestic, and English. As Rafe ventures into Moldavia or the realm of giants, he never is allowed to kick free from mimesis, London, the home, or his status as mastered boy. Instead the play mires fantasies about submission, escape, and mastery to the absolute particularities of English life. Domesticity thus develops into a kind of national ground zero, the blueprint on which social and theatrical relations are mapped, and the ur-storehouse for dreams and nightmares.

Part of the comedy of Rafe's story, like that of Don Quixote, rests in his ability to translate unexceptional events into adventures. The barber-surgeon's shop becomes an ogre's castle; the Bell Inn, geographically fixed in Waltham's town end, mutates into an ancient castle filled with squires, damsels, and errant knights. The double-consciousness that audiences maintained with regard to theatrical and dramatic space is foregrounded in the play, for the citizens enjoy the fantastical scenario while also allowing that castles are "really" inns. They thus insist on an overtly artificial violation of the intractable "real" – both of events and dramatic conventions – but in doing so, they consolidate the bedrock reality of prosaic English habits, places, and sites. The joke, that is, depends on the rooted nature of English methods and goods, which are thrown into relief by their fleeting incarnation within the sometimes Italianate, sometimes northern European, and sometimes mythical landscape of romance. When Rafe "tips" the princess of Moldavia for her domestic comforts, he foregrounds the hominess of his foreign adventures: "There's twelve pence for your father's chamberlain," he says, and then details his accommodations so fully that the castle is radically reshaped into a customary English house, complete with cook, butter, hay, ostler, launderer, and bootcleaner. Rafe's attempt at hospitable behavior uncostumes the "princess" and locates her squarely back in London. The shimmer of Moldavia dissolves into a familiar English domain.

The play thus extends its spirited juxtaposition of the "exotic" and "familiar" realms generated out of quixoticism to encompass lines of nationality. Why else would the Cracovian/Moldavian princess insist on seeing Rafe as an exemplary Englishman and question him about national foods and habits? "Oft have I heard of your brave countrymen," the Princess confesses, "And fertile soil and store of wholesome food; / My father oft will tell me of a drink / In England found, and 'nipitato' called" (4.76–9). Only after Rafe has discussed powdered beef, mustard, and ale is the princess' anthropological curiosity about Rafe's homeland satisfied. Rejecting the foreign princess for Susan the cobbler's maid on Milk Street, Rafe pronounces on the satisfactions of home. Up to this point, the citizens have relentlessly converted fictions into home staples, but now "home" is tied to patriotic English rituals, morris dances, cakes, ale, and the glories of St. George. In fact the citizens' arsenal of theatrical devices gradually serves as an index of native foods, national rituals, and historic sites. The result is that an expansive if vexed conception of domesticity becomes the hallmark of true Englishness. As the citizens call for "rare things" that they already know, the play attempts to suture individual consciousness to a national identity founded on the imagined commonality of daily life. Rafe's adventures, then, end on a note of high national fervor in which rites like May Day rituals, military battles, folk traditions, civic institutions, and domesticity blend indiscriminately."Rejoice oh English hearts," Rafe cries (Interlude, 4.34).[60]

While wittily putting the "stranger" housewife on stage to protest the rash of comedies bound to hyperreal and unrealistic representations of city life, *Burning Pestle* also vivifies the Wife's contradictory desires for theatrical sameness and difference; these desires found many of the play's psychic, social, and sexual fantasies. If, as Judith Butler writes, "Fantasy . . . is to be understood not as an activity of an already formed subject, but of the staging and dispersion of the subject into a variety of identificatory positions," then the play's representation of housewifery prompts the audience's flickering identifications with both the domestic supervisor and the submissive dependants she manages.[61] Emotions spiraling out of "normative" heterosexual domestic relationships – longings for mastery, submission, role-reversal, indulgence, sadism, comfort – become the "psychic glue" of national fantasy; for the play inscribes these mixed fantasies within a decidedly domestic Englishness.

Desiring that her servant Rafe *almost* escape her control, Nell shows the domestic scene to harbor a wide range of potentially disruptive erotic investitures. Yet in importing these desires to the stage, the housewife insists that the spectacle of domesticity is no more or less queer than the fantasies that children's theater regularly offered viewers. The play as a whole founds a national vision out of Nell's homey, if slightly perverse, guardianship. It is no wonder that the printed account of the play continues the fantasy of a return to unstable but foundational familial origins. The publisher's introduction to *Burning Pestle* names the printed text as a child, who, having been maintained by "father, foster-father, nurse" now looks to be adopted by patrons and readers. The chain of surrogate authorities continues: Nell's invitation for everyone to return home echoes in print, as *Burning Pestle* ventures into English households to enlarge and disperse the fantasy.

# 6    Blood in the kitchen: service, taste, and violence in domestic drama

> Bedtime came and I stirred my husband's vat of milk and put in the powder as directed. My husband came crashing over to the stove and gulped the milk in one draught. As soon as he had finished he began to swell up. He swelled out of the house, cracking the roof, and within a few moments had exploded. Out of his belly came a herd of cattle and a fleet of pigs, all blinking in the light and covered in milk.
>
> Jeanette Winterson, *Sexing the Cherry*[1]

In Thomas Heywood's *The English Traveller*, a servant named Roger narrates for his master and mistress a spectacular battle at a neighbor's house, one that involves mutilation, maiming, and even cannibalism. "As I came along by the doore," he says,

> I was call'd up amongst them; Hee-Gallants, and Shee-Gallants, I no sooner look'd out, but saw them out with their Knives, Slashing of Shoulders, Mangling of Legs, and Lanching of Loynes, till there was scarce a whole Limbe left amongst them ... One was hacking to cut off a Necke ... [O]ne was picking the Braines out of a Head, another was Knuckle deepe in a Belly, one was Groping for a Liver, another Searching for the Kidneyes.[2]

Alternately recalling epic battle scenes and the dissections of popular anatomy theaters, Roger describes an orgy of bloodshed in which body parts fly so furiously that actual subjects are hard to identify. Mutating into an array of visceral interiors – brains, kidneys, livers – individual bodies blur into an indistinguishable mass of adulterated and edible flesh: "There was such biting and tearing with their teeths," Roger notes, "that I am sure, I saw some of their poore Carcasses pay for't ... There was no stitching up of those Wounds, where Limbe was pluckt from Limbe" (25).

The humor of this narrative rests in the fact that the scene of violence is, in fact, merely a "Massacre of meat" (26), as one character terms it, simply the daily work of food preparation and consumption. Roger's audience, the Wincotts, gradually understand the comic nature of their servant's conceit, but only after inquiring about the origins of the battle, the arrival of surgeons, and the fate of the ladies. Roger spends over fifty lines embellishing his story with graphic descriptions of scarred flesh, a body staked from mouth to anus and, finally, the tasting of sundry limbs. First "Broacht in the Kitchin" by a "Colloricke" cook, the fight apparently stirs up free-floating passions, for, as Roger says blandly, "one had a Stomacke, and another had a Stomacke" (26, 25). While "having a stomach" could simply mean being hungry, it also referred more abstractly to having affections, dispositions, and cravings, and, more specifically, to feelings of resentment, courage, irritation, haughtiness, or pride.[3] As militant servants spark a battle that spreads to passionate gallants, everyone indiscriminately mixes into the flesh they battle. Having stomachs (tantamount to being driven by unspecified longings and resentments) makes household members turn into stomachs. For the women, this entails being force fed with recycled food until they appear pregnant: they were, Roger reports, "forc'd to swallow what is not yet digested, yet every one had their share, and shee that had least, I am sure by this time, hath her belly full" (26). Domesticated bodies, in this servant's imagination, are those literally positioned on the food chain as entities caught up in an appetitive world of pleasurable destruction and consumption that substitutes for reproduction; eating smacks of the aggression that made Freud term the oral stage "cannibalistic."[4]

If we juxtapose this tale of banqueting to Firk's vision of "live food" in *Shoemaker's Holiday* (discussed in Chapter 4) we see the different features of daily life that each highlights. Roger initially echoes Firk's euphoria about the culinary cornucopia of a place "where for Pints, w'are served in Pottles; and in stead of Pottle-pots, in Pailes; in stead of Silver-tanckards, we drinke out of Water-tanckards" (25). The super-amplification of goods, so abounding that their immense containers miniaturize ordinary objects, underscores the prodigality of this house. But Roger goes behind the scenes to reveal the grotesquely brutal *work* underpinning extravagant dining, for he has the battle begin in the kitchen and spread slowly to dinner guests. Firk's interest in foodstuffs that willingly sacrifice themselves for human consumption touches on the fantasy of Jonson's "To Penshurst," where partridges and eels eagerly volunteer to be dinner. Roger instead amplifies the arduous labor required to maintain daily life. Though comic, his description follows the deep structural logic that Isabella uses when she interweaves the protocols of animal slaughter with human execution in *Measure for Measure*. Arguing for her brother's life, Isabella points to affinities between the spiritual and domestic projects of "attending to the flesh." "Even for our kitchens / We kill the fowl of season," she pleads to Angelo, "Shall we serve heaven / With less respect than we do minister / To our gross selves?" (2.2.84–7). Given that only mature animals are fit for slaughter, God's "feast" of death should be supplied with fully prepared human dishes, Isabella argues. In her plea for mercy, the "grossness" or full materiality of the body comes into view. Inverting the Eucharist so that the heavens consume flesh, Isabella, like Roger, lodges the specter of animal butchery in the imaginative neighborhood of human mortality. When cooking and eating are perceived as the ingestion of live beings, household routines acquire a conspicuously ominous if monumental aura.

What type of violence does *The English Traveller* describe? Since it occurs in a play that has retrospectively been labeled a "domestic tragedy," this passage raises the question of how scholars define both "domesticity" and "violence" as they analyze early modern representations. Roger's comic narration at first seems to defamiliarize ordinary acts; that is, he can be seen as fantasizing about disorder so as to render strange the mundane practices that typically defined domestic subjects. Reinterpreting daily life as violence might throw into relief the importance of a stable domestic structure. The post-Reformation household, as we have seen, was heralded as the microcosm and training ground for political order, the "School wherein are taught and learned the principles of authoritie and subjection."[5] The household was the primary institution for teaching subjects where they fit into early modern society and how they should properly experience a sense of dependency.

As part of this mission, the household was often represented as an organism composed of carefully hierarchized yet interdependent parts (indeed the human body provided the quintessential cognitive grid in Renaissance cosmic, legal, medical, religious, and social ideologies).[6] The Pauline conception of marriage involved the unequal yoking of individuals to form "one flesh," as conduct books reiterated. "Everie *Wife* should bee then as *a part* of her *Husband*; as a *limme* of him that hath her," writes Thomas Gataker in *A Good Wife Gods Gift*.[7] In the marital body, that is, the wife serves as a necessary though subordinate part. In *A Health to the Gentlemanly Profession of Servingmen*, I. M. characteristically uses the analogy between body and household/commonwealth to warn against rebellion: "for all desiring to be Heades, then the body must needes fall for want of Eyes to direct him; and if all Eyes, then it must needes perish for want of a mouth to feede him: But being devided into members, every one using his office, and resting contented with his estate, the body remaynes in perfect health & happines."[8] Clearly Roger, as a domestic subordinate, is happy to counter this image of organic harmony by describing a full-scale bodily fragmentation, one that disrupts the intertwined process of familial and civic "subjection." After all, in Roger's story there are no discrete subjects to be ordered into a unified domestic body.

Many representations of domesticity did indeed feed early modern ideologies which created normative categories.[9] Roger's defamiliarizing of household practice thus might be said to consolidate the idea that everyday tasks should be unremarkable. But "ordinary" tasks, as we have seen, could already be estranged in the early modern imagination. What if bodies were routinely imagined to be divisible, unmanageable, and recyclable? What if the lived experience of domesticity suggested alternative ways of thinking about the body and relations of dependency? Examining Heywood's two domestic tragedies, *A Woman Killed with Kindness* (1609) and *The English Traveller* (1633), in the context of the first printed cookbooks in England, we see that representations of household practice could trouble conventional domestic ideologies. For when embodiment is represented as a fraught domestic experience, it pressures conceptions of "proper" early modern subjects as they are constructed in somatic terms. And while Heywood's plays show that domesticity trailed the threat of mortality and disorder, they also make clear that housewifery was not confined to the work of women; it was instead part and parcel of the free-floating appetites circulating among household inhabitants.

### Domestic flesh

Cookbooks and guides could pressure orthodox conceptions of domesticity by describing practices that either undid *oeconomia* (those elaborate desserts, for example) or emphasized the domestic worker's power over life and death. In the previous chapter, I noted that the regimens of household physic made people subject to the painful, embarrassing, and/or infantilizing care of the housewife and her squadron of servants. Attending to medical care, cooking and butchery meant spending considerable time thinking about the relation between bodily fluids, anatomy, and diet. Here I want to return to the fact that animal and human bodies were not separated taxonomically in cookbooks, medical guides, or actual household space; and I want to foreground the proximity of medical care to butchery and carving.

In one sense Roger reminds his audience that the early modern kitchen could become a slaughterhouse reeking of blood and strewn liberally with animals waiting to be killed, plucked, and dressed (Fig. 15). Devoid of refrigeration or packaged meats, the Renaissance kitchen, as well as its textual elaboration in advice literature, everywhere marked the live origins of food. Markham tells his housewife to "take the Blood of an Hogge whilest it is warme, and steepe in it a quarte, or more, of great Oat meale grotes [grits]"; and Murrell offhandedly advises the housewife to haul in, decapitate, and sauce a huge hog.[10] While it might give modern readers pause to imagine a freshly killed or live donor hog draping the kitchen workspace, carnage was a household commonplace at this time. Woolley thus can recommend that the housewife make a cure for consumption by plucking a live cock. "Slit him down the back," she continues, "and take out his Intrals, cut him in quarters, and bruise him in a Mortar, with his Head, Legs, Heart, Liver and Gizard; put him into an ordinary Still with a Pottle of Sack."[11] Having killed the cock, either by slitting it open or wringing its neck, the housewife disembowels, beats, and boils the animal parts. When Woolley revises this recipe in a later guide, she heightens the liveness of the dismembered animal: "Take two Running Cocks, pull them alive, then kill them," she begins,

Fig. 15   Scene of cooking in which we see housework being done among the corpses of various animals. From the title page to Hannah Woolley, *The Accomplisht Ladys Delight* (London, 1675).

"Cut them Cross on the Back, when they are almost cold take their Guts, and after you have made them clean break them all to pieces."[12] Noting baldly that "the fleshe sustaineth the fleshe, and the bloude sustaineth the bloud," one 1582 medical guide offers a version of this same recipe: "Take a great fatt Capon that is well fleshed, and pull it while it is alive, and take forthe onely the guttes and the bellie, and when he is dead, stamp it in a Morter grostly."[13] Emptying and dismembering bodies when they are almost cold, trafficking in warm blood, and ripping guts from live chickens, the housewife isolated and manipulated the boundary between animation and death.[14]

Whether housewives actually did butcher animals regularly or not (and we have reason to believe that they sometimes did), Renaissance cookbooks depict domestic work as both aggressive and visceral. Beating fledgling swallows fresh from the nest was the first step in the prized "oil of swallows"; and cutting the head and tail off a live snake improved the famed Gascony powder.[15] While housewives purchased meat from butchers, and, on country estates, animals were slaughtered by farm workers, domestic guides make knowledge of butchery part of the kitchen worker's purview. *The Queens Closet Opened* offers a cure for kidney stones that depends on "proper" slaughter, the recycling of animal excretions, and astrological animation:

In the moneth of *May* distill Cow-dung, then take two live Hares, and strangle them in their blood, then take the one of them, and put it into an earthen vessel of pot, and cover it well with mortar made of horse dung and hay, and bake it in an Oven with houshold bread, and let it still in an Oven two or three dayes, baking a new with any thing, untill the Hare be baked or dried to powder; then beat it well, and keep it for your use. The other Hare you must flea [flay], and take out the guts onely; then distill all the rest, and keep this water: then take at the new and full of the Moon, or any other time, three mornings together as much of this powder as will lie on six pence, with two spoonfuls of each water; and it will break any stone in the Kidneys. (7–8)

In fortifying the human bodies under her care, the housewife might routinely work with bouncing animals that had to be strangled "in their blood," stuffed in an oven to rot for several days, flayed, and/or distilled. These procedures enabled her to extract and preserve various creatures' vital spirits. Crystallized in a potent powder, marinated in excrement, and perhaps activated by a full moon, animal spirits lingered in the material ingested by humans. Despite a clear difference in attitude toward animals and humans in some contexts, medical and culinary practice emphasize their *shared* elements. What people consumed was identifiably flesh; and the act of killing a creature *just so* was critical to the maintenance of healthy human life. One recipe in *The Queens Closet Opened*, for instance, highlights the method of slaughter: "Take the fat of a young Dog one pound, it must be killed well, that the blood settle not into the fat, then let the outer skin be taken off before it be opened, lest any of the hair come to the fat" (212). These instructions were not meant to improve a dish's taste, but instead to make the flesh assimilable to the human body.

As Markham's instructions for the "ordering of meats to be roasted" indicates, the housewife and kitchen worker became authorities on carnage, as they were to contort, amputate, and decapitate bodies. "For in all joints of meat except a shoulder of mutton," writes Markham,

you shall crush and break the bones well, from pigs and rabbits you shall cut off the feet before you spit them and the heads when you serve them to table, and the pig you shall chine, and divide into two parts ... Hens, stock-doves, and house-doves, you shall roast with the pinions folded up, and the legs cut off by the knees and thrust into the bodies ... woodcocks, snipes, and stints shall be toasted with their heads and necks on ... bitterns shall have no necks but their heads only. (88)

The housewife or cook regularly is to squeeze blood from animals, "crush and break" bones, "thrust" amputated legs into body cavities, decapitate fowl, and remove large bladders. Markham indulges in a vocabulary that makes cooking repeat prior acts of slaughter; for the worker contorts bodies to produce bitterns with heads (but no necks), rabbits with no heads, or hens with amputated legs secreted in bellies. "Thrust in your Knife betwixt the Ribs and the Kidney," Woolley writes of carving a rabbit.[16] Given the visceral imagery evident in these guides, Roger's view of servants and dinner guests as enmeshed in severed limbs begins to resemble actual practice. In linking medicine with

butchery, cookbooks invited early modern people to glimpse connections between eating and the anatomist's dissection theater. Health smacked of licensed
bloodshed.[17]

It is worth returning to Woolley's linguistic glee in tutoring her reader on
the lexicon of butchery. "In cutting up small Birds it is proper to say thigh
them, as thigh that Woodcock, thigh that Pigeon," Woolley writes, before
offering increasingly surreal verbs that make the processes of dissection intensely vivid – "disfigure," "dismember," "splat," "spoyl," "unlace," "break,"
and "barb" (*Compleat Servant-Maid*, 35). Her description of shaving wattles
from fish, binding poultry's wings, and unfurling limbs takes on an urgent if
somewhat delirious tone. "Take slugs," advises Grey's *Choice Manual* in a poetical rendering of food preparation, "such as when you touch them [they] will
turn like the pummel of swords."[18] What type of "subjection" did household
workers learn in imbibing a decorum of violence and dissection, we might
ask?

The housewife's brushes with mortality could extend to trolling for human
parts to fill her pharmacy. *The Queens Closet Opened* recommends giving
chronic bedwetters beer laced with a dried and powdered umbilical cord, taken
fresh from the infant.[19] While it isn't hard to imagine that midwives might
supply umbilical cords for needy housewives, it is more troubling to think of
how a housewife might follow Grey's recipe for curing epilepsy. After mixing
gold with pearl, amber, coral, and peony seeds, the housewife is instructed:

you must put in some powder of a dead mans Scull that hath been an Anatomy for a
woman, and the pouder of a woman for a man, compound all these together; and make as
much of the pouder of all these, as will lie upon a two-pence, for nine mornings together
in Endive water and drink a good draught of Endive-water after it. (3)

Grey's book, which displays this remedy prominently as its third recipe, was
popular enough to be reprinted eight times in the decades after it was first
published. What would it mean to use cranial powder as a kitchen ingredient?
When Woolley presents a version of this remedy in her *Compleat Servant-
Maid*, she erases the gender requirement of the human donor but elaborates the
practitioner's violation of human remains; for her reader doesn't just buy cranial
powder but is instructed to pound an actual skull into particles: "Take the Skull
of a Man or Woman," she advises, "wash it clean, then dry it in your Oven,
after your Bread is drawn, beat it to Powder, and boyl it in Posset drink, then
let the Party drink thereof Morning and evening, or as oft as need requireth"
(151). Lady Grace Mildmay similarly advises grinding six drams of "a man's
skull" with a stone mortar, mixing it into an herbal syrup, and serving it to
children who suffered from epilepsy.[20] Lest we think that Grey's, Woolley's,
and Mildmay's cannibalistic tastes would have been considered purely exotic
to readers, we might turn to Timothy Bright's 1580 medical treatise, which

advocates only simple and readily available English ingredients. Bright advises his reader to cure the "falling sickness" with a mixture of "the roote of the *Missleto* of the *Oake*, the runnet of an *Hare*, the *Peonie* roote, *Enula Campana*, the scalpe of a Man, an Asse hoofe, *Hissope* ... five leaved grasse, the juice of the *Cowslippe*, the juice of *Horehound* with *Honie*."[21] Along with flowers, grasses, roots, and the curdling milk found in a rabbit's stomach, Bright includes a human scalp as an example of the "home-grown" remedies accessible to everyone.

According to Piero Camporesi, continental intellectuals and physicians recognized the medicinal properties of cranial powder, blood, mummia (the fluid drawn from embalmed corpses), and *aqua divina* (the distillation of corpses).[22] *A Choice Manual* does call for one admittedly unusual "polychrest" panacea recipe for "Paracelsus Salve" which blends mummia with gold, silver, oils, lead, wax, rosins, gums, myrrh, and vinegar. Not hindered by Bright's concern for home-grown simples, *The Queens Closet Opened* describes a balsam in which "mummey" is mixed with imported herbs, olive oil, conduit water, and rosewater (95). Mummia (either drawn from imported fermented bodies or made more cheaply from baked corpses) was widely recognized as a precious if repulsive elixir. *The Charitable Physitian*, addressed to lay practitioners, includes a lengthy section on embalming corpses tucked neatly beside recipes for fruit preserves. And though he ends up recommending against the practice, Thomas Muffet discusses the relative advantages of drinking human blood as a source of revitalization.[23]

It makes sense, then, that early modern plays joke anxiously that the housewives' restoratives might have mortal costs. In *The Nice Valour*, a Clown complains about being beaten, as he says, to a pulpy "cullis. I am nothing ... but very pap, / And jelly." "I've no Bones, / My Body's all one Bruise," he laments, "whoever lives to see me / Dead, Gentlemen, shall find me all one Mummy / Good to fill Gallipots, and long dildo Glasses."[24] Since gallipots were the household earthen jars used to store ointments, and dildo glasses the cylindrical tubes used in home distilling, the Clown's reverie about violence revolves around the transformative powers of the housewife and her ghastly goods. The "cullis" to which the Clown refers (a strong broth in which the "strength" of meat was thought to transfer through liquid to a weak patient) could even serve as a verb meaning "to beat," shorthand for the phrase "to beat to a cullis." "Quit thy father ... or Ile cullice thee With a battoun," threatens Lord Rainebow in Shirley's *The Ball*.[25] Like the cullis, mummia was paradoxically associated with both restorative value and violence.

Yet was it truly possible for a shopper to obtain a human skull in seventeenth-century London? According to Jonathan Sawday, there was in all probability a growing corpse economy in Europe created to supply anatomists. Although statutes severely restricted the number of bodies that the Barbers-Surgeons

Company or the College of Physicians could dissect, private researchers, guilds (butchers, tailors, and wax chandlers), and universities all sought "human material," as it was termed, for experimentation and scientific inquiry. Louis de Bils's proposal for an anatomy theater in Rotterdam envisioned fifty cadavers to be processed yearly; and an Edinburgh town statute assigned monetary values to various bodies for dissection.[26] The corpses of suicides, unclaimed foundlings who died at nurse, persons with no families who died violent deaths, and criminals supplied the increasingly popular anatomy theaters. In fact, criminals were designated as anatomy subjects precisely as a deterrent to crime, since this fate was increasingly seen as obviating the possibility of Christian resurrection. When there weren't enough criminals to go around, some anatomists took to grave-robbing and trafficking in stolen corpses, feats made easier by the dire overcrowding of cemeteries. This problem resulted in the unintended exhuming of human bones, much like Yorick's skull.[27] It seems likely that human remains visibly circulated in the early modern world.

Although scholars are well aware of how Renaissance *memento mori* drilled in the lessons of mortality (for example, those emblematic skulls that grace portraiture, jewelry, and tombs), we rarely contemplate human remains within the home.[28] Yet, according to Camporesi, this was indeed the case in early modern Italy where an openness to death made the presence of bones unremarkable in many walks of life. Camporesi argues that the cannibalism that Europeans obsessively condemned in other cultures surfaced in their own preoccupation with a "sacrilegious gastronomy" (20). He takes his evidence largely from Italian intellectuals, like Ficino, who recommended drinking human blood as a guard against aging, or from erudite books that praised violent death as retaining precious spirits within a corpse (44–7). What is startling about the recipes from Grey's, Bright's, and Woolley's English guides is the classification of a scaled-down version of these practices as *housewifery* rather than the arcane work of learned doctors. The household, it seems, was spacious enough to embrace the work of recycling corpses; cookbooks placed the human body imaginatively in proximity to death, carnality, and orality.

The very fact that recipes calling for human skulls and mummia could be printed alongside conventional salves suggests how customary it was to think of body parts in the kitchen. Since cures regularly involved dung, breastmilk, human urine, and animal organs, housewifery involved a world of interchangeable, absorbable, and consumable body parts, extracted from live and dead beings. Plunged into the thick of mortality, the housewife was to repair and butcher flesh in its different incarnations. But might such practices have triggered alarm, at moments? Might Markham's cure for diarrhea, which has the housewife dry and grate a stag's penis to be served steaming hot in a beer concoction, have elicited a few qualms about castration (30)? The body's precariousness might well have registered in the everyday work of cooks, servants, and housewives.

How else might we read the scenes that crop up in plays like Middleton's *A Chaste Maid in Cheapside*, where babies substituting for legs of lamb comically underscore controversies over eating and bodily care? Where sustenance goes hand in hand with the threat of injury? The violence of my title, then, points to practices other than spousal murder and suicide, the typical fare of domestic tragedies. Instead routine tasks might be estranged temporarily, in plays, guides, and, perhaps, in practice, so that their affinities with conventionally defined violence were made apparent.

Such recipes steer us toward Renaissance fictions in which household bodies are threatened, consumed, or violently "subjected" as part of daily life. Jonson's description of the devil's feast in *The Gypsies Metamorphosed* (1640), for instance, satirically anatomizes social types by recasting people as food. In this masque, Satan's favorite dishes surface in their full particularity: fat usurers stewed in their own marrow, lawyers' heads smothered in green sauce, midwives folded in a pasty, and poached Puritans. The feast continues:

> Then carbonado'd, and Cookt w^th paines,
> Was brought up a Cloven serieante face;
> The sawce was made of his yeomans braines,
> That had beene beaten out w^th his owne mace.
>
> Two rosted Sheriffes came whole to the bord;
> (The feast had nothing beene without 'em)
> Both living and dead, they were foxt, and furd,
> Their Chaines like sausages hung about 'em.
>
> The nexte dishe, was the Maior of a Towne,
> W^th a pudding of mainetenance thrust in his bellie;
> Like a goose in the feathers, drest in his gowne,
> And his Couple of Hinch-boyes boyld to a jellie.[29]

Like Roger's "Massacre," the humor of this passage turns on the incongruity of humans standing in for food. But while it contemplates the joke of cannibalism, Jonson's mockery of social types doubles as an inventory of English kitchen *practices* – carbonados, roasts, puddings, and jellies – refracted into a highly particularized if demonic incarnation; that is, this passage holds up to scrutiny not just food but specific culinary methods not usually readable as violence – such as the dressing, beating, and roasting of flesh.

The 1599 *Patient Grissill*, on the other hand, exposes power struggles surrounding eating and cooking. Peeking into the kitchen, Sir Owen's servant Farnezie reports that there will be no dinner that night:

Nay there's no matter in it, the fire's quencht, the victuals giuen to beggers, Sir Owens Kitchin lookes like the first Chaos, or like a Brokers stall, full of odde endes: or like the

end of some terrible battle, for upon euery dresser lyes legges and feathers, and heads
of poore Capons and wilde foule that haue bin drawne and quartred, and now mourne
that their carkasses are carried away . . . heere lye fish in a pittifull pickle, there standes
the coffins of pyes, wherein the dead bodies of birdes should haue been buried, but their
ghostes haue forsaken their graues & walkt abroad.[30]

Criminally punished fowl and ravished food bespeak the fact that Owen's
wife Gwyneth has abdicated her wifely duties and exposed her husband to
the ridicule of his guests. With a tone more mournful than indignant, Farnezie
describes leftovers as empty coffins, dishes as graves forfeited by wandering
ghosts, shards as the remnants of a "terrible battle"; in short, the wife's unruliness leads to a palpable nothingness likened to the "first Chaos." Culinary
carnage, linked to the rubble of the material world, takes on a decidedly
human cast, and a crisis in marital hierarchy produces this excursus on mortality in the kitchen. When Dekker and Middleton's *Honest Whore, Pt. 1* (1604)
turns to the scene of the wife's negligence, and thus her authority, in food provision, it has one angry man imagine a tasty revenge in the war between men
and the domus: "'I should he' played mad tricks with my wife and family:
first, I would ha' spitted the men, stewed the maids, and baked the mistress,
and so served them in."[31] The kitchen's barrenness unmasks affinities between
butchery and human mortality while revealing deep aggressions circulating
around the kitchen.

Perhaps it is not surprising that critics have found a powerful and widespread
early modern association of domesticity with witchcraft. *Macbeth* has received
much commentary in this regard, since it speaks forcefully to the crossover between heath and hearth.[32] As they create a witchy brew, the weird sisters appear
to make familiar household tasks into the uncanny; that is, malevolence, in this
play, seems grounded in an inversion of everyday life. Lady Macbeth's breastmilk only horrifically appears as gall because it is expected to be nurturing, just
as the Macbeths' evil domesticity throws into relief the value of the orthodox
household. But seen through the lens of cookbooks, these witchcraft scenes
take on a slightly more complicated valence; for when the witches call for body
parts in their grotesque brew, they don't *invert* medical remedies as much as ex-
aggerate their sinister nature. After all, some of the ingredients in the cauldron –
"Eye of newt and toe of frog, / Wool of bat and tongue of dog, / Adder's fork and
blind-worm's sting, / Lizard's leg and howlet's wing" – aren't that different from
the body parts that surface in household guides (4.1.14–17). Even when bats
and owls do not appear as ordinary staples, cookbooks assume that housewives
will work with frogs, dogs, reptiles, and snakes. *Macbeth* simply demonizes an
already alarming domestic practice by freighting its materials with an added
characteristic: instead of requiring mere human skulls or umbilical cords, the
witches' concoction calls specifically for the limbs of foreigners, heretics, and
murder victims ("liver of blaspheming Jew," "Nose of Turk and Tartar's lips,"

"Finger of birth-strangled babe" – 4.1.26, 29–30). My focus on the *work* of domesticity thus takes me close to Dolan's conclusion about the fluid boundaries between home and moral wasteland in *Macbeth* – "The antifamily is *the* family" (230). If early modern representations freely show the antihousehold to be the household (meaning that its potential disorder is rendered monstrous), then the witches are more than scapegoating devices for internal disharmony. In showing that housewifery didn't just involve the comforting transfer of the milk of human kindness, *Macbeth* borders on an acknowledgment of domesticity's frightening power.

This recognition becomes the impetus for a sustained joke in Fletcher's comedy, *The Elder Brother*, when Charles, a scholar fresh from the university, questions his servant Andrew about the "earthquake" emanating from the kitchen. When Andrew explains that "the Cookes / Are chopping hearbs and mince meat to make pies, / And breaking Marrow-bones," Charles interrupts: "Can they set them again?" Andrew replies blithely: "Yes, yes, in Brothes and Puddings, and they grow stronger / For th'use of any man." Damaged animal skeletons are "set," or healed, when converted into edible puddings that strengthen human bones. Yet in this economy, animal and human bodies exchange under the auspices of militant workers rather than unruly witches or wives.

CHARLES. What squeaking's that? Sure there is a massacre.
ANDREW. Of Pigs and Geese Sir,
    And Turkeys for the spit. The Cookes are angry Sir
    And that makes up the medly.[33]

In this "massacre," the cooks' hostility, animal sacrifice, and male fright merge in a "medly" of comic terror. Since at this point in the play Charles is a firm bachelor, and since the flurry of activity to which he objects is a wedding preparation, Charles's fright at the sound of kitchen knives suggests broad anxieties about domesticity's potency; that is, this play makes visible the transference of affect, from dying animals to hostile carvers and fearful bachelors. As concern about bodily submission moves up and down the food chain from animal to worker to householder, we discover a fantasy about aggressive agency not confined to the housewife. This scene pushes us to expand investigations of the war between the sexes in order to consider the place of servants. Nightmarish representations of domestic combat could, as Roger's tale suggests, revolve around the potential violence of everyday service.

Nervousness about household work provides a clue toward understanding Heywood's representation of domestic cannibalism. Rewriting his first domestic tragic plot, *A Woman Killed with Kindness*, in *The English Traveller*, Heywood tellingly employs the vocabulary of exchanged body parts as a means of accentuating the intertwined sexual, economic, and domestic relationships in the early modern household. While these plays dramatize adultery, they locate spousal relations within other social relations (i.e., including servants of different ranks, neighbors, kinship systems, companions, guests, and children). Rather than the fantasy of the unruly housewife seen in *Knight of the Burning Pestle*, Heywood's tragedies consider other domestic workers wielding kitchen knives. These plays highlight the threat posed by servants who sustain the household with their labors and who engage in intimate relationships with household inhabitants. As such, these works make visible the potentially chaotic nature of even normative domestic worlds. Playing off the conception of the household as the microcosm of the body politic, Heywood's tragedies point to the fragility and incoherence of what might be termed "domesticated bodies," entities that mark the constant, often eroticized, flux of dependencies in the household; that is, they show fantasies of interdependence that clash with prescriptive idealizations of the organically unified home.

### Look in your heart and fight

> Incorporation: whereby the subject, more or less on the level of phantasy, has an object penetrate his body and keeps it "inside" his body ... although it has a special relationship with the mouth and with the ingestion of food, it may also be lived out in relation with other erotogenic zones and other functions. Incorporation provides the corporal model for introjection and identification.[34]

*A Woman Killed with Kindness* tells the story of the investiture of the Frankford household through marriage, the master's acquisition of a servant-companion named Wendoll, the ensuing adulterous liaison between his wife Anne and Wendoll, and a conclusion in which the husband banishes his wife, she starves herself to death, and the marital couple reconciles at her deathbed. The play follows the template of other domestic tragedies in attributing household disorder to adultery, but instead of culminating in murder, the scandal causes the wife's self-destruction along with the renewal of extended male familial bonds. A subplot narrates the tale of a legal/financial crisis in a landowning aristocratic family, which is resolved through a marriage that seals kinship alliances.

The play foregrounds the critical role played by Nick, a wage-earning servant who takes an instant dislike to Frankford's new gentleman companion Wendoll and refuses to be his "man": "I do not like this fellow by no means: / I never see him but my heart still earns. / 'Zounds, I could fight with him, yet know not why."[35] How are we to read Nick's unexplained antipathy toward a man that Frankford praises for affability and refined manners? While in moral terms, Nick functions as the play's ethical barometer (cleverly anticipating Wendoll's fall) he displays, in social terms, the competitive relationships existing between servants of different classes. Such conflict, as Lena Orlin and Mark Burnett observe, was a consequence of the shift from a mode of service based on obligation, hospitality, and feudal allegiance to different set of domestic principles organized around production and the maintenance of property.[36] The institution of service was rapidly changing in the early seventeenth century as "gentle" servants became a casualty of the shrinkage of great households.

Nick's choice of phrase is telling, for when he says that his heart "earns" upon seeing Wendoll, he uses a word, derived from the Old English word ("esne") for serf or laborer, to mean "to grieve, tremble or curdle like sour cheese" (*OED*). The word's central meaning, compensation for labor, resonates in his narration of his soluble and fragile heart; and appropriately, given the play's focus on homey detail, a dairy phrase infiltrates the heart's deep-seated passions. Frankford's presentation of his "table" to an outsider (4.65) might well have sparked resentment that household resources should be misspent on a servant who appears to do no work. Perhaps Nick "earns" at the sight of Wendoll because Wendoll, in one sense, doesn't earn at all. Nick isolates his emotional response in a body part that registers his discontent – his earning heart.

The only character privy to his mistress' affair, Nick eventually orchestrates Frankford's discovery of the adulterous lovers. The servant's prominence in detecting household disorder (as he becomes the "eye" (6.179) or "I" of the house) is seconded when Anne Frankford is discovered in bed with Wendoll, for here an unidentified "maid in her smock" (whom Orlin astutely reads as the "genius domus") prevents Frankford from killing his wife. "I thank thee, maid," says Frankford, "Thou like the angel's hand / Hath stayed me from a bloody sacrifice" (13.69–70). While her allegorical significance is not to be overlooked, the maid also makes visible the cadre of servants who have a privileged view of the gentry's shame. She is the invisible "hand" that reaches out almost supernaturally to shape the play's action. Nick's tutoring of Frankford about domestic governance is thus completed by the maid's physical pedagogy about the bounds of violence; and this experience is again registered somatically – as the "hand" of God working through the servant's body part.

In the discovery scene, household servants are the primary choric voices to the gentry's crises. When Anne attempts to transform herself into emblem – "O women . . . Make me your instance: when you tread awry, / Your sins like mine will on your conscience lie" (13.142, 144–5) – the response is for a group of servants to take the stage and witness her mortification. Servants, coded as "women," are given the task of demanding an account of the sin that has collapsed the household. As Rebecca Bach notes, a modern representation might have privatized this moment by confining it to the marital bedroom (508), but *Woman Killed* demonstrates that the early modern domestic world revolved around communal supervision. Unseen by Anne, and standing in for the theater audience, servants enable the performance of nothing less than morality itself. "See what guilt is: here stand I in this place, / Ashamed to look my servants in the face," she laments (13.151–2). The circuit of knowledge has thus come full circle – from one servant's initial detection, through the husband's verification, and back to rest in servants as privileged beholders of the action. It is thus appropriate that Nick offers the prototype for the community's forgiveness of Anne. Acting as detectives, spectators, instructors, and model audiences, servants in *Woman Killed* occupy a fundamental place in domestic and dramatic ordering.

The moral righting enabled by the servants involves the expulsion of the gentleman-servant as well as household mistress. This ousting is no frivolous task, since Wendoll has been profoundly "wed" to the household, in the play's terms, in ways that echo prominent representations of the symbiotic marital unit. The title page to Gataker's *A Good Wife Gods Gift* (1623), for instance, cites Proverbs 12:4: "A vertuous Woman is a Crowne to her Husband: But she that shameth him is as rottenness in his Bones." The corporeal motif continues in Gataker's description of the couple as "one flesh" and the wife as her husband's limb.[37] The negligent housewife becomes, according to Gataker, a prosthetic limb rendering the household vulnerable. Wendoll's entry into the Frankford home marks just this kind of intimate merger; for Frankford eagerly opens his household to the financially pressed son of a gentleman: "He esteems you," Anne says to Wendoll of her husband, "Even as his brain, his eye-ball, or his heart" (6.113–14). Esteemed as a vital bodily organ, Wendoll exposes fractures in the householder's self-integrity. Frankford's engrafting of a companion/limb calls attention to potential danger posed by the older system of gentlemanly service. "Hast thou the power straight with thy gory hands," Wendoll asks himself, "To rip thy image from [Frankford's] bleeding heart?" (6.45–6). Orlin thus persuasively reads the play as a critique of the older domestic ethic of liberality based on Ciceronian male friendship in light of a new post-Reformation domestic ethic. This ethic, which constitutes an oeconomic imperative to "keep" property, should make the householder wary of adopting non-instrumental alliances or embedding a dependant too deeply into the household nerve center.

Wendoll anatomizes his relationship with Frankford specifically in terms of digestion: "He cannot eat without me," says Wendoll, "Nor laugh without me; I am to his body / As necessary as his digestion, / And equally do make him whole or sick" (6.40–43). Unified thus into the husbandly body, the gentleman servant profits by seemingly losing his self-identity, but this subsumption erodes the mark of his subordination in the domestic hierarchy. The play's emphasis on separable and cannibalized body parts – brain, eyeball, heart, belly – raises the specter of household relations as an ever-shifting set of dissected corporeal exchanges.[38] The verticality of domestic hierarchy necessarily falters as agents dissolve into limbs caught in furious circuits of exchange.

This process becomes readable in terms of Freud's theory that the oral stage allows the subject to obtain erotic mastery over an object by destroying it.

The oral stage leads to the process of incorporation whereby the subject takes pleasure in having the "other" penetrate the body in ways that redefine the assimilating "host" body. In incorporation, according to Laplanche and Pontalis, "the subject, more or less on the level of phantasy, has an object penetrate his body and keeps it 'inside' his body." This process, in Freudian terms, constitutes the corporeal model for the abstract process of identification. Laplanche and Pontalis continue: "[I]ncorporation contains three meanings: it means to obtain pleasure by making an object penetrate oneself; it means to destroy the object; and it means, by keeping it within oneself, to appropriate the object's qualities" (212). Frankford's incorporation of Wendoll – though not yet legible as the combined orality, homosexuality, sophistication, and "taste" that Joseph Litvak reads astutely in modern representations – forges a homoerotic service bond transgressive because of its intensity.[39]

It is no wonder that Nick, who has been in the household since Frankford's youth, experiences the arrival of Wendoll as a potential heart attack, for he senses the way that the new companion is engrafted so powerfully onto the household that existing lines of dependency are exposed and endangered. Not only does Wendoll usurp the place of existing servants and wife, but he reveals Frankford to be a penetrable authority – blazoned fragments capable of self-destruction or of contamination by his "lowers." "Did I not lodge thee in my bosom? / Wear thee here in my heart?" Frankford demands of Anne after discovering her infidelity (13.113–14). But he joined Wendoll *and* his wife as one flesh. When Wendoll penetrates Anne's body sexually, he seems only, I think, to repeat his prior invasion into Frankford's bodily recesses. And when Anne decides to commit suicide, she picks self-starvation as her means, not only to symbolize a necessary denial of appetite and the flesh but also to seal her body from now suspect incorporations. When Anne begs Frankford not to spot her flesh because she wants to die *whole*, she unwittingly interprets adultery and its consequences as a replaying of Frankford's faulty opening of his body. To understand the play's rhetorical logic, we might turn to conduct book writer William Whately, who warns against the sin of adultery by labeling taboo bodies as "strange flesh": "the covenant that passeth between yoke-fellowes, doth make it utterly unlawful for them upon any occasion, at any time," he writes, "to give their bodies to any other in all the world, besides, themselves; therefore the Scripture calleth all other, strange flesh."[40]

We might be inclined to read the play as a critique of homoeroticm's "strange flesh." But this interpretation fails to account for Nick's unchallenged position in the heart of the household body. Instead the play is skeptical of Frankford's over-identification with one particular male bond – one that opens the household to the status-confusing gentlemanly serving man. Regular servants were *supposed* to be subsumed almost wholly within their master's identity. In *The*

*Servants Dutie*, Thomas Fosset argues that, with the exception of refusing an immoral command, the servant must relinquish his own autonomy, promising to "obey and to be in subjection, to have no will of his own or power over himself, but wholly to resign himself to the Will of his Master."[41] William Gouge concurs: "Servants ought to forbeare doing of things on their owne heads without or against consent of their masters, because while the time of their service lasteth, they are not their owne."[42] But the gentleman-servant's reserve of status (his claim to be his own "head") made him less incorporable within the household organism. Certainly the metaphors of incorporation prevalent in conduct books represented spousal and parent/child relations more easily than master/servant relations; for references to physical resemblance, shared blood, and exchanged fluids in sexual union made the conceit work smoothly. But when the household was imagined as an organism, servants might undermine the body from within. Frankford's excessive dependence on Wendoll makes subsumption (in Renaissance legal terms) or incorporation (in Freudian terms) into a two-way process that erodes the master's, as well as the servant's, self-definition.[43]

This is why is it important that Nick, rather than the master, spearheads the ousting of the servingman and expresses the play's moral rage over Anne's adultery. He puts in place a coup from below designed to protect the institution of marriage and the clear lines of dependency constructed in the household. While other domestic tragedies link wives and servants as rebellious subordinates whose familiarity in the household becomes their means of insurrection, *Woman Killed* points to the frightening instrumentality of the loyal servant.[44] It is Nick who turns the play's somatic tropes of incorporation into overt threats of dismemberment and cannibalism. When Wendoll joins the household, Nick threatens, "If I pluck off his boots," he says, "I'll eat the spurs, / And they shall stick fast in my throat like burrs" (4.97–8). Using this graphic trope, Nick imagines consuming Wendoll's accouterments as an act of self-mutilation. In doing so, he anticipates and parodies Frankford's dependence on Wendoll for digestion. "My master shall not pocket up this wrong," Nick later says of the affair (6.169):

> I'll eat my fingers first. What sayest thou metal? (Drawing his dagger)
> Does not the rascal Wendoll go on legs
> That thou must cut off? Hath he not hamstrings
> That thou must hough? Nay metal, thou shalt stand
> To all I say. I'll henceforth turn a spy
> . . .
>
> I'll have an eye
> In all their gestures.                                                    (6.170–4, 179–80)

Calling forth and then disavowing self-ingestion in lieu of a plan to hack off Wendoll's legs, Nick positions his bodily integrity against Wendoll's dissolution. Later he combines these two impulses by uttering a dramatic threat: "I cannot eat, but had I Wendoll's heart / I would eat that" (8.17–18). If Frankford consumes Wendoll with love, Nick deftly reads the potentially destructive nature of that identification by mimicking it in an expression of hostility. He exposes a link between pleasurable orality and self-division, injury and nourishing cannibalism. His portrayal of a hunger that cannot be satisfied except with a human feast constitutes a nightmarish version of the appetites circulating in this domestic world. Ending his tirade by projecting his "eye" onto household space, Nick attempts to subsume a domestic world composed of body pieces into his expansive vision. This desperate conversion of synecdochal parts into a whole, however, is undone by its own terms, for the servant's detached "eye" lingers like the Cheshire cat's smile as an inappropriate marker of the drive for integrity.

The bond between Wendoll and Frankford thus triggers fears about the erasure of difference that gets played out within somatic discourse. Approaching Frankford with news of Anne's infidelity, for instance, Nick threatens to make his master's heart imitate his own fearful "earning": "I will tell you, master, / That which will make your heart leap from your breast," he warns (8.39–40). Frankford's response is first to strike his servant and then to mystify his own violence: "Thou has killed me," he declares to his servant, "with a weapon whose sharpened point / Hath pricked quite through and through my shivering heart" (8.59–60). In terms of the play's vocabulary, Frankford attributes the imminent loss of his "brain," "eyeball," or "heart" to Nick's penetrating words. The working servant has slain the master. Yet Nick responds by glossing their conversation and his injury as a curative vomit: "now that I have eased my stomach, / I will go fill my stomach," he declares at the end of this conversation (8.96–97). Given his previous threat to "eat ... Wendoll's heart" as the alternative to self-mutilation, Nick's impulse to *consume* is suggestive, for his initiative in educating his master enables him to replace Frankford's voluntary incorporation of Wendoll with Nick's forced penetration into Frankford's heart. One model of ingestion gives way to another.

The violent terms of the servant's re-identification with the master reveal latent aggressions harbored in even the most loyal bonds. In this cycle of incorporation, Nick's faulty heart is substituted for Frankford's psychic wound, which is then exchanged for Nick's healthy humoral purging. What is compelling about the play's metaphoric tissue is its graphic exposure of the vulnerability of human bonds and emotional investments. But abstract emotions are also, within this topos, specifically mapped corporeally and domestically; that is, subjects are framed by particular household roles and realized in the bodily exchange constituting lines of power. When he revisits the genre of domestic tragedy in *The English Traveller* years later, Heywood renders both features of this intersubjectivity transparent, for he adds to these tropes of bodily exchange a pleasurable fantasy of all-consuming kitchen slaughter, the joys of "strange flesh" lodged in the mouth of the servant.

### Proliferating limbs

*The English Traveller* consists of two plots, a prodigal son city comedy story drawn wholesale from Plautus' *Mostellaria* (*The Haunted House*) annexed onto the plot sketched in *Woman Killed with Kindness*. *English Traveller* retells the plot of *Woman Killed* with a few variations: the Frankfords become the Wincotts, differentiated by a January/May marriage; the Wendoll figure is split between Geraldine and his friend Dalavill, neither of whom are financially strapped enough to become actual serving men but both of whom move in and out of the Wincott household in undefined subordinate positions; Geraldine and his childhood sweetheart Mistress Wincott forge a secret but chaste marriage-within-a-marriage by exchanging a vow that they will marry when Mr. Wincott dies; and the householder's desire for his guest-companion Geraldine is intensified. But Dalavill upsets this erotic network by engaging in a furtive affair with "the Wife," as she is identified in the play. Strangely, the guest Geraldine assumes the role of wronged husband, and, with the help of an informing servant, discloses the shame of the two lovers to household members and neighbors. Mistress Wincott dies of shame, Dalavill flees the country, and the husband repledges his devotion to Geraldine. It would be hard to see the righting of patriarchal authority as the moral and ideological telos for this play, since the cuckolded figure in the erotic foursome is a guest, the husband desires his male companion more than his wife, and the wife is punished not as much for adultery as for desiring two guests simultaneously. The erotic triangle of *Woman Killed* thus expands into a quadrangle, with the result that the prominence of marriage diminishes in lieu of the proliferation of extramarital rivals, primarily gentlemanly guest-companions.

Domestic chaos takes a different form in the citizen comedy plot where a merchant named Lionnel leaves his house in the hands of his wayward son while traveling. Upon his return, the father is duped by his son's unruly steward, who assumes control of the estate and concocts artful fables to cover the son's financial transgressions. After Lionnel Sr. forgives his penitent son and servant, he brings his family in tow to the Wincott's, where the two plots fold together as mirror images of oddly configured all-male households.

Both plots in *The English Traveller* invoke culinary violence. Initially the play presents food merely as an index of contrasting lifestyles. Roger answers his master's casual question – "what's new?" – with a lively domestic tableaux: "Dancing newes sir, / For the meat stands piping hot upon the dresser, / The kitchin's in a heat, and the Cooke hath so bestir'd himselfe, / That hee's in a sweat. The Jacke plaies Musicke, and the Spits / Turne round too't" (13). Roger makes the kitchen into the convivial site of all news, the place where the rhythm of turning spits mutates into a frenzied dance. The sweat of labor blurs, in his account, into a bodily revelry that links the cook to the hot meat he prepares; both stew in a festive but arduous rhythm. After commenting on the cook toiling behind the scenes, Roger then converts sweaty labor into a sign of good householding. Equating moral husbandry with the possession of culinary provisions, he makes work signify status. The Wincotts take definition from their ability to command the dance of labor that twins hot bodies and eaten objects as property.

The Wincotts' moderately festive husbandry is allied with neighbor Lionnel Sr.'s merchandising, and both contrast with the orgiastic banqueting initiated by Lionnel Jr., whose house is described as a "House of Hospitality and a Pallace of Plenty; Where there's Feeding like Horses, and Drinking like Fishes" (25). The difference between acquisitive father and over-consuming son is displayed in terms of their contrasting dinners. Before the father's return from his business ventures, Lionnel's steward Reignald and his country servant Robin (modeled on Plautus' Tranio and Grumio) establish the terms by which the father–son conflict will be expressed. When Robin travels to the city to denounce Lionnel for surfeiting, Reignald brands him as coarse foodstuff and banishes him roundly to the countryside: "Adue good Cheese and Oynons, stuffe thy guts / With Specke and Barley-pudding for digestion, / Drinke Whieg and sowre Milke, whilest I rince my Throat, / With Burdeaux and Canarie" (16). Labeling Robin one of the "hinds of the country that comes prying /To see what dainty fare our kitchin yields," Reignald debates values by reference to contrasting menus. Reignald's transformation of the servant into a "hind" and a cheese not only renders humans and food indistinguishable, but also signals the breakdown of household order. Lionnel is eventually reunited with his father (without killing any fatted calf, now surely depleted), but only after he promises to be a "thrifty son," which means giving up the compulsion to eat, shop, and consort with harlots. The popular story of prodigality becomes, in this incarnation, the tale of a penitent gourmand, with consumption standing in for a range of sexual and social transgressions.

Lionnel Jr. is unsurprisingly fascinated with cataloguing his riches as dinner courses. Commanding his steward, Lionnel fantasizes about an endless purchase of entrées:

> LIONNEL. Let me have to Supper, Let mee see, a Ducke –
> REIGNALD. Sweet Rogue.
> LIONNEL. A Capon –
> REIGNALD. Geld the Rascall.
> LIONNEL. Then a Turkey –
> REIGNALD. Now spit him for an Infidell. (17)

Filling out his list of what to "have to Supper" with plovers, partridges, larks, pheasants, caviar, sturgeon, anchovies, pickle oysters, and a potato pie, Lionnel luxuriates in imaginatively stocking the house with goods. Yet while his master obsesses on the menu, Reignald playfully makes shopping into violence; that is, he endows each dish with social characteristics ("rogue," "Infidell," "Rascall") and details their impending injuries (castration, execution). While abundant food signals status and pleasure for Lionell, it suggests to Reignald an exoticized feast in which "others" are sacrificed to satisfy the collective appetites of servant and master; for the servant redraws the boundaries to include himself in a domestic unit contrasted with infidels and eunuchs. The master's autoerotic compulsions about eating are matched by the servant's equally pleasurable reinterpretation of cooking as sacrificial violence.

Roger's subsequent description of domestic "Massacre" echoes Reignald's animation of dinner, with the result that both complicate a familiar moral fable. For, as Wincott's servant, Roger does not creates the topos of the "massacre" to critique excesses in expenditure. Imagining gallants and servants as biting mongrels taking advantage of the weaponry of the kitchen, Roger mockingly hints at phantasmatic inversions in the home. Moral indignation thus doesn't account for Roger's pleasure in frightening the Wincotts with the image of home slaughter waged by subordinates and guests out of control. Instead both Reignald and Roger present unruly forms of embodiment that underscore the potential disarray of service.

We might not be surprised, given this focus, that the story of prodigal Lionell turns into the tale of an upstart servant. Banishing Robin to the countryside, Reignald utters a threat that highlights the rebellious component of Roger's fantasy: "I, as the mighty Lord . . . Of this great house and castle, banish thee/The very smell ath' kitchin, bee it death, / To appear before the dresser" (14–15). Although Reignald simply means that the garlic-scented servant will be killed if he dares to taint the subtlety of their delicacies, his ambiguous phrase – "bee it death / To appear before the dresser" – opens the door for another meaning: the agent of violence seems to be the cook whose ability to "dress" people recovers the etymological tie between cooking and beating.[45] Appearing before the "dresser," the sideboard in the kitchen on which food was prepared, rings of a juridical appearance before an unacknowledged magistrate.

Reignald's playful allusion to the cook's power, marshaled within his claim to mastery, foreshadows his later usurpation of the household. As an early modern steward, itself an intimate and liminal position between householder and "lower" servants, Reignald is enjoined to supervise personnel and budgets, regulate provisions, keep accounts, and serve as a "factor" in business deals.[46] As such, he occupies a position that intensifies the threat that servants generally were thought to pose. Dolan notes in *Dangerous Familiars*:

Because of their intimate relationship with their employees, servants were confusing even threatening, figures. The threat lay not in their stark opposition to their masters or their demonized otherness but in their very familiarity and their insinuation into all social groups and situations . . . Dependent yet depended upon, familiar yet not wholly known or controlled, a class yet not one, servants blurred boundaries and confused categories. (66–67)

We may think of *Twelfth Night*'s Malvolio, *Duchess of Malfi*'s Antonio, or *Volpone*'s Mosca when considering the fantasized consequences of this "in-between" intimate service position. Following Plautus' *Mostellaria* where slave Trania usurps the household, this play presents Reignald as household governor, director and exchequer. Using "inventions, Braines, / Wits, Plots, Devices, [and] Stratagems," he locks Lionnel and his drunken acquaintances in a jailed sanctuary and concocts the ingenious fiction that the Lionnel house is haunted by the previous householder's murder of a subordinate (35). Like Roger, Reignald has knives on the mind, for he describes the slain ghost as having a "body gasht, and all ore-stuck with wounds" (40); but Reignald here indicts the *master* of the household as the agent of illegitimate violence (perhaps because he has heard his own master threaten to amputate his guests' tongues). Holding the purse, undertaking violent shopping, governing militant cooks, and fictionalizing bloodthirsty masters, the steward makes domestic routine appear sinister. Hubristically reveling in his mastery, Reignald compares himself to Alexander, Agathocles, and Caesar: "These commanded / Their subjects, and their servants; I my Master" (61). The city comedy plot thus foregrounds master–servant and father–son conflicts rather than heterosexual discord.

The crisis in the Lionnel plot concludes when the father agrees to reconcile with his son on one condition. Departing from Plautus' play, where the father demands repayment, *English Traveller* presents Lionnel Sr. as readily forgiving his son's male comrades but banishing Lionnel's female companions from the home. Clearing the house of women might create a gynophobic all-male preserve, but it doesn't pave the way for easy domestic order; for Old Lionnel shows that the servant–master relationship is an ongoing and vexed one; this resolution occurs, for instance, after he almost beats Reignald. The hint of the master's barely averted violence lingers, heard clearly by neighboring servant Roger who has already shown himself to be acquainted with blood in the kitchen. Nick's vision of domestic cannibalism in *Woman Killed* thus resurfaces as Roger's delight in a violent dinner; and the aggressivity of housewifery evidenced in cookbooks becomes the story of domestic crisis in *The English Traveller.*

Although the Wincott plot concerns adultery rather than upstart servants, it shares with the citizen comedy a focus on bodily partition and human food, in part because embodiment is the play's key vocabulary for describing human bonds. In ways that echo *Woman Killed*, Geraldine's integration in the Wincott household is described as an affective incorporation: "He studies to engrosse mee to himself," says Geraldine of Wincott, "And is so wedded to my company, / Hee makes mee stranger to my Father's house" (9). With "engross" meaning "to make the body gross, fat, or bulky" as well as "to take possession or absorb," Geraldine's subsumption is imagined in corporeal, marital, and spatial terms. Despite the fact that he "love[s], nay almost doate[s] on" Geraldine, Wincott isn't fully able to engross (or wed) his neighbor, as he admits: "Oh had my youth bin blest with such a sonne, / To have made him my estate to my name hereditary, / I should have gone contented to my grave, / As to my bed" (13). Offering his guest free reign over the household, including his wife's bedchamber, Wincott attempts futilely, as he admits, to install a second domestic master to substitute for his lack of a son. His wife complies by furtively lodging Geraldine in her "Bosome" alongside her husband (31). The Wincotts adopt Geraldine into the household, as the brother (33), son (13), and lover (31) each claims to have never had. Recalling the "choice favours" that he "taste[s] in abundance" at the Wincotts, Geraldine responds in kind by using the language of subsumption (87). The play suggests that Wincott's opening of his body/home, like Frankford's, sets into motion a passionate and potentially destructive cycle of human absorption that spirals beyond his control.

Dalavill, Geraldine's rival for Mistress Wincott's affections, later brings out the potential brutality of this incorporation when he reports to Geraldine the effects of his absence from the Wincott home:

> The House
> Hath all this time seem'd naked without you;
> The good Old Man doth never sit to meat,
> But next his giving Thankes, hee speakes of you;
> There's scarce a bit, that he at Table tastes,
> That can digest without a Geraldine,
> You are in his mouth so frequent: Hee and Shee
> Both wondering, what distaste from one, or either,
> So suddenly, should alienate a Guest,
> To them, so deerely welcome. (54–5)

The first hint that we have of the Wincotts' yearning for the absent Geraldine is told as the story of table talk. Having engrossed Geraldine, the Wincotts cannot eat without recalling their companion as present food or the absent object of speech. How can Wincott "digest without a Geraldine" in his mouth? (And does this constitute talking with his mouth full?) Is longing another name for hunger? The Wincotts speculate on the cause for Geraldine's "distaste" while indulging their tastes, plaintively demonstrating that he has become a constituent part of their collective digestion and appetite. While other Renaissance plays mention names lodged in speakers' mouths,[47] Dalavill's modified phrase smacks of cannibalism. Affection, desire, and love are made to speak the language of ingestion; and mourning is represented as the dinner that fails to satisfy.

As in *Woman Killed*, it falls to a servant to provide parodic commentary on the play's pervasive corporeal language. Heywood emphasizes service by replacing the aristocratic crisis over dynastic lineage found in the subplot to *Woman Killed* with Plautus' citizen-based mercantile comedy about a wayward servant. Shifting the location from the Yorkshire countryside to a market town, Heywood makes the merchant's financial peril the crux of the Lionnel family crisis. As the aristocratic plot gives way to the horror of social inversion, the economic bonds of service come into full view. Roger's tale of a kitchen massacre, replete with detachable limbs and gluttonous passions, mocks not only Lionnel's appetitive expenditure (as we might expect) but the Wincott's network of consuming desire. Rather than simply pointing to the servant's importance within the fiction, however, I want to suggest that both plays, to different degrees, open up sites in which the vantage point of the servant can be elaborated. In Heywood's plays, hospitality is imagined as stuffing a friend's guts, shame as a heart bursting from a rib cage, anger as a trembling organ, terror as the thought of being plucked, and desire as the ingestion of bodies. The potential adulteration of the flesh, hardly restricted to a simple act of sexual betrayal, pervades all of household life. Going out of its way to designate the kitchen massacre as a servant's fantasy, *English Traveller* allows Roger to give these antagonisms a local habitation and a name.

### Family values

Both *Woman Killed* and *English Traveller* end with households newly reconstituted through the expulsion of the adulterous mistress and gentleman-companion and the cementing of "proper" male alliances. Forming what Orlin terms a "gynophobic fantasy," both plays inaugurate an all-male household. In *English Traveller* Heywood modifies the nature of the final community by heightening the violence attending to the wife's death: while Anne Frankford's self-starvation enables her to absent herself from a perilous world of consumption, the narrative of Mrs. Wincott's heart bursting from her ribs intensifies the economy of exchanged body parts operative in the play as a whole. The scapegoat symbolically bearing the weight of the household's corporeal trauma is thus Mistress Wincott. After Geraldine plays the "Doctor" to purge her sin, she commands, "Swell sicke Heart, / Even till thou burst the ribs that bound thee in; / So, there's one string crackt, flow, and flow high, / Even till thy blood distill out of mine eyes, / To witnesse my great sorrow" (92). Using a language associated with housewifery (distilling) to describe a "sicke Heart" rupturing into tears, Mistress Wincott reimagines the fragmented flesh that her adultery causes. But Heywood minimizes Mistress Wincott's importance to the final social resolution in this later play. While Anne Frankford's penitent death unveils the moral stature of her husband and the affective center of a new community, Mrs. Wincott's death, reported off stage, does not rehabilitate her or the social world. Instead her death creates a vacuum to be filled with newly consolidated male bonds. Her disintegration points not only to the adulterous opening of her body but implicitly to her husband's and her own problematic engrossment of Geraldine. Yet her corporeal breakdown unexpectedly paves the way for Wincott to "marry" Geraldine in the finale and thus legitimate a homoerotic dyad.

Both plays end with the performance of matrimonial vows that recasts the institution of marriage. "Wedding" his wife again as she dies, Frankford creates a necrophiliac union elasticized to accommodate Anne's brother Sir Francis. "O Master Frankford," says Francis, "all the near alliance / I lose by her shall be supplied in thee" (17.101–102). In *English Traveller*, Wincott gives his wife's death only a thought before realizing with elation that his true love Geraldine will no longer go into exile:

> This meeting that was made
> Onely to take of you a parting leave,
> Shall now be made a Marriage of our Love,
> Which none save onely Death shall separate. (94)

In sealing this marriage, he names Geraldine as heir, a feat not possible when his wife had a claim to his property.[48] Coldly labeling the final gathering as a celebratory feast, Wincott then compares his dead wife to a stingy father whose death inspires more joy than sorrow. The dynastic merging of households forged in *Woman Killed* thus gives way to an eroticized, financial, and domestic bond between men in *English Traveller*. No longer a guest, Geraldine moves into the Wincott household as combined son, mistress, and duplicate owner; and thus the play reconceives the nuclear family through the reapportionment of property rather than through kinship alliances. While the "normative" domestic order produced in both plays rests on a newly consolidated homosocial imaginary, *English Traveller* accentuates the monetary and queer nature of domestic relations and thus diminishes the homiletic framework and dynastic network that made homoeroticism properly readable in *Woman Killed*. And if Heywood's earlier tragedy critiqued the interpenetration of householder's and male subordinate's body, his later play makes that relationship the model for a newly authorized normative subject. Bereft of a wife, Wincott now fully engrosses Geraldine to himself. Feasting and mourning, very near the body of Mistress Wincott and the letter she wanted to write in "blood," the new household is still immersed in consumption and mortality.

The reconstruction of the family also involves a consolidation of the servant/master bond, for servants are conspicuously present to fill the void left by the wife's death. When the family members yearn to join Anne in her heartbreaking suicide, Nick demurs: "So will not I" (17.99). In keeping with his frustration with extraneous household members, Nick sports a Falstaffian pragmatism and refuses to engage in sacrificial if hollow emotional investments. His presence in the scene, however, suggests how vital he is to the new household. Having cleansed the domus of potential rivals – guest and interloping wife – he has proven his talent at ferreting out domestic disorder. Although Nick eschews an identification with gentlemen based on sentiment, he stands within the emergent "family" as its privileged viewer. And, as the link between audience and stage, he interpellates the audience into the odd position of being the guardian of household order – from below.

In *English Traveller*, neighboring servant Reignald occupies a similarly choric position in the final scene at the Wincott estate; instead of using sarcasm to rupture the community's identification with the household dissident, he has the audacity to compare Mistress Wincott's death with his own upstart behavior: "Burying of Wives," says Reignald, is "As stale as shifting [changing] shirts, or for some servants, / To flout and gull their Masters" (93). Blurring the positions of servant and master, Reignald merges the loss of a dependant with the mockery of social inversion. Unlike moral fables such as *Volpone* where overreaching servants receive due punishment, this play reinstalls the unruly servant into the very nerve center of domestic life. The final domestic order fails to model the ideal hierarchy advocated in domestic guides, for in both plays, Heywood creates non-normative, all-male households whose meaning is governed by powerful servants.[49]

Contrasting the subplots of these domestic tragedies shows just how far this later play goes in reconstructing the family. In *Woman Killed*, the two plots resolve in ways that position women differently: the Mountford–Acton feud is healed through a dynastic marriage, while Frankford replaces marriage with male kinship alliances. But the city comedy subplot in *English Traveller* stages a family crisis whose resolution *reduplicates* the all-male complexion of the Wincott family. Without "household servants," as Lionnel's companions are called, domesticity becomes an all-male preserve. Yet domesticity remains unstable since servants and guests (as extra body parts) trail threats of conflict. In the play's discourse, domestic subjects must be continually sacrificed, self-divided, partitioned, and consumed for the system to work.

As these plays suggest, domestic disorder isn't attributable simply to unruly wives but also to prodigal children, ambitious servants, and even obedient subordinates whose place renders them alarmingly indispensable. As well, domestic order requires the negotiation of "proper" homoerotic bonds. The plays also allow us to see how "women's work" could be variously articulated and disarticulated from "service." While English cookbooks hail the wife as the ultimate manager of flesh, these plays transfer her power to workers and other subordinates. If we read the play with an eye to constructions of gender, we discover the subordination and erasure of the wife. Yet this reading fails to account for the representation of *domestic practice* as wayward, internally conflicted, and highly unstable.[50] The violent potential of daily acts – imaged as knives in the kitchen – hints at an overdetermined fantasy available to many: nervous householders who fear insurrection, masters and mistresses who seek masochistic identification with their "lowers," servants and housewives who resent being mastered, household subordinates who jockey for position. Countering the deep structural logic of the well-running domus as a harmoniously ordered and hierarchized body, *English Traveller* vividly portrays the *pleasures* of domestic/corporeal fragmentation, partition, and conflict. Describing the delights of mutiny, rage, abjection, and mastery in bodily terms, *English Traveller* enjoins its audience to experience a domestic world in which traumatic brushes with brutality coexist with the joys of malleability. The homiletic framework of sin and repentance may have allowed female unruliness to be represented and expelled, but appetite and labor remain as requisite parts of a stubbornly material household life.

Taking up the issues of violence and service in *Woman Killed* with *Kindness* and *The English Traveller* may help us to reread a genre retroactively dubbed domestic tragedy. Dramatic representations of disorder in the non-elite household flourished on the London stage between 1590 and 1610, seen in such plays as *Arden of Faversham*, *A Warning for Fair Women*, *Two Lamentable Tragedies*, and *A Yorkshire Tragedy*.[51] Challenging standard definitions of tragedy as espoused by Donatus, Diomedes, and Sidney, these plays located protagonists of the middling sort and comic situations in tragic frameworks.[52] According to Henry Hitch Adams, this genre presents "common people, ordinarily set in the domestic scene, dealing with personal and family relationships rather than with large affairs of state, presented in a realistic fashion, and ending in a tragic or otherwise serious manner" (1–2). While Heywood's plays aren't based on true stories, they are generally catalogued in this grouping. Yet how is violence connected to "personal and family" relationships in *Woman Killed*? Aside from superficial bruises inflicted in a brawl and the wife's self-starvation, the only specified acts of violence depicted are masters beating and murdering servants. Since historical evidence shows that women, children, and servants were overwhelmingly the primary victims of violence in the home, Heywood's depiction of ever-present mutual *aggressiveness* simply diffuses this historical reality.[53]

Since earlier domestic tragedies centered on spousal murders, critics have un-
derstandably read the genre through an analysis of marital relations.[54] Feminist
scholars have found these plays to be a rich repository for unearthing the stage's
construction and contestation of marital, domestic, and gender ideologies.[55] But
as Heywood disperses spousal conflict into a network of domestic relations,
ritual, and practices, and as he locates sexual betrayal within a competitive
"homosocial imaginary," he invites consideration of this already hybrid genre.[56]
Perhaps this isn't surprising. Even in his conventional argument for domestic
ordering in *Christian Oeconomie*, Perkins defines the family as at "least three;
because two cannot make a societie."[57] Thus it is that the most capacious fantasy
of violence in these plays is conceived by a servant who takes pleasure in frag-
menting "a societie" into non-autonomous parts. Marital friction, it seems, bears
the consequences for an assortment of domestic desires and aggressions. Or as
Roger observes, "One had a Stomacke, and another had a Stomacke." While his
story of gallants consuming each other sidesteps the authority of housewives,
it nevertheless exposes the unsettling place of household subordinates and the
radically alienating quality of early modern domestic practice.

### Knowing home

> A good poet differs nothing at all from a Master-Cooke ... I am by my place, to
> know how to please the palates of ghests; so, you, are to know the palate of the
> times: study the several tasts, what every Nation, the Spaniard, the Dutch, the
> French, the Walloun, the Neapolitan, the Brit[t]an, the Sicilian, can expect from
> you ... I would have had your Ile brought floting in, now, In a brave broth.
>
> The Cook to the Poet, *Neptune's Triumph for the Return of Albion*[58]

Even as *English Traveller* reframes violence as the domestic unconscious, it
registers the national discourse evident in some household manuals; for it lav-
ishly stakes a claim to domesticity as the ultimate ground of knowledge. The
play's representation of bodily rupture is thus not bereft of a pull toward another
kind of cohesion; severed bodies are integrated thematically, if associatively,
into a national body politic secured by shared place. This framing gesture is
evident in the scene where Geraldine discovers his mistress in bed with Dalavill,
for he analyzes his "passions" by reassigning affect from persons to place:

> You have made mee
> To hate my very Countrey, because heere bred:
> Neere two such monsters; First I'le leave this House,
> And then my Fathers; Next I'le take my leave,
> Both of this Clime and Nation, Travell till
> Age snow upon this Head: My passions now,
> Are unexpressable. (70)

Moving from the scene of betrayal in the bedroom to the conjoined spaces of home and nation, Geraldine transforms his "divorce" (89) from the Wincotts into a national exile. Why should his disaffection with love and marriage – indeed his bodily disjoining from the household – become a renunciation of England? In *Woman Killed*, by contrast, the wife is expelled from home and the adulterous Wendoll flees the country, wandering "like a Cain, / In foreign countries and remoted climes" (16.127–28). But since Geraldine has not committed any offense, his national disgust and self-imposed exile appears inexplicable. Arguing that an exodus implies guilt, Geraldine's father puzzles, "why [do] you desire to steale out of your Countrey, / Like some malefactor?" (86). Geraldine's silent answer, of course, is that the whole country has absorbed the guilt of the "monsters" it births; and thus only national disarticulation can save him from becoming heir to a land capable of breeding corruption. Geraldine's logic rests on his easy cognitive leap from nation to domus as well as his sense of "place" as the ultimate determinant of moral action.

Both plays associate domesticity with a distinctly English order, so that household intruders and wronged guests alike read their disaffection in national terms. What England "breeds" is in fact precisely the subject that opens *English Traveller*, since Geraldine's position as the titled figure gives him occasion to compare national tastes and inclinations. Envying Geradine's cosmopolitanism, his audience translates national knowledge into *erotic* terms, suggesting that the sum of his travels rests in his ability to compare appetites, foods, beauties, and culturally distinct sexual proclivities. When pressured to say which country produces the best women, Geraldine turns the conversation to the issue of food. Since each climate and soil determines men's "stomachs," he argues, men naturally prefer native wives: "what is most pleasing to the man [is] there borne," Geraldine concludes. Climate and nationality, in this logic, determine "appetites" (12). The "stomach" that will later be linked to domestic bloodshed, and "taste," which will later be linked to eroticism, are introduced first as the product of the nation. It is no wonder that Geraldine later reads "monstrous" desire as inherently English, or that the play's title frames the story in national terms.[59] For the first scene intermeshes culinary, sexual, and national appetite. When Wincott asks what has caused Geraldine's "strangeness" and "distaste," he evidences the play's deep intertwining of orality and familiarity. Returning to England only to find domestic disorder, travelers in both plots – Geraldine and Lionnel – make a final decision to "stay at home"; and their reaffiliation marks the terms of domestic redemption.

What Geraldine learns is supposedly the truth of home's monstrosity; that is, heterosexual infidelity precipitates a rupture that bleeds into but then finds reparation in the fantasy of national exile. Geraldine's reconciliation with Wincott in the finale thus constitutes a national reunion as well as a homoerotic marriage. Lover to his surrogate father, Geraldine is engrossed back into a community defined specifically as English. After Wincott pledges a "marriage of [their] love," Geraldine finalizes its terms: "It calles me from all Travell, and from henceforth, / With my Countrey I am friends" (94). With the seeming depravity of England giving way to national affiliation, the play ends with an authorized and eroticized national union that compensates for the tragedy of unauthorized heterosexual desire. As the play uses Mistress Wincott's death to absorb the potential injury posed broadly by domesticity, it revises the discourse nominating the housewife as guardian of national culture.

In imprinting sexual themes onto a domestic and national graph, this play also comments on the fact that domestic tragedies routinely compel audience identification by reference to a particular location. Domestic tragedy, as we have seen, is defined not only by its subject matter but also by its realistic style of representation. What this usually entails is attention to the minute details of life, with the authenticity of this "slice of life" style bolstered by an overtly English setting. In this vein, taxonomically different features – prosaic acts, common persons, domestic themes, and realistic style – are made to seem "naturally" related to the plays' native settings. The morphing of recognizably English plots into highly particularized household spaces fashions a specific form of audience identification, the creation of a recognizable "us." Although domesticity obviously has no inherent relationship to "realistic" representation, Englishness illogically emerges from within the supposedly "ordinary" and "true-to-life" features of household life. In *A Warning for Fair Women*, for instance, Lady Tragedy makes a case for the play's local realism: "My sceane is London, native and your owne," she declares, "I sigh to thinke, my subject too well knowne, / I am not faind."[60] Verisimilitude, familiarity and native setting, Lady Tragedy implies, lend dignity to tragic form. Since the audience is said to possess the dramatic world as its "owne," habitation and property converge to create a special intimacy between spectators and represented place, an intimacy that compensates for the lack of "noble" subject matter. In the concluding chorus, Tragedy explains why she has not presented a revenge narrative: "The reason is, that now of truth I sing ... Beare with this true and home-borne Tragedie, / Yeelding so slender argument and scope, / To build a matter of importance on" (2725, 2729–31). While seemingly trivializing its "slender" subject, the play in fact lauds its accomplishment in laying tragedy on an unexpected foundation. Apparently being "home-borne" – meaning both domestic and English – is its salient claim.[61] Through these gestures, domestic tragedies invite audiences to ratify what is already "known," not only the plays' native content but the circumstantial everydayness in which these stories were saturated.[62]

Critics have been fascinated with the "authenticity-effect" that Heywood creates. Offering a "bare stage" comparable to "coarse fare," the Prologue introduces *Woman Killed* as unadorned and homey. Instead of simulating exotic locations, Heywood litters the stage space with the stock of the everyday imaginary: salt cellars, voiders, trenchers, table cloths, napkins, stools, cards, and candlesticks. The most famous example of the play's particularizing verisimilitude is found in the stage direction commanding Frankford to enter a scene "as it were brushing the crumbs from his clothes with a napkin" (8.22).[63] By having the moral crux of *English Traveller* rest in a character's decision to "stay home," Heywood casts a sly glance at the genre that he has belatedly revisited, as if winking at the way that domestic plays routinely enfranchise their audiences. In commenting on a common, national, and "home-borne" taste, *English Traveller* brilliantly weaves the themes of appetite, consumption, and community-formation into an acknowledgment of its own form of address.

Heywood's domestic tragedies don't conventionally take meaning, as we might expect, from the sacrificial violence found in their closing scenes. Both plays endorse a male community founded on the eradication of women, and community consolidates around a scene of death. But the play's fictional networks remain in flux at the end, represented dramatically as organs and limbs circulating in an eroticized body politic. Frankford's heart must bleed routinely, servants must cut flesh to stay life, and dinner must be served. As the audience is asked to acknowledge this daily aggressivity, the phantasmatic sites of identification that this knowledge enables are anchored to the familiarity of shared place. By making violence rest on everyday practice, the play thus triggers two key fantasies: that the labor of male and female servants produces a fully penetrable household body more complex and negotiable than dominant models suggest; and that even a disorderly household life is compensatorily reassuring, for it fortifies the "real" bonds shared by English people.

### The playhouse

Let me conclude by considering the moment when servant Reignald, caught red-handed in his schemes, scrambles to temporary safety on the roof of Lionnel's house and declares that he stands like "Dame Fortune / Before the Fortune Playhouse" (84). In Plautus' *Haunted House* the cheeky slave Tranio ascends an "altar" to find safe haven. In *English Traveller*'s most metatheatrical moment, however, the household is converted into a London amphitheater (in a northern suburb) with the trickster servant as its cross-gendered figurehead. The fantasy of power reversal that everywhere hovers close to violence in this play, is, in this moment, mapped onto the particularized space of London theater, the disarrayed "household" serving as a refuge for the servant threatened with injury. Looking at Reignald, who directs their gazes back to the playhouse space they occupy, the Renaissance audience is invited to interpret their theatrical experience as a naughty domestic rebellion. The comfort of the play's "home-borne" knowledge (*you, like Reignald, are at a theater*), paired with its insistence that this is a familiar story, makes palpable the complex way in which the play embraces the imaginary violence, violation, and repair of the everyday world it celebrates. The play thus exposes the peculiarity of the world that it nevertheless insists is commonplace. With theories of national taste transmuting everywhere into images of live food, *English Traveller* converts the destructive power of the desires it so vividly portrays into a final investment in a place called home.

# Notes

## INTRODUCTION: IN THE NATION'S KITCHEN

1. Jacqueline Rose, *States of Fantasy* (Oxford: Clarendon Press, 1996), 4.
2. Scholars debate whether conceptions of the family changed significantly in the wake of the Reformation. Lawrence Stone has famously argued that Catholic idealizations of celibacy gave way to celebrations of the spiritual potential of the companionate conjugal union (*The Family, Sex and Marriage in England 1500–1800* [London: Weidenfeld and Nicolson, 1977]; see also Christopher Hill, *Society and Puritanism in Pre-Revolutionary England* [NY: Schocken Books, 1964], 443–81). On the value of Stone's work for literary analyses, see Mary Beth Rose, *The Expense of Spirit: Love and Sexuality in English Renaissance Drama* (Ithaca: Cornell University Press, 1988). For skeptical critiques of Stone, see J. A. Sharpe, *Early Modern England: A Social History 1550–1760* (London: Edward Arnold, 1987); Ralph Houlbrooke, *The English Family 1450–1700* (NY: Longman, 1984); Kathleen Davies, "The Sacred Condition of Equality – How Original were Puritan Doctrines of Marriage?" *Social History* 5 (1977): 563–81; and Karen Newman, *Fashioning Femininity and English Renaissance Drama* (University of Chicago Press, 1991). One can appreciate Stone's grasp of discontinuities in "the family" over time without validating all of his conclusions (e.g., the novelty of idealizations of marriage; the rise of affective individualism; the shift from an open lineage family to restricted nuclear family; increased power granted the wife in companionate marriage).
3. William Perkins, *Christian Oeconomie: Or, A Short Survey of the Right Manner of Erecting and Ordering a Familie* (1609), ¶3$^{r-v}$. Even orthodox early modern writing on domesticity shows that its financial, ethical, and social dimensions could conflict. Conduct book writers, for instance, argued for strict hierarchies that were largely untenable given their prescriptions for a symbiotic home economy; they emphasized the public/private continuum at a time in which property was demarcating a privatized household; and they positioned domesticity unevenly in arguing for humanism's civic utility. On these contradictions, see Lena Cowen Orlin, *Private Matters and Public Culture in Post-Reformation England* (Ithaca: Cornell University Press, 1994), 126–30; Susan Amussen, *An Ordered Society: Gender and Class in Early Modern England* (NY: Columbia University Press, 1988), 41–7; and Lorna Hutson, *The Usurer's Daughter: Male Friendship and Fictions of Women in Sixteenth-Century England* (London: Routledge, 1994), esp. 17–51.
4. Hugh Plat, *Delightes for Ladies* (1602), A2$^v$-A3$^r$.
5. *Epulario, or The Italian Banquet* (1598), B4$^r$.

6. John Partridge, *Treasurie of Commodious Conceites, & Hidden Secrets, and may be called the Huswives Closet, of Healthful Provision* (1584), A8$^r$.

7. Michel de Certeau, *The Practice of Everyday Life*, trans. Steven Randall (Berkeley, Los Angeles, London: University of California Press, 1984), xiii. On banqueting, see Patricia Fumerton, *Cultural Aesthetics: Renaissance Literature and the Practice of Social Ornamentation* (University of Chicago Press, 1991), 111–68.

8. On the humoral body, see Gail Kern Paster, *The Body Embarrassed: Drama and the Disciplines of Shame in Early Modern England* (Ithaca: Cornell University Press, 1993), esp. 1–22, 113–62; and Michael Schoenfeldt, *Bodies and Selves in Early Modern England: Physiology and Inwardness in Spenser, Shakespeare, Herbert and Milton* (Cambridge University Press, 1999), 1–39.

9. See excerpts of Lady Catherine Sedley's manuscript receipt book in A. W. Sloan, *English Medicine in the Seventeenth Century* (Durham: Durham Academic Press, 1996), 136; Elizabeth Grey's (Countess of Kent's) posthumous guide, *A Choice Manual, or Rare and Select Secrets in Physick and Chyrurgery: Collected, and practised by the Right Honourable, the Countess of Kent, late deceased* (1653), 92; and Lady Mildmay's manuscript receipts, reprinted in Linda Pollock, *With Faith and Physic: The Life of a Tudor Gentlewoman, Lady Grace Mildmay, 1552–1620* (London: Collins and Brown, 1993).

10. Hannah Woolley, *The Compleat Servant-Maid* (1683), 174.

11. Hilary Spurling, *Elinor Fettiplace's Receipt Book* reproduced in *Elizabethan Country House Cooking* (London: Viking Salamander, 1986), 42; introduction, 20.

12. *The Widdows Treasure, Plentifully furnished with sundry precious and approved secrets in Phisicke* (1595), prefatory gathering, irregular pagination.

13. Jonathan Sawday, *The Body Emblazoned: Dissection and the Human Body in Renaissance Culture* (London and NY: Routledge, 1995), especially 1–15.

14. Patricia Fumerton, introduction to Patricia Fumerton and Simon Hunt (eds.), *Renaissance Culture and the Everyday* (Philadelphia: University of Pennsylvania Press, 1999), 6.

15. On the "middling sort," see Theodore Leinwand, "Shakespeare and the Middling Sort," *Shakespeare Quarterly* 44 (1993): 283–303; Keith Wrightson, "Estates, Degrees, and Sorts: Changing Perceptions of Society in Tudor and Stuart England," in Penelope J. Corfield (ed.), *Language, History and Class* (Oxford: Basil Blackwell, 1991), 30–52; and Wrightson, *English Society 1580–1680* (New Brunswick, NJ: Rutgers University Press, 1982). On the social complexity of the London population, see Ian W. Archer, *The Pursuit of Stability: Social Relations in Elizabethan London* (Cambridge University Press, 1991).

16. Jacqueline Rose conceives of fantasy as both a structuring principle for "social reality" and an intermediary process binding subjects to the "real" they structure.

17. On the value of using the term "class," a nineteenth-century analytical category, for an interpretation of early modern culture, see David Scott Kastan, "Is there a Class in this (Shakespearean) Text?" in *Shakespeare After Theory* (NY: Routledge, 1999), 149–64.

18. Gordon J. Schochet, *Patriarchalism in Political Thought* (Oxford: Basil Blackwell, 1975), 55. For different accounts of patriarchalism, see Richard Mocket, *God and the King* (London, 1615); Dudley Digges, *The Unlawfulnesse of Subjects* (London, 1643), William Gouge, *Of Domesticall Duties* (London, 1622); and Richard Filmer,

*Patriarcha, of the Natural Power of Kings* (written in 1640s, published London, 1680).

19. On the multiplicity of patriarchalism and its contradictions, see Schochet, *Patriarchalism*; Amussen, *An Ordered Society*, 34–66; Orlin, *Private Matters and Public Culture*, 85–136; Margaret Ezell, *The Patriarch's Wife* (Chapel Hill, NC: University of North Carolina Press, 1987), 36–61, 161–2; Deborah Shuger, *Habits of Thought in the English Renaissance: Religion, Politics, and the Dominant Culture* (Berkeley: University of California Press, 1990), 218–49; Wrightson, *English Society*, 89–118; and Louis Montrose, *The Purpose of Playing: Shakespeare and the Cultural Politics of Elizabethan Theatre* (University of Chicago Press, 1996), 109–23.

20. See Orlin, *Private Matters*, esp. 1–13, 182–89; Mark Girouard, *Life in the English Country House: A Social and Architectural History* (New Haven, CT: Yale University Press, 1978); Alice T. Friedman, *House and Household in Elizabethan England: Wollaton Hall and the Willoughby Family* (University of Chicago Press, 1989); Amy Louise Erickson, *Women and Property in Early Modern England* (NY: Routledge, 1993), esp. 6–20, 187–203; Susan Cahn, *Industry of Devotion: The Transformation of Women's Work in England, 1500–1650* (NY: Columbia University Press, 1987); David Underdown, *Revel, Riot, and Rebellion: Popular Politics and Culture in England, 1603–1660* (NY: Oxford University Press, 1985); Sara Mendelson and Patricia Crawford (eds.), *Women in Early Modern England, 1550–1720* (Oxford: Clarendon Press, 1998); and Amussen, *An Ordered Society*, 67–94.

21. On the difficulty in defining the household (e.g., as a physical site of residency or extended kinship alliance), see Suzanne Westfall, "'A Commonty a Christmas gambold or a tumbling trick': Household Theater," in John D. Cox and David Scott Kastan (eds.), *A New History of Early English Drama* (NY: Columbia University Press, 1997), 39–58; Diane Henderson, "The Theater and Domestic Culture," *A New History of Early English Drama*, 173–94; Jean-Louis Flandrin, *Families in Former Times*, trans. Richard Southern (Cambridge University Press, 1979); and Peter Laslett and Richard Wall (eds.), *Household and Family in Past Time* (Cambridge University Press, 1971).

22. The term "economy" initially referred to the financial, ethical, and domestic responsibilities of household management. On shifts in the family industry during the early modern period, see Alice Clark, *The Working Life of Women in the Seventeenth Century* (NY: E. P. Dutton & Co., 1919); Cahn, *Industry of Devotion*; and Roberta Hamilton, *The Liberation of Women* (London: George Allen and Unwin, 1978). For assessments of Clark's argument, see Judith Bennett, "Medieval Women, Modern Women: Across the Great Divide" in David Aers (ed.), *Culture and History, 1350–1600: Essays on English Communities, Identities, and Writing* (Detroit: Wayne State University Press, 1992), 146–67; Amy Louise Erickson, introduction to Clark's *Working Life* (NY: Routledge, 1992); and Lindsey Charles, introduction, in Lindsey Charles and Lorna Duffin (eds.), *Women and Work in Pre-Industrial England* (London: Croom Helm, 1985), 1–23.

23. Amussen, *An Ordered Society*, 64–6; Schochet, *Patriarchalism*, 268–81.

24. Feminist work documenting early modern domesticity's material features includes Clark, *Working Life*; Orlin, *Private Matters*; Amussen, *An Ordered Society*; Frances

E. Dolan, *Dangerous Familiars: Representations of Domestic Crime in England, 1550–1700* (Ithaca: Cornell University Press, 1994); Natasha Korda, "Household Kates: Domesticating Commodities in *The Taming of the Shrew*," *Shakespeare Quarterly* 47:2 (1996): 109–31; Kim F. Hall, "Culinary Spaces, Colonial Spaces: The Gendering of Sugar in the Seventeenth Century," Valerie Traub, M. Lindsay Kaplan, and Dympna Callaghan (eds.) *Feminist Readings of Early Modern Culture* (Cambridge University Press, 1996), 168–90; Ezell, *The Patriarch's Wife*; Laura Gowing, *Domestic Dangers: Women, Words and Sex in Early Modern London* (Oxford: Clarendon Press, 1996); Charles and Duffin (eds.), *Women and Work in Pre-Industrial England*; Amy Louise Erickson, *Women and Property in Early Modern England* (NY: Routledge, 1993); Louise A. Tilly and Joan W. Scott (eds.), *Women, Work and the Family* (NY: Routledge, 1987); Lisa Jardine, *Reading Shakespeare Historically* (NY: Routledge 1996), esp. 65–77, 148–57; and Cahn, *Industry of Devotion*. On the need for a materialist feminism, see Jean E. Howard, *The Stage and Social Struggle in Early Modern England* (NY: Routledge, 1994); and Valerie Wayne, introduction, in Wayne (ed.), *The Matter of Difference: Materialist Feminist Criticism of Shakespeare* (Ithaca: Cornell University Press, 1991), 1–26.

25. Scholarship that pushes critics to queer domesticity includes Alan Bray, *Homosexuality in Renaissance England*, 2nd edn. (London: Gay Men's Press, 1988), esp. 51–3; Bray, "Homosexuality and the Signs of Male Friendship in Elizabethan England," in Jonathan Goldberg (ed.), *Queering the Renaissance* (Durham: Duke University Press, 1994), 40–61; Bruce Smith, *Homosexual Desire in Shakespeare's England* (University of Chicago Press, 1991; rpt. 1994), esp. 84–8, 191–7; Jeffrey Masten, "Playwrighting: Authorship and Collaboration," in Cox and Kastan (eds.), *A New History of Early English Drama*, 357–82; Masten, "My Two Dads: Collaboration and the Reproduction of Beaumont and Fletcher," in Goldberg (ed.), *Queering the Renaissance*, 280–309; Rebecca Ann Bach, "The Homosocial Imaginary of *A Woman Killed with Kindness*," *Textual Practice* 12:3 (1998): 503–24; Mario DiGangi, "Queering the Shakespearean Family," *Shakespeare Quarterly* 47:3 (1996): 269–90 and his *The Homoerotics of Early Modern Drama* (Cambridge University Press, 1997), 64–99; Alan Stewart, *Close Readers: Humanism and Sodomy in Early Modern England* (Princeton, NJ: Princeton University Press, 1997), esp. 161–87. Scholarship that has refined homoeroticism includes Stephen Orgel, *Impersonations: The Performance of Gender in Shakespeare's England* (Cambridge University Press, 1996); Goldberg, *Sodometries: Renaissance Texts/Modern Sexualities* (Stanford University Press, 1992); and Valerie Traub, *Desire and Anxiety: Circulations of Sexuality in Shakespearean Drama* (NY: Routledge, 1992).

26. In hierarchies of early modern England, desire was refracted through the prism of social verticality. On eros as implicated in social place, see Jardine, *Reading Shakespeare*, 65–77; Jean Howard, "Sex and Social Conflict: The Erotics of *The Roaring Girl*," in Susan Zimmerman (ed.), *Erotic Politics: Desire on the Renaissance Stage* (NY: Routledge, 1992); Bray, *Homosexuality in Renaissance England*; and Smith, *Homosexual Desire*, esp. 79–115 and 189–223.

27. I use the word "queer" to mean both explicitly homoerotic relationships and the non-normative potential of early modern domesticity generally. "Queer domesticity"

is one in which subject positions and the erotic desires that accompany those positions are disorienting, fluid, and disruptive of traditional techniques for social ordering. On queerness, see Michael Warner's introduction, *Fear of a Queer Planet: Queer Politics and Social Theory* (Minneapolis: University of Minnesota Press, 1993). On how all national identity, indeed all *identity*, can be said to be "queer," see Antony Easthope, *Englishness and National Culture* (NY: Routledge, 1999), 22.

28. For commentary on the "business" of housewifery, see William Perkins, *The Workes of That Famous and Worthy Minister of Christ in the University of Cambridge, Mr. William Perkins*, 3 vols. (1612), Vol. I: 391. Barnabe Rich *The Excellency of Good Women* (1613), 23; Thomas Gainford, *The Rich Cabinet* (1616), 102; Ezell, *The Patriarch's Wife*; Cahn, *Industry of Devotion*; and Michael Roberts, "'Words they are Women, and Deeds they are Men': Images of Work and Gender in Early Modern England," Charles and Duffin (eds.), *Women and Work in Pre-Industrial England*, 122–80.

29. When Benedict Anderson writes that "nation-ness is the most universally legitimate value in the politics life of our time," he points to a key difference between modern and early modern periods. *Imagined Communities: Reflections on the Origins and Spread of Nationalism* (London: Verso, 1983), 3.

30. See Jean Howard and Phyllis Rackin, *Engendering A Nation* (NY: Routledge, 1997), 11–19; Richard Helgerson, *Forms of Nationhood* (University of Chicago Press, 1992); Easthope, *Englishness*; Anderson, *Imagined Communities*, 37–46; Andrew Hadfield, *Literature, Politics and National Identity: Reformation to Renaissance* (Cambridge University Press, 1994). Modern political theorists see the political fiction of the monarch's "two bodies" as a transitional state between the medieval theological doctrine that all Christendom was a collective *corpus mysticum* and the distinctively modern state, which is a power separate from both the ruled and ruler. See Quenten Skinner, *The Foundations of Modern Political Thought*, 2 vols. (Cambridge University Press, 1978), Vol. II: 353.

31. Claire McEachern, *The Poetics of English Nationhood, 1590–1612* (Cambridge University Press, 1996), 1.

32. For a sample of the scholarship on Queen Elizabeth as "text," see Leah Marcus, *Puzzling Shakespeare: Local Reading and Its Discontents* (Berkeley: University of California Press, 1988), 51–105; Louis Montrose, "The Elizabethan Subject and the Spenserian Text," in Patricia Parker and David Quint (eds.), *Literary Theory/Renaissance Texts* (Baltimore, MD: Johns Hopkins University Press, 1986), 303–40; and Susan Frye, *Elizabeth I: The Competition for Representation* (Oxford University Press, 1993).

33. For critics who have investigated ways in which gender functions to produce (highly unstable) racial and national differences, see Montrose, "The Work of Gender in the Discourse of Discovery," *Representations* 33 (1991): 1–41; Ann Rosalind Jones and Peter Stallybrass, "Dismantling Irena: The Sexualizing of Ireland in Early Modern England," in Andrew Parker, Mary Russo, Doris Sommer, and Patricia Yaeger (eds.), *Nationalisms and Sexualities* (NY: Routledge, 1992), 157–71; Phyllis Rackin, *Stages of History: Shakespeare's English Chronicles* (Ithaca: Cornell University Press, 1990); and Jean Howard, "An English Lass Amid the Moors: Gender, Race, Sexuality, and National Identity in Heywood's *The Fair Maid*

*of the West*," in Margo Hendricks and Patricia Parker (eds.), *Women, "Race," & Writing in the Early Modern Period* (NY: Routledge, 1994), 101–17.

34. Lauren Berlant, *Anatomy of National Fantasy: Hawthorne, Utopia and Everyday Life* (University of Chicago Press, 1991).

35. Among others, Jacqueline Rose, Easthope, and Berlant argue powerfully for the viability of collective fantasy (though I should note, as a point of contrast, that Berlant's work posits the "everyday" as potentially disruptive of the National Symbolic, while in my account it becomes a building block in an emergent middling-class formation of nationhood). For a model of how to blend psychoanalytic and historicist methods, see Mark Breitenberg, *Anxious Masculinity in Early Modern England* (Cambridge University Press, 1996).

36. In his account of early modern "shaping fantasies," Montrose sees representations as dialectically shaped by the cultural fantasies that they then reconfigure. "Fantasies," in his usage, are specific appropriations of social discourses. See *The Purpose of Playing*, 1–16 and 109–10.

37. Judith Butler, *Bodies that Matter: On the Discursive Limits of "Sex,"* (NY: Routledge, 1993), 267, fn. 7; Slavoj Žižek, *Looking Awry: An Introduction to Jacques Lacan through Popular Culture* (Cambridge, MA: MIT Press, 1997), 6. "Fantasy . . . is not the object of desire, but its setting," state Laplanche and Pontalis, "In fantasy the subject does not pursue the object or its sign: he appears caught up himself in the sequence of images. He forms no representation of the desired object, but is himself represented as participating in the scene although, in the earliest forms of fantasy, he cannot be assigned any fixed place within it." "Fantasy and the Origins of Sexuality," in Victor Burgin, James Donald, and Cora Kaplan (eds.), *Formations of Fantasy* (NY: Methuen, 1986), 26.

38. Here we might turn to the work of Diana Fuss, who helpfully theorizes identity formation as predicated on crisscrossing identifications and desires that construct but nevertheless exceed and thus destabilize identity. The term "identification" has different meanings for scholars. In brief: psychoanalytic critics tend to see "identification" as a process of self-recognition based on loss; one incorporates the lost object to produce a self-differentiation that enables self-recognition (or *identification of*). In this sense, identification is the mechanism for the subject knowing itself based on an internalized other. Historicist critics tend to think in terms of a transparent process of *identification with* (e.g., a person, object, group, or institution), the phenomenon of recognizing an affinity. In work such as Fuss's, both uses of the term are in play and are explained in relation to one another. Diana Fuss, *Identification Papers* (NY: Routledge, 1995), 1–19.

39. Since identification is predicated on a particular view of "everydayness," my study echoes in part Fumerton's call for a critical practice that focuses on "the common," a capacious term, as she notes. Unlike Fumerton, I don't see "everydayness" as separable from something called politics. But I engage the constellation of terms that she astutely traces. "Introduction: A New New Historicism," *Renaissance Culture*, 4.

40. *The Civile Conversation of M. Steeven Guazzo*, trans. George Pettie, 2 vols. (London: Constable and Co., Ltd, 1925), Vol. II: 40–41.

41. Richard Hyrde, preface to Desiderius Erasmus, *A Devout Treatise Upon the Pater Noster*, trans. Margaret Roper (1526).

42. Sir Thomas Overbury, *His Wife with Additions of New Characters* (1614) rpt. *The Miscellaneous Works in Prose and Verse of Sir Thomas Overbury*, ed. Edward F. Rimbault (London: Reeves and Turner, 1890), 41.

43. Miles Coverdale, *Goostly Psalmes and Spirituall Songes* (1635), *2$^v$.

44. Elizabeth Grey (Countess of Kent), *A Choice Manual*, (1661), 75. *The Ladies Cabinet Enlarged* (1655) also hints at the almost mythic element of physic when it instructs readers to create a potion to preserve youthfulness, purify blood, and prevent miscarriage: "Take of the biggest and fatest Snakes, Adders or Vipers which you can get in June or July, cutt off their heads, take off their skins, and unbowel them," the recipe begins, thus making the worker master hazardous creatures associated with primal temptation and danger (69).

45. When Volpone glosses his final punishment as "the mortifying of the fox," he chooses a word that could mean "humiliating," "rendering the flesh dead," or "seasoning meat to make it tender." Cookery, spiritual humbling, and violence mingle in this linguistic register. Ben Jonson, *Volpone*, ed. Philip Brockbank (NY: W.W. Norton New Mermaids Series, 1992), 5.12.125.

46. With the new affordability of printed books, the popularity of London drama, and the growth of provincial touring, the possibility of a national *culture* was enhanced. Theater historians suggest, for instance, that up to 24,000 people attended the theater weekly in 1600 London, that a person living in Bath might see 15–20 plays a year performed by touring companies, and that peddlers' trade made cheap quarto playtexts available outside the capital. Alfred Harbage's famous case for the "popularity" of drama (in *Shakespeare and the Rival Traditions* [NY: Macmillan Co., 1952]) may have been rooted in misconceptions about the exclusivity of coterie plays and Shakespeare's purported transpolitical nature, but it persuasively establishes drama's broad appeal.

47. Martin Butler, *Theater and Crisis, 1632–1642* (Cambridge University Press, 1984).

48. William Shakespeare, *Othello* in *The Riverside Shakespeare* (Boston, MA: Houghton Mifflin Co., 1974), 2.1.109–12.

## 1 FAMILIARITY AND PLEASURE IN THE ENGLISH HOUSEHOLD GUIDE, 1500–1700

1. Sigmund Freud, "The Uncanny" (1919), in *Collected Papers*, general trans., Joan Riviere, 5 vols. (London: The Hogarth Press, 1934), Vol. IV: 368–407.

2. Fumerton discusses aristocratic banqueting in *Cultural Aesthetics*, 111–68, and animal torture in *Renaissance Culture and the Everyday*, 1–3. Fumerton's most dramatic example of early modern domestic difference – the torment of animals for culinary pleasure – isn't typical in English household guides of the period. With the exception of her indirect reference to Muffet's *Health's Improvement*, Fumerton's examples come from continental cookbooks and eighteenth-century sources, many of which overlap with those discussed by Phillipa Pullar in *Consuming Passions: Being An Historic Inquiry into Certain English Appetites* (Boston and Toronto: Little, Brown and Company, 1970), 150–51. On the brutality of kitchen butchery, see chapter 6 below.

3. My description of this hypothetical housewife's activities is pieced together from the following texts: Plat, *Delightes for Ladies*; Gervase Markham, *The English Housewife* (1631; first published as *The English Hus-wife* in 1615); Thomas Tusser, *Fiue Hundreth Points of Good Husbandry*; Partridge, *The Treasurie of Hidden Secrets* (1600); W. M., *The Queens Closet Opened* (1655); *A Closet for Ladies* (1608); Grey, *A Choice Manual*; Margaret Hoby, *Diary of Lady Margaret Hoby, 1599–1605*, ed. Dorothy M. Meads (Boston and NY: Houghton Mifflin Co., 1930); Woolley, *The Compleat Servant-Maid*; John Cotta, *A Short Discouerie of the Unobserved Dangers of... Unconsiderate Practisers of Physicke*; *Ladie Borlase's Receiptes Booke* (1612), ed. David E. Schoonover (Iowa City: University of Iowa Press, 1998), and Spurling, *Elinor Fettiplace's Receipt Book*.

4. Margaret Hoby, entry "The 4 day the :20 [week]," *Diary of Lady Margaret Hoby, 1599–1605*, 109. Almost daily, Hoby mentions her dedication to "being busy" and "dispatching" household affairs; and her medicinal recipes circulated widely enough to be cited in *The Queens Closet Opened* (11).

5. *The Diaries of Lady Anne Clifford*, ed. D. J. H. Clifford (Wolfeboro Falls, NH: Alan Sutton Publishing Ltd., 1990), esp. 57, 68, 122–3. Clifford's diary spans from 1603–76. Maria Thynne's letters are reprinted in Suzanne Trill, Kate Chedgzoy and Melanie Osborne (eds.), *Lay By Your Needles Ladies, Take the Pen: Writing Women in England, 1500–1700* (NY: Arnold, 1997), 77. Spurling discusses Fettiplace's home remedies. On ladies who engaged in medical practice, see Doreen Nagy, *Popular Medicine in Seventeenth-Century England* (Bowling Green, OH: Bowling Green State University Press, 1988), 54–78; and Pollock, *With Faith and Physic*.

6. See, for example, Kenelme Digby, *The Closet of Sir Kenelme Digby Opened*, ed. Anne MacDonnell (London: Philip Lee Warner, 1910).

7. See Nagy, *Popular Medicine*, 43–53.

8. Woolley claims that her experience in housewifery was augmented by reading published guidebooks provided by her employer. See *Supplement to the Queen-like Closet*, bound with *The Queen-like Closet* (1675), 10–11.

9. See Clark, *Working Life*.

10. John Dod and John Cleaver, *A Godly Forme of Houshold Government* (London, 1630), F6$^r$.

11. Ezell, *The Patriarch's Wife*, 36–61.

12. See Patrick Hannay, *A Happy Husband*, 2nd edn (1622) rpt. in *The Poeticall Works of Patrick Hannay* (Glasgow: Hunterian Club Publication, Vol. XIV, 1875), 168.

13. "The Good and the Badde," in *The Works in Verse and Prose of Nicholas Breton*, ed. Alexander B. Grosart, 2 vols. (Edinburgh: A. Constable, 1879), Vol. II: 12.

14. Andrew McRae, "Husbandry Manuals and the Language of Agrarian Improvement," in Michael Leslie and Timothy Raylor (eds.), *Culture and Cultivation in Early Modern England: Writing and the Land* (Leicester University Press, 1992), 35–62; Joan Thirsk (ed.), *The Agrarian History of England and Wales*, vol. IV: 1500–1640 (Cambridge University Press, 1967); and Thirsk, "Making a Fresh Start: Sixteenth-Century Agriculture and the Classical Inspiration," in Leslie and Raylor (eds.) *Culture and Cultivation*, 15–34.

15. See Wrightson, *English Society, 1580–1680*; and Cahn, *Industry of Devotion*, 11–32.

16. Though the first English printed cookbook, *This is the Boke of Cokery* (1500), was medieval in character and addressed elite male readers, subsequent English cookbooks did not fit this model.
17. Barbara Ketcham Wheaton, *Savoring the Past: The French Kitchen and Table from 1300 to 1789* (Philadelphia: University of Pennsylvania Press, 1983), 28.
18. Nancy Armstrong, *Desire and Domestic Fiction* (Oxford University Press, 1987) and Armstrong and Leonard Tennenhouse (eds.), *The Ideology of Conduct* (NY: Methuen, 1987) are examples of two books that elaborate the work of Norbert Elias, *The Civilizing Process*, trans. Edmund Jephcott (Oxford: Basil Blackwell, 1978–82).
19. Woolley, *The Queen-like Closet* (1675), 314.
20. Fitzherbert, *The Boke of Husbandry*. I cite from the 1534 edition, rpt. ed. Walter W. Skeat (London: Trubner & Co. for the English Dialect Society, 1882). Although there has been a lively debate about whether to attribute the book to the judge and author of surveying books, Anthony Fitzherbert, or his brother John, critical consensus leans toward John.
21. See Barnabe Googe, *The Whole Art and Trade of Husbandry* (1614), *4$^r$.
22. For passages in which Fitzherbert disputes common wisdom, see *The Boke of Husbandry*, 18, 59, 91; for passages in which he accepts "olde sayings" because verified by experience, see *ibid*. 24, 73, 74.
23. *Fitzharberts Booke of Husbandrie* (1598), 147.
24. Richard Surflet, *The Countrie Farme* (1600), 206–207, 24; Partridge, *Treasurie of Commodious Conceites* (1573), B5$^r$.
25. Perkins, *Christian Oeconomie*, 126; Dod and Cleaver, *A Godly Forme of Household Government*, L6$^v$-L7$^r$; Whately, *The Bride Bush, Or Direction for Married Persons* (1619), 152.
26. William Turner, *A new Herball* (1551), A3$^v$.
27. This same rationale for publishing medical advice is offered in the preface to *A Compendium of the rationall Secretes of the worthie Knight and moste excellent Doctour of Physicke and Chirurgerie, Leonardo Phioravante Bolognese* (1582).
28. B[artholomew] D[owe], *A Dairie Booke for Good Huswives* (1588), A3$^r$. Bound with Torquato Tasso, *The Householders Philosophie. Wherein is perfectly and profitably described the true Oeconomeia and forme of Housekeeping*, trans. T.K.
29. Juliet Fleming, "Memory, Method, and the Female Self in the English Domestic Guide, OR Mistress Duffield's Capon," unpublished paper, The Sixteenth Century Studies Conference, 1990. Fleming's provocative paper, which was the starting point for my project as a whole, cites Dowe's text to critique readings that look for transparent representations of female experience in the early modern period. As Fleming notes, these texts construct the *illusion* of a female practitioner's experience as an authorizing pre-text for erecting various systems of knowledge.
30. See chapter 2, for an overview of humanist pedagogy's denigration of female labor.
31. All quotations subsequently cited in the text are from the 1984 edition.
32. McRae, "Husbandry Manuals," 45. Tusser's *Fiue Hundreth Points of Good Husbandry* (1573) was reprinted in 1577, 1580, 1586, 1599, 1610, 1614, 1620, 1630, 1638 and 1672.
33. McRae, *God Speed the Plough: The Representation of Agrarian England, 1500–1600* (Cambridge University Press, 1996), 247.

34. *The Nice Valour, or, The Passionate Madman* in *The Works of Mr. Francis Beaumont and Mr. John Fletcher*, 10 vols. (London: J. and R. Tonson and S. Draper, 1750), Vol. X: 358.
35. In the Folger edition of *The English Hus-wife* (1615), the publisher R. I. includes this caveat: "Thou mayst say (gentle Reader) what hath this man to doe with Huswifery, he is now out of his element; and to be so generall for all the Huswives qualities, is to expresse more in one Book then can be found exprest in two women. I shall desire thee therfore to understand, that this is no collection of his whose name is prefixed to this work, but an approved Manuscript which he happily light on, belonging sometime to an honorable Personage of this kingdome, who was singular amongst those of her ranke for many of the qualities here set forth. This onely he hath done, digested the things of this booke in a good method" (verso to title page). This disclaimer, which suggests the domestic writer's threat in being "out of his element," vanished in the wake of the book's popularity and did not appear in subsequent editions.
36. K.R. Fussell, *The Old English Farming Books from Fitzherbert to Tull. 1523–1730* (London: Crosby Lockwood & Son, 1947), 21. Markham's opus covered six books on husbandry (including two translations), four on country recreations, four on military discipline, one housewifery book, one romance, one instructional guide to letter-writing, a 1400–line poem, and two plays.
37. Markham, *The English Husbandman* (1613), A1$^r$.
38. Markham's modern editor Michael Best details exchanges between these texts. *The English Housewife*, ed. Best (Kingston and Montreal: McGill-Queen's University Press, 1986), xx.
39. Markham, *Maison Rustique, Or, The Countrey Farme* (1616), "Epistle Dedicatorie," irregular signatures.
40. This exchange is evident in Markham's subsequent husbandry books. In 1631 he re-publishes a translated German husbandry book, *The Whole Art of Husbandry*, in order to correct the previous editor's (Googe's) attempt to introduce foreign plants and ideas to English soil. The title page to Markham's *Cheap and Good Husbandry* (1623) declares that the information is "Gathered together for the general good and profit of this whole Realm, by exact and assured experience from English practices, both certain, easy, and cheap: differing from all former and foreign experiments."
41. *The English Hus-Wife* was published three times as part of *Countrey Contentments* and six more times before 1683 as a stand-alone text. I cite here from the 1631 text (*The English House-wife*), unless otherwise noted. On conflicting ideals of femininity and housewifery, see Ann Rosalind Jones, "Nets into Bridles: Early Modern Conduct Books and Sixteenth-Century Women's Lyrics," in Armstrong and Tennenhouse (eds.), *The Ideology of Conduct*, 39–72.
42. *The English House-wife*, 155. See also Best's 1986 introduction to *The English Housewife*, xliii.
43. *Ibid.*, xlii–xliii.
44. Cahn, *Industry of Devotion*, 45–6; Clark, *Working Life*, 223–5. In 1500 most households brewed beer and ale for domestic use, but by 1650 the trade in these products was so great that its taxation was an important source of royal revenue. Basically, brewing equipment had become too expensive (relative to the price of tavern beer) for small landholders to own, too bulky to be carried between country estate and

London, and too large to be kept in cramped city quarters, where taverns were plentiful. With the development of hops, beer technology was refined in ways that outstripped home production. While country gentry and yeoman continued to brew beer at home, most middling and poorer sorts would have availed themselves of local brewers for *part* of their consumption. Beer was, after all, the staple drink for all members of the household, and as such, was needed in great quantities. While Markham's advice on brewing retains some practical value, it fails to acknowledge the reality of professionalization.

45. In Cahn's reading, Markham responds to a transitional moment when women are trained unevenly and thus are in need of professional advice. But she discounts the fact that Markham is "impractical" at points in the guide in recommending chores that housewives did not do.

46. On the transformation of the family economy into a family wage economy, see Tilly and Scott, *Women, Work and Family*, 18–21. On the importance of female labor in the preindustrial family, see Clark, *The Working Life of Women*; Wally Secombe, "The Housewife and her Labour under Capitalism," *New Left Review* 83 (1974): 3–24; and Richard T. Vann, "Toward a New Lifestyle: Women in Pre-Industrial Capitalism," in Renate Bridenthal and Claudia Koonz (eds.), *Becoming Visible: Women in European History* (Boston, MA: Houghton Mifflin Co., 1977), 192–216.

47. England consolidated its ties to a global market with the formation of the Russia, Eastland, Levant, and East India Companies. Levels of importation seem to have been exaggerated by writers who blame economic chaos on a desire for luxury goods. See Gerrard de Malynes, *The Canker of England's Commonwealth* (1601), ctd. in *Tudor Economic Documents*, ed. R.H. Tawney and Eileen Power (London: Longmans, Green & Co., 1924), Vol. III: 395; John Stow, *A Survey of the cities of London and Westminster* (1580), A4$^v$; E. Misselde, *Free Trade, or The Means to Make Trade Flourish* (1622); and William Harrison, *The Description of England* (1577), rpt. ed. Georges Edelen (Washington, DC: The Folger Shakespeare Library, 1994), 129–30. For a discussion of levels of importation, see Malcolm Thick, "Root Crops and the Feeding of London's Poor in the late Sixteenth and Early Seventeenth Centuries," in John Chartes and David Hey (eds.), *English Rural Society, 1500–1800* (Cambridge University Press, 1990), 279–96; and Wrightson, *English Society* 222–9.

48. Shakespeare, *Henry V*, 2.2.62.

49. See Paster, *The Body Embarrassed*, 23–63; Peter Stallybrass, "Patriarchal Territories: The Body Enclosed," in Margaret W. Ferguson, Maureen Quilligan, and Nancy J. Vickers (eds.), *Rewriting the Renaissance: Discourses of Sexual Difference in Early Modern Europe* (University of Chicago Press, 1986), 123–42. On the sovereign's body as a site of enclosure, see Louis Montrose, "The Elizabethan Subject and the Spenserian Text," in Patricia Parker and David Quint (eds.), *Literary Theory/Renaissance Texts* (Baltimore MD: Johns Hopkins University Press, 1986), 303–40.

50. It might seem that Markham's disdain for shopping belies his attempt to patrol the gendered division of labor. The division of "within/without" was the central way of categorizing household labor in manuals (and it persists today in the middle-class husband's jobs of barbecuing, lawn care, and emptying the garbage). It was conventional to advise couples, as Thomas Becon did, that "All provision and

whatsoever is to be done without the house belongs to the man; and the woman ought to take charge within" (Becon, *Golden Book of Matrimony* [1564], 676). But few advice books actually adhere to this definition, since women were to go to market, tend livestock, and help at harvest. While Markham's subscription to a traditional gendered division of labor comes at cross purposes with his interest in efficient production. I don't think we can chalk Markham's decision up to an attempt to confine women, for his text assigns the housewife tasks that were culturally controversial. Instead we should read this contradiction in terms of Markham's desire to cling to the *family* productive unit as a simulacrum of the self-sufficient nation

51. See G.E. and K.R. Fussell, *The English Countrywoman* (London: Andrew Melrose, 1953); Christina Hole, *The English Housewife in the Seventeenth Century* (London: Chatto & Windus, 1953).

52. Hall, "Culinary Spaces, Colonial Spaces: The Gendering of Sugar in the Seventeenth Century," in Traub, Kaplan, and Callaghan (eds.), *Feminist Readings of Early Modern Culture: Emerging Subjects*, 168–90. On the sugar trade, see the now classic work by Sidney W. Mintz, *Sweetness and Power: The Place of Sugar in Modern History* (NY: Viking, 1985).

53. Tryon, *The Good Housewife Made a Doctor* (1685), 70.

54. The Folger Library's copy of the 1600 edition of Partridge, *The Treasurie of Hidden Secrets* is inscribed "Catheren Tattemache oweth this boock" (E1$^v$); the 1573 Huntington Library copy of Partridge's *Treasurie of Commodious Conceites* is signed by "Mary"; and other cookbooks contain female as well as male signatures.

55. Partridge, *Treasurie of Commodious Conceites* (1573), A3$^v$.

56. *A Closet for Ladies and Gentlewomen, or, The Art of Preserving, Conserving, and Candying* (London, 1608; rpt. 1635), 38.

57. M.B., *The Ladies Cabinet Enlarged* (1655), 30.

58. See *Epulario, or The Italian Banquet*, B4$^r$.

59. *The Whole Duty of a Woman: Or a Guide to the Female Sex* (1707), 167.

60. M.B., *Ladies Cabinet Enlarged*, 158.

61. C. Anne Wilson, "The Evolution of the Banquet Course," in Wilson (ed.), *'Banquetting Stuffe': The Fare and Social Background of the Tudor and Stuart Banquet* (Edinburgh University Press, 1991), 29–31. Sugarworks date to the medieval period but the late fifteenth-century introduction of a Mediterranean resin called gum tragacanth allowed for a more complex compound to be used in molding desserts.

62. *A Closet for Ladies* (1635), B11$^r$.

63. "The Honourable Entertainment gieven to the Queenes Maiestie in Progresse, at Elvetham," in *The Complete Works of John Lyly*, ed. R. W. Bond, 3 vols. (Oxford: Clarendon Press, 1902), Vol. I: 448–9.

64. On banquetting's intersection with loss and mortality, see Fumerton, *Cultural Aesthetics*, 111–46. Dawson similarly describes the pleasures of smashing virtual tableware. *The Second Part of the Good Huswives Jewell* (1597), C8$^r$.

65. On this contradiction, see Michel Jeanneret, *A Feast of Words: Banquets and Table Talk in the Renaissance*, trans. Jeremy Whitely and Emma Hughes (University of Chicago Press, 1987), 1–10.

66. *Delightes for Ladies* was published in 1602, 1608, 1609, 1611, 1615, 1630, 1632, 1636, 1647, 1651, 1656, and 1683. I cite from the first edition unless noted otherwise.

67. Juliet Fleming, "Memory, Method, and the Female Self."

68. Plat, *The Jewell House of Art and Nature: Containing Divers Rare and Profitable Inventions* (1594), 13.

69. Fleming, "Memory."

70. See, for instance, M.B.'s preface to *The Ladies Cabinet Enlarged* (1655), which describes the reader/housewife as wandering in a pleasure palace or garden of "fancies" (A3$^r$). See also *A Gentlewomans Delight*, (1682, L12$^v$).

71. William Davenant, *Unfortunate Lovers* (1643), 2.1.220–1.

72. William Cartwright, *The Siege, or Love's Convert* (1651), 1.4.295–7, in *The Plays and Poems of William Cartwright*, ed. G. Blakemore Evans (Madison: University of Wisconsin Press, 1951), 373.

73. John Crowne, *The Married Beau* (1694), 51. Polidor, a friend of Mrs. Lovely's, amplifies the sexualization of housewifery when he ferrets out the hidden intruder "I'll see what you ha'got,/Whether it be a Flower or a wee, / Which you are stilling in this Limbeck here,/For I believe he's in a dripping Sweat" (51). In Nicholas Breton's poem, "Not long agoe as I at supper sat," the narrator dreams of attractive women by associating them with particular banquet comfits. *The Woorkes of a Young Wit* (1577), 35–40.

74. Robert Anton, *The Philosophers Satyrs* (1616), 52.

75. *The Diary of Samuel Pepys*, ed. Robert Latham and William Matthews, 5 vols. (Berkeley: University of California Press, 1971), Vol. IV: 272–3. On the cookbooks in Pepys's collection, see Margaret Spufford, *Small Books and Pleasant Histories: Popular Fiction and its Readership in Seventeenth-Century England* (Athens, GA: University of Georgia Press, 1981), 61.

76. Lynette Hunter, "'Sweet Secrets' from Occasional Receipt to Specialised Books: The Growth of a Genre," in C. Anne Wilson (ed.), *'Banquetting Stuffe,'* 39.

77. Robert May, *The Accomplisht Cook, or the Art & Mystery of Cookery* (1685), A8. Later books emphasizing courtly cuisine include Patrick Lamb, *Royal Cookery or the Complete Court Cook* (1710); Robert Smith, *Court Cookery* (1723); and Charles Carter, *The Complete Practical Cook* (1730).

78. Stephen Mennel, *All Manners of Food: Eating and Taste in England and France from the Middle Ages to the Present* (NY: Basil Blackwell, 1985), 67.

79. Because of Woolley's disclaimer in her published writing, there is dispute about her authorship of *The Gentlewomans Companion*, a text attributed to her in the period.

80. See *The Queen-like Closet* (1675), *Supplement*, A3$^v$-A3$^r$ (irregular pagination).

81. "Instead of Song and Musicke, let them learne Cookery and Laundrie. And in stead of reading *Sir Philip Sidneys Arcadia*, let them read the grounds of good housewifery. I like not a female Poetess at any hand," writes Thomas Powell, *Tom of All Trades, Or The Pathway to Preferment* (1631), G3. He recommends that ambitious men send a few of their daughters out for training in "sempstrie, confectionary & all requistes of Huswifery" (G3). See also Thomas Salter, *The Mirror of Modesty* (1578), B5$^v$-B8$^r$.

82. Elite households turned increasingly to French cooking, which developed a *haute cuisine* only in the seventeenth century. After mid-century, books of cookery addressed male specialists and often based their recipes on French methods.

## 2 NEEDLES AND BIRCHES: PEDAGOGY, DOMESTICITY, AND THE ADVENT OF ENGLISH COMEDY

1. *What You Will*, in *The Works of John Marston*, ed. Arthur H. Bullen, 5 vols. (London: John C. Nimmo, 1887), Vol. I: 2.2.41–3.
2. Quoted by Frederick Boas, *University Drama in the Tudor Age* (Oxford: Clarendon Press, 1914), 323.
3. On the importance of Latin to the Renaissance curriculum, see J. Howard Brown, *Elizabethan Schooldays: An Account of the English Grammar Schools in the Second Half of the Sixteenth Century* (Oxford: Basil Blackwell, 1933), 156. Kenneth Charlton argues that prohibitions on the vernacular (the Oundle, Rivington, and Hawkhead statutes) were not always borne out in practice (*Education in Renaissance England* [London: Routledge & Kegan Paul, 1965], 119–22). In 1643, John Robotham argued for using the vernacular in the classroom: "it is mere folly, to be curious and expert in *foreign* cunning, and be a stranger *at home:* and it should be the care of every teacher, as well to accustom a child betimes to the practice of *good English* as of *good Latin*." Robotham, *Janua Linguarum Reserata* (1643), preface.
4. Although its authorship and exact date are hotly contested, scholars use the 1575 title page as evidence that *Gammer Gurton's Needle* was performed at Christ's College, Cambridge, in the 1550s or early 1560s. On the play's dating, see Howard B. Norland, *Drama in Early Tudor Britain, 1485–1558* (Lincoln: University of Nebraska Press, 1995), 280–3. Based on the fact that the title page attributes the play to Mr. S., Master of Arts, scholars speculate that the author may have been Christ College Master, William Stephenson, but this issue is by no means settled. On debates about the play's authorship, see the editor's introduction to *Three Sixteenth Century Comedies*, ed. Charles W. Whitworth (NY: W.W. Norton Mermaids Series, 1984), xxii–xxix; and Boas, *University Drama*, 80–88. I cite the play to Whitworth's edition by act, scene and line number.
5. Perhaps this explains the antipathy that Gossip Mirth, Gossip Tattle, and Gossip Expectation have for schoolmasters. See Ben Jonson, *The Staple of News*, in *Ben Jonson*, ed. C.H. Herford and Percy and Evelyn Simpson, 11 vols. (Oxford: Clarendon Press, 1925–52), Vol. VI: intermean after the third act, lines 33–56.
6. The other candidate for "first English play" is Nicholas Udall's *Ralph Roister Doister*, which was performed by grammar school boys at Eton in 1553 and which also offers the fantasy of a return to cross-gendered domesticity. But this fantasy has less to do with squaring linguistic nationalism with pedagogical sex/gender identifications and more to do with reconciling education with middle-class theories of citizenship.
7. Walter Ong, "Latin Language Study as a Renaissance Puberty Rite," *Studies in Philology* 56 (1959): 103–24; Juliet Fleming, "Dictionary English and the Female Tongue," in Richard Burt and John Michael Archer (eds.), *Enclosure Acts: Sexuality, Property, and Culture in Early Modern England* (Ithaca: Cornell University Press, 1994), 290–325.
8. On grammar schools and universities, see Brown, *Elizabethan Schooldays*; Charlton, *Education in Renaissance England*; and Joan Simon, *Education and Society in Tudor England* (Cambridge University Press, 1966).

9. Roger Ascham, *The Schoolmaster* (1570), rpt., ed. Lawrence V. Ryan (Ithaca: Cornell University Press for the Folger Shakespeare Library, 1967), 114, my emphasis.

10. "By the Queen" (1561), reprinted in David Cressy's collection of documents, *Education in Tudor and Stuart England* (London: Edward Arnold, 1975), 125–6, my emphasis.

11. William Hawkins, *Apollo Shroving* (1627). My thanks to Juliet Fleming for calling this text to my attention.

12. Steven Mullaney, *The Place of the Stage* (University of Chicago Press, 1988), 76–87. "The voice of the Other, of the *barbaros*, sounded in the throat whenever the mother tongue was spoken," Mullaney writes, "one's own tongue was strange yet familiar, a foreigner within, a quite literal *émigré*" (79).

13. E.K., "Epistle to Harvey" prefacing *The Shepheardes Calendar* in *The Yale Edition of the Shorter Poems of Edmund Spenser*, ed. William Oram, Einar Bjorvand, Ronald Bond, Thomas H. Cain, Alexander Dunlop, and Richard Schell (New Haven, CT: Yale University Press, 1989), 16–17. E.K.'s metaphor was not exceptional, as Richard Foster Jones documents (*The Triumph of the English Language* [Stanford University Press, 1953], 19–21).

14. *Gammer Gurton's Needle*, in *Three Sixteenth-Century Comedies*, 2.1.59–60.

15. In *The Body Embarrassed*, Paster states this point nicely: "To be a laborer like Hodge is to have clothes full of holes . . . labor will always reopen holes in clothes Gammer will always work to repair. From this perspective, the sexual division of labor in the household appears rational and interdependent" (118). Broadly concerned with the formation of affective psychic structures in the early modern subject, Paster places *Gammer* in the context of the Renaissance medical practice of the alimentary purge. She argues that eroticized anality, an important feature of childhood, fashioned structures of psychic dependence on maternal authority. The play presents humorally fashioned ideas of pleasure and identity only to reveal how a socially produced shame can naturalize gender and economic relations.

16. See Cahn, *An Industry of Devotion*, 33.

17. Richard Mulcaster, *Positions* (1581), abgd., ed. Richard L. DeMolen (NY: Columbia Teacher's College Press, 1971), 138.

18. *A Critical Edition of Anthony Munday's Fedele and Fortunio*, ed. Richard Hosley, 5.4.156–60.

19. On how women used these forms as a means of female expression, see Susan Frye, "Sewing Connections: Elizabeth Tudor, Mary Stuart, Elizabeth Talbot, and the Seventeenth-Century Anonymous Needleworkers," in Susan Frye and Karen Robertson (eds.), *Maids and Mistresses, Cousins and Queens* (NY and Oxford: Oxford University Press, 1999), 165–82.

20. John Taylor, "In Praise of the Needle," prefatory poem to *The Needle's Excellency*, rpt. in *The Works of John Taylor* (Manchester: Charles Simms for the Spenser Society, 1870), A1[r].

21. Robert Greene, *The Scottish History of James the Fourth* (1598) rpt., ed. J. A. Lavin (London: Ernest Benn Ltd., 1967), 2.1.16–71. On the needle as a weapon, see also Munday, *Fedele and Fortunio*, 2.2.89–92.

22. Cartwright, *The Siege, or Love's Convert* (1651), 1.4.250–4, in *The Plays and Poems of William Cartwright*, 373.

23. Amy Erickson, *Women and Property in Early Modern England*, 195. While this figure includes predominantly young people housed in service, it also prompts scholars to consider single-headed households in their accounts of early modern domesticity.

24. Cahn writes, "Written laws, the statutes of Parliaments, guilds and municipalities, and customs show that the English recognized that women were important contributors to the English economy, both as housewives and as individuals with economic functions outside the home, partly because the housewife's role in guaranteeing her family's subsistence could take her outside the realm of subsistence production and into the world of markets and skilled labor" (35). But see Judith M. Bennett's critique of rosy accounts of the family economy, articulated in strong form in Clark's pioneering *Working Life of Women in the Seventeenth Century*, in Bennett, "Medieval Women, Modern Women: Across the Great Divide," in Aers (ed.), *Culture and History, 1350–1600: Essays on English Communities, Identities, and Writing*, 146–67. Both supporters and attackers of the myth of women's "fall" from productivity tend to blend the economic with the political; that is, they move from questions about women's economic contributions to debates about their unquestioningly unequal status.

25. Heywood, *A Pleasant conceited Comedie, wherein is shewed, how a man may choose a good wife from a bad* (1602), C1ᵛ.

26. Hodge, Tib, and Dr. Rat enter the play complaining about the "rotten rags" that shamefully display their impoverishment and subordination; the two town matriarchs threaten to "dress" each other when fighting (3.3.32); Rat insists on being "re-dressed" with ale for his suffering; and he describes the play's conflicts as a covered beating: "the villain knave hath dressed us round about" (5.2.180).

27. For an example of a literary beggar, see *King Lear*, 2.2.6–20. On vagrancy, see John Pound, *Poverty and Vagrancy in Tudor England* (NY: Longman, 1971; rpt. 1986).

28. On Diccon as a revealer of truths, see J. W. Robinson, "The Art and Meaning of *Gammer Gurton's Needle*," *Renaissance Drama* 14 (1983): 45–77. While I attempt a more historical reading than Robinson, I appreciate his sense that the play was not simply a farce produced to entertain academics sick of the niceties of intellectual work.

29. For a revisionist reading of Bakhtin's binary of grotesque body, see Peter Stallybrass and Allon White, *The Politics and Poetics of Transgression* (Ithaca: Cornell University Press, 1986), 1–26.

30. Ben Jonson, George Chapman, and John Marston, *Eastward Ho*, in *Ben Jonson*, ed. Herford, Simpson, and Simpson, Vol. IV: 1.2.55.

31. I use the term "sodomy" to refer to all sexual practices not aimed at procreation. N. Lindsay McFayden sees the needle as a phallus, but connects this symbolism to an adolescent's "natural" sense of gender insecurity. Robinson responds by commenting that this identification is "illogical." When critics have outlined, or been baffled by, connections between body parts and the needle, they have been stymied by their inability to acknowledge that a woman can possess the phallus. McFayden, "What Was Really Lost in *Gammer Gurton's Needle*," *Renaissance Papers* (1982): 9–13; Robinson, "Art and Meaning in *Gammer*," 45–77.

32. See Stallybrass, "Transvestism and the 'Body Beneath': Speculating on the Boy Actor," in Zimmerman (ed.), *Erotic Politics*, 64–83.

33. The play reveals the "plasticity," "transferability," and "expropriability" of Hodge's (and the audience's) phalluses while also demonstrating the normative phallic terms by which Gammer's power must be imagined. I draw these terms from Judith Butler's reading of Freud's "On Narcissism: An Introduction," in *Bodies That Matter: On the Discursive Limits of "Sex"* (NY: Routledge, 1993), 59–62.

34. In *The Poetics of Primitive Accumulation: English Renaissance Culture and the Genealogy of Capital* (Ithaca: Cornell University Press, 1991), Richard Halpern observes that the figure of the nurse reveals "not just a double threat of class and gender but a threat of class embedded in or mediated through gender"(275, fn. 23). Halpern is centrally concerned with the way in which a juridical notion of authority (the sovereign model) is revised by the humanist mode of imitation privileged in sixteenth-century pedagogy; he argues that "the schools' exclusionary function was . . . complemented by a hegemonic one in which the behavioral disposition of the 'middle sort' was imposed on a relatively broad array of classes" (26).

35. Richard Wilson, *Will Power: Essays on Shakespearean Authority* (Detroit: Wayne State University Press, 1993), 170–75.

36. Erasmus, *De Pueris Instituendis* in William Harrison Woodward, *Desiderius Erasmus Concerning the Aim and Method of Education* (NY: Teacher's College, Columbia University Press, 1964), 214, 182. According to Fildes, concerns about the wetnurse's influence over speech increases in the seventeenth century and then disappears as a concern in the eighteenth century. See Valerie Fildes, *Breasts, Bottles and Babies* (Edinburgh University Press, 1986), 152–212.

37. Thomas Elyot, *The Book named The Governor* (1962), rpt. ed. S. E. Lehmberg (London: Dent, Everyman's Library, 1966), 18. On the gendering of speech, see Patricia Parker, "On the Tongue: Cross-Gendering, Effeminacy and the Art of Words," *Style* 23 (1989): 445–65.

38. Spenser, *A View of the Present State of Ireland* (1596), rpt., ed. W. L. Renwick (London: Eric Partridge, 1934), 88, my emphasis. Halpern argues that some Renaissance writers urged a continuum between female infant care and male education (30), but they are more typically opposed, with the schoolmaster expected to compensate for domesticity's lack.

39. Mulcaster, *Positions*, 45, 44.

40. On controversies about the English language – which centered on its perceived inadequacy and the issue of linguistic borrowing – see Richard Foster Jones, *Triumph of the English Language*; Richard W. Bailey, *Images of English: A Cultural History of the Language* (Ann Arbor: University of Michigan Press, 1991), esp. 37–57; and Fleming, "Dictionary English," 296–9.

41. On the need to install material conditions into psychoanalytic problematics, see John Brenkman, *Straight Male Modern: A Cultural Critique of Psychoanalysis* (NY: Routledge, 1993), 129–47; and Stallybrass and White's reading of the maid and family romance, *The Politics and Poetics of Transgression*, 149–70. For an example of these theories in practice, see Paster's reading of the nurse and the "dug" in early modern English culture (*The Body Embarrassed*, 215–80).

42. Thomas Wilson, *The Art of Rhetoric* (1553), rpt. ed. G.H. Mair (Oxford: Clarendon

Press, 1909), 162. The "naturalizing" of plain speech and of the English language partook of common tropes. "No man is so wel indued with the knowledge of forren tongues," Stanislaus Hozyusz argued, "but when a matter of great importaunce is told hym . . . [he] had rather haue it declared in his natural and mother tonge be it never so barbarouse, then in a straunge language be it never so eloquent." *A Most Excellent Treatise of the Begynnyng of Heresyes in Oure Tyme* (Antwerp, 1565).

43.  Shakespeare, *Richard II*, 1.3.159–62, 170–1.

44.  Janet Adelman, *Suffocating Mothers: Fantasies of Maternal Origin in Shakespeare's Plays, "Hamlet" to "The Tempest"* (NY: Routledge, 1992), 5. Adelman's provocative psychoanalytic readings are implicitly revised by historicist work such as Paster's.

45.  Stephen Orgel discusses the Renaissance belief in women's potential transformation into men, a belief enabled by medical theories of conception and replayed through the practice of breeching: "The frightening part of the teleology for the Renaissance mind, however, is precisely the fantasy of its reversal," Orgel writes, "the conviction that men can turn into – or be turned into – women; or perhaps more exactly, can be turned *back* into women, losing the strength that enabled the male potential to be realized in the first place"(14). Orgel, "Nobody's Perfect: Or Why Did the English Stage Take Boys for Women?" *South Atlantic Quarterly* 88 (1989): 7–29.

46.  Thomas Nashe, *Summer's Last Will and Testament* in *The Works of Thomas Nashe*, ed. R. B. McKerrow, 5 vols. (London: A.H. Bullen, Vols. I–II; Sidgwick and Jackson, Vols. III–V, 1904–1910), Vol. III: 279–80.

47.  *Gammer Gurton's Needle*, in *Three Sixteenth-Century Comedies*, 5.2.307.

48.  Bray, *Homosexuality in Renaissance England*, 51–53; Bruce Smith, *Homosexual Desire in Shakespeare's England*, esp. 84–8, 191–7; Goldberg, *Sodometries*, 79–80, 163; and Stone, *Family, Sex, and Marriage in England*, 516–17. Smith notes that "Schools, colleges, and the inns of court were *households* in both the literal and figurative senses of the word: young men studied together, played together, ate together, and, like everybody else in the sixteenth century, slept together two to a bed . . . [the Renaissance boy] came to maturity in an all-male household that had a sharp sense of its own identity, its own traditions, even its own language" (84). John Marston writes that he would subject his sons to Catholics "Before some pedant Tutor, in his bed / Should use my frie, like Phrigian Ganimede" (*Scourge of Villainie*, in *Works*, C7ʳ). While Stewart criticizes Stone and Bray for relying on literary evidence in arguing for the bedroom intimacy of educational institutions (91), he finds Marston's poetry useful at times (*Close Readers*, 103).

49.  Harrison, *Description of England*, ed. Edelen, 70.

50.  Edward Chamberlayne, *The Second Part of the Present State of England* (1682), 313.

51.  On alterations in the grammar school system, see Brown, *Elizabethan Schooldays*, 38–44; Simon, *Education and Society*, 302–16; and Charlton, *Education in Renaissance England*, 89–130. On changes in universities, see Charlton, *Education*, 131–68; Simon, *Education and Society*, 333–53; and Mark H. Curtis, *Oxford and Cambridge in Transition 1558–1642* (Oxford: Clarendon Press, 1959). Although Charlton disagrees with Curtis' argument that changes in the class makeup of universities caused a cultural revolution, he does finally endorse Curtis' point that

universities diversified in terms of class composition.

52. Brown, *Elizabethan Schooldays*, 89–90, 114–15.

53. For a discussion of pedagogical violence, see Halpern, *Poetics of Primitive Accumulation*, 21–9; Mary Thomas Crane, *Framing Authority: Sayings, Self, and Society in Sixteenth-Century England* (Princeton, NJ: Princeton University Press, 1993), 55–6; and Stewart, *Close Readers*, 84–121. Stewart reads violence in terms of new unequal social relationships between aspiring schoolmaster and elite students.

54. See Goldberg's critique of Smith (*Sodometries*, 68–72, 273, fn. 42). In *Textual Intercourse: Collaboration, Authorship, and Sexualities in Renaissance Drama* (Cambridge University Press, 1997), Masten distinguishes his work from critics such as Smith and Bray by noting that he attempts to locate "sites" and "structures" of homoeroticism rather than the *identity* of the homosexual as located in individuals, subjects, or even "acts." Following work that disengages the homo/hetero binary, Masten investigates socio-erotic discursive systems.

55. Ascham, *The Schoolmaster*, 80. This passage is discussed by Goldberg, *Sodometries*, 79; Smith, *Homosexual Desire*, 84; and Stewart, *Close Readers*, 125–160. Ascham argues against corporal punishment and urges schoolmasters to use pleasure to incite pupils to labor. "Young children," he advises, "were sooner allured by love than driven by beating to attain good learning" (7).

56. In his analysis of Thomas Kyd's representation of his relationship with Marlowe, Masten provides further evidence for how *De amicitia* was coded. Masten, "Playwrighting: Authorship and Collaboration."

57. Erasmus, *De Ratione Studii*, in Woodward, *Desiderius Erasmus*, 164. On the word "intercourse," see Masten, *Textual Intercourse*, 197, fn. 41.

58. Bray discusses ways in which distinctions in age, status, and economic position subtended what we now call homosexual practices (*Homosexuality*). For critiques of Bray's book, see Goldberg, *Sodometries*, 68–70; and Elizabeth Pittenger, "'To Serve the Queere': Nicholas Udall, Master of Revels," in Goldberg (ed.), *Queering the Renaissance*, 162–89, esp. 166–70. On apprenticeship, see Charlton, *Education in Renaissance England*, 254–6.

59. I refer to Mulcaster's famous feminization of the birch in his plea that parents and teachers work together: "for the rod may no more be spared in schools than the sword in the prince's hand. By the rod I mean correction and awe . . . For the private, whatsoever parents say, my lady birchely will be a guest at home, or else parents shall not have their wills . . . The same faults must be faults at home which be faults at school" (*Positions*, 155).

60. Steven Bateman, *A Crystal Glass of Christian Reformation* (1569).

61. "Ingles" are catamites; "cracks," are both lively lads and fissures (and here we might recall Hodge's "hole"). For puns on these words in Marston's play, see 3.3.30–40, 126; 5.1.58–68, 177–80. Noose also satirizes his master's desires: "He loves his boy and the rump of a cramm'd capon" (3.3.50–1). On the eroticization of dependency, see Lisa Jardine, "Twins and Travesties: Gender, Dependency and Sexual Availability in *Twelfth Night*," in Zimmerman (ed.), *Erotic Politics*, 27–38.

62. That early modern persons identified homoerotic pedagogical relationships as "sodomy" only when its practitioners were charged with some other transgressive behavior is evidenced by the case of Nicholas Udall, who was reported to have committed sodomy repeatedly with one of his students only when that student

confessed to robbery. See Pittenger, "'To Serve the Queere,'" 162–89. The image of the schoolmaster as a sadistic sodomite was consolidated in the late seventeenth century, Stewart argues, in texts concerned that beatings exposed the boys' buttocks to view and thus to unwanted sexual practices (88). Stewart argues that it was rare for sixteenth-century texts to query the "normative" male homoerotic alliances of pedagogy, even when boys saw beatings as potentially erotic (100), but the wealth of textual examples Stewart cites confirm a pervasive connection between "lewdness" and beating. Although Stewart's *Close Readers* covers some of the same ground that I do, his primary interest is in disentangling pedagogical violence from eroticization so as to counter modern representations of Renaissance schoolmasters as sadistic rapists. He reads citations to pedagogical force as exposing unequal social and knowledge "transactions" surrounding humanist theory.

63. Bray, "Homosexuality and the Signs of Male Friendship," 40–61. For discussions of the relationship between the monstrous sodomite and male–male desire, see Goldberg *Sodometries*, 18–23; and Gregory W. Bredbeck, *Sodomy and Interpretation: Marlowe to Milton* (Ithaca: Cornell University Press, 1991), 3–30.

64. On sodomy as an accusation, see Stewart, *Close Readers*, xxi–xxii, who draws from Michael Warner, "New English Sodom," *American Literature* 64 (1992): 19–47. While my reading fails to critique *Gammer*'s construction of sodomy as a comic effect, I wouldn't want to extrapolate from this particular *situation* a general definition in the period; that is, while I read "sodomy" as produced within the context of male–male academic relations and made visible as a crisis about language, other accounts emphasize it as part of a normative homoeroticism.

65. Paster sees the fact that the needle was "never really lost" as a sign of its ultimate consolidation of the sex/gender system. In uncovering the cultural meanings of anality – the purges given to Renaissance males and females in common domestic medical practice – Paster's work qualifies my reading of the play's anality as connected specifically with pedagogical pederasty. But Paster's reading tends to dissolve sexual practice into the category of gender. For a discussion of this problem in feminism, see Traub, *Desire and Anxiety*, 91–116; Gayle S. Rubin, "Thinking Sex: Notes for a Radical Theory of the Politics of Sexuality," in Henry Abelove, Michéle Aina Barale, and David M. Halperin (eds.), *The Lesbian and Gay Studies Reader* (NY: Routledge, 1993), 3–41. See also, however, Judith Butler's critique of the *Reader*'s separation of feminism and queer theory, "Against Proper Objects," in *More Gender Trouble: Feminism Meets Queer Theory*, a volume of *Differences* 6 (1994), 1–26; and Eve Kosofsky Sedgwick's response to Rubin, "Across Gender, Across Sexuality: Willa Cather and Others," in Ronald R. Butters, John M. Clum, and Michael Moon (eds.), *Displacing Homophobia*, 53–72.

66. The invasion of cross-gendered domesticity into academia was a fantasy reinforced by the visual staging of plays, as we know from college account books. In 1551–52, a carpenter was paid for removing the tables from the hall in Christ's College and "setting them up again, With the houses & other things" for "S. Stephenson play" (281). This citation suggests a three-dimensional set for the performances. The placement of rustic houses in scholarly confines visually consolidated the oddity of the "proper" household within the "private" halls of knowledge. See Norland, *Drama in Early Tudor Britain*, 281; and Richard Southern, *The Staging of Plays before Shakespeare* (London: Faber and Faber, 1973), 399–423.

67. Slavoj Žižek, *Looking Awry: An Introduction to Jacques Lacan through Popular Culture* (Cambridge, MA: MIT Press, 1992), 6–8.

68. See Freud, *Jokes and their Relation to the Unconscious*, trans. James Strachey (NY: W. W. Norton, 1960). The audience might have experienced this fantasy through the lens of what Freud terms a "tendentious joke," one that has a particular aim and that allows a release from repressive internal and external prohibitions. As in all the jokes Freud examines, its pleasure depends on its economy. While cultural associations between the vernacular and a non-heterosexual domesticity persist in the structure of the play's joke, these associations are pressured. "With tendentious jokes we are not in a position to distinguish by our feeling what part of the pleasure arises from the sources of their technique and what part from those of their purpose. Thus, strictly speaking, we do not know what we are laughing at," Freud writes (102). In keeping with the economy of the joke, *Gammer* suggests ambivalent comic effects that I have not even begun to exhaust.

69. de Certeau, *The Practice of Everyday Life*, xiii.

70. But see Curtis and Charlton for a debate about the nationalist effects of the educational system, which seems to have promoted a homogenous national culture at least among the elite groups of England. My analysis needs to be augmented by a discussion of how *Gammer* blends various *regional* dialects into an imagined unified rural and national speech, as well as an exploration of how the play locates enabling origins within a rural England notorious for its resistance to centralizing structures. In this chapter, however, I am interested in how the fantasy of domesticity offered a register in which Englishness could be associated with a common, though alien, language; that is, how it could generate a linguistic community that erodes the class differences often marked precisely through the linguistic ridicule (malapropisms, dialect, slang) that the play circulates.

71. See Halpern, *Poetics of Primitive Accumulation*, 205–208.

72. See Anderson, *Imagined Communities*. On how the break-up of Latinate medieval culture in post-Reformation England motivated the creation of vernacular languages as expressions of territorial integrity, see Hadfield, *Literature, Politics and National Identity*, 9. On writers' awareness of the importance of mobilizing the vernacular, see Michael Neill, "Broken English and Broken Irish," *Shakespeare Quarterly* 45 (1994): 14–16.

73. Timothy Brennan writes: "As for the 'nation,' it is both historically determined and general. As a term, it refers both to the modern nation-state and to something more ancient and nebulous – the '*natio*' – a local community, domicile, family, condition of belonging." "The National Longing for Form," in Homi K. Bhabha (ed.), *Nation and Narration* (NY: Routledge, 1990), 45. Comedy is, of course, traditionally defined in connection with "the domestic," in that it is understood to signify a "real life" imagined in mundane events. Donatus, Cicero, and Horace argue that comedy mirrors daily life.

74. See Whitworth, introduction to *Three Sixteenth-Century Comedies* (NY: W.W. Norton and Co., 1984,) xxix, xxxi; Boas, *University Drama*, 49; Thorndike, *English Comedy*, 59; and Felix E. Schelling, *Elizabethan Drama, 1558–1642*, 2 vols. (NY: Russell & Russell, 1959), Vol. I: 86, 92, and 104.

75. William Gager, letter to John Rainolds, July 31, 1595, Corpus Christi College MS 352, 49. This letter is reprinted in full in Karl Young, "William Gager's Defence of

the Academic Stage," *Transactions of the Wisconsin Academy of Science, Arts and Letters* 18 (1916): 593–630. On statutes mandating the performance of plays for colleges founded in the sixteenth century, see James W. Binns, *Intellectual Culture in Elizabethan and Jacobean England* (Leeds: Francis Cairn Publications, 1990), 121–23.

76. See Martin Mueller, *Children of Oedipus* (University of Toronto Press, 1980), 12–17; Halpern, *Poetics of Primitive Accumulation*, 24; Binns, *Intellectual Culture*, 120–5; Richard Mulcaster, *Mulcaster's Elementarie*, ed. E. T. Campagnac (Oxford: Clarendon Press, 1925), 18; and Norland, *Drama in Early Tudor Britain*, 65–83. On *Gammer*'s citation of Terence, see Douglas Duncan, *Gammer Gurton's Needle* and the Concept of Human Parody," *Studies in English Literature* 27 (1987): 177–93. Insisting on the spiritual and intellectual seriousness of the play, Duncan eschews claims that the play's "shitty" thematics were created simply to amuse adolescents and instead suggests that *Gammer*'s parody of learned concepts points out the foibles of intellectual pride.

77. For a discussion of Cambridge town/gown controversy, see Boas, *University Drama*, 322–46.

78. *A Chaste Maid in Cheapside*, in Thomas Middleton, *Five Plays* (London: Penguin Books, 1988), 4.1.18. I would like to thank David Kaye for reminding me of the christening scene in this play.

79. Patricia Parker, "*The Merry Wives of Windsor* and Shakespearean Translation," *Modern Language Quarterly* 52 (1991): 225–61; and Parker, *Literary Fat Ladies: Rhetoric, Gender, Property* (NY: Methuen, 1987), 26–31.

80. Pittenger, "Dispatch Quickly: The Mechanical Reproduction of Pages," *Shakespeare Quarterly* 42 (1991): 389–408.

81. As *Chaste Maid* and *Merry Wives* exemplify, cross-dressing is relevant to an analysis of pedagogy, sexuality, gender, and domesticity, but perhaps not as the *privileged* site of sexual or of gender identifications. Instead critics might read cross-dressing unevenly – that is, as defined differently within particular frameworks (e.g., pedagogy, professional theater, antitheatrical literature).

82. I discuss scholarly debates about *Merry Wives*' inscription of the court in Chapter 3.

83. It is tempting to see the model for Dr. Caius as a physician of the same name who resided at Cambridge in the 1570s, a man reputed to suffer difficulties because he was suckled by two wetnurses with different humors when he fell ill as an adult (wetnursing for the elderly and ill was an accepted medical practice). "What made Dr. *Caius* in his last sickness so peevish and so full of frets at Cambridge, when he suckt one woman (whom I spare to name) froward of conditions and of bad diet; and contrariwise so quiet and well, when he suckt another of contrary disposition? verily the diversity of their milks and conditions, which being contrary one to the other, wrought also in him that sucked them contrary effects," reports Thomas Muffet in *Health's Improvement* (rpt. 1655), 123.

84. In arguing that the play demonstrates how local power can shape a national identity based on shared language rather than allegiance to the crown, I draw support from Rosemary Kegl's different analysis of the play's promotion of "the regional and national authority of the towns' official representatives – their governing burgesses." Kegl is concerned with how the play's exchange of insults creates political alliances among people with diverse interests. Kegl, *The Rhetoric of Concealment:*

*Figuring Gender and Class in Renaissance Literature* (Ithaca: Cornell University Press, 1994), 77–102.

85. Leah S. Marcus, *Unediting the Renaissance: Shakespeare, Marlowe, Milton* (NY: Routledge, 1996), 68–101. I take up this issue and Marcus' reading in Chapter 3.

86. In fact the play's allusion to Order of the Garter is suggestive, for in the legendary origins of this ritual we find a deep concern for the astonishing power of the feminine trifle (like *Gammer*'s needle, perhaps). In this legend, Edward III supposedly insisted on retrieving a garter dropped unwittingly by his Queen in public. When courtiers objected to his inexplicable interest in a "trifle," he announced his intention to build a prestigious political order from this object. From a "slender occasion" was born a signifier of honor. In mocking the Order of the Garter, *Merry Wives* may allude to this ritual's revaluation of the trifle. The legend is recounted in William Harrison, *The Description of England*, 103–106.

3 WHY DOES PUCK SWEEP? SHAKESPEAREAN FAIRIES
AND THE POLITICS OF CLEANING

1. My terminology is drawn from de Certeau, *The Practice of Everyday Life*, esp. 1–28. Scholars have questioned "popular" as an intelligible critical term of analysis or a distinct culture, noting that it sometimes refers to the origin of production, sometimes to cultural objects consumed exclusively by lower classes but produced elsewhere, and sometimes to the most widely shared aspects of any given culture. Arguing that popular forms are not finally extricable from the culture at large and thus can't be distributed to one set social group, Stuart Hall has suggested that we think of popular culture either as a process (the culture of a people as they actively interweave forms and customs from material and social conditions) or a shifting designation ("Notes on Deconstructing 'The Popular,'" in Raphael Samuel (ed.), *People's History and Socialist Thought* [London: Routledge & Kegan Paul, 1981], 227–41). Since people label practices as "popular" for strategic reasons, it seems foolhardy to assume in advance its definition (as authentic, indigenous, politically resistant, or conservative). On debates over the notion of the "popular," see Peter Burke, "The 'Discovery' of Popular Culture," in Samuel (ed.), *People's History and Socialist Thought*, 216–26; Jacques Le Goff, "The Learned and Popular Dimensions of Journeys in the Otherworld in the Middle Ages," in Steven L. Kaplan (ed.), *Understanding Popular Culture: Europe from the Middle Ages to the Nineteenth Century* (NY: Mouton Publishers, 1984), 19–38; David Hall, introduction to Kaplan (ed.), *Understanding Popular Culture*, 5–18; Tim Harris, "The Problem of 'Popular Political Culture' in Seventeenth-Century London," *History of European Ideas* 19 (1989): 43–58; Tessa Watt, *Cheap Print and Popular Piety, 1550–1640* (Cambridge: University Press, 1991), 2–4; and Roger Chartier, *The Cultural Uses of Print in Early Modern France*, trans. Lydia C. Cochrane (Princeton, NJ: Princeton University Press, 1987), esp. 3.

2. Montrose, *The Purpose of Playing*, 125.

3. Although we cannot with any surety evaluate the level or breadth of early modern belief in fairies, we can attend to conflicting ways in which that belief, as well as the changing shape of its content, was represented in the culture. On fairylore and its

connection to other status-laden forms of ritual, see Mary Ellen Lamb, "Taken by the Fairies: Fairy Practices and the Production of Popular Culture in *A Midsummer Night's Dream,*" *Shakespeare Quarterly* 51 (2000): 277–312.

4. Erasmus, *De pueris statim ac liberaliter instituendis* (1529), in William Harrison Woodward (ed.), *Desiderius Erasmus Concerning the Aim and Method of Education*, 214.

5. Reginald Scot, *The Discoverie of Witchcraft* (Carbondale, IL: Southern Illinois University Press, 1964), 88, 139.

6. Richard Tarlton, *Tarltons Newes out of Purgatory* (1630), B1$^v$.

7. Michael Drayton, *Nimphidia: The Court of Fayrie*, lines 9–16, in *Minor Poems of Michael Drayton*, ed. Cyril Brett (Oxford: Clarendon Press, 1907), 124.

8. George Puttenham, *The Arte of English Poesie* (1589 rpt. fac. Kent, OH: Kent State University Press, 1988), 183–4.

9. Thomas Churchyard, *A Handeful of Gladsome Verses, given to the Queenes Maiesty at Woodstocke this Prograce* (Oxford, 1592), B3$^v$.

10. Minor White Latham, *The Elizabethan Fairies* (NY: Columbia University Press, 1930), 10. Latham argues that there were few references to fairies in English literature before mid–sixteenth century but abundant allusions in Scottish literature. After the 1553 English publication of the Scottish translation of *The Aeneid*, fairies began to appear in English translations of Virgil and Ovid, and then saturated English literary texts.

11. Katharine Briggs, *The Anatomy of Puck: An Examination of Fairy Beliefs among Shakespeare's Contemporaries and Successors* (London: Routledge & Kegan Paul, 1959), 12–24.

12. The current critical debate among scholars of fairylore seems to be about chronology: was a native tradition of large and dangerous spirits erased when Renaissance writers penned darling and diminutive fairies? Latham argues that Shakespeare's *Midsummer Night's Dream* single-handedly destroyed a living belief system by reducing fairies to inconsequential beings (176–218). Briggs counters this argument by pointing out that a tradition of tiny beings already existed on the continent before *Dream* was performed, so Shakespeare can only be indicted for importing a foreign fairylore into England (12–24).

13. On changes in fairylore, see Keith Thomas, *Religion and the Decline of Magic* (NY: Scribner's Sons, 1971), 608. Thomas defines fairylore as a "store of mythology" rather than a "corpus of living beliefs" in the Elizabethan period (608).

14. See Latham, *Elizabethan Fairies*, 8, 25–7, 222.

15. Ibid., 26 and 222. In Ben Jonson's masque *Oberon the Fairy Prince* the satyrs identify Oberon and his fairies as having "rough & rude" forms (*Ben Jonson*, ed. Herford, Simpson, and Simpson, Vol. VII: 351.

16. *Robin Good-fellow his mad prankes, and merry iests* (London, 1628), A4$^r$.

17. Briggs argues that fairies became a popular motif for literary writers because church prosecution of heresy declined enough in the Elizabethan era to permit an older belief system to surface in benign form (18). Briggs's theory perhaps naively assumes a time when fairies didn't hover unstably between the real and fantastical, when they were not the product of avid belief tainted by skepticism. Nevertheless, she convincingly tracks ways in which fairies increasingly became identified as "literary" machinery, the stuff of self-conscious legend.

18. Samuel Rowlands, "Of Ghoasts and Goblins" in *More Knaues Yet* (London, 1613), F2ᵛ.
19. The poetry of Robert Herrick may seem an exception, for Herrick includes fairy antics in his descriptions of popular rural pastimes. Despite the occasional poem devoted to cleaning, Herrick's evocations of the countryside emphasize the *festivity* of popular rituals rather than daily work: his poetic creatures are more inclined to go a'maying than to wash pails; e.g., "The Fairies" in *The Poetical Works of Robert Herrick*, ed. L. C. Martin (Oxford: Clarendon Press, 1956), 201. Leah Marcus argues that Herrick creates a self-conscious rural mythology that smacks of seventeenth-century royalism. But at the turn of the century, the court's interests were not yet so insistently identified with those of the countryside; indeed yeomanry were often in tension with the court about regulation of land and taxation. Since the fractious political tensions that would split the realm in civil war had not yet solidified into the ideological faultline that Marcus suggests, these invocations of fairies gracing the countryside didn't necessarily indicate a cavalier outlook. See Marcus, *The Politics of Mirth: Jonson, Herrick, Milton, Marvell, and the Defense of Old Holiday Pastimes* (University of Chicago Press, 1986), 140–68.
20. In Drayton's poem, Oberon, fearful of the amorous designs that Pigwiggen has on Queen Mab, dons an acorn cap and battles valiantly with a wasp. While Drayton uses mock heroic language to emphasize the humor of these aristocratic creatures, he can't help mentioning their rustic interest in sweeping; they "make our Girles their sluttery rue, / By pinching them both blacke and blew, / And put a penny in their shue, / The house for cleanly sweeping" (126, lines 65–8).
21. Ben Jonson, "Entertainment at Althrope,"*Ben Jonson*, ed. Herford, Simpson, and Simpson, Vol. VII: 122.
22. Jonson, *Love Restored*, in *ibid.*, 378
23. *Grim the Collier of Croydon* (1662); fac. rpt. (Amersham, England: Old English Drama Students' Facsimile, 1912), 51–2.
24. Hence the humor of *Eastward Ho*, where two city ladies bemoan the fact that "there are no *Fayries* now adayes" when they run into financial trouble. Feeling entitled, they recoil from the idea of working and instead fantasize that fairies might deliver them from poverty if they themselves consent to do minimal domestic tasks: "Sure, if wee lay in a cleanly house, they would haunt it," says Gyrtrude, "Ile sweepe the chamber soon eat night, & set a dish of water o' the Hearth. A *Fayrie* may come, and bring a Pearle, or a Diamonde" (*Ben Jonson*, Vol. IV: 599).
25. *The Maydes Metamorphosis* (1600), C4ᵛ.
26. Thomas Campion, *The Book of Ayres*, in *The Works of Thomas Campion*, ed. Walter R. Davis (Garden City, NY: Doubleday and Co., 1967), 44.
27. Although Maureen Duffy exaggerates the implications of some of her research and relies on vaguely defined universal archetypes, her *Erotic World of Faery* (London: Hodder and Stoughton, 1972) persuasively uncovers texts that link fairies with eroticism. On the etymological connection between "puck" and "fuck," see Duffy, 92.
28. See Thomas Heywood, *The Hierarchie of the Blessed Angels* (1635), 574.
29. It is easy to locate fairy tales within the broader narratives that historians offer about the widening split between popular and elite cultures and the decline of magic in the

early modern period. According to Peter Burke, elite people withdrew from the world of popular festivity and traditional beliefs between 1500 and 1800, as popular culture was gradually replaced by a mass culture that served the interests of the ruling classes (*Popular Culture in Early Modern Europe* [London: T. Smith, 1978], 270–86). The invention of folklore as an intellectual enterprise in the late eighteenth century became the core of a romantic nationalism founded on the category of the vulgar. But scholars have quibbled with Burke's two-tiered model of elite and popular cultures, noting the potent presence of a "middling sort" as well as the problems that ensue when one tries to distribute cultural objects to fixed social classes. See critiques by T. Harris, Watt, and D. Hall. On the problems of naming exclusionary practices as "popular," see Miri Rubin, *Corpus Christi: The Eucharist in Late Medieval Culture* (Cambridge University Press, 1991), 266; as well as Montrose's discussion of this problem (*Purpose of Playing*, 23).

30. See Jonathan Gil Harris, "Puck/Robin Goodfellow," in Vicki K. Janik (ed.), *Fools and Jesters in Literature, Art, and History: A Bio-bibliographical Sourcebook* (Westport, CT: Greenwood Press, 1998), 351–62.

31. See Montrose, who reads the play's anxieties about the sex/gender system in terms of domestic practices, the phenomenon of a female monarch, and the Galenic "one-sex" model (*Purpose of Playing*, 109–78).

32. C. L. Barber, *Shakespeare's Festive Comedy: A Study of Dramatic Form and its Relation to Social Custom* (Princeton, NJ: Princeton University Press, 1959).

33. See Montrose, *Purpose of Playing*, 121–3 and 33–4n; and Annabel Patterson, *Shakespeare and the Popular Voice* (Oxford: Basil Blackwell, 1989). In arguing against Barber's reading of the popular, Patterson shifts Barber's focus from the fairies to the workers and restores the vexed social history that made holidays politically controversial in the period.

34. Jonson, *The Alchemist*, *Ben Jonson*, Vol. V:297. See also John Fletcher, *The Night Walker* (1649), B1$^v$; and John Cooke, *Greenes Tu quoque or The Cittie Gallant* (1614), E4$^v$. While the broom was mainly identified as a peddled good, it was sometimes associated with witches and/or discipline (besoms, or birch instruments of punishment).

35. *Dream*'s sprites are an amalgam of variant traditions: Oberon has roots in German folklore, Oberon and Titania in classical mythology; the miniature floral fairies come from Welsh tradition; and Robin Goodfellow is a native English hobgoblin. When Puck warns Oberon that night spirits must flee daylight (and thus shows vestiges of his medieval heritage), Oberon insists that they are "spirits of another sort" (3.2.388).

36. *The Englishmans Doctor or the School of Salerne*, trans. John Harington (1617), B6$^r$ and B8$^r$.

37. Paster astutely unpacks the scene in which Bottom is returned to an eroticized childhood dependency (*The Body Embarrassed*, 125–43).

38. As Kim Hall suggests, the early modern English household invisibly functioned as a clearinghouse for foreign products newly touted as homegrown. "Culinary Spaces, Colonial Spaces: The Gendering of Sugar in the Seventeenth Century," in Traub, Kaplan, and Callaghan (eds.), *Feminist Readings of Early Modern Culture*, 168–90.

39. Robert Weimann divides the play into interlocking groups of airy fairies, earthy workers, and royal courtiers: "It is through the intimate interplay of delicately

woven threads (one silken, one homespun, one sheer gossamer, as the Victorians might have said) that the varied attitudes and moods are made to merge in one complex perspective … When the muddy boots of the mechanicals thump through the airy wood of the fairies, the result is much more than a series of colorful contrasts: their imaginative interrelation is such that the varied attitudes and statements illuminate one another, and the play as a whole achieves a poetic substance infinitely larger than the sum of its parts" (Weimann, *Shakespeare and the Popular Tradition in the Theater: Studies in the Social Dimension of Dramatic Form and Function,* trans. Robert Schwartz [Baltimore, MD: Johns Hopkins University Press, 1978], 174–5).

40. On the play's cross-specied sexuality, see Bruce Boehrer, "Bestial Buggery in *A Midsummer Night's Dream*," in David Lee Miller, Sharon O'Dair, and Harold Weber (eds.), *The Production of English Renaissance Culture* (Ithaca: Cornell University Press, 1994), 123–50. On Bottom's infantilization, see Paster, *The Body Embarrassed,* 125–43.

41. For opposite readings of the play's inscription of gender and of class, see Peter Erickson, "The Order of the Garter, the Cult of Elizabeth, and Class-Gender Tension in *The Merry Wives of Windsor*," in Jean E. Howard and Marion F. O'Connor (eds.), *Shakespeare Reproduced: The Text in History and Ideology* (NY: Methuen, 1987), 116–40; and Carol Thomas Neely, "Constructing Female Sexuality in the Renaissance: Stratford, London, Windsor, Vienna," in Richard Feldstein and Judith Roof (eds.), *Feminism and Psychoanalysis* (Ithaca: Cornell University Press, 1989), 208–29.

42. Steeped in Arthurian mythology, the exclusive Order of the Garter was used to ensure the loyalty of feudal aristocratic factions to the sovereign, and to display that ritual of allegiance to a larger populace. The chapel in which members were inducted had originally been located in the Windsor court, but Elizabeth moved the ritual to London. On the Order, see Roy Strong, *The Cult of Elizabeth: Elizabethan Portraiture and Pageantry* (London: Thames and Hudson, 1977), 179; Erickson, "The Order of the Garter," 124–8; and Fumerton, *Cultural Aesthetics,* 20.

43. Richard Helgerson, "The Buckbasket, the Witch, and the Queen of Fairies: The Women's World of Shakespeare's Windsor," in Fumerton and Hunt (eds.), *Renaissance Culture and the Everyday,* 162–82. Helgerson's essay, which appeared after this chapter was written, dovetails with mine in details the way that a localizable and English domesticity is produced in the play. But he finally sees the play's representation of women's work as supporting the interests of the court.

44. On how the final scene reinscribes court ritual within the public's voyeuristic "hideous imagination," see Leslie Katz, "*Merry Wives of Windsor*: Sharing the Queen's Holiday," *Representations* 51 (1995): 77–93, esp. 79 and 81. While I appreciate Katz's reading of how the play enables collective fantasy (which she embeds in a reading of dramatic intertextuality), I disagree with her final assessment that *Merry Wives* primarily indulges the desires of its audience to speculate on the lifestyles of the rich and famous. Instead I see the play as showing the court's desirability positioned strategically to serve the interests of the citizenry.

45. Erickson argues that the play's politics can be read in one of three ways: "as the victory of bourgeois solidarity over the aristocratic court, as the reconciliation of the best of both bourgeois and aristocratic worlds, or as the consolidation of aristocratic power through a populist approach" ("Order of the Garter," 124).

46. As Helgerson notes, "*Merry Wives* is not only uniquely English as a simple fact of its setting; it also works at its Englishness, insists on it, makes it fundamental to the definition of domestic space that court and town can share" (168). In examining the play's version of national identity, I consider Homi K. Bhabha's warning that critics lose sight of the nation as a "modern Janus": "There is a tendency to read the Nation rather restrictively; either, as the ideological apparatus of state power, somewhat redefined by a hasty, functionalist reading of Foucault or Bakhtin; or, in a more utopian inversion, as the incipient or emergent expression of the 'national-popular' sentiment preserved in radical memory" ("Introduction," Homi K. Bhabha (ed.), *Nation and Narration* [NY: Routledge, 1990], 3).

47. In *Unediting the Renaissance*, Marcus argues that the quarto *Wives* presents a play not set clearly in Windsor, despite its title, but instead laden with references to London or a large provincial town. Stripped of references to the Order of the Garter with a Fenton who is no longer a courtier, the quarto version is less eager than the folio to harmonize court and countryside, and more interested in the work of urban citizens. Responding to Marcus' call to attend to both textual versions of the play steers me to conclusions about the folio's representation of the court that differ from hers (68–100).

48. Jeanne Addison Roberts, *Shakespeare's English Comedy: The Merry Wives of Windsor in Context* (Lincoln: University of Nebraska Press, 1979), esp. 74–83; Northrop Frye, *Anatomy of Criticism: Four Essays*, (Princeton, NJ: Princeton UP, 1957), 183.

49. *Shakespeare, A Most pleasaunt and excellent conceited Comedie, of Syr John Falstaffe, and the merrie Wives of Windsor* (1602), $G2^{r-v}$. In Marcus' reading, the quarto emerges as the political hero, suppressed by editors interested in preserving the folio's courtly prominence. I would temper her claims for the ideological differences between the plays while endorsing her sense of their distinct features. While allusions to the Garter in the folio text posit a world of honor from which Falstaff has fallen, that ideal is evidently constructed as part of a fantasy controlled by village citizens.

50. After receiving their royal charter in 1518, the Royal Academy of Physicians began to ward off the barber-surgeons, apothecaries, and laywomen (known as "old wives" or "wise women") who historically controlled healthcare. On conflicts between professional and domestic medical practitioners, see Clark, *Working Life of Women in the Seventeenth Century*, 253–65; Nagy, *Popular Medicine*, and Nancy G. Siraisi, *Medieval and Early Renaissance Medicine* (University of Chicago Press, 1990).

51. In discussing *translatio* as a figure for numerous types of transfer, Patricia Parker charts how *Merry Wives*' linguistic puns address the vector where the gendered language of humanist learning and patriarchal property meet. In my reading, housewifery provides a complementary set of controling metaphors that shape the action of the play. Parker, "*The Merry Wives of Windsor*."

52. In *The English House-wife*, Markham writes of whitening yarn: "Put all the yarne againe into a bucking tubbe without ashes, and cover it as before with a bucking cloth, and lay thereupon good store of fresh ashes, and drive that buck as you did before, with very strong seething lies" (188). For a similar pun on bucking, see Jonson's *Tale of a Tub* in *Ben Jonson*, Vol. III: 3.9.75–7. Helgerson discusses the buckbasket's significance in a tradition of male paranoia stories, "The Buckbasket," 169–71.

53. On the importance of keys in the period, see Orlin, *Private Matters and Public Culture*, 182–9.
54. On the play's "imaginative configurations" at many levels, see Katz, *"Merry Wives of Windsor,"* 82–4; and William Carroll, "'A Received Belief': Imagination in *The Merry Wives of Windsor,"* *Studies in Philology* 74 (1977): 186–215.
55. See 2.2.155–8 and 172–3. Editors who condemn the quarto but still choose the "bad" quarto's name "Brooke" probably do so in order to enable a set of puns on aquatics.
56. Ralph Knevet, *Rhodon and Iris* (1631), E3$^{\text{v}}$.
57. Partridge, *The Treasurie of Hidden Secrets* (1600), D2$^{\text{r}}$; Dawson, *The Second Part of the Good Huswifes Jewell* (1597), 48. One of the 38 distillation recipes in Markham's *English House-wife* illustrates the multiple uses to which such waters were put: when applied topically, rosemary water clarified skin and prevented hair loss; when drunk, it drove venom out of blood, stabilized wandering ovaries, and increased fertility; and when used as a bath, it decreased fatigue (131). For other examples of distillation recipes, see *A Closet for Ladies and Gentlewomen* (1608), 48–52; Partridge, *Treasurie*, 1–58; and Markham, *The English House-wife* (1631), ch. 3.
58. Paster notes that almanacs warned against bathing in particular thermal conditions and that bodily events of "like evacuation" – bleeding, purging, and sexual activity – could be seen as hazardous (134–8). On the sweating tub as a cure for venereal disease, see *Henry V*, 2.1.75; *Timon of Athens*, 4.3.85–8; and Pompey's characterization of Mistress Overdone in *Measure for Measure*: "she hath eaten up all her beef, and she is herself in the tub" (3.2.556–7). For a description of the sweating tub, see F. David Hoeniger, *Medicine and Shakespeare in the English Renaissance* (Newark: University of Delaware Press, 1992), 243–5.
59. Paster, *The Body Embarrassed*, 115.
60. John Cotta, *A Short Discouerie*, 32–3.
61. James Shirley, *The Humorous Courtier* (1640), H1$^{\text{v}}$.
62. Helgerson asks: "What then are we to make of a play that uses the same female control of domestic space to correct this male fantasy in both its paranoid and its wishful versions?" ("The Buckbasket," 171). He argues that two of the play's three domestic playlets – the buckbasket and Brainford witch scenes – demonstrate that women's rule over the household can merge the local and domestic harmoniously. But for Helgerson the third fairy playlet signals the erosion of the wives' domestic control. "The local and the domestic are thus subsumed into the national," and the national is, according to Helgerson, defined by the Queen's presence (176). I suggest instead that the domestic defines the way that fantasies of the court are shaped.
63. In Thomas Dekker and John Webster's *Westward Ho*, Mrs. Justiano cries to her husband when he threatens to throw her out of the house: "What would you haue me do? Would you haue mee turne common sinner, or sell my apparell to my wastcoat and become a Landresse?" He replies, "No Landresse deere wife, though your credit would goe farre with Gentlemen for taking vp of Linnen." *The Dramatic Works of Thomas Dekker*, ed., Fredson Bowers, 4 vols. (University of Cambridge Press, 1953–61). Vol. II 2: 324 (1:1.177–81).
64. Richard Brathwait, *The Whimzies: or, a New Cast of Characters*, 83. For a history of modern laundresses that sheds light on early modern meanings, see Patricia E. Malcolmson, *English Laundresses: A Social History, 1850–1930* (Urbana: University of Illinois Press, 1986). Laundering was included in housewifery

guides, with starching and washing silks, points, laces, and stockings seen as a more prestigious activity than regular washing. On this hierarchy of labor, see Woolley, *The Compleat Servant-Maid* (1683), 62–9 and 141–2.

65. William Haughton, *Englishmen for My Money* (1616) rpt. (Oxford University Press for the Malone Society, 1912), G3$^{r-v}$, and H4$^{v-r}$.

66. John Taylor, *All the Workes of John Taylor The Water Poet Collected into one Volume by the Author* (1630), 165.

67. Ibid., 164. While imagining the laundress as a noble warrioress, Taylor describes her valor in way that nevertheless sexualize her: "she strikes, she poakess and thrusts, she hangs and drawes, She stiffens stiffly" (169).

68. Francis Dickinson, *A Pretious Treasury of Twenty Rare Secrets* (1649), A3$^{v}$. On laundering, see also Woolley, *The Compleat Servant-Maid*, 62–9.

69. Arguing for a symbiotic domestic unit, post-Reformation conduct books stressed the wife's economic importance, which was often at odds with her prescribed place in the marital hierarchy. Thomas Tusser's bestseller jauntily says: "Take weapon awaye, of what force is a man? / Take huswife from husband, and what is he than? / As lovers desireth, together to dwell, / So husbandrie loveth, good huswiferie as well." Tusser, *Fiue Hundreth Points of Good Husbandry* (1580), 66. See also Thomas Gainford, *The Rich Cabinet Furnished* (1616), 102.

70. Coppélia Kahn's remark that Falstaff's horns are a "richly multivalent" symbol (*Man's Estate: Masculine Identity in Shakespeare* [Berkeley: University of California Press, 1981]) is nicely borne out by the profusion of symbolic meanings critics have found in them – as references to a fertility spirit, satyr, sexual potency, devil, hunted deer, Actaeon, the victim of a charivari ritual, and male impotence. See also Anne Parten, "Falstaff's Horns: Masculine Inadequacy and Feminine Mirth in *The Merry Wives of Windsor*," *Studies in Philology* 82 (1985): 184–99.

71. For an analysis of the play's meditation on pure transmission, multiplication, authenticity, and circulation, see Pittenger, "Dispatch Quickly: The Mechanical Reproduction of Pages."

72. See Patricia Parker, "Shakespeare and Rhetoric: 'Dilation' and 'Delation' in *Othello*," in Parker and Geoffrey Hartman (eds.), *Shakespeare and the Question of Theory* (NY: Methuen, 1985), 54–74.

73. The play concludes with what Jeanne Addison Roberts terms decidedly "English" materials, the fairy "Cricket" and the folio Herne the Hunter (*Shakespeare's English Comedy*, 58). While Roberts is mistaken in thinking that *Merry Wives'* satiric presentation of cuckoldry and city sharpers is "peculiarly English" (59), her assessment follows the play's witty construction of its own Englishness.

74. Felix E. Schelling, *Elizabethan Drama, 1558–1642*, 2 vols. (NY: Russell & Russell, 1959), Vol. II: 324.

75. While Marcus' central argument is that the rural landscape so dear to this mythology is located only in the folio version, she makes visible the extent to which the "Merry England" ideal is premised on the play's "realistic" portrayal of everyday life and country manners (*Unediting*, 80–92).

76. Marcus' argument in *Unediting* against a critical tradition that assumes the hygienic superiority of the folio is particularly interesting for my purposes, since she frames her textual analysis in terms of Mary Douglas' work on the conceptual uses of dirt

and cleanliness. Asserting that the editorial tradition's condemnation of the quarto as "textual filth" belies an over-investment in purity, Marcus notes that editors-turned-housewives explicitly use metaphors of cleaning in their work without seeing how these tropes fit into the ideological project of affirming the play's "proper" presentation of social hierarchy. Editors sanitize the play, that is, by affirming a folio text respectful of the court.

77. The terms I have chosen may seem anachronistically colored by modern nationalism and folklore studies precisely because the play offers a thematic blueprint on which these concepts are elaborated.

78. Marcus, *Unediting*, 70–1.

## 4 THE EROTICS OF MILK AND LIVE FOOD, OR, INGESTING EARLY MODERN ENGLISHNESS

1. Sidney, Sonnet 71, *Sir Philip Sidney: Selected Poems*, ed. Katherine Duncan-Jones (Oxford: Clarendon Press, 1973), 153.
2. Harrison, *The Description of England*, 123–4.
3. See Paster, *The Body Embarrassed*, 8–13. On the national and gendered aspects of climate theory, see A. J. Hoenselaars, *Images of Englishmen and Foreigners in the Drama of Shakespeare and his Contemporaries* (London and Toronto: Associated University Presses, 1992), esp.17–19. Since continental writers usually stipulated that intelligence declined as one traveled north through the three zones, English writers sought to dispute or revise the theory.
4. Tryon, *The Good Housewife Made a Doctor*, 90. "Here you will . . . find Physical Recepts for the most reigning Distemperes, Diseases, and Grievances, incident to English Bodies," writes J. H. in *The Family-Dictionary; Or Houshold Companion* (1695), A3$^r$.
5. Markham, *The English Husbandman* (1613), A1$^v$.
6. *The Good Huswifes Handmaide for the Kitchin* (1594), 42, 46.
7. Plat, *Delightes For Ladies* (1609), F8$^r$; *The Jewell House of Art and Nature* (1594), 157–8.
8. Wrightson, *English Society, 1580–1680*, 40.
9. I am indebted to Juliet Fleming's unpublished commentary on Dowe. ("Memory, Method and the Female Self in the English Domestic Guide"); and her "Ladies' Men, the Ladies' Text, and the English Renaissance" (Ph.D. diss., University of Pennsylvania, 1991).
10. Bright, *A Treatise Wherein is declared the sufficiencie of English Medicines* (1580), 30–31. Bright elaborates the specificity of the "English body" as well as the home-grown simples (rosemary, basil, sage, saffron, thyme) that compare favorably to their foreign counterparts (cinnamon, cloves, nutmeg, ginger, musk). On the social meanings of food in the period in general, see Stephen Mennell, *All Manners of Food*, 40–101.
11. Markham, *English House-wife* (1631), 12, 39–40. For additional recipes calling for human milk, see ibid., 11, 47–8; W. M., *The Queens Closet Opened* (1658), 130, 139; Thomas Phaire, *The Boke of Chyldren* (1545; rpt. Edinburgh and London:

E. & S. Livingstone Ltd., 1957), 27; Grey, *A Choice Manual* (1661), 103, 147; and Woolley, *The Compleat Servant-Maid* (1683), 149.

12. Morris Palmer Tilly, *Dictionary of the Proverbs*, 45. On how the breast signified food in the medieval period, see Caroline Bynum, *Holy Feast and Holy Fast: The Religious Significance of Food to Medieval Women* (Berkeley: University of California Press, 1987).

13. Clark, *Working Life of Women*, 53–9. Gainford includes cheesemaking in his list of a housewife's primary duties (*The Rich Cabinet*, 103$^v$-104$^r$).

14. Cahn, *An Industry of Devotion*, 36; Clark, *Working Life*, 54.

15. Tusser, *Five Hundred Points of Good Husbandrie* (Oxford University Press, 1984), 119.

16. Thomas Lodge and Robert Greene, *A Looking Glasse for London and England*, ed. George Alan Clugston (NY and London: Garland, 1980), 143.

17. Historians almost uniformly refer to the dairy as the sole province of women, and dairying as one of the few tasks not undertaken by male servants. See Michael Roberts, "'Words they are Women, and Deeds they are Men': Images of Work and Gender in Early Modern England," in Charles and Duffin (eds.), *Women and Work in Pre-Industrial England*, 140 and 149.

18. Robert Greene, *Friar Bacon and Friar Bungay*, ed. Daniel Seltzer (Lincoln: University of Nebraska Press, 1963), 1.72–80. One type of charivari (European shaming rituals designed to enforce community standards) was named for the slotted spoon that women used to skim milk in making butter and cheese – the skimming ladle. The "skimmington" involved a procession filled with discordant "rough music" that was directed at either a cuckold or a scold. As David Underdown argues, skimmingtons were recorded more frequently in pasture country (where domestic disorder abounded) than in arable farming lands, for women in pasture lands made greater contributions to the family income through dairying and spinning. Cheese production, in the early modern imagination, was linked to a potentially unruly female independence. In working with her naked hands rather than a skimming ladle, Margaret mitigates the threat of her labor. See Underdown, *Revel, Riot, and Rebellion: Popular Politics and Culture in England, 1603–1660* (Oxford: Clarendon Press, 1985), 99–103.

19. On Spenser's use of pastoral, see David Lee Miller, "Authorship, Anonymity, and *The Shepheardes Calendar*," *Modern Language Quarterly* 40 (1979): 219–36; Richard Helgerson, *Self-Crowned Laureates: Spenser, Jonson, Milton and the Literary System* (Berkeley: University of California Press, 1983); and Louis Montrose, "'The perfecte paterne of a Poete': The Poetics of Courtship in *The Shepheardes Calendar*," *Texas Studies in Language and Literature* 21 (1970): 34–67. For a survey of English Renaissance pastoralism, see Walter W. Greg, *Pastoral Drama and Pastoral Poetry* (NY: Russell & Russell, 1959); and Hallett Smith, *Elizabethan Poetry* (Ann Arbor: University of Michigan Press, 1968), 1–63.

20. On Queen Elizabeth's desire to be a milkmaid, see Montrose, "'Eliza Queene of Shepheardes,' and the Pastoral of Power," *English Literary Renaissance* 10 (1980), 153–82, esp. 154–60.

21. Montrose, "Of Gentlemen and Shepherds: the Politics of Elizabethan Pastoral Form," *ELH* 50 (1983): 415–59; and his "'Eliza, Queen of Shepheardes.'" For a sweeping argument about the erasure of labor in the countryside, see Raymond

Williams' classic *The Country and the City* (NY: Oxford University Press, 1973).

22. Philip Sidney, *Astrophel and Stella*, Sonnet 91 and "Pyrocles Praises Philoclea," both in *Sir Philip Sidney*, ed. Duncan-Jones, 176 and 48. See also Shakespeare, *Two Gentlemen of Verona* (3.1.252); *Venus and Adonis* (902); *Midsummer Night's Dream* (2.1.167); and *Pericles* (4. Gower. 22).

23. *The Gentlewomans Companion* (1673), 33.

24. On how urban dwellers got milk and on its dangers to the body, see Dorothy Davis, *A History of Shopping* (London: Routledge, 1966), 91. On how cow's milk was seen as filthy, see Pullar, *Consuming Passions*, 155.

25. See Phaire, *Boke of Chyldren*, 19; Gouge, *Of Domesticall Duties*, 515.

26. Muffet, *Health's Improvement*, 122. On testing the nurse's milk, see *ibid.*, 121–8; James Guillimeau, *Child-birth, or, The Happy Deliverie of Women* (1612; rpt. 1635), 7; and Phaire, *Boke of Chyldren*, 19.

27. On the use of puppies for drawing out what was considered dangerous early breast-milk, see Guillimeau, *Child-birth*, 18–19.

28. Henry Smith, *A Preparative to Marriage* (1591), 77. See also Muffet, *Health's Improvement*, 121–8; Phaire, *Boke of Chyldren*, 18.

29. Fildes, *Breasts, Bottles and Babies*, 170–1.

30. Spenser, *A View of the Present State of Ireland*, 88.

31. E.K., Epistle to Harvey, prefacing Spenser, *The Shepheardes Calendar*, in *Yale Edition of the Shorter Poems*, ed. Oram *et al.*, 16–17.

32. In Jonson's "Kings Entertainment at Welbeck" (performed in the 1620s), gentlemen say of James's return to Scotland: "Our *King* is going now to a great worke / Of highest Love, Affection, and Example, / To see his Native *Countrey*, and his Cradle, / And find those manners there, which he suck'd in / With Nurses Milke, and Parents pietie!" (309–13). In *Ben Jonson*, ed. Herford, Simpson and Simpson, Vol. VII: 802.

33. "That first and tender age of infancy, apt to be molded of any fashion, oftentimes with the milk sucketh the conditions of the Nurse," writes Kyd in translating Tasso's *The Householder's Philosophy* in *The Works of Thomas Kyd*, ed. Frederick S. Boas (Oxford: Clarendon Press, 1901), 259. Tasso explicitly warns mothers that wetnurs-ing denies children their proper class status.

34. Laurent Joubert, *Popular Errors*, trans. Gregory de Rocher (Tuscaloosa: The Univer-sity of Alabama Press, 1989), 192. In *Child-birth*, Guillimeau also writes that milk "hath as much power to make the children like the Nurse, both in bodie, and mind; as the seed of the Parents hath to make the children like them" (Ii4); and William Yonger takes non-maternal lactation as his sustained metaphor for the magistrate's spiritual and secular governance. Yonger, *The Nurses Bosome. A Sermon Within the Greene-Yard in Norwich* (1616).

35. Paster writes: "The lactating breast never completely loses the class and other at-tributes of the body of which it is part, thus never becomes completely fungible with any other woman's breast" (*The Body Embarrassed*, 200). On the nurse's diet, see Muffet, *Health's Improvement*, 126 and Guillimeau, *Child-birth*, 9.

36. In *The Compleat Mother* (1695), Henry Newcome considers the possible "hazard" and "dimunition" that an infant gentleman suffers at the hands of the nurse (79, 80). In *The English Gentlewoman* (1631), Richard Brathwaite warns against a "strangers" milk: "No marvell then, if they [descendents] degenerate, when they partake of the

natures of other women." "With the milke of the Nurse," he continues, "they suck the quality or condition of her life" (361).

37. Gouge, *Of Domesticall Duties*, 512.
38. Newcome, *Compleat Mother*, 57. On milk as shaping personality and character, see Thomas Deloney, *The Gentle Craft* in *The Novels of Thomas Deloney*, ed. Merritt E. Lawlis (Indiana University Press, 1961), 212; and Philip Massinger, *The Guardian* (1655) in *The Poems and Plays of Philip Massinger* (Oxford: Clarendon Press, 1976), 159.
39. Thomas Overbury, *Characters* in *The Miscellaneous Works in Prose and Verse of Sir Thomas Overbury, Knt.*, ed. Rimbault, 118–19.
40. See my discussion of Markham in Chapter 1. See also Juan Luis Vives, *A Fruteful and pleasant boke called the Instruction of Christen Woman* (1529; rpt. 1557), 108.
41. John Dunton *Voyage Round the World* (1691), 375–6.
42. Richard Head, *The English Rogue* (1665) rpt. ed. Michael Shinagel (Boston, MA: New Frontiers Press, 1961), 147–8.
43. *A Pleasant Comedie, Called The Two Merry Milke-Maids* (1620), 1.3.98–9.
44. Philip Sidney, *Certain Sonnets*, no. 9, in *The Poems of Sir Philip Sidney*, ed. William A. Ringler (Oxford: Clarendon Press, 1961), 141.
45. Robert Herrick, "The Descripcion: Of a Woman" and "Upon Julia's Breasts" in *Hesperides*, in *The Poetical Works*, 405, 96. This language was not restricted to one courtly genre or Herrick's psychopathology. For instance, see Robert Burton's description of the milkiness of the idealized female body in *Anatomy of Melancholy* (*c*. 1624), III.65–87.
46. Thomas Lodge, *Phillis* (1593), Sonnet 39, H2$^{\text{v}}$.
47. When Joubert counters objections to maternal breastfeeding on the grounds that husbands don't like the smell of milk on their wife's breasts, he points out that eroticism and milkiness might in fact have gone hand in hand, for men make love to nurses: "The sagging breasts of the nurse, or the smell of milk on her, do not disgust them" (204). Paster argues that courtly love poetry attempts to protect the breast from *mutability* (the breast's changes and links to the humorally uncontained womb) by evoking Petrarchan metonymies – lillies, ivory, and snow (208). I want to consider moments when love poetry represents milky breasts and thus accentuates the very feature of the breast that it might be expected to downplay.
48. *The Rape of Lucrece* in *The Dramatic Works of Thomas Heywood*, 6 vols. (London: John Pearson, 1874), Vol. V: 209. I cite this edition by page number since there are no line numbers given.
49. Anthony Munday, "Camp-bell" (1609), in *Pageants and Entertainments of Anthony Munday*, ed. David M. Bergeron (NY: Garland, 1985), 27.
50. *The Englishmans Doctor*, A3$^{\text{r}}$.
51. See Montrose, "The Elizabethan Subject and the Spenserian Text," in Parker and Quint (eds.), *Literary Theory/ Renaissance Texts* (Baltimore, MD: Johns Hopkins University Press, 1986), 315. On "enclosure" as a multivalent symbol fundamental to conceptions of early modern class, gender, sexuality, and nationality see Peter Stallybrass, "Time space and unity: The Symbolic of *The Faerie Queene*" in Samuel (ed.), *Patriotism: The Making and Unmaking of British National Identity*, 3 vols. (London and NY: Routledge, 1989), vol. III: 199–214; and "Patriarchal Territories," 123–44. My work is also indebted to critics who discuss Elizabeth's body as a

signifier for the nation. See Leonard Tennenhouse, *Power on Display: The Politics of Shakespeare's Genres* (NY: Routledge, 1986), 102–12; Linda Woodbridge, "Palisading the Body Politic," in Woodbridge and Edward Berry (eds.), *True Rites and Maimed Rites: Ritual and Anti-Ritual in Shakespeare and his Age* (Urbana: University. of Illinois Press, 1992), 270–98; and Marie Axton, *The Queen's Two Bodies: Drama and the Elizabethan Succession* (London: Royal Historical Society, 1977).

52. In the second plot, the foreign entourage celebrates Oxford's pastures as the heart of true Englishness while watching a national contest between Friar Bacon and the German scholar Vandermast waged over the inviolability of the Hesperides garden; this mythic site is connected to England by writers such as Harrison (*Description of England*, 331).

53. By presenting the central social and moral conflict as Ned's desire for a commoner, the play unsurprisingly mystifies the range of existing conflicting social groups *within* England. While we glimpse struggles among copyholder, landowner, and tenant, and between king and aristocrat, the diverse socioeconomic interests of the countryside, court, companies, merchants, and municipal powers largely vanish in Greene's dreamy world.

54. Dekker and Webster, *Westward Ho,* in *Dekker*, ed. Bowers, Vol. II: 2.2.204–205.

55. The term is Laura Stevenson's, used in *Praise and Paradox: Merchants and Craftsmen in Elizabethan Popular Literature* (Cambridge University Press, 1984), 204.

56. See Stephen Maynard, "Feasting on Eyre: Community, Consumption and Communion in *The Shoemaker's Holiday*," *Comparative Drama* 32 (1998): 327–64.

57. Thomas Dekker, *The Shoemaker's Holiday*, ed. Anthony Parr (London: A.C. Black and NY: Norton, 1990), 18.194–200. "Dry-fats" and scuttles are large casks or barrels used to contain goods.

58. Stevenson is right to caution against reading scenes such as this one as evidence of a bourgeois mentality distinct from aristocratic beliefs. But, as I argue below, the scene ends with a business transaction and not just a show of liberality.

59. Googe, adaptation of Heresbach, *The Whole Art and Trade of Husbandry* (1614), 46.

60. See Steven Smith, "The London Apprentices as Seventeenth-Century Adolescents," *Past and Present* 61 (1973): 149–61; and Olive Jocelyn Dunlop, *English Apprenticeship and Child Labour, A History* (NY: Macmillan, 1912). On the workplace as a surrogate family, see Ilana Krausman Ben-Amos, *Adolescence and Youth in Early Modern England* (New Haven, CT: Yale University Press, 1994), 54–67.

61. I thank the participants of my graduate seminar at Northwestern University, particularly Glenn Sucich, for a valuable discussion of food metaphors in this play.

62. Martha Howell, *Women, Production and Patriarchy in Late Medieval Cities* (University of Chicago Press, 1986), 27–30.

63. Tilly and Scott, *Women, Work and the Family*, 12.

64. As critics have noted, the play denies antagonisms between English craftsmen and Dutch immigrant workers that often resulted in bloodshed; instead the shoemakers beg Simon to hire the Dutch Hans for their amusement. For examples of power struggles among apprentices and domestic workers, see Ben-Amos, *Adolescence and Youth*, 101. For other dramatic representations, see Thomas Dekker, *The Honest Whore, Pt. I* (authored with Thomas Middleton) in *The Dramatic Works of Thomas Dekker*, Vol. II: 1.5.

65. I am reading Simon's aside, when he offers cans of ale to his men ("no more Madge, no more"), as spoken to his wife Margery and not to the maid named Madge who isn't in this scene (7.79). Confusion about women's names arises in the first scene when Simon seems to call his wife a pet name, Cecily Bumtrincket, but this turns out to be the name of one of her (absent) maids. At some level, this confusion suggests the interchangeability of household mistress and domestic workers.

66. Natalie Zemon Davis, "Women in the Crafts in Sixteenth Century Lyon," in Barbara Hanawalt (ed.), *Women and Work in Pre-industrial Europe* (Indiana University Press, 1986).

67. Ben-Amos, *Adolescence and Youth*, 106–107.

68. Drawing on the common analogy of social hierarchy and body politic, Prospero in Shakespeare's *Tempest* scolds his daughter for insubordination by simply saying: "What, I say, / My foot, my tutor?" (1.2.469–70). On feet, see Peter Stallybrass, "Footnotes," in David Hillman and Carlo Mazzio (eds.) *The Body in Parts: Fantasies of Corporeality in Early Modern Europe* (NY: Routledge, 1997), 317.

69. See Clark, *Working Life of Women in the Seventeenth Century*, as well as a critique of Clark by Bennett, "Medieval Women, Modern Women: Across the Great Divide," 146–67.

70. David S. Kastan, "Workshop and/as Playhouse," in Kastan and Peter Stallybrass (eds.), *Staging the Renaissance: Reinterpretations of Elizabethan and Jacobean Drama* (NY: Routledge, 1991), 151–63.

71. *Friar Bacon* was produced on stage at least seven times in 1592 and 1593, revived in 1594 by the Queen's Men and Sussex's Men, entered into the Stationers' Register in May and subsequently printed as a quarto. Probably revived as a court performance in 1602, it was reprinted twice before 1655. The play, then, ran in five different seasons, spanning thirteen years; and it was probably acted during the reigns of James and Charles (see Seltzer's introduction to *Friar Bacon*, xi). Although we don't have records documenting the performance history of *A Shoemaker's Holiday*, its appearance six times in quarto between 1600 and 1657 made it extremely popular in print. Entered in Henslowe's diary in 1599, it was probably first performed at the Rose Theater that year and was revived as a court entertainment for the Queen in 1600.

72. Jean-Louis Flandrin, *Families in Former Times: Kinship, Household, and Sexuality*, trans. Richard Southern (Cambridge University Press, 1979), 4. His conclusion, however, lays bare the presentism that I hope to avoid. "We are not . . . prevented from giving a privileged place in our historical researches to the relations between spouses and between them and their children, *because it is these relations that lie at the heart of our preoccupations today.* It is, however, important to emphasize that what was referred to in past times as the 'family' was not identical with the father – mother – children triad, and that one cannot study this triad, in the sixteenth, seventeenth, and eighteenth centuries, without taking into account its relations with *lignage* or kindred on the one hand, and the domestic staff on the other" (10, my emphasis). On the history of the family, see Rayna Rapp, Ellen Ross, and Renate Bridenthal, "Examining Family History," in Judith L. Newton, Mary P. Ryan, and Judith R. Walkowitz (eds.), *Sex and Class in Women's History* (NY: Routledge & Kegan Paul, 1983), 232–58.

73. *The Diary of Samuel Pepys*, 1.

74. Henslowe, *Henslowe's Diary*, ed. R. A. Foakes and R. T. Rickert (Cambridge University Press, 1961), 319. This appendix, "Playhouse Inventories Now Lost," is derived from Edmund Malone's 1790 publication of Henslowe's loose papers. Given the cost of sugar, it is unlikely that a theatrical company would use it simply as the raw material for making objects unless its status as a sugar object was obvious to the audience.

## 5 TENDING TO BODIES AND BOYS: QUEER PHYSIC IN *KNIGHT OF THE BURNING PESTLE*

1. Francis Beaumont, *The Knight of the Burning Pestle*, ed. Michael Hattaway (NY: W.W. Norton New Mermaids Series, 1969), induction, 25–6. While I cite an edition of the play that attributes the play to Beaumont, I am persuaded by Jeffrey Masten's argument for the play's more ambiguous and collaborative authorship. The first quarto offers no attribution; the second and third quartos attribute the play both to Beaumont and Fletcher; and the prefatory apparatuses for these texts refer to both a single and plural author. See Masten, "Beaumont and/or Fletcher: Collaboration and the Interpretation of Renaissance Drama," *ELH* 59 (1992), 337–57. The play was probably performed by the Children of the Chapel Royal, also called the Children of the Queen's Revels and the Children of Blackfriars.
2. See Raymond S. Burns, introduction to John Day, *Isle of Guls* (NY: Garland Publishing Co., 1980), 40–2, esp. 41 fn. 66. Jonson's inductions include *Every Man Out of His Humor*, *Bartholomew Fair*, *Cynthia's Revels*, *The Staple of News*, and *The Magnetic Lady or Humours Reconciled*.
3. Day, *Isle of Guls*, Induction, lines 53–6. Day mocks gallants' tastes for satire, sex, and exaggerated acting styles as well as their propensity to sleep late, leave plays in the middle, and hiss.
4. Jonson imitates this scenario in his *Staple of News* by having four "gossips" seek "delights" by climbing on stage and defying noblemen's expectations. One of the choric women, Gossip Mirth, defends a woman's right to take the stage with gentlemen by pointing to the shared experience of maternity and nursing: "Why, what should they think? But that they had mothers, as we had, and those mothers had gossips, if their children were christened, as we are, and such as had a longing to see plays and sit upon them, as we do, and arraign both them and their poets." Jonson, *The Staple of News* (1631), rpt. in *Ben Jonson*, ed. Herford, Simpson and Simpson, Vol. VI, Induction, 23; 17–21.
5. Romance was often identified as the literary fare of non-elite women. The chambermaid in Overbury's *Characters*, for instance, "reads *Greenes* works over and over, but is so carried away with the *Mirror of Knighthood*, she is many times resolv'd to runne out of her selfe, and become a lady errant." Overbury, *Characters* in *The Miscellaneous Works in Prose and Verse of Sir Thomas Overbury*, 101.
6. Michael Hattaway, introduction, *Knight of the Burning Pestle*, xiv.
7. See note 58 below.
8. Vives, *A Fruteful and pleasant boke called the Instruction of a Christen Woman*, 108.

9. Tusser, *Five Hundred Points of Good Husbandry* (1984), 179.

10. See Lucinda McCray Beier, *Sufferers and Healers: The Experience of Illness in Seventeenth-Century England* (NY: Routledge & Kegan Paul, 1987), 172–3; Pollock, *With Faith and Physic*, 97–8; and Nagy, *Popular Medicine*, 54–78.

11. Linda Pollock reprints portions of Mildmay's manuscripts, including this comment. *With Faith and Physic*, 92 (manuscript, Pt. 1, fol. 46).

12. See *ibid.*, 92–7; 169, fn. 2.

13. Ann Windsor, Nottingham Record Office, Saville MS 221/97/7, ctd. by Pollock, *With Faith and Physic*, 94.

14. Hoby, *Diary of Lady Margaret Hoby*, ed. Meads, 184. On how women's medical practice extended beyond the home and beyond prescribed measures, see Nagy, *Popular Medicine*, 45–47.

15. Cotta, *A Short Discouerie . . .* , 29.

16. Markham, *The English House-wife*, 5.

17. Charles Stevens, *The Countrey Farm*, revised by Markham, in *Maison Rustique*, (1616), 39; Partridge, *The Treasurie of Hidden Secrets* (1600), title page.

18. Murrell, *Daily Exercise* (1617), D7$^r$. See also Partridge, *Treasurie* (1600), H5$^r$; W. M., *Queens Closet Opened*, 5, 27, 122; *A Closet for Ladies* (1635), B8$^r$, D5$^r$; and Guibert, *The Charitable Physitian*, 160.

19. *The Charitable Physitian* recommends that the housewife have pestles of different sizes composed of materials such as wood or iron (41). See also Grey, *A Choice Manual* (1661), 84.

20. Dod and Cleaver, *A Godly Forme of Houshold Government*, L6$^v$-L7$^r$.

21. Woolley, *The Compleat Servant-Maid*, 166, 175; *Queens Closet Opened*, 132, 160; and Grey, *A Choice Manual*, 24–5. *The Ladies Cabinet Opened* offers a typical recipe for an enema to "loosen the body being bound": "Take Mallows and Mercury, unwashed, of each two handfuls, half a handful of barly, clean rubbed and washed: boile them in a pottle of running water to a quart, then straine out the water, and put it in a skillet, and put to it three spoonfuls of sallet oyl, two spoonfuls of honey and a little salt: then make it lukewarme, and so minister it" (1655), 153.

22. George Hartman, *The Family Physitian* (1696), 330–43. In *The Kitchin Physitian* T. K. recommends a monthly purge, 133. See also Everard Maynwaringe, *The Efficacy and Extent of True Purgation . . . Distinguished from Promiscuous Evacuations; injuriously procured, and falsely reported Purging* (1696).

23. Thomas Elyot, *The Castel of Health* (1541), 58. Elyot lists nearly one hundred simples that work as digestives and purgatives (57–60).

24. Cotta, *A Short Discouerie*, 32–3.

25. *Diary of Lady Margaret Hoby, 1599–1605*, 131, 88, and 115.

26. See, for instance, Mildmay's recipe for the pox, in Pollock, *With Faith*, 138–9.

27. Paster, *The Body Embarrassed*, 115; Paster discusses the eroticization of the purge, 132–43.

28. John Ford, *Loves Sacrifice* (1633), D1$^v$.

29. Cosmo Manuche, *The Loyal Lovers* (1652), 24.

30. Johnson, *Academy of Love* (1641), 70–71.

31. See Pollock, *With Faith*, 114–15, 119.

32. Markham includes a recipe for setting a broken bone that requires soaking a linen

in raw egg whites to make a plaster that remains on the bone for at least nine days and then is reheated and reapplied (*The English House-wife*, 55–6). Poultices and curative liquids were routinely comprised of mouse, peacock, dog, and horse dung, since it was said to retain the animal's vital spirits. *The Closet for Ladies*, for instance, instructs a patient to drink mouse dung beaten into a powder and mixed with sugar daily in order to eliminate spitting blood (G5$^r$).

33. On licorice as aiding digestion and breathing, see John Ford, *The Fancies Chaste and Noble* (1638), D3$^r$.

34. See Partridge, *Treasurie of Hidden Secrets* (1600), G4$^r$.

35. Robert Greene and Thomas Lodge, *A Looking Glasse for London and England* (1594; rpt. 1598), lines 249–53. On the qualities of ginger, see *The Gentlewomans Companion* (1673), 161–2; and *A Warning for Fair Women*, ed. Charles Dale Cannon (The Hague and Paris: Mouton, 1975), 139. M. B., *The Ladies Cabinet Enlarged* includes a typical recipe for candying ginger (1655), 19.

36. John Webster, *The Duchess of Malfi*, ed. Elizabeth M. Brennan (NY: W.W. Norton New Mermaids Series, 1990), 4.2.200–202.

37. Lee Bliss argues that the Duchess attempts to "establish a private sphere, a world of intimate relationship and family concerns to which she can devote herself as a private individual" (*The World's Perspective: John Webster and the Jacobean Drama* [New Brunswick, NJ: Rutgers University Press, 1983], 148). Emily Bartels notes that the Duchess makes claims of self-assertion within social circumscriptions ("Strategies of Submission: Desdemona, the Duchess, and the Assertion of Desire," *Studies in English Literature* 36 [1996]: 417–33). Reading the play as constructing a bourgeois liberal subjectivity dependent on the separation of domestic and public spheres, Catherine Belsey comments, "The Duchess's final words to Cariola identify her as a nurturing, loving mother" (*The Subject of Tragedy*: *Identity and Difference in Renaissance Drama* [London: Methuen, 1985], 199). Lisa Jardine looks at the Duchess' final speech as evidencing a "stereotyped nurturing mother" stripped of dynastic power (*Still Harping on Daughters* [NY: Barnes and Noble, 1983], 82). While the play certainly reveals an attempt to cordon off intimacy from a broader spectrum of relations, these are not *a priori* separate. My point is that the Duchess' reference to cough syrup neither simply points to a privatizing moment that insulates the family from the outside world nor does it necessarily instantiate modern ideas of motherhood.

38. See Tryon, *The Good Housewife Made a Doctor*, 2.

39. Ben Jonson, George Chapman, and John Marston, *Eastward Ho* in *Ben Jonson*, Vol. IV: 293–8.

40. Lording Barry, *Ram-Alley* (1611), E2$^r$.

41. Thomas Dekker and John Webster, *Westward Ho* (1607), rpt. in *The Dramatic Works of Thomas Dekker*, ed. Fredson Bowers, 4 vols. (Cambridge University Press, 1955), Vol. II: 1.1.76–80.

42. See Ben-Amos, *Adolescence and Youth in Early Modern England*, 85. On service and youth, see Ben-Amos, ch. 1; and Mark Thornton Burnett, *Masters and Servants in English Renaissance Drama and Culture* (London: Macmillan Press, 1997), 14–53.

43. On the history of the children's companies, see Michael Shapiro, *Children of the Revels: The Boy Companies of Shakespeare's Time and Their Plays* (NY: Columbia

University Press, 1977), esp. 1–30; Harbage, *Shakespeare and the Rival Traditions*; and Harold Newcomb Hillebrand, *The Child Actors* (Urbana: University of Illinois Studies in Language and Literature by the University of Illinois Press, 1926).

44. On Henry Clifton's 1601 lawsuit against the company for impressing his 13–year-old son, see Hillebrand, *Child Actors*, 160–163; Shapiro, *Children of the Revels*, 24–25; and Orgel, *Impersonations*, 66.

45. The culturally noted antagonism between housewife and educator is discussed above. On the housewife's figurative position in the production of masculinist humanism, see Lorna Hutson, *The Usurer's Daughter: Male Friendship and Fictions of Women in Sixteenth-Century England* (London and NY: Routledge, 1994), 17–51.

46. Jonson, *Staple of News*, in *Ben Jonson*, Vol. IV, 3rd intermean, 43–4, 46–7.

47. Shapiro, *Children of the Revels*, 104–12.

48. *Lingua, or the Combat of the Tongue* (1607; rpt. Amersham, England: Old English Drama Students' Facsimiles issued by John S. Farmer, 1913), D4$^v$.

49. Thomas Heywood, *An Apology for Actors* (Shakespeare Society Publications III, 1841), 61.

50. Jonson, *Cynthia's Revels*, in *Ben Jonson*, Vol. IV, Induction, 97, 102–103.

51. On the erotics of service, see Goldberg, *Sodometries*, 143; Bray, *Homosexuality in Renaissance England*, 51–3; Stewart, *Close Readers*, esp. 84–121; and Bruce Smith, *Homosexual Desire*.

52. Jardine, *Reading Shakespeare Historically*, 65–77.

53. The now lost *Children of the Chapel Stript and Whipt* is cited by Thomas Warton, *The History of English Poetry*, 3 vols. (1824; rpt. London: Thomas Tegg, 1840), Vol. III: 240–1, fn. t.

54. "Commission for the Chapel," *Malone Society Collections*, ed. E.K. Chambers (1911), Vol. I, Parts 4 and 5, 362. ctd. by Harbage, *Shakespeare*, 80.

55. As one point of entry for the difficult project of locating female–female relationships in the household, we might look to Tusser, who suggests that the wife had hands-on interaction in managing servants. He warns the maid that the mistress may "uncover [her] bare" if she fails to arise early: "Maides, up I beseech yee / Least Mistress doe breech yee," he then advises (*Fiue Hundred Points*, 162). While critics have discussed the boy's period of "breaching" as a sex/gender initiation ritual, Tusser's words steer us to consider the implications of different kinds of female "breaching" turning on clothing (uncovering) and beating (being breeched). On same-sex female eroticized domestic sites, see Fiona McNeill, "Gynocentric London Spaces: (Re)Locating Masterless Women in Early Stuart Drama," *Renaissance Drama* 28 (1997): 195–244.

56. David Samuelson comments on the Wife's "carnal longings," for instance, in "The Order in Beaumont's *Knight of the Burning Pestle*,"*English Literary Renaissance* 9 (1979): 302–18.

57. For a scene that pairs purging with salacious storytelling, see James Shirley, *The Polititian* (1655), 7.

58. While I am sensitive to critics who wish to reserve the word "queer" to describe homoerotic relations, I join critics who use the term to signify non-normative sexual practices. Since queer theory has galvanized feminists to disarticulate gender and sexuality, feminism in turn offers the possibility of broadening the way in which we understand "non-normative" desires in the early modern world. Attending to and

demasculinizing the potentially pederastic relationship of housewife to children and young servants is one place to start this project.

59. On the association of violence with apprentices, see Mark Thornton Burnett, "Apprentice Literature and the Crisis of the 1590s," *The Yearbook of English Studies* 21 (1991): 27–38.

60. I join critics who argue against reading *Knight of the Burning Pestle* as a simple critique of bourgeois naivete. See Leinwand, "Shakespeare and the Middling Sort"; and Sheldon Zitner's introduction to Francis Beaumont, *Knight of the Burning Pestle* (Manchester University Press, 1984), 31–9. While at first glance, "The London Merchant" seems to be about "real" social problems and is thus defined against the citizens' discredited desire for unrealistic romance, *Burning Pestle* pressures this opposition. The citizens' failure to read Jasper's "love test" and fake death correctly, for instance, points to the artificiality of the conventions of city comedy.

61. Butler, *Bodies that Matter*, 267, fn. 7.

## 6 BLOOD IN THE KITCHEN: SERVICE, TASTE, AND VIOLENCE IN DOMESTIC DRAMA

1. Jeanette Winterson, *Sexing the Cherry* (NY: Grove Press, 1989), 55.

2. Heywood, *The English Traveller* in *Heywood's Dramatic Works*, Vol. IV: 25. I will cite all references to this play by page number.

3. See *OED* entries for "stomach," 5b, 6a, 7a, 8a, 8b, 8c.

4. Laplanche and Pontalis, *The Language of Psycho-Analysis*, trans. Nicholson-Smith, 55.

5. Perkins, *Christian Oeconomie*, ¶3$^r$. On scholarly debates about the function of the post-Reformation household, see my introduction, esp. note 2.

6. On the metaphorics of the body in the period, see Leonard Barkan, *Nature's Work of Art: The Human Body as Image of the World* (New Haven, CT: Yale University Press, 1975); Sawday, *The Body Emblazoned*; Stallybrass, "Patriarchal Territories: The Body Enclosed"; Jonathan Gil Harris, *Foreign Bodies and the Body Politic* (Cambridge University Press, 1998); and Caroline Walker Bynum, *Fragmentation and Redemption: Essays on Gender and the Human Body in Medieval Religion* (NY: Zone Books, 1992). In their introduction to *The Body in Parts: Fantasies of Corporeality in Early Modern Europe* (NY: Routledge, 1997), Hillman and Mazzio argue that early modern fascination with the isolated body part might constitute a new "logic of the fragment."

7. Thomas Gataker, "A Wife Indeed," in *A Good Wife Gods Gift* (1623), 9.

8. I. M., *A Health to the Gentlemanly Profession of Servingmen*, B2$^v$.

9. The best account of how domestic violence functioned in the period is Dolan's *Dangerous Familiars*. On domestic ideology, see Orlin, *Private Matters*; and Gowing, *Domestic Dangers*, 206–31.

10. Markham, *The English House-wife*, 77; Murrell, *New Booke of Cookerie*, 2; see also Leonardo Fioravanti, *A Compendium of the rationall Secretes of . . . Leonardo Phioravante Bologuese*, trans. J. Hertes (London, 1582), 112.

11. Woolley, *The Queen-like Closet* (1675), 11. This recipe appears twenty years earlier in W. M., *The Queens Closet Opened*, with the cock identified as "running" and the injunction, "then kill him" included for clarification (14).

12. Woolley, *The Compleat Servant-Maid*, 174.

13. *A Compendium of the rationall Secretes*, 59.

14. Early modern practices could involve baiting, skinning, and pounding live animals. See Fumerton, "Introduction: A New New Historicism," *Renaissance Culture and the Everyday*, 1–4. On animal torture, see Muffet, *Healths Improvement*, 45–7, 65–7.

15. W.M., *The Queens Closet Opened*, 182, 187.

16. *Compleat Servant-Maid*, 38.

17. One recipe in M. B., *The Ladies Cabinet Enlarged* (1655) begins, "Kill your chickens" (220); and another advises, "Take a live Carp, and when you have scaled it with your knife, and dryed it very wel with a cloth, open the belly, and take out the entrails" (226). See also Dawson, "The stilling of a Cappon" in *The Good Huswifes Jewell* (1596), 48; and W. G., *A True Gentlewomans Delight* (1661), 131.

18. Grey, *A Choice Manual* (1661), 50–51.

19. "A medicine for a childe that cannot hold his or her Water" advises the reader to "take the Navil string of a child which is ready to fall from him, dry it and beat it to a powder, and give it to the patient childe Male or Female in two spoonfuls of small Beer to drink fasting in the morning." W. M., *The Queens Closet Opened*, 91.

20. Mildmay's manuscript recipe is reprinted in Pollock, *With Faith and Physic*, 114.

21. Bright, *A Treatise wherein is declared the sufficiencie of English Medicines*, 37.

22. Piero Camporesi, *Bread of Dreams: Food and Fantasy in Early Modern Europe*, trans. David Gentilcore (Cambridge: Polity Press, 1989), 40–55. Camporesi presents a society of nearly starved inhabitants who were narcotically stimulated by hunger, fermented bread, hallucinogenic potions, vampirism, and bloodletting as well as the consumption of dung, dirt, and mind-altering herbs. Arguing that early modern people collectively conjured up fantasies of the supernatural largely through the mind-shaping power of diet, Camporesi discusses belief in the medicinal properties of corpses. My thanks to Gail Paster for pointing out this book to me.

23. Muffet, *Healths Improvement*, 139–40. One translated Italian medical book includes a panacea that calls for a "pound of mans blood of the bodie of a very healthfull and fleshy man" to be distilled with herbs (*The Secrets of Alexis*, 207).

24. Beaumont and Fletcher, *The Nice Valour, or, The Passionate Madman* in *The Works of Mr. Francis Beaumont and Mr. John Fletcher*, Vol. X: 326. For other references to mummia, see Ben Jonson, *Volpone*, ed. Philip Brockbank (NY: W.W. Norton New Mermaids Series, 1992), 4.4.14; and John Webster, *The White Devil* in *John Webster: Three Plays* (NY: Penguin Books, 1986), 1.1.16.

25. Shirley, *The Ball* (1632), 4.1.204, 209–10.

26. Sawday, *The Body Emblazoned*, 54–66.

27. On burial practices, see Vanessa Harding, "'And one more may be laid there': The Location of Burials in Early Modern London," *The London Journal* 14 (1989): 112–29; Katherine Parks, "The Criminal and the Saintly Body: Autopsy and Dissection in Renaissance Italy," *Renaissance Quarterly* 42 (1994): 1–33; and David Cressy, *Birth, Marriage & Death: Ritual, Religion, and the Life-Cycle in Tudor and Stuart England* (Oxford University Press, 1997), 465–7.

28. On *memento mori* tradition, see Roland Mushat Frye, "Ladies, Gentlemen, and Skulls: Hamlet and the Iconographical Traditions," *Shakespeare Quarterly* 30 (1979): 15–28; and Marjorie Garber, "'Remember Me': Memento Mori Figures in Shakespeare's Plays," *Renaissance Drama* 12 (1981): 3–25.

29. Ben Jonson, "The Metamorphosed Gypsies," in *Ben Jonson*, ed. Herford, Simpson, and Simpson, Vol. VII: 602.

30. Thomas Dekker, William Haughton, and Henry Chettle, *The Pleasant Comedie of Patient Grissill* (1603), I1ʳ.

31. Thomas Dekker, *Honest Whore*, Pt. *1* in *The Dramatic Works of Thomas Dekker*, Vol. II:107.

32. Criticism on early modern witchcraft is too extensive to cite; and I keep my commentary on *Macbeth* brief since it has received ample critical attention. On domesticity's link to witchcraft, see Dolan, *Dangerous Familiars*, 171–236; Adelman, *Suffocating Mothers*, 130–47; and Deborah Willis, *Malevolent Nurture: Witch-Hunting and Maternal Power in Early Modern England* (Ithaca: Cornell University Press, 1995).

33. Fletcher, *The Elder Brother* in *The Dramatic Works in The Beaumont and Fletcher Canon*, ed. Fredson Bowers, 9 vols. (Cambridge University Press, 1994), Vol. IX: 3.3.1–14.

34. Laplanche and Pontalis, *Language of Psycho-Analysis*, 211.

35. Heywood, *A Woman Killed with Kindness*, ed. Brian Scobie (NY: W.W. Norton New Mermaids Series, 1985), 4.85–7. I cite this play by scene and line number.

36. Orlin, *Private Matters*, esp. 137–81; Burnett, *Masters and Servants*, 4–5, 8–9. See Walter Darell's *A Short Discourse of the Life of Serving-men* (1578) for a lament on the decay of feudal liberality caused by the emergent contract-based system of service turning on mobile, lower-class wage earners.

37. Gataker, *Good Wife*, 9, who draws from Matthew 4:10. The "one flesh" marital conceit is elaborated by Perkins, *Christian Oeconomie*, 10; and Dod and Cleaver, *A Godly Forme of Houshold Government*, F8ᵛ.

38. Alexandra Halasz notes of the play, "One body substitutes for another, body parts circulate, are incorporated, expelled, cannibalized, self-cannibalized." "Servants and the Circulation of Gentlemen," unpublished paper, *Shakespeare Association of America*, 1998.

39. Joseph Litvak, *Strange Gourmets: Sophistication, Theory and the Novel* (Durham: Duke University Press, 1997).

40. Whately, *The Bride Bush*, B2ʳ.

41. Thomas Fosset, *The Servants Dutie* (1613), B7ᵛ.

42. Gouge, *Of Domesticall Duties*, 604.

43. The term "servant" could apply to people at many points on the social spectrum – stablehands, chambermaids, apprentices, waiting women, stewards, housekeepers, scullery maids, companions, and noble secretaries. Most servants were unmarried persons who didn't distinguish themselves as a class but instead saw themselves moving through a transitional stage on the road to adulthood. As such, their central identification was as household "dependant."

44. In *Arden of Faversham* (ed. Martin White [NY: W.W. Norton New Mermaid Series, 1990]) and *A Warning for Fair Women* (ed. Charles Dale Cannon [The Hague and Paris: Mouton, 1975]), servants along with women mastermind the plays' central criminal activities, and they call upon their privileged information about the master's schedule and access to household materials in planning homicides.

45. To "dress" someone is to treat him or her "properly," meaning (ironically) with deserved severity, hence, to give a thrashing, chastise, reprimand (*OED* I.9). "To dress" also means "to prepare for use as food, by making ready to cook" (*OED*

II.13.a). Both definitions stem from the meaning "to prepare or set straight" (Old French "dresser," "drecier," or "drescer," deriving from the Latin "directiare").

46. Burnett remarks that the male servant "proved a convenient vehicle for testing the stability of early modern social formations" (*Masters and Servants*, 93). On service relations generally, see Burnett, *Masters and Servants*, 156–7; Dolan, *Dangerous Familiars*, esp. 66–7; Ann Kussmaul, *Servants in Husbandry in Early Modern England* (Cambridge University Press, 1981), and Ben-Amos, *Adolescence and Youth*.

47. See Jonson, *Volpone*, ed. Brockbank, 1.5. 8–9.

48. As Kathleen McLuskie notes, Geraldine's secret betrothal to the Wife had already made him heir to the estate but her death allows him to bypass the "dubious undertaking" of marriage to become beneficiary by permission of the father/husband. McLuskie, *Dekker and Heywood: Professional Dramatists* (Basingstoke and London: St. Martin's Press, 1994), 158.

49. On homoeroticism as an element in domestic contestations of power, see Mario DiGangi, *The Homoerotics of Early Modern Drama*, 64–99.

50. Orlin writes of *English Traveller*: "the aim of this text is its arduous reclamation of the domestic sphere from the intrusive female" (*Private Matters*, 252). But Orlin contextualizes this move by demonstrating that the newly reconfigured all-male household is one that must finesse economic discrepancies between the "old orders of patriarchy and privilege" and the new forces of commodification (267). She attributes the masculine ethos of domestic tragedy to the inevitable "feminization" that the householder undergoes in a fluid market economy.

51. For a list of non-extant plays that document the popularity of this tradition, see Andrew Clark, "An Annotated List of Lost Domestic Plays, 1578–1624," *Research Opportunities in Renaissance Drama* 18 (1975): 29–44.

52. Philip Sidney, *The Defense of Poesie*, 1595, E4$^{r-v}$. Sidney's differentiation between "grand" subjects of tragedy and "common" subjects of comedy was conventional. On definitions of domestic tragedy, see Orlin, *Private Matters*, 75; Henry Hitch Adams, *English Domestic, or Homiletic Tragedy 1575–1642* (NY: Columbia University Press, 1943); Andrew Clark, *Domestic Drama: A Survey of the Origins, Antecedents, and Nature of the Domestic Play in England, 1500–1640* (Salzburg: Institut für Englische Sprache und Literatur, Universität, 1975); and Chilton Latham Powell, *English Domestic Relations, 1487–1653* (NY: Columbia University Press, 1917).

53. On domestic violence in the period, see Gowing, *Domestic Dangers*, 206–31; Dolan, *Dangerous Familiars*.

54. Building on important critical work done by Orlin, Dolan, and Ann Christensen, I consider how Heywood presents a domestic discord that cannot be restricted to the murderous fantasies of wives or husbands. Christensen reads *A Woman Killed* as negotiating changes in the household economy and concepts of vocation ("Business, Pleasure and the Domestic Economy in Heywood's *A Woman Killed with Kindness*," *Exemplaria* 9 [1997]: 315–40). In *Domestic Familiars*, Dolan maps the evolution of the discourse of domestic violence, locating a shift from stories of husband-murder at the beginning of the century to tales of the husband's petty tyranny after the civil war. Dolan's interest is in showing how plays offer criminalized but nevertheless intelligible subject positions for household subordinates. Attending to the materiality of the early modern household, Orlin reads domestic drama as part of her analysis of the conjoined emergence of privacy and property.

55. See Nancy Gutierrez, "The Irresolution of Melodrama: The Meaning of Adultery in *A Woman Killed with Kindness*," *Exemplaria* 1 (1989): 265–91; Laura Bromley, "Domestic Conduct in *A Woman Killed with Kindness*," *SEL* 26 (1986): 259–76; Leanore Lieblein, "The Context of Murder in English Domestic Plays, 1590–1610," *SEL* 23 (1983): 181–96; McLuskie, "'Tis But a Woman's Jar': Family and Kinship in Elizabethan Domestic Drama," *Literature and History* 9 (1983): 228–39; and Dolan, "Gender, Moral Agency, and Dramatic Form in *A Warning for Fair Women*," *SEL* 29 (1989): 201–18.

56. Rebecca Ann Bach, "The Homosocial Imaginary of *A Woman Killed with Kindness*," *Textual Practice* 12:3 (1998): 503–24. Bach provocatively suggests that there is no domesticity in domestic tragedies at all, if we mean by "domestic" a nuclear family built on a privileged and privatized heterosexual relationship. Instead, as she argues for *Woman Killed*, the "homosocial imaginary" structures household life. Bach positions the play to expose how inadequate modern terminology is for describing early modern domesticity. I want to extend and refine her analysis of male bonds by showing that master–servant relationships conflict with aristocratic kinship networks, that is, that the homosocial imaginary is itself fraught.

57. Perkins, *Christian Oeconomie*, ¶2v, ¶2$^r$.

58. Jonson, *Neptune's Triumph for the Return of Albion*, in *Ben Jonson*, Vol. VII: 682, 687.

59. On the term "queer," see my introduction, note 27. Geraldine's unruly and eroticized place in the household – as married to both mistress and master – is an example of a "queer" domestic subject position. But since the play also suggests that Geraldine's role in the household is the logical extreme of orthodox prescription, it shows that early modern proper domestic roles slide into potentially disruptive deviance.

60. *A Warning for Fair Women*, ed. Cannon, 95–7.

61. *Arden of Faversham* similarly concludes with Franklin's argument for the unadorned truth of "this naked tragedy"; for, he states, "simple truth is gracious enough." *Arden of Faversham*, ed. White, Epilogue, 14, 17.

62. There has been a lively debate about *Woman Killed*'s vaunted "realism." Lisa Hopkins argues that the play presents only a faux "slice of life," since its seemingly shapeless events of everyday experience in fact are marshaled to fulfill symbolic ends ("The False Domesticity of *A Woman Killed with Kindness*," *Connotations* 4 [1994–95]: 1–7). But Hopkins relies on the questionable binary of realistic as opposed to symbolic modes, as Diane Henderson notes (Henderson, "*A Woman Killed with Kindness* and Domesticity, False or True: A Response to Lisa Hopkins*," *Connotations* 5 [1995–96]: 49–54). Given that post–structuralism has tutored scholars to be suspicious of a clear opposition between journalism and fiction, allegory and realism, mimesis and artifice, these terms might productively be seen as interdependent and relational. Gutierrez, for instance, looks at the symbiosis of "realistic representation and emblematic meaning"; and Adams reads domestic tragedies both in terms of their homiletic impulse and their anticipation of theatrical realism. More recently this issue has been taken up by McLuskie, "'Tis But a Woman's Jar'"; and Catherine Belsey, *The Subject of Tragedy*.

63. McLuskie notes the "physical details of the settings of these plays [domestic drama] contrive to place them in a clearly identified and authentic social milieu which often corroborates the findings of modern social history" (231).

# Bibliography

EARLY MODERN WORKS

Anton, Robert. *The Philosophers Satyrs*. London, 1616.

*Arden of Faversham* (1592) rpt. ed. Martin White. New York: W. W. Norton New Mermaids Series, 1990.

Ascham, Roger. *The Schoolmaster* (1571) rpt. ed. Lawrence V. Ryan. Ithaca: Cornell University Press for the Folger Shakespeare Library, 1967.

B. M., *The Ladies Cabinet Enlarged and Opened, Containing Many Rare Secrets and Rich Ornaments, of several kindes and different uses*. London, 1655.

Barry, Lording. *Ram-Alley*. London, 1611.

Bateman, Steven. *A Crystal Glass of Christian Reformation*. London, 1569.

Beaumont, Francis. *The Knight of the Burning Pestle* (1613) rpt. ed. Michael Hattaway. New York: Norton New Mermaids Series, 1969.

and John Fletcher. *The Works of Mr. Francis Beaumont and Mr. John Fletcher*. 10 vols. London: J. and R. Tonson and S. Draper, 1750.

Becon, Thomas. *Golden Book of Matrimony*. London, 1564.

Borlase, Lady. *Ladie Borlase's Receiptes Booke*, ed. David E. Schoonover. Iowa City: University of Iowa Press, 1998.

Brathwait, Richard. *The English Gentlewoman*. London, 1631.

*The Whimzies, or a New Cast of Characters*. London, 1631.

Breton, Nicholas. *The Woorkes of a Young Wit*. London, 1577.

*The Works in Verse and Prose of Nicholas Breton*, ed. Alexander B. Grosart, 2 vols. Edinburgh: A. Constable, 1879.

Bright, Timothy. *A Treatise Wherein is declared the sufficiencie of English Medicines*. London, 1580.

Burton, Robert. *Anatomy of Melancholy*. London, 1624.

Campion, Thomas. *The Works of Thomas Campion*, ed. Walter R. Davis. Garden City, New York: Doubleday and Co., 1967.

Carter, Charles. *The Complete Practical Cook*. London, 1730.

Cartwright, William. *The Plays and Poems of William Cartwright*, ed. G. Blakemore Evans. Madison: University of Wisconsin Press, 1951.

Chamberlayne, Edward. *The Second Part of the Present State of England*. London, 1682.

Churchyard, Thomas. *A Handeful of Gladsome Verses, given to the Queenes Maiesty at Woodstocke this Prograce*. Oxford, 1592.

Clifford, Anne. *The Diaries of Lady Anne Clifford*, ed. D. J. H. Clifford. Wolfeboro Falls, NH: Alan Sutton Publishing Ltd., 1990.

A *Closet for Ladies and Gentlewomen, or, The Art of Preseruing, Conseruing, and Candying.* London, 1608; rpt. 1635.

Cooke, John. *Greenes Tu quoque or The Cittie Gallant.* London, 1614.

Cotta, John. *A Short Discouerie of the Unobserved Dangers of Several Sorts of Ignorant and Unconsiderate Practisers of Physicke in England.* London, 1612.

Coverdale, Miles. *Goostly Psalmes and Spirituall Songes.* London, 1635.

Crowne, John. *The Married Beau.* London, 1694.

Darell, Walter. *A Short Discourse of the Life of Serving-men.* London, 1578.

Davenant, William. *Unfortunate Lovers.* London, 1643.

Dawson, Thomas. *The Good Huswifes Jewell. Wherein is to be found most excellent and rare Devises, for conceites in Cookery.* London, 1585; rpt. 1596 and 1597.

*The Second Part of the Good Huswifes Jewell.* London, 1597.

Day, John. *Isle of Guls* (1606) rpt. ed. and introduction by Raymond S. Burns. New York: Garland Publishing Co., 1980.

Dekker, Thomas. *The Shoemaker's Holiday* (1600) rpt. ed. Anthony Parr. London: A.C. Black and New York: Norton, 1990.

—— and Thomas Middleton. *The Honest Whore, Pt. I* (1604) rpt. *The Dramatic Works of Thomas Dekker*, ed. Fredson Bowers, 4 vols. Cambridge University Press, 1955, Vol. II.

—— and William Haughton and Henry Chettle. *The Pleasant Comedie of Patient Grissill.* London, 1603.

—— and John Webster. *Westward Ho* (1607) rpt. *The Dramatic Works of Thomas Dekker*, ed. Fredson Bowers, 4 vols. Cambridge University Press, 1955, Vol. II.

Deloney, Thomas. *The Gentle Craft. The Novels of Thomas Deloney*, ed. Merritt E. Lawlis. Indiana University Press, 1961.

Dickinson, Francis. *A Pretious Treasury of Twenty Rare Secrets.* London, 1649.

Digby, Kenelme. *The Closet of Eminently Learned Sir Kenelme Digby Kt. Opened* (1669) rpt. *The Closet of Sir Kenelme Digby Opened*, ed. Anne MacDonnell. London: Philip Lee Warner, 1910.

Digges, Dudley. *The Unlawfulnesse of Subjects.* London, 1643.

Dod, John and John Cleaver. *A Godly Forme of Houshold Government.* London, 1630.

D[owe], B[artholomew]. *A Dairie Booke for Good Huswives.* London, 1588.

Drayton, Michael. *Minor Poems of Michael Drayton*, ed. Cyril Brett. Oxford: Clarendon Press, 1907.

Dunton, John. *Voyage Round the World.* London, 1691.

Elyot, Thomas. *The Book named The Governor* (1531) rpt. ed. S. E. Lehmberg. London: Dent, Everyman's Library, 1962.

*The Castel of Health.* London, 1541.

*The Englishmans Doctor or the School of Salerne.* Trans. John Harington. London, 1608; rpt. 1617.

*Epulario, or The Italian Banquet.* London, 1598.

Erasmus, Desiderus. *A Devout Treatise Upon the Pater Noster.* Trans. Margaret Roper. Introduction by Richard Hyrde. London, *c.* 1526.

*De Pueris statim ac liberaliter instituendis* (1529) in William Harrison Woodward, *Desiderius Erasmus Concerning the Aim and Method of Education.* New York: Columbia University Press, 1964.

Fettiplace, Elinor. *Elinor Fettiplace's Receipt Book.* In Hilary Spurling, *Elizabethan Country House Cooking.* London: Viking Salamander, 1986.

Filmer, Richard. *Patriarcha, or the Natural Power of Kings.* London, 1680.

Fioravanti, Leonardo. *A Compendium of the rationall Secrets of ... Leonardo Phioravante Bolognese.* Trans. J. Hester. London, 1582.

Fitzherbert, John. *The Boke of Husbandry.* London, 1523, rpt. 1534. Rpt. ed. Walter W. Skeat. London: Trubner & Co. for the English Dialect Society, 1882.

*Fitzharberts Booke of Husbandrie.* London, 1598.

Fletcher, John. *The Elder Brother* (1637) rpt. *The Dramatic Works in The Beaumont and Fletcher Canon,* ed. Fredson Bowers, 9 vols. Cambridge University Press, 1994, Vol. IX.

*The Night Walker.* London, 1649.

Ford, John. *Loves Sacrifice.* London, 1633.

*The Fancies Chaste and Noble.* London, 1638.

Fosset, Thomas. *The Servants Dutie.* London, 1613.

G., W. *A True Gentlewomans Delight, wherein is contained all manner of cookery. Together with preserving, conserving, drying and candying. Very necessarie for all ladies and Gentlewomen.* London, 1661; rpt. 1682.

Gainford, Thomas. *The Rich Cabinet.* London, 1616.

*Gammer Gurton's Needle* (1575) rpt. In *Three Sixteenth-Century Comedies,* ed. Charles Walters Whitworth. New York: W.W. Norton and Co., 1984.

Gardiner, Richard. *Profitable instructions for the manuring, sowing and planting of kitchin gardens.* London, 1599.

Gataker, Thomas. *A Good Wife Gods Gift.* London, 1623.

*The Gentlewomans Companion. Or, a Guide to the Female Sex.* London, 1673 [attributed to Woolley].

*A Gentlewomans Delight.* London, 1682.

*The Good Huswifes Handmaide for the Kitchin. Containing Manie principall pointes of Cookerie, as well how to dresse meates, after sundrie of the best fashions used in England and other Countries, with their apt and proper sawces, both for flesh and fish, as also the orderly serving of the same to the table.* London, 1594.

Googe, Barnabe. *The Whole Art and Trade of Husbandry.* London, 1614.

Gouge, William. *Of Domesticall Duties.* London, 1622.

Greene, Robert. *Friar Bacon and Friar Bungay* (1594) rpt. ed. Daniel Seltzer. Lincoln: University of Nebraska Press, 1963.

*The Scottish History of James the Fourth* (1598) rpt. ed. J. A. Lavin. London: Ernest Benn Ltd., 1967.

and Thomas Lodge. *A Looking Glasse for London and England.* London, 1598.

Grey, Elizabeth (Countess of Kent). *A Choice Manual, or Rare and Select Secrets in Physick and Chyrurgery: Collected, and practised by the Right Honourable, the Countess of Kent, late deceased.* London, 1653; rpt. 1655, 1661, 1682.

*Grim the Collier of Croydon; OR The Devil and his Dame* (1662) fac. rpt. Amersham, England: Old English Drama Students' Facsimile, 1912.

Guazzo, Steven. *The Civile Conversation of M. Steeven Guazzo.* Trans. George Pettie (1581); rpt. 2 vols. London: Constable and Co. Ltd., 1925.

Guibert, Philbert. *The Charitable Physitian.* Trans. I.W. London, 1639.

Guillimeau, James. *Child-birth, or, The Happy Deliverie of Women.* London, 1612; rpt. 1635.

H., J. *The Family-Dictionary; Or Houshold Companion.* London, 1695.

Hannay, Patrick. *The Poeticall Works of Patrick Hannay.* Glasgow: Hunterian Club Publication Vol. XIV, 1875.

Harrison, William. *The Description of England*, ed. Georges Edelen. Washington DC: Folger Shakespeare Library, 1968; rpt. 1994.

Hartman, George. *The Family Physitian.* London, 1696.

Haughton, William. *Englishmen for My Money* (1616) rpt. Oxford University Press for the Malone Society, 1912.

Hawkins, William. *Apollo Shroving.* London, 1627.

Head, Richard. *The English Rogue* (1665) rpt. ed. Michael Shinagel. Boston: New Frontiers Press, 1961.

Henslowe, Philip. *Henslowe's Diary*, ed. R. A. Foakes and R. T. Rickert. Cambridge University Press, 1961.

Heresbach, Conrad. *The Whole Art and Trade of Husbandry.* Trans. and ed. Barnabe Googe. London, 1614.

Herrick, Robert. *The Poetical Works of Robert Herrick*, ed. L. C. Martin. Oxford: Clarendon Press, 1956.

Heywood, Thomas. *An Apology for Actors* (1612) rpt. Shakespeare Society Publications III. London, 1841.

*The Dramatic Works of Thomas Heywood*, 6 vols. London, John Pearson, 1874.

*The Hierarchie of the Blessed Angels.* London, 1635.

*A Pleasant conceited Comedie, wherein is shewed, how a man may choose a good wife from a bad.* London, 1602.

*A Woman Killed with Kindness* (1607) rpt. ed. Brian Scobie. New York: W.W. Norton New Mermaids Series, 1985.

Hoby, Margaret. *Diary of Lady Margaret Hoby, 1599–1605*, ed. Dorothy M. Meads. Boston and New York: Houghton Mifflin Co., 1930.

Hozyusz, Stanislaus. *A Most Excellent Treatise of the Begynnyng of Heresyes in Oure Tyme.* Antwerp, 1565.

Johnson, John. *Academy of Love.* London, 1641.

Jonson, Ben. *Ben Jonson*, ed. C. H. Herford and Percy and Evelyn Simpson, 11 vols. Oxford: Clarendon Press, 1925–52.

*The Devil is an Ass.* London, 1640.

*Volpone* (1605) rpt. ed. Philip Brockbank. New York: W.W. Norton New Mermaids Series, 1992.

Joubert, Laurent. *Popular Errors.* Trans. Gregory de Rocher. Tuscaloosa: The University of Alabama Press, 1989.

K., T. *The Kitchin Physitian, or, A guide for good-housewives in maintaining their families in health.* London, 1680.

Knevet, Ralph. *Rhodon and Iris.* London, 1631.

Kyd, Thomas. *The Works of Thomas Kyd*, ed. Frederick S. Boas. Oxford: Clarendon Press, 1901.

Lamb, Patrick. *Royal Cookery or the Complete Court Cook.* London, 1710.

*Lingua, or the Combat of the Tongue* (1607) rpt. Amersham, England: Old English Drama Students' Facsimiles issued by John S. Farmer, 1913.

Lodge, Thomas. *Phillis.* London, 1593.

and Robert Greene, *A Looking Glasse for London and England* (1594) rpt. ed. George Alan Clugston. New York and London: Garland, 1980.

Lyly, John. *The Complete Works of John Lyly*, ed. R. W. Bond, 3 vols. Oxford: Clarendon Press, 1902.

M., I. *A Health to the Gentlemanly Profession of Servingmen*. London, 1598.

M., W. *The Queens Closet Opened*. London, 1655; rpt. 1658.

Malynes, Gerrard de. *The Canker of England's Commonwealth*. London, 1601, ctd. in *Tudor Economic Documents*, ed. R.H. Tawney and Eileen Power. London: Longmans, Green & Co., 1924.

Manuche, Cosmo. *The Loyal Lovers*. London, 1652.

Markham, Gervase. *Cheap and Good Husbandry*. London, 1623.

    *The English House-wife*. London, 1631. Rpt. from *The English Hus-wife*. In *Countrey Contentments*. London, 1615.

    *The English Housewife*, ed. Michael Best. Kingston and Montreal: McGill-Queen's University Press, 1986.

    *The English Husbandman*. London, 1613.

    *Maison Rustique, Or, The Countrey Farme*. London, 1616.

    *The Whole Art of Husbandry*. London, 1631.

Marston, John. *The Works of John Marston*, ed. Arthur H. Bullen, 5 vols. London: John C. Nimmo, 1887.

Massinger, Philip. *The Poems and Plays of Philip Massinger*. Oxford: Clarendon Press, 1976.

May, Robert. *The Accomplisht Cook, or the Art & Mystery of Cookery*. London, 1685.

*The Maydes Metamorphosis*. London, 1600.

Maynwaringe, Everard. *The Efficacy and Extent of True Purgation . . . Distinguished from Promiscuous Evacuations; injuriously procured, and falsely reported Purging*. London, 1696.

Middleton, Thomas. *Five Plays*. London: Penguin Books, 1988.

Misselde, E. *Free Trade, or The Means to Make Trade Flourish*. London, 1622.

Mocket, Richard. *God and the King*. London, 1615.

Muffet, Thomas. *Health's Improvement: OR, Rules Comprizing and Discovering the Nature, Method, and Manner of Preparing all sort of Food used in this Nation*. London, 1584; rpt. 1655.

Mulcaster, Richard. *Mulcaster's Elementarie* (1582) rpt. ed. E. T. Campagnac. Oxford: Clarendon Press, 1925.

    *Positions* (1581) abgd., ed. Richard L. DeMolen. New York: Columbia Teacher's College Press, 1971.

Munday, Anthony. *A Critical Edition of Anthony Munday's Fedele and Fortunio*, ed. Richard Hosley. New York: Garland Publishers, 1981.

    *Pageants and Entertainments of Anthony Munday*, ed. David M. Bergeron. New York: Garland, 1985.

Murrell, John. *A Daily Exercise for Ladies and Gentlewomen. Whereby they may learne and practise the whole Art of making Pastes, Preserves, Marmalades, Conserves, Tarstuffes, Gellies, Breads, Sucket candies, Cordiall waters, Conceits in Sugarworkes of severall kindes*. London, 1617.

    *Murrells Two Books of Cookerie and Carving*. London, 1638.

    *A New Booke of Cookerie;Wherein is set forth the newest and most commendable Fashion for Dressing or Sowcing, eyther Flesh, Fish or Fowle. Together with making of all sorts of Jellyes, and other made-Dishes for service, both to beautifie and adorne eyther Nobleman or Gentlemans Table*. London, 1615.

Nashe, Thomas. *The Works of Thomas Nashe*, ed. R. B. McKerrow, 5 vols. London: A.H. Bullen, Vols. I–II, Sidgwick and Jackson, Vols. III–V, 1904–1910.

Newcome, Henry. *The Compleat Mother.* London, 1695.

Overbury, Sir Thomas. *The Miscellaneous Works in Prose and Verse of Sir Thomas Overbury, Knt.*, ed. Edward F. Rimbault. London: Reeves and Turner, 1890.

Partridge, John. *The Treasurie of Commodious Conceites & Hidden Secrets. and may be called, The Huswives Closet, of Healthful Provision.* London, 1573; rpt. 1584.

*The Treasurie of Hidden Secrets, Commonlie called, The Good-huswives Closet of Provision . . . Not impertinent for every good Huswife to use in her house, amongst her own familie.* London 1600 rpt. 1627.

Pepys, Samuel. *The Diary of Samuel Pepys. A New and Complete Transcription*, ed. Robert Latham and William Matthews. 11 vols. Berkeley: University of California Press, 1970–83.

Perkins, William. *Christian Oeconomie: Or, A Short Survey of the Right Manner of Erecting and Ordering a Familie.* London, 1609.

*The Workes of That Famous and Worthy Minister of Christ in the University of Cambridge, Mr. William Perkins*, 3 vols. London, 1612.

Phaire, Thomas. *The Boke of Chyldren* (1545) rpt. Edinburgh and London: E. & S. Livingstone Ltd., 1957.

Plat, Hugh. *Delightes for Ladies, to Adorne their Persons, Tables, Closets, and Distillatories: With Beauties, Banquets, Perfumes, & Waters.* London, 1602.

*The Jewell House of Art and Nature: Containing Divers Rare and Profitable Inventions.* London, 1594.

*A Pleasant Comedie, Called The Two Merry Milke-Maids.* London, 1620.

Powell, Thomas. *Tom of All Trades, Or The Pathway to Preferement.* London, 1631.

Puttenham, George. *The Arte of English Poesie* (1589) fac. Kent, OH: Kent State University Press, 1988.

Rabisha, William. *The Whole Body of Cookery Dissected, Taught and fully manifested.* London, 1673.

Rich, Barnabe. *The Excellency of Good Women.* London, 1613.

*Robin Good-fellow his mad prankes, and merry iests.* London, 1628.

Robotham, John. *Janua Linguarum Reserata.* London, 1643.

Rowlands, Samuel. *More Knaues Yet.* London, 1613.

Salter, Thomas. *The Mirror of Modesty.* London, 1578.

Scot, Reginald. *The Discoverie of Witchcraft* (1584) rpt. Carbondale: Southern Illinois University Press, 1964.

*The Secrets of Alexis: Containing Many Excellent Remedies against divers Diseases, wounds, and other Accidents.* London, 1615.

Shakespeare, William. *A Most pleasaunt and excellent conceited Comedie, of Syr John Falstaffe, and the merrie Wives of Windsor.* London, 1602.

*The Riverside Shakespeare.* Boston, MA: Houghton Mifflin Co., 1974.

Shirley, James. *The Ball.* London, 1632.

*The Humorous Courtier.* London, 1640.

*The Polititian.* London, 1655.

Sidney, Philip. *The Defense of Poesie.* London, 1595.

*The Poems of Sir Philip Sidney*, ed. William A. Ringler. Oxford: Clarendon Press, 1961.

*Sir Philip Sidney: Selected Poems*, ed. Katherine Duncan-Jones. Oxford: Clarendon Press, 1973.

Smith, Eliza. *The Compleat Housewife*. London, 1727.

Smith, Henry. *A Preparative to Marriage*. London, 1591.

Smith, Robert. *Court Cookery*. London, 1723.

Spenser, Edmund. *A View of the Present State of Ireland*, (c. 1596) rpt. ed. W. L. Renwick London: Eric Partridge, 1934.

*The Yale Edition of the Shorter Poems of Edmund Spenser*, ed. William Oram, Einar Bjorvand, Ronald Bond, Thomas H. Cain, Alexander Dunlop, and Richard Schell. New Haven, CT: Yale University Press, 1989.

Stow, John. *A Survey of the cities of London and Westminster*. London, 1580.

Surflet, Richard. *The Countrie Farme*. London, 1600.

Tarlton, Richard. *Tarltons Newes out of Purgatory*. London, 1630.

Tasso, Toquato. *The Householders Philosophie*. London, 1588.

Taylor, John. *All the Workes of John Taylor The Water Poet Collected into one Volume by the Author*. London, 1630.

*The Needle's Excellency* (1640) rpt. *The Works of John Taylor*. Manchester: Charles Simms for the Spenser Society, 1870.

*This is the Boke of Cokery*. London, 1500.

Tryon, Thomas. *The Good Housewife Made a Doctor, Or Health's choice and sure friend: Being a Plain Way of Nature's own prescribing, to Prevent & Cure Most Diseases incident to men, women and Children, by Diet and Kitchin-Physick only*. London, 1685.

Turner, William. *A new Herball*. London, 1551.

Tusser, Thomas, *Fiue Hundreth Points of Good Husbandry*. London 1573; rpt. 1580. Rpt. *Five Hundred Points of Good Husbandry*. Oxford University Press, 1984.

*A Hundreth Good Pointes of Husbandrie*. London, 1557.

Udall, Nicholas. *Ralph Roister Doister*. In *Three Sixteenth-Century Comedies*, ed. Charles W. Whitworth. New York: W. W. Norton, 1984.

Vives, Juan Luis. *A Fruteful and pleasant boke called the Instruction of Christen Woman*. London, 1529; rpt. 1557.

*A Warning for Fair Women* (1599) rpt. ed. Charles Dale Cannon. The Hague and Paris: Mouton, 1975.

Warton, Thomas. *The History of English Poetry*, 3 vols. London: Thomas Tegg, 1840, Vol. III.

Webster, John. *The Duchess of Malfi* (1623) rpt. ed. Elizabeth M. Brennan. New York: Norton New Mermaids Series, 1990.

*John Webster: Three Plays*. New York: Penguin Books, 1986.

Whately, William. *The Bride Bush, Or Direction for Married Persons*. London, 1619.

*The Whole Duty of a Woman: Or a Guide to the Female Sex*. London, 1707.

*The Widdowes Treasure, Plentifully furnished with sundry precious and approved secrets in Phisicke*. London, 1595.

Wilson, Thomas. *The Art of Rhetoric* (1553) rpt. ed. G.H. Mair. Oxford: Clarendon Press, 1909.

Woolley, Hannah. *The Accomplisht Ladys Delight in Preserving, Physick, Beautifying and Cookery*. London, 1675.

*The Compleat Servant-Maid, or the Young Maidens Tutor. Directing them how they may fit, and qualifie themselves for any of these Employments. Viz.*

*Waiting Women, House-keeper, Chamber-Maid, Cook-Maid, Under Cook-Maid, Nursery-Maid, Dairy-Maid, Laundry-Maid, House-Maid, Scullery-Maid.* London, 1683.

*The Queen-like Closet, or Rich Cabinet: Stored with all Manner of Rare Receipts for Preserving, Candying and Cookery.* Bound with *A Supplement to the Queen-like Closet; or A Little of Every Thing. Presented to All Ingenious Ladies and Gentlewomen.* London, 1675.

Yonger, William. *The Nurses Bosome. A Sermon Within the Greene-Yard in Norwich.* London, 1616.


CRITICAL WORKS

Adams, Henry Hitch. *English Domestic, or Homiletic Tragedy 1575–1642.* New York: Columbia University Press, 1943.

Adelman, Janet. *Suffocating Mothers: Fantasies of Maternal Origin in Shakespeare's Plays, "Hamlet" to "The Tempest."* New York: Routledge, 1992.

Anderson, Benedict. *Imagined Communities: Reflections on the Origins and Spread of Nationalism.* London: Verso, 1983.

Amussen, Susan. *An Ordered Society: Gender and Class in Early Modern England.* New York: Columbia University Press, 1988.

Archer, Ian W. *The Pursuit of Stability: Social Relations in Elizabethan London.* Cambridge University Press, 1991.

Armstrong, Nancy. *Desire and Domestic Fiction: A Political History of the Novel.* London: Oxford University Press, 1987.

and Leonard Tennenhouse, eds. *The Ideology of Conduct: Essays in Literature and the History of Sexuality.* New York: Methuen, 1987.

Axton, Marie. *The Queen's Two Bodies: Drama and the Elizabethan Succession.* London: Royal Historical Society, 1977.

Bach, Rebecca Ann. "The Homosocial Imaginary of *A Woman Killed with Kindness.*" *Textual Practice* 12:3 (1998): 503–24.

Bailey, Richard W. *Images of English: A Cultural History of the Language.* Ann Arbor: University of Michigan Press, 1991.

Barber, C. L. *Shakespeare's Festive Comedy: A Study of Dramatic Form and its Relation to Social Custom.* Princeton, NJ: Princeton University Press, 1959.

Barkan, Leonard. *Nature's Work of Art: The Human Body as Image of the World.* New Haven, CT: Yale University Press, 1975.

Bartels, Emily. "Strategies of Submission: Desdemona, the Duchess, and the Assertion of Desire." *Studies in English Literature* 36 (1996): 417–33.

Beier, Lucinda McCray. *Sufferers and Healers: The Experience of Illness in Seventeenth-Century England.* New York: Routledge & Kegan Paul, 1987.

Ben-Amos, Ilana Krausman. *Adolescence and Youth in Early Modern England.* New Haven, CT: Yale University Press, 1994.

Bennett, Judith. "Medieval Women, Modern Women: Across the Great Divide." In David Aers (ed.), *Culture and History, 1350–1600: Essays on English Communities, Identities, and Writing.* Detroit: Wayne State University Press, 1992. 146–67.

Berlant, Lauren. *Anatomy of National Fantasy: Hawthorne, Utopia and Everyday Life.* University of Chicago Press, 1991.

Bhabha, Homi K. "Introduction: Narrating the Nation." In Bhabha, ed. *Nation and Narration*. New York: Routledge, 1990. 1–7.

Binns, James W. *Intellectual Culture in Elizabethan and Jacobean England: The Latin Writings of the Age*. Leeds: Francis Cairn Publication, 1990.

Bliss, Lee. *The World's Perspective: John Webster and the Jacobean Drama*. New Brunswick, NJ: Rutgers University Press, 1983.

Boas, Frederick. *University Drama in the Tudor Age*. Oxford: Clarendon Press, 1914.

Boehrer, Bruce. "Bestial Buggery in *A Midsummer Night's Dream*." In David Lee Miller, Sharon O'Dair, and Harold Weber eds. *The Production of English Renaissance Culture*. Ithaca, NY: Cornell University Press, 1994. 123–50.

Bray, Alan. "Homosexuality and the Signs of Male Friendship in Elizabethan England." In Jonathan Goldberg, ed. *Queering the Renaissance*. Durham: Duke University Press, 1994. 40–61.

    *Homosexuality in Renaissance England*, 2nd edn London: Gay Men's Press, 1988.

Bredbeck, Gregory W. *Sodomy and Interpretation: Marlowe to Milton*. Ithaca: Cornell University Press, 1991.

Breitenberg, Mark. *Anxious Masculinity in Early Modern England*. Cambridge University Press, 1996.

Brenkman, John. *Straight Male Modern: A Cultural Critique of Psychoanalysis*. New York: Routledge, 1993.

Brennan, Timothy. "The National Longing for Form." In Homi K. Bhabha, ed., *Nation and Narration*. New York: Routledge, 1990. 44–70.

Briggs, Katharine. *The Anatomy of Puck: An Examination of Fairy Beliefs among Shakespeare's Contemporaries and Successors*. London: Routledge & Kegan Paul, 1959.

Bromley, Laura. "Domestic Conduct in *A Woman Killed with Kindness*." *Studies in English Literature* 26 (1986): 259–76.

Brown, J. Howard. *Elizabethan Schooldays: An Account of the English Grammar Schools in the Second Half of the Sixteenth Century*. Oxford: Basil Blackwell, 1933.

Burke, Peter. *Popular Culture in Early Modern Europe*. London: T. Smith, 1978.

    "The "Discovery" of Popular Culture." In Raphael Samuel, ed., *People's History and Socialist Thought*. London: Routledge & Kegan Paul, 1981. 216–26.

Burnett, Mark Thornton. "Apprentice Literature and the Crisis of the 1590s." *The Yearbook of English Studies* 21 (1991): 27–38.

    *Masters and Servants in English Renaissance Drama and Culture*. London: Macmillan Press, 1997.

Butler, Judith. "Against Proper Objects." *More Gender Trouble: Feminism Meets Queer Theory*, a volume of *Differences* 6 (1994): 1–26.

    *Bodies that Matter: On the Discursive Limits of "Sex."* New York: Routledge, 1993.

Butler, Martin. *Theater and Crisis, 1632–1642*. Cambridge University Press, 1984.

Bynum, Caroline Walker. *Fragmentation and Redemption: Essays on Gender and the Human Body in Medieval Religion*. New York: Zone Books, 1992.

    *Holy Feast and Holy Fast: The Religious Significance of Food to Medieval Women*. Berkeley: University of California Press, 1987.

Cahn, Susan. *Industry of Devotion: The Transformation of Women's Work in England, 1500–1650.* New York: Columbia University Press, 1987.

Camporesi, Piero. *Bread of Dreams: Food and Fantasy in Early Modern Europe.* Trans. David Gentilcore. Cambridge: Polity Press, 1989.

Carroll, William. "'A Received Belief': Imagination in *The Merry Wives of Windsor.*" *Studies in Philology* 74 (1977): 186–215.

Charles, Lindsey, and Lorna Duffin, eds. *Women and Work in Pre-Industrial England.* London: Croom Helm, 1985.

Charlton, Kenneth. *Education in Renaissance England.* London: Routledge & Kegan Paul, 1965.

Chartier, Roger. *The Cultural Uses of Print in Early Modern France.* Trans. Lydia C. Cochrane. Princeton, NJ: Princeton University Press, 1987.

Christensen, Ann. "Business, Pleasure and the Domestic Economy in Heywood's *A Woman Killed with Kindness.*" *Exemplaria* 9 (1997): 315–40.

Clark, Alice. *The Working Life of Women in the Seventeenth Century.* New York: E. P. Dutton & Co., 1919.

Clark, Andrew. "An Annotated List of Lost Domestic Plays, 1578–1624." *Research Opportunities in Renaissance Drama* 18 (1975): 29–44.

*Domestic Drama: A Survey of the Origins, Antecedents, and Nature of the Domestic Play in England, 1500–1640.* Salzburg: Institut für Englische Sprache und Literatur, Universität, 1975.

Crane, Mary Thomas. *Framing Authority: Sayings, Self, and Society in Sixteenth-Century England.* Princeton, NJ: Princeton University Press, 1993.

Cressy, David. *Birth, Marriage & Death: Ritual, Religion, and the Life-Cycle in Tudor and Stuart England.* Oxford University Press, 1997.

*Education in Tudor and Stuart England.* London: Edward Arnold, 1975.

Curtis, Mark H. *Oxford and Cambridge in Transition 1558–1642.* Oxford: Clarendon Press, 1959.

Davies, Kathleen. "The Sacred Condition of Equality – How Original were Puritan Doctrines of Marriage?" *Social History* 5 (1977): 563–81.

Davis, Dorothy. *A History of Shopping.* London: Routledge, 1966.

Davis, Natalie Zemon. "Women in the Crafts in Sixteenth-Century Lyon." In Barbara Hanawalt, ed., *Women and Work in Pre-industrial Europe.* Indiana University Press, 1986. 167–97.

de Certeau, Michel. *The Practice of Everyday Life.* Trans. Steven Randall. Berkeley: University of California Press, 1984.

DiGangi, Mario. *The Homoerotics of Early Modern Drama.* Cambridge University Press, 1997.

"Queering the Shakespearean Family," *Shakespeare Quarterly* 47:3 (1996): 269–90.

Dolan, Frances E. *Dangerous Familiars: Representations of Domestic Crime in England, 1550–1700.* Ithaca: Cornell University Press, 1994.

"Gender, Moral Agency, and Dramatic Form in *A Warning for Fair Women.*" *Studies in English Literature* 29 (1989): 201–18.

Duffy, Maureen. *Erotic World of Faery.* London: Hodder and Stoughton, 1972.

Duncan, Douglas. "*Gammer Gurton's Needle* and the Concept of Human Parody." *Studies in English Literature* 27 (1987): 177–93.

Dunlop, Olive Jocelyn. *English Apprenticeship and Child Labour, a History; with a supplementary section on the modern problem of juvenile labour by O.J. Dunlop and R.D. Denman.* New York: Macmillan, 1912.

Easthope, Antony. *Englishness and National Culture.* New York: Routledge, 1999.

Elias, Norbert. *The Civilizing Process.* Trans. Edmund Jephcott. Oxford: B. Blackwell, 1978–82.

Erickson, Amy Louise. Introduction to Alice Clark, *The Working Life of Women in the Seventeenth Century.* New York: Routledge, 1992.

*Women and Property in Early Modern England.* New York: Routledge, 1993.

Erickson, Peter. "The Order of the Garter, the Cult of Elizabeth, and Class-Gender Tension in *The Merry Wives of Windsor.*" In Jean E. Howard and Marion F. O'Connor, eds., *Shakespeare Reproduced: The Text in History and Ideology.* New York: Methuen, 1987. 116–42.

Ezell, Margaret. *The Patriarch's Wife.* Chapel Hill, NC: University of North Carolina Press, 1987.

Fildes, Valerie. *Breasts, Bottles and Babies.* Edinburgh: Edinburgh University Press, 1986.

Flandrin, Jean-Louis. *Families in Former Times: Kinship, Household, and Sexuality.* Trans. Richard Southern. Cambridge University Press, 1979.

Fleming, Juliet. "Dictionary English and the Female Tongue." In Richard Burt and John Michael Archer, eds., *Enclosure Acts: Sexuality, Property, and Culture in Early Modern England.* Ithaca: Cornell University Press, 1994. 290–325.

*Ladies' Men, the Ladies' Text, and the English Renaissance.* Ph.D. diss., University of Pennsylvania, 1991. Ann Arbor: University of Michigan Microfilms, 1991.

"Memory, Method, and the Female Self in the English Domestic Guide, OR Mistress Duffield's Capon." Paper, The Sixteenth Century Studies Conference, 1990.

Freud, Sigmund. "The Uncanny." *Collected Papers.* Trans. Joan Riviere, 5 vols. London: The Hogarth Press, 1934, Vol. IV. 368–407.

Friedman, Alice T. *House and Household in Elizabethan England: Wollaton Hall and the Willoughby Family.* University of Chicago Press, 1989.

Frye, Northrop. *Anatomy of Criticism: Four Essays.* Princeton, NJ: Princeton University Press, 1957.

Frye, Roland Mushat. "Ladies, Gentlemen, and Skulls: Hamlet and the Iconographical Traditions." *Shakespeare Quarterly* 30 (1979): 15–28.

Frye, Susan. *Elizabeth I: The Competition for Representation.* London: Oxford University Press, 1993.

"Sewing Connections: Elizabeth Tudor, Mary Stuart, Elizabeth Talbot, and the Seventeenth-Century Anonymous Needleworkers." In Susan Frye and Karen Robertson, eds., *Maids and Mistresses, Cousins and Queens.* New York: Oxford University Press, 1999. 165–82.

Fumerton, Patricia. *Cultural Aesthetics: Renaissance Literature and the Practice of Social Ornamentation.* University of Chicago Press, 1991.

"Introduction: A New New Historicism." In Patricia Fumerton and Simon Hunt, eds., *Renaissance Culture and the Everyday.* Philadelphia: University of Pennsylvania Press, 1999. 1–17.

Fuss, Diana. *Identification Papers.* New York: Routledge, 1995.

Fussell, G.E. and K.R. *The English Countrywoman.* London: Andrew Melrose, 1953.

Fussell, K.R. *The Old English Farming Books from Fitzherbert to Tull. 1523–1730.* London: Crosby Lockwood & Son, 1947.

Garber, Marjorie. "'Remember Me': Memento Mori Figures in Shakespeare's Plays." *Renaissance Drama* 12 (1981): 3–25.

Girouard, Mark. *Life in the English Country House: A Social and Architectural History.* New Haven, CT: Yale University Press, 1978.

Goldberg, Jonathan. *Sodometries: Renaissance Texts/Modern Sexualities.* Stanford University Press, 1992.

ed. *Queering the Renaissance.* Durham: Duke University Press, 1994.

Gowing, Laura. *Domestic Dangers: Women, Words and Sex in Early Modern London.* Oxford: Clarendon Press, 1996.

Greg, Walter W. *Pastoral Drama and Pastoral Poetry.* New York: Russell & Russell, 1959.

Gutierrez, Nancy. "The Irresolution of Melodrama: The Meaning of Adultery in *A Woman Killed with Kindness.*" *Exemplaria* 1 (1989): 265–91.

Hadfield, Andrew. *Literature, Politics and National Identity: Reformation to Renaissance.* Cambridge University Press, 1994.

Halasz, Alexandra. "Servants and the Circulation of Gentlemen," unpublished paper, *Shakespeare Association of America*, 1998.

Hall, David. Introduction, in Steven L. Kaplan, ed., *Understanding Popular Culture: Europe from the Middle Ages to the Nineteenth Century.* New York: Mouton Publishers, 1984. 5–18.

Hall, Kim F. "Culinary Spaces, Colonial Spaces: The Gendering of Sugar in the Seventeenth Century." In Valerie Traub, M. Lindsay Kaplan, and Dympna Callaghan, eds., *Feminist Readings of Early Modern Culture: Emerging Subjects.* Cambridge University Press, 1996. 168–190.

Hall, Stuart. "Notes on Deconstructing 'The Popular.'" In Raphael Samuel, ed., *People's History and Socialist Thought.* London: Routledge & Kegan Paul, 1981. 227–41.

Halpern, Richard. *The Poetics of Primitive Accumulation: English Renaissance Culture and the Genealogy of Capital.* Ithaca: Cornell University Press, 1991.

Hamilton, Roberta. *The Liberation of Women.* London: George Allen and Unwin, 1978.

Harbage, Alfred. *Shakespeare and the Rival Traditions.* New York: Macmillan Co., 1952.

Harding, Vanessa. "'And one more may be laid there': The Location of Burials in Early Modern London." *The London Journal* 14 (1989): 112–29.

Harris, Jonathan Gil. *Foreign Bodies and the Body Politic.* Cambridge University Press, 1998.

"Puck/Robin Goodfellow." In Vicki K. Janik, ed., *Fools and Jesters in Literature, Art and History: A Bio-bibliographical Sourcebook.* Westport, CT: Greenwood Press, 1998. 351–62.

Harris, Tim. "The Problem of 'Popular Political Culture' in Seventeenth-Century London." *History of European Ideas* 19 (1989): 43–58.

Helgerson, Richard. "The Buckbasket, the Witch, and the Queen of Fairies: The Women's World of Shakespeare's Windsor." In Patricia Fumerton and Simon Hunt, eds., *Renaissance Culture and the Everyday.* Philadelphia: University of Pennsylvania Press, 1999. 162–82.

*Forms of Nationhood: The Elizabethan Writing of England.* University of Chicago Press, 1992.

*Self-Crowned Laureates: Spenser, Jonson, Milton and the Literary System.* Berkeley: University of California Press, 1983.

Henderson, Diane. "The Theater and Domestic Culture." In John D. Cox and David Scott Kaplan, eds., *A New History of Early English Drama.* New York: Columbia University Press, 1997. 173–94.

"*A Woman Killed with Kindness* and Domesticity, False or True: A Response to Lisa Hopkins." *Connotations* 5 (1995–96): 49–54.

Hill, Christopher. *Society and Puritanism in Pre-Revolutionary England.* New York: Schocken Books, 1964.

Hillebrand, Harold Newcomb. *The Child Actors.* Urbana: University of Illinois Studies in Language and Literature by the University of Illinois Press, 1926.

Hillman, David and Carla Mazzio, eds. *The Body in Parts: Fantasies of Corporeality in Early Modern Europe.* New York: Routledge, 1997.

Hoeniger, F. David. *Medicine and Shakespeare in the English Renaissance.* Newark: University of Delaware Press, 1992.

Hoenselaars, A. J. *Images of Englishmen and Foreigners in the Drama of Shakespeare and his Contemporaries.* London: Associated University Presses, 1992.

Hole, Christina. *The English Housewife in the Seventeenth Century.* London: Chatto & Windus, 1953.

Hopkins, Lisa. "The False Domesticity of *A Woman Killed with Kindness.*" *Connotations* 4 (1994–95): 1–7.

Houlbrooke, Ralph. *The English Family 1450–1700.* New York: Longman, 1984.

Howard, Jean E. "An English Lass Amid the Moors: Gender, Race, Sexuality, and National Identity in Heywood's *The Fair Maid of the West.*" In Margo Hendricks and Patricia Parker, eds., *Women, "Race," & Writing in the Early Modern Period.* New York: Routledge, 1994. 101–17.

"Sex and Social Conflict: The Erotics of *The Roaring Girl.*" In Susan Zimmerman, ed., *Erotic Politics: Desire on the Renaissance Stage.* New York: Routledge, 1992. 170–90.

*The Stage and Social Struggle in Early Modern England.* New York: Routledge, 1994.

and Phyllis Rackin. *Engendering A Nation: A Feminist Account of Shakespeare's English Histories.* New York: Routledge, 1997.

Howell, Martha. *Women, Production and Patriarchy in Late Medieval Cities.* University of Chicago Press, 1986.

Hunter, Lynette. "'Sweet Secrets' from Occasional Receipt to Specialised Books: The Growth of a Genre." In Anne Wilson, ed., *'Banquetting Stuffe': The Fare and Social Background of the Tudor and Stuart Banquet.* Edinburgh University Press, 1991.

Hutson, Lorna. *The Usurer's Daughter: Male Friendship and Fictions of Women in Sixteenth-Century England.* London: Routledge, 1994.

Jardine, Lisa. *Reading Shakespeare Historically.* New York: Routledge 1996.

*Still Harping on Daughters.* New York: Barnes and Noble, 1983.

"Twins and Travesties: Gender, Dependency and Sexual Availability in *Twelfth Night.*" In Susan Zimmerman, ed., *Erotic Politics: Desire on the Renaissance Stage.* New York: Routledge, 1992. 27–38.

Jeanneret, Michel. *A Feast of Words: Banquets and Table Talk in the Renaissance.* Trans. Jeremy Whitely and Emma Hughes. University of Chicago Press, 1987.

Jones, Ann Rosalind. "Nets into Bridles: Early Modern Conduct Books and Sixteenth-Century Women's Lyrics." In Nancy Armstrong and Leonard Tennenhouse, eds.,

*The Ideology of Conduct: Essays in Literature and the History of Sexuality.* New York: Methuen, 1987. 39–72.

and Peter Stallybrass. "Dismantling Irena: The Sexualizing of Ireland in Early Modern England." In Andrew Parker, Mary Russo, Doris Sommer, and Patricia Yaeger, eds., *Nationalisms and Sexualities.* New York: Routledge, 1992. 157–71.

Jones, Richard Foster. *The Triumph of the English Language.* Stanford University Press, 1953.

Kahn, Coppélia. *Man's Estate: Masculine Identity in Shakespeare.* Berkeley: University of California Press, 1981.

Katz, Leslie. "*Merry Wives of Windsor:* Sharing the Queen's Holiday." *Representations* 51 (1995): 77–93.

Kegl, Rosemary. *The Rhetoric of Concealment: Figuring Gender and Class in Renaissance Literature.* Ithaca: Cornell University Press, 1994.

Kastan, David Scott. *Shakespeare After Theory.* New York: Routledge, 1999.

"Workshop and/as Playhouse." In David Scott Kastan and Peter Stallybrass, eds., *Staging the Renaissance: Reinterpretations of Elizabethan and Jacobean Drama.* New York: Routledge, 1991. 151–64.

Korda, Natasha. "Household Kates: Domesticating Commodities in *The Taming of the Shrew.*" *Shakespeare Quarterly* 47 (1996): 109–31.

Kussmaul, Ann. *Servants in Husbandry in Early Modern England.* Cambridge University Press, 1981.

Lamb, Mary Ellen. "Taken by the Fairies: Fairy Practices and the Production of Popular Culture in *A Midsummer Night's Dream.*" *Shakespeare Quarterly* 51 (2000): 277–312.

Laplanche, Jean and J.-B. Pontalis. "Fantasy and the Origins of Sexuality." In Victor Burgin, James Donald and Cora Kaplan, eds., *Formations of Fantasy.* New York: Methuen, 1986.

*The Language of Psycho-Analysis.* Trans. Donald Nicholson-Smith. New York: W. W. Norton & Co., 1973.

Laslett, Peter and Richard Wall, eds. *Household and Family in Past Time.* Cambridge University Press, 1971.

Latham, Minor White. *The Elizabethan Fairies.* New York: Columbia University Press, 1930.

Le Goff, Jacques. "The Learned and Popular Dimensions of Journeys in the Otherworld in the Middle Ages." In Steven L. Kaplan, ed., *Understanding Popular Culture: Europe from the Middle Ages to the Nineteenth Century.* New York: Mouton Publishers, 1984. 19–37.

Leinwand, Theodore. "Shakespeare and the Middling Sort." *Shakespeare Quarterly* 44 (1993): 284–303.

Leslie, Michael and Timothy Raylor, eds. *Culture and Cultivation in Early Modern England: Writing and the Land.* Leicester University Press, 1992. 15–34.

Lieblein, Leanore "The Context of Murder in English Domestic Plays, 1590–1610." *Studies in English Literature* 23 (1983): 181–96.

Litvak, Joseph. *Strange Gourmets: Sophistication, Theory and the Novel.* Durham: Duke University Press, 1997.

Malcomson, Patricia E. *English Laundresses: A Social History, 1850–1930.* Urbana: University of Illinois Press, 1986.

Marcus, Leah. *The Politics of Mirth: Jonson, Herrick, Milton, Marvell, and the Defense of Old Holiday Pastimes.* University of Chicago Press, 1986.

　*Puzzling Shakespeare: Local Reading and Its Discontents.* Berkeley: University of California Press, 1988.

　*Unediting the Renaissance: Shakespeare, Marlowe, Milton.* New York: Routledge, 1996.

Masten, Jeffrey. "Beaumont and/or Fletcher: Collaboration and the Interpretation of Renaissance Drama." *ELH* 59 (1992): 337–57.

　"My Two Dads: Collaboration and the Reproduction of Beaumont and Fletcher." In Jonathan Goldberg, ed., *Queering the Renaissance.* Durham: Duke University Press, 1994. 280–309.

　"Playwrighting: Authorship and Collaboration." In John D. Cox and David Scott Kaplan, eds., *A New History of Early English Drama.* New York: Columbia University Press, 1997. 357–82.

　*Textual Intercourse: Collaboration, Authorship, and Sexualities in Renaissance Drama.* Cambridge University Press, 1997.

Maynard, Stephen. "Feasting on Eyre: Community, Consumption and Communion in *The Shoemaker's Holiday.*" *Comparative Drama* 32 (1998): 327–64.

McEachern, Claire. *The Poetics of English Nationhood, 1590–1612.* Cambridge University Press, 1996.

McFayden, N. Lindsay. "What Was Really Lost in *Gammer Gurton's Needle.*" *Renaissance Papers* (1982): 9–13.

McLuskie, Kathleen. *Dekker and Heywood: Professional Dramatists.* Basingstoke and London: St. Martin's Press, 1994.

　"'Tis But a Woman's Jar': Family and Kinship in Elizabethan Domestic Drama." *Literature and History* 9 (1983): 228–39.

McNeill, Fiona. "Gynocentric London Spaces: (Re)Locating Masterless Women in Early Stuart Drama." *Renaissance Drama* 28 (1997): 195–244.

McRae, Andrew. *God Speed the Plough: The Representation of Agrarian England, 1500–1600.* Cambridge University Press, 1996.

　"Husbandry Manuals and the Language of Agrarian Improvement." In Michael Leslie and Timothy Raylor, eds., *Culture and Cultivation in Early Modern England: Writing and the Land.* Leicester University Press, 1992. 35–62.

Mendelson, Sara and Patricia Crawford, eds. *Women in Early Modern England, 1550–1720.* Oxford: Clarendon Press, 1998.

Mennel, Stephen. *All Manners of Food: Eating and Taste in England and France from the Middle Ages to the Present.* New York: Basil Blackwell, 1985.

Miller, David Lee. "Authorship, Anonymity, and *The Shepheardes Calendar.*" *Modern Language Quarterly* 40 (1979): 219–36.

Mintz, Sidney W. *Sweetness and Power: The Place of Sugar in Modern History.* New York: Viking, 1985.

Montrose, Louis. "'Eliza Queene of Shepheardes,' and the Pastoral of Power." *English Literary Renaissance* 10 (1980): 153–82.

　"The Elizabethan Subject and the Spenserian Text." In Patricia Parker and David Quint eds., *Literary Theory/Renaissance Texts.* Baltimore, MD: Johns Hopkins University Press, 1986. 303–40.

　"Of Gentlemen and Shepherds: The Politics of Elizabethan Pastoral Forms." *ELH* 50 (1983): 415–59.

"'The perfecte paterne of a Poete': The Poetics of Courtship in *The Shepheardes Calendar.*" *Texas Studies in Language and Literature* 21 (1970): 34–67.

*The Purpose of Playing: Shakespeare and the Cultural Politics of Elizabethan Theatre.* University of Chicago Press, 1996.

"The Work of Gender in the Discourse of Discovery." *Representations* 33 (1991): 1–41.

Mueller, Martin. *Children of Oedipus.* University of Toronto Press, 1980.

Mullaney, Steven. *The Place of the Stage.* University of Chicago Press, 1988.

Nagy, Doreen. *Popular Medicine in Seventeenth-Century England.* Bowling Green, OH: Bowling Green State University Press, 1988.

Neely, Carol Thomas. "Constructing Female Sexuality in the Renaissance: Stratford, London, Windsor, Vienna." In Richard Feldstein and Judith Roof, eds., *Feminism and Psychoanalysis*, Ithaca: Cornell University Press, 1989. 208–29.

Neill, Michael. "Broken English and Broken Irish: Nation, Language, and the Optic of Power in Shakespeare's Histories." *Shakespeare Quarterly* 45 (1994): 1–32.

Newman, Karen. *Fashioning Femininity and English Renaissance Drama.* University of Chicago Press, 1991.

Norland, Howard B. *Drama in Early Tudor Britain, 1485–1558.* Lincoln: University of Nebraska Press, 1995.

Ong, Walter. "Latin Language Study as a Renaissance Puberty Rite." *Studies in Philology* 56 (1959): 103–24.

Orgel, Stephen. *Impersonations: The Performance of Gender in Shakespeare's England.* Cambridge University Press, 1996.

"Nobody's Perfect: Or Why Did the English Stage Take Boys for Women?" *South Atlantic Quarterly* 88 (1989): 7–29.

Orlin, Lena Cowen. *Private Matters and Public Culture in Post-Reformation England.* Ithaca: Cornell University Press, 1994.

Parker, Patricia. *Literary Fat Ladies: Rhetoric, Gender, Property.* New York: Methuen, 1987.

"*The Merry Wives of Windsor* and Shakespearean Translation." *Modern Language Quarterly* 52 (1991): 225–61.

"On the Tongue: Cross-Gendering, Effeminacy and the Art of Words." *Style* 23 (1989): 445–65.

"Shakespeare and Rhetoric: 'Dilation' and 'Delation' in *Othello.*" In Patricia Parker and Geoffrey Hartman, eds., *Shakespeare and the Question of Theory.* New York: Methuen, 1985. 54–74.

Parks, Katherine. "The Criminal and the Saintly Body: Autopsy and Dissection in Renaissance Italy." *Renaissance Quarterly* 42 (1994): 1–33.

Parten, Anne. "Falstaff's Horns: Masculine Inadequacy and Feminine Mirth in *The Merry Wives of Windsor.*" *Studies in Philology* 82 (1985): 184–99.

Paster, Gail Kern. *The Body Embarrassed: Drama and the Disciplines of Shame in Early Modern England.* Ithaca: Cornell University Press, 1993.

Patterson, Annabel. *Shakespeare and the Popular Voice.* Oxford: Basil Blackwell, 1989.

Pittenger, Elizabeth. "Dispatch Quickly: The Mechanical Reproduction of Pages." *Shakespeare Quarterly* 42 (1991): 389–408.

"'To Serve the Queere': Nicholas Udall, Master of Revels." In Jonathan Goldberg, ed., *Queering the Renaissance.* Durham: Duke University Press, 1994. 162–89.

Pollock, Linda. *With Faith and Physic: The Life of a Tudor Gentlewoman, Lady Grace Mildmay, 1552–1620.* London: Collins and Brown, 1993.

Pound, John. *Poverty and Vagrancy in Tudor England.* New York: Longman, 1971; rpt. 1986.

Powell, Chilton Latham. *English Domestic Relations, 1487–1653.* New York: Columbia University Press, 1917.

Pullar, Phillipa. *Consuming Passions: Being An Historic Inquiry into Certain English Appetites.* Boston and Toronto: Little, Brown and Company, 1970.

Rackin, Phyllis. *Stages of History: Shakespeare's English Chronicles.* Ithaca: Cornell University Press, 1990.

Rapp, Rayna, Ellen Ross, and Renate Bridenthal, "Examining Family History." In Judith L. Newton, Mary P. Ryan, and Judith R. Walkowitz, eds., *Sex and Class in Women's History.* New York: Routledge & Kegan Paul, 1983.

Roberts, Jeanne Addison. *Shakespeare's English Comedy: The Merry Wives of Windsor in Context.* Lincoln: University of Nebraska Press, 1979.

Roberts, Michael. "'Words they are Women, and Deeds they are Men': Images of Work and Gender in Early Modern England." Lindsey Charles and Lorna Duffin, eds., *Women and Work in Pre-Industrial England.* London: Croom Helm, 1985. 122–80.

Robinson, J. W. "The Art and Meaning of *Gammer Gurton's Needle.*" *Renaissance Drama* 14 (1983): 45–77.

Rose, Jacqueline. *States of Fantasy.* Oxford: Clarendon Press, 1996.

Rose, Mary Beth. *The Expense of Spirit: Love and Sexuality in English Renaissance Drama.* Ithaca: Cornell University Press, 1988.

Rubin, Gayle S. "Thinking Sex: Notes for a Radical Theory of the Politics of Sexuality." In Henry Abelove, Michèle Aina Barale, and David M. Halperin, eds., *The Lesbian and Gay Studies Reader.* New York: Routledge, 1993. 3–44.

Rubin, Miri. *Corpus Christi: The Eucharist in Late Medieval Culture.* Cambridge University Press, 1991.

Samuelson, David. "The Order in Beaumont's *Knight of the Burning Pestle.*" *English Literary Renaissance* 9 (1979): 302–18.

Sawday, Jonathan. *The Body Emblazoned: Dissection and the Human Body in Renaissance Culture.* New York: Routledge, 1995.

Schelling, Felix E. *Elizabethan Drama, 1558–1642: A history of the Drama in England from the accession of Queen Elizabeth to the Closing of the theaters . . . ,* 2 vols. New York: Russell & Russell, 1959.

Schochet, Gordon J. *Patriarchalism in Political Thought.* Oxford: Basil Blackwell, 1975.

Schoenfeldt, Michael. *Bodies and Selves in Early Modern England: Physiology and Inwardness in Spenser, Shakespeare, Herbert and Milton.* Cambridge University Press, 1999.

Secombe, Wally. "The Housewife and her Labour under Capitalism." *New Left Review* 83 (1974): 3–24.

Sedgwick, Eve Kosofsky. "Across Gender, Across Sexuality: Willa Cather and Others." In Ronald R. Butters, John M. Clum, and Michael Moon, eds., *Displacing Homophobia: Gay Male Perspectives in Literature and Culture.* Durham: Duke University Press, 1989. 53–72.

Shapiro, Michael. *Children of the Revels: The Boy Companies of Shakespeare's Time and Their Plays.* New York: Columbia University Press, 1977.

Sharpe, J. A. *Early Modern England: A Social History 1550–1760.* London: Edward Arnold, 1987.

Shuger, Deborah. *Habits of Thought in the English Renaissance: Religion, Politics, and the Dominant Culture.* Berkeley: University of California Press, 1990.

Simon, Joan. *Education and Society in Tudor England.* Cambridge University Press, 1966.

Siraisi, Nancy G. *Medieval and Early Renaissance Medicine.* University of Chicago Press, 1990.

Skinner, Quentin. *The Foundations of Modern Political Thought*, 2 vols. Cambridge University Press, 1978.

Sloan, A. W. *English Medicine in the Seventeenth Century.* Durham Academic Press, 1996.

Smith, Bruce. *Homosexual Desire in Shakespeare's England.* University of Chicago Press, 1991; rpt. 1994.

Smith, Hallett. *Elizabethan Poetry.* Ann Arbor: University of Michigan Press, 1968.

Smith, Steven. "The London Apprentices as Seventeenth-Century Adolescents." *Past and Present* 61 (1973): 149–61.

Southern, Richard. *The Staging of Plays before Shakespeare.* London: Faber, 1973.

Spufford, Margaret. *Small Books and Pleasant Histories: Popular Fiction and its Readership in Seventeenth-Century England.* Athens: GA: University of Georgia Press, 1981.

Spurling, Hilary. *Elinor Fettiplace's Receipt Book: Elizabethan Country House Cooking.* London: Viking Salamander, 1986.

Stallybrass, Peter. "Footnotes." In David Hillman and Carla Mazzio, eds., *The Body in Parts: Fantasies of Corporeality in Early Modern Europe.* New York: Routledge, 1997. 313–25.

"Patriarchal Territories: The Body Enclosed." In Margaret W. Ferguson, Maureen Quilligan, and Nancy J. Vickers, eds., *Rewriting the Renaissance: Discourses of Sexual Difference in Early Modern Europe.* University of Chicago Press, 1986. 123–142.

"Time space and unity: The Symbolic of *The Faerie Queene.*" In Raphael Samuel, ed., *Patriotism: The Making and Unmaking of British National Identity.* 3 vols. London and New York: Routledge, 1989. Vol. III: 199–214.

"Transvestism and the 'Body Beneath': Speculating on the Boy Actor." In Susan Zimmerman, ed., *Erotic Politics: Desire on the Renaissance Stage.* New York: Routledge, 1992. 64–83.

and Allon White. *The Politics and Poetics of Transgression.* Ithaca: Cornell University Press, 1986.

Stewart, Alan. *Close Readers: Humanism and Sodomy in Early Modern England.* Princeton, NJ: Princeton University Press, 1997.

Stevenson, Laura. *Praise and Paradox: Merchants and Craftsmen in Elizabethan Popular Literature.* Cambridge University Press, 1984.

Stone, Lawrence. *The Family, Sex, and Marriage in England, 1500–1800.* London: Weidenfeld and Nicolson, 1977.

Strong, Roy. *The Cult of Elizabeth: Elizabethan Portraiture and Pageantry.* London: Thames and Hudson, 1977.

Tennenhouse, Leonard. *Power on Display: The Politics of Shakespeare's Genres.* New York: Routledge, 1986.

Thick, Malcolm. "Root Crops and the Feeding of London's Poor in the late Sixteenth and Early Seventeenth Centuries." In John Chartes and David Hey, eds., *English Rural Society, 1500–1800.* Cambridge University Press, 1990. 279–96.

Thirsk, Joan. *Agrarian History of England and Wales,* vol. IV: *1500–1640.* Cambridge University Press, 1967.

"Making a Fresh Start: Sixteenth-Century Agriculture and the Classical Inspiration." In Michael Leslie and Timothy Raylor, eds., *Culture and Cultivation in Early Modern England: Writing and the Land.* Leicester University Press, 1992. 15–34.

Thomas, Keith. *Religion and the Decline of Magic.* New York: Charles Scribner's Sons, 1971.

Thorndike, Ashley H. *English Comedy.* New York: Macmillan, 1929.

Tilly, Louise A. and Joan W. Scott. *Women, Work and the Family.* New York: Routledge, 1987.

Tilly, Morris Palmer. *Dictionary of the Proverbs in England in the Sixteenth and Seventeenth Centuries.* Ann Arbor: University of Michigan Press, 1950.

Traub, Valerie. *Desire and Anxiety: Circulations of Sexuality in Shakespearean Drama.* New York: Routledge, 1992.

Trill, Suzanne, with Kate Chedgzoy and Melanie Osborne, eds. *Lay By Your Needles Ladies, Take the Pen: Writing Women in England, 1500–1700.* New York: Arnold, 1997.

Underdown, David. *Revel, Riot, and Rebellion: Popular Politics and Culture in England, 1603–1660.* Oxford: Clarendon Press, 1985.

Vann, Richard T. "Toward a New Lifestyle: Women in Pre-Industrial Capitalism." In Renate Bridenthal and Claudia Koonz, eds., *Becoming Visible: Women in European History.* Boston, MA: Houghton Mifflin, 1977. 192–216.

Warner, Michael. *Fear of a Queer Planet: Queer Politics and Social Theory.* Minneapolis: University of Minnesota Press, 1993.

"New English Sodom." *American Literature* 64 (1992): 19–47.

Watt, Tessa. *Cheap Print and Popular Piety, 1550–1640.* Cambridge University Press, 1991.

Wayne, Valerie. Introduction. In Wayne, ed., *The Matter of Difference: Materialist Feminist Criticism of Shakespeare.* Ithaca: Cornell University Press, 1991. 1–27.

Weimann, Robert. *Shakespeare and the Popular Tradition in the Theater: Studies in the Social Dimension of Dramatic Form and Function.* Trans. Robert Schwartz. Baltimore, MD: Johns Hopkins University Press, 1978.

Westfall, Suzanne. "'A Commonty a Christmas gambold or a tumbling trick': Household Theater." In John D. Cox and David Scott Kastan, eds., *A New History of Early English Drama.* New York: Columbia University Press, 1997. 39–58.

Wheaton, Barbara Ketcham. *Savoring the Past: The French Kitchen and Table from 1300 to 1789.* Philadelphia: University of Pennsylvania Press, 1983.

Whitworth, Charles W. Introduction to *Three Sixteenth-Century Comedies*. New York: W. W. Norton and Co., 1984.

Willams, Raymond. *The Country and the City*. New York: Oxford University Press, 1973.

Willis, Deborah. *Malevolent Nurture: Witch-Hunting and Maternal Power in Early Modern England*. Ithaca: Cornell University Press, 1995.

Wilson, C. Anne. "The Evolution of the Banquet Course." In Wilson, ed., *'Banquetting Stuffe': The Fare and Social Background of the Tudor and Stuart Banquet*. Edinburgh University Press, 1991.

Wilson, Richard. *Will Power: Essays on Shakespearean Authority*. Detroit: Wayne State University Press, 1993.

Winterson, Jeanette. *Sexing the Cherry*. New York: Grove Press, 1989.

Woodbridge, Linda. "Palisading the Body Politic." In Linda Woodbridge and Edward Berry, eds., *True Rites and Maimed Rites: Ritual and Anti-Ritual in Shakespeare and his Age*. Urbana: University of Illinois Press, 1992. 270–98.

Wrightson, Keith. *English Society 1580–1680*. New Brunswick, NJ: Rutgers University Press, 1982.

"Estates, degrees, and sorts: changing perceptions of society in Tudor and Stuart England." In Penelope J. Corfield, ed., *Language, History and Class*. Oxford: Basil Blackwell, 1991. 30–52.

Young, Karl. "William Gager's Defence of the Academic Stage." *Transactions of the Wisconsin Academy of Science, Arts and Letters* 18 (1916): 593–630.

Zitner, Sheldon. Introduction to Francis Beaumont, *Knight of the Burning Pestle*. Manchester University Press, 1984.

Žižek, Slavoj. *Looking Awry: An Introduction to Jacques Lacan through Popular Culture*. Cambridge, MA: MIT Press, 1997.

# Index